Joel Barlow

JOEL BARLOW

American Citizen in a Revolutionary World

RICHARD BUEL JR.

The Johns Hopkins University Press

Baltimore

The Johns Hopkins University Press
2715 North Charles Street
Baltimore, Maryland 21218-4363
www.press.jhu.edu

Library of Congress Cataloging-in-Publication Data

Buel, Richard, 1933–
Joel Barlow : American citizen in a revolutionary world /
Richard Buel Jr.
p.   cm.
Includes bibliographical references and index.
ISBN-13: 978-0-8018-9769-6 (hardcover : alk. paper)
ISBN-10: 0-8018-9769-6 (hardcover : alk. paper)
1. Barlow, Joel, 1754–1812. 2. Poets, American—18th century—Biography.
3. Diplomats—United States—Biography. 4. Politicians—United
States—Biography. I. Title.
PS705.B84   2011
811'.2—dc22
[B]
2010017552

A catalog record for this book is available from the British Library.

*Special discounts are available for bulk purchases of this book.
For more information, please contact Special Sales at 410-516-6936
or specialsales@press.jhu.edu.*

The Johns Hopkins University Press uses environmentally friendly
book materials, including recycled text paper that is composed of
at least 30 percent post-consumer waste, whenever possible.
All of our book papers are acid-free, and our jackets and covers
are printed on paper with recycled content.

For those in the Wesleyan community
who have supported my scholarly career

Contents

Illustrations

Joel Barlow

Introduction

Picture the crowded, still medieval city of Algiers in July 1796. Joel Barlow had recently accepted appointment as the U.S. consul there, at the urging of his long-time friend and fellow Yale graduate, David Humphreys, then U.S. minister to Portugal. The administration of George Washington needed someone of Barlow's stature to resolve an urgent problem. Before 1793 only a few American vessels venturing into the Mediterranean had fallen victim to North African piracy. But after Britain had arranged a truce between Algeria and Portugal toward the end of that year, armed vessels from the Barbary states started seizing American merchantmen in the eastern Atlantic and enslaving their crews. Pleas for help from the 150 American seamen incarcerated at Algiers had appeared in American newspapers.

Barlow and his wife had just returned to Paris after fourteen months' residence in Hamburg, but the summons from Humphreys, a man Barlow had long admired, was hard to refuse. Both men feared that if the new U.S. government could not defend its citizens against enslavement, it would not be worthy of their allegiance. Though Britain posed a more immediate, strategic challenge to the United States, failure to free American citizens from North African slavery could seriously compromise the still fragile authority of the federal government.

Barlow brought unusual qualities to the job of U.S. consul. Though at home he was known for *The Vision of Columbus* (1787), his epic poem about America and its recent revolution, in Europe he had achieved notoriety as a defender of the French Revolution. His wholehearted endorsement of the revolution's early republican phase had led the National Convention to confer French citizenship on him in 1793. That status gave him a diplomatic advantage because France was the European power best able to influence the North African appendages of the Ottoman Empire. Barlow initially assumed his mission would take only a few months, but he soon found that being the American consul in Algiers was more taxing than he had expected. Commitments had already been made by Joseph Donaldson—an advance agent—about the payment of tribute to the dey of Algeria, which could not be fulfilled. To placate this impatient, capricious tyrant, Barlow resorted to expedients for which he lacked formal authorization. To compound his difficulties, the bubonic plague broke out three months after his arrival in Algiers.

The plague's seasonal appearance, later in 1796 than usual, was accepted by the Islamic denizens and rulers of the region as a visitation of Allah. Although a good Moslem was supposed to submit to such judgments, those who were able left the city for the countryside. Barlow could have taken this precaution, but it was not an option for the American sailors held prisoner in unhealthy conditions, some of whom contracted the disease. Barlow felt obliged to visit them and to render both the sick and the well any assistance he could, despite the risk of contracting the disease himself. In early July, Barlow drafted a long letter to his wife Ruth, who had remained in Paris.[1] After explaining his situation, he warned Ruth that he might never return. But he was unlikely to unnecessarily alarm her because, as he noted, the letter would not "come into your hands unless & untill by some other channel you shall have been informed of the event which it anticipates." Because Barlow assumed Ruth valued his life "more than you do your own," as he did hers, he sought to explain the "pressing duty of humanity" he felt "to expose my self . . . in endeavouring to save as many of our unhappy citizens as possible. . . . Though they are dying very fast, yet it is possible that my exertions may be the means of saving a number who otherwise would perish." If Barlow died in the course of helping them, he begged Ruth not to "upbraid my memory by even thinking that I did too much. . . . [M]any of these persons have wives at home as well as I. . . . If their wives love them as mine does me (a thing which I cannot believe, but have no right to deny) ask these lately disconsolate and now joyful families, whether I have done too much."

Barlow found drafting this farewell letter difficult since he could think of no "word of tenderness, of gratitude, of counsel, of consolation" that could compensate for "robbing you of, the husband whom you cherish." The only thing he could do, since they were childless, was to make Ruth his sole heir. He estimated his estate might come to as much as $120,000, from which Ruth would derive an annual income of between $5,000 and $7,000. That would make her richer than most other American women, whose claims on their husband's estates were usually limited to a dower third. Barlow had never been bound by the usual, but he felt obliged to explain to Ruth his reasons so that she could parry the criticism he expected his bequest to generate.

"In a view of justice and equity," Barlow felt that "whatever we possess at this moment is a joint property between ourselves and ought to remain to the survivor." When they had married, "I was destitute of every other possession as of every other enjoyment. I was rich only in the fund of your affectionate economy and the sweet consolation of your society." Looking back upon "our various struggles and disappointments," particularly since 1790—when Ruth had joined him in Europe—Barlow marveled how often he had been "rendered happy by misfortunes; for the heaviest were turned into blessings by the opportunities they gave me to discover new virtues in you, who taught me how to bear them." Barlow had become "happier in [Ruth] during the latter years of our union" because he had learned to love "you better; my heart has been more full of your excellence, & less agitated with objects of ambition, which used to devour me too much." He attributed "the acquisition of the competency which we seem at last to have secured . . . more to your energy than mine: I mean the energy of your virtues, which gave me consolation and even happiness under circumstances, wherein, if I had been alone, or with a partner no better than myself, I should have sunk." Since Ruth deserved to enjoy the "fruits of our joint exertions <u>with me</u>. . . . if by my death you are to be deprived of the greater part of the comfort you expected, it would surely be unjust and cruel" to give "any portion . . . to others."

Barlow could not resist advising her about disposing of the wealth she might inherit. He assumed she would want to relieve the wants of others, not just needy relations and their close friends but also the deserving poor. "One of the principal gratifications . . . I intended . . . [was] to succor the unfortunate of every description as far as possible." Barlow had in mind going beyond simple charity to "advising . . . poor persons" about how to "employ their own industry," and extending them small loans. He thought $50 loaned in rotation over a dozen years could liberate a dozen families from possible imprisonment for debt. He also predicted that Ruth's charitable example would prove contagious and that her "benevolence, . . . character and connexions . . . [would] put in motion a much greater fund of charity than you will yourself possess . . . benefiting thousands whom you might never hear of."

Barlow had many reasons for wanting to remain alive; he intended to "use every precaution for my safety, as well for your sake as for mine. But if you should see me no more, my dearest friend, you will not forget I loved you." Recognizing that if Ruth ever received this letter, it would then be out of his power to further her happiness, he begged her to submit "with patience to a destiny that is unavoidable" and to "transfer your affections to some worthy person who shall supply my place in the relation I have borne to you." Though he did not customarily sign his letters to her, on this occasion it seemed "proper that the last characters that this hand shall trace for your perusal should compose the name of your most faithful, most affectionate & and most grateful husband—Joel Barlow."

Few modern nations have been as blessed as the United States with the quality of its founders. George Washington, John Adams, Thomas Jefferson, James Madison, and James Monroe each played a pivotal role in our Revolution and then contributed in distinctive ways to consolidating its achievements. Today all are widely celebrated in historical writing. No less attention has been lavished on Benjamin Franklin and Alexander Hamilton, whose influence in shaping our national destiny rivals that exerted by our first four presidents. In addition, the reading public has access to multiple biographies of their more prominent associates, such as John Jay, John Marshall, and Gouverneur Morris, while students can explore in depth the recently published correspondence of important individuals like Robert Morris (no relation to Gouverneur) and Nathaniel Greene.

The life of Joel Barlow—a member of the founding generation whose renown depended on his activities in Europe as much as in America—has escaped recent notice. Yet Barlow won a reputation on both continents for trumpeting the redemptive promise of representative republicanism. During the French Revolution and its Napoleonic aftermath, he was involved either as actor or observer on both continents in many of the transforming events that shaped the world we live in today. He interacted with virtually every prominent figure in the American and French Revolutions, from the first U.S. presidents to Lafayette, Talleyrand, and Napoleon, as well as with leading scientific and economic innovators like Robert Fulton and prominent literary personalities like Tom Paine, Mary Wollstonecraft, and Constantine Volney.

Barlow lived to free the American seamen in Algiers, return to his wife, and with her share many later adventures in Europe and America. His wide-ranging career finally made him a firsthand witness to more important events of this climactic age than perhaps any other American of his generation. Although Jefferson, among others, urged him to write the histories of the two revolutions he had observed, Barlow was too much of a visionary simply to record events that had already happened. Today he is remembered as a minor literary figure. During the age of revolution, however, he enjoyed international renown for his vision of a republican future. Aided by free commerce, republicanism would lead to the abolition of wars that monarchies used as engines of subjugation. That Barlow lost his life while trying to promote peace as the U.S. minister to Napoleon's regime lends his story a tragic air.

Even so, he epitomized the character of his time better than did many of its most prominent heroes. Barlow's story captures wonderfully the multilayered, cosmopolitan, and tumultuous character of the revolutionary age itself.

CHAPTER ONE

Beginnings

In 1754 the first Sabbath of spring, March 24, coincided with the fourth Sunday in Lent. On that day Esther (Hester) Barlow, second wife of Samuel Barlow, gave birth to their fourth and last son in their Redding farmhouse in western Connecticut. At the time Redding was an outlying part of northwestern Fairfield, a dozen miles from the shoreline where the original European settlers had established a town a century before. Redding would not formally separate from Fairfield until 1767. However, in 1729 the colonial legislature set off as a separate parish the southern portion of what would eventually become a new town. That enabled its inhabitants to gather their own church and in 1733 to settle a Congregational minister who was supported by parish rates.

Samuel Barlow had his new son christened Joel, the first use of that name in a family given to calling its males John, Joseph, Samuel, Daniel, and Nathaniel. To those familiar with the Bible, "Joel" came freighted with meaning. The Hebrew prophet of that name had called on the people of Israel to repent in response to a plague of "locusts" invading from the north. New Englanders at the time felt threatened by French Canada, and the rivalry between Britain and France for control of North America would lead to the last great colonial war in 1755. For the average colonist, though, the religious dimension of the looming conflict was as important as its geopolitical implications. Catholic France posed a threat to Protestant Britain nowhere more immediately than in Britain's New England colonies.

The religious identity of New Englanders had recently been sharpened by a surge of piety known as the Great Awakening. The Awakening spawned millennial expectations about the imminent second coming of Christ that paralleled the biblical prophesy of Joel. The prophet and the New Englanders both expected divine intervention to be preceded by a climactic struggle between the forces of good and evil. Although Samuel Barlow left no religious testament, when he chose the name "Joel" for his son, it seems likely he was mindful of the name's biblical implications.

Between 1734 and 1760 Samuel had seven sons and two daughters by two wives. The mother of Samuel's first four children (three sons and one daughter) was Eunice Bradley, daughter of Daniel Bradley, the scion of a prominent Fairfield family. Samuel had married Eunice in August 1731, when he was 21 and she was 23. The newlyweds had then waited an unusually long time (three and a half years) for their first child, Daniel. After Daniel, a daughter, Ruhamah, and a son, James, arrived in the more normal interval of two years. Jabez, the last child, was separated from his nearest brother by three years. When Eunice died not long afterwards in 1743, Samuel moved from a house near the center of Fairfield to Redding parish. In 1744 he married Esther, the daughter of a local resident, Nathaniel Hull. Whereas Eunice had been two years older than Samuel, Esther was eleven years his junior. Their first born, Nathaniel, arrived forty weeks after the wedding. Then a five-year lapse ensued, at least in the surviving record, before Aaron, Samuel, and Joel came along in rapid succession between 1750 and 1754. Another daughter, Huldah, was born in 1760.[1]

Esther's first interval of childlessness was possibly due to miscarriages. But the interruption in childbearing after Joel's birth in 1754 was more likely the result of parental restraint. Samuel already had more progeny to provide for than he had resources. The death of his first born, Daniel, left him with six sons. To establish one's sons in separate households was a patriarchic duty. Samuel's move from Fairfield to Redding in the mid-1740s had been dictated by the lower price of interior lands. He sold several small plots he owned in Fairfield to finance the 1749 purchase of a farmhouse with adjacent lands in the southwestern portion of Redding know as "Boston" district, about a mile west of the Saugatuck River. This acquisition was only a first step in establishing each of his male offspring on his own farm. Between 1751 and 1773, he bought ten additional parcels of unimproved land. Some of the purchases were contiguous to the family farm in Redding, some more distant. But the most remote was no further away than Ridgefield, just to the west of Redding.[2]

Daughters had less claim on parental resources, but a family so top heavy with males presented problems for Esther. There were fewer female helpers to assist her with those household functions that women ordinarily performed: caring for young children, tending the vegetable garden, manufacturing clothing for the entire family, preparing food on a daily basis, and nursing the sick. Ruhamah's marriage to Daniel Gray, who lived nearby, heightened Esther's difficulties, which is probably why Samuel purchased a slave girl around that time.

As Joel began exploring the world, he would have been most aware of Esther and the other females helping her care for her young brood of male children. Only after weaning would Joel's brothers have gradually supplanted women as the principal influence on him. The historical record is largely mute about eighteenth-century Americans' earliest years, even though we now regard this period as decisive in shaping human personality. All we know is that as Joel matured he became his mother's favorite child. We can also infer from his adventurous intellect and sanguine disposition that he eluded most of the destructive traumas to which humans are vulnerable in their early years. As a mature adult he was never afraid of his feelings, and shortly after graduating from Yale he described himself as "determined to love mankind if they kill me."[3] He also avoided the serious accidents to which farm youth are prone as they learn to handle draft animals and agricultural tools. Every boy growing up in a gaggle of male siblings has adventures to which a certain amount of physical peril is attached.

That no more than four years separated Aaron, little Samuel, and Joel in their early childhood created tensions as well as a warm bond between them. Male children were expected to begin working on the farm after they passed their seventh birthday. With three growing sons coming along at two-year intervals, Samuel senior could rely on each to instruct the next youngest in the round of chores. One began with collecting eggs from the hen house and driving livestock to and from pasture, moved on to heavier tasks like bringing in wood for fuel and repairing fences, to working alongside grown men in clearing land, plowing, and harvesting. Being the youngest boy in the family allowed Joel to be cared for without having to care for others, but the downside was the absence of someone to whom each newly acquired function could be passed on. He must at times have felt as if the tasks his brothers were instructing him in would become life-long sentences, and this diminished his enthusiasm for farm life.

Infinitely preferable to agricultural duties were mental activities that gave his imagination free play. Redding parish had begun making provision for the schooling of its male children shortly after settling a minister. In 1737 it voted to hire a schoolmaster who would periodically visit three separate districts to instruct youths in reading, writing, and arithmetic. Joel's instruction probably began at home because of his close association with his two older brothers and the indulgence of his mother. By the early 1760s, when he had reached the appropriate age to attend the town's common school, each of Redding's districts had its own schoolmaster. References in his poetry suggest he relished the time he spent in a small schoolhouse more than his work in the fields.

At the time, most New England children were introduced to literacy through the *New England Primer*. Next to the Bible and psalm books, the *Primer* was the most widely read book in eighteenth-century America. The *Primer* associated letters simultaneously with images, sounds, and familiar narratives. Its alphabet began with the juxtaposition of the image of a man and "A," followed by the first verse of the catechism, "In Adam's Fall / We Sinned all." Next came the image of a book bearing the letter "B," accompanied by the admonitory verse, "Thy Life to Mend / This Verse Attend." Not all image-verse linkages were biblical or even Christian, but they all connected the visual and the aural with abstract symbols to assist the child in learning the alphabet. The primer was designed to introduce a new dimension of language to those whose linguistic experience had previously been wholly aural. The association of the unfamiliar with the familiar, of letters and printed words with their oral rendition, enhanced the power of that experience.[4]

To judge from Joel Barlow's later preference for expressing himself in verse, a penchant his brother-in-law repeatedly urged him to abandon, the poetic configuration of the primer's alphabet made a powerful impression on him. Although contemporaries would find his prose more memorable than his poetry, Barlow remained convinced that the poetic rendering of an idea had more power to persuade than its prose counterpart. His tenacious preference for poetry is worth stressing because, as a leading republican ideologue of his age, Barlow could hardly be described as wedded to tradition. Yet in this respect he seems to have been determined to cling to a venerable but waning aesthetic.

The meter and, where present, the rhyme of poetry inescapably imbeds it in an aural world. One cannot speed read a poem for the same reason that one cannot paraphrase it. Poetry has to be recited. Barlow's facility for picking up foreign languages simply by listening to them demonstrates his sensitivity to the sound of words. His first published poem, *The Prospect of Peace* (1778), celebrated the mystery of word sounds and called for a "rising Sage" (129)

To find the cause, in secret nature bound,
The unknown cause, and various charms of sound?
What subtil medium leads the devious way:
Why different tensions different sounds convey;

Why harsh, rough tones in grating discord roll,
Or mingling concert charms th' enraputr'd soul.   (131–36)

Literacy often weakens attachment to the aural world, but in Barlow's case his early exposures to the written word strengthened that attachment.

Local folklore claimed that Barlow's penchant for rhyming and his sense of the rhythms of the language eventually attracted the attention of the local minister, Nathaniel Bartlett, who prepared him for college. If one did not live in one of the few towns that had a grammar school, the local minister was often the only person who could teach a boy the classical languages required for entering college. Bartlett had come to Redding a year before Joel's birth, but the boy did not become Bartlett's pupil until the early 1770s, when Joel was in his late teens. Until then Samuel Barlow needed the unpaid services of his youngest son to help provide for the others.

In 1770, as Samuel approached 60, he decided he could no longer postpone settling his sons. His own father's death at 63 served as a warning. On March 30, 1770, he deeded over to James, the oldest surviving son, who at the time was over 30, a 110-acre farm in Ridgefield. Around that time, Nathaniel married Jane Bradley, a kinswoman of Samuel's first wife, and settled on lands contiguous to the Redding homestead. Jabez, Samuel's youngest child by Eunice, would get the remainder of the Redding farm with the obligation of providing for Esther for the rest of her life. Aaron married Rebecca Sanford on December 17, 1772. Ten months later Aaron purchased a large saltbox dwelling (which still stands as a listed property on the National Register) at the northern end of Umpawaug Hill in Redding. The house, for which Aaron paid £135 in hard money, had originally been built in 1725 by Rebecca's prosperous grandfather. In the early 1770s, it was owned by her uncle, Nehemiah Sanford.[5] Rebecca's father and Samuel probably assisted with this purchase. But Samuel had not made full provision for either Aaron or Samuel Jr. before dying in December 1773.

That it took the better part of four years to settle Samuel's estate partially explains Aaron's and Samuel's enlistment in Connecticut's Seventh Continental Regiment, commanded by Colonel David Waterbury, in 1775. They were recruited by Captain Zalmon Read into the Tenth Company that was composed almost entirely of young Redding men. Assuming Joel's two brothers were able to equip themselves, their tour promised to yield each £17 in addition to their subsistence over the course of the next seven months. Although £17 was not a princely sum, it was comparable to what they could have expected to earn as farm laborers.

That the two brothers were prepared to accept this form of employment set them apart from James and Nathaniel, the oldest surviving sons from Samuel's two marriages. They eschewed military service, suggesting Samuel had provided better for them. Nathaniel probably would not have been welcome in Captain Read's company because of a loyalist declaration he signed early in 1775.[6]

Samuel may also have delayed preparing Joel for college until the lad approached 17 because he wanted to be sure that a college education constituted an appropriate patrimony. Nathaniel Bartlett probably helped persuade Samuel of the wisdom of such a choice, and Esther undoubtedly weighed in on Joel's behalf, sensing that her favorite son could do better than a life behind the plow. Once Samuel had made his decision in 1772, he placed Joel under Bartlett's supervision. However, a rural ministry provided neither the need nor the occasion to maintain the linguistic skills Bartlett had acquired for his Yale education, and after a year Samuel chose to enroll Joel in Eleazar Wheelock's school in distant New Hampshire.

Originally established in Lebanon, Connecticut, in 1754 as Moor's Indian Charity School, Wheelock's school had met with enough success by the mid-1760s to expand its operations. After his prize Indian pupil, Samson Occum, managed to raise substantial sums of money in Britain, Wheelock decided to establish an institution that would provide the graduates of his charity school with a college education. In 1769 he moved the Indian school from Lebanon to the northern frontier town of Hanover, New Hampshire, for the same reasons that Samuel Barlow had moved from Fairfield proper to Redding in the 1740s. Land in Lebanon was far more expensive than land in Hanover, which up until a few years before the founding of Dartmouth College had been uninhabited wilderness. Wheelock hoped the missionaries issuing from his institutions would pave the way for the millennium by converting the heathen to Christianity.

Moor's Indian Charity School recommended itself to Samuel for several reasons. If Joel were conscientious in pursuing his studies, the school's one-year preparatory course offered admission to Dartmouth sooner than attending the Hopkins Grammar School in New Haven would enable him to enter Yale. The college in New Haven had also suffered after student disorders forced President Clap's resignation in 1766. When the trustees proved unable to secure a suitable replacement, student enrollment declined. By the early 1770s, when Samuel was looking for a college for Joel, Yale classes often had fewer than twenty students, and the total student body hovered around one hundred. Wheelock's wilderness institutions had overtaken Yale's enrollment in the course of four short years.

Hanover's isolation was an additional recommendation because it would preserve Joel's morals and his health. New Haven, though not a major port, nonetheless had direct contact with the West Indies, as well as with New York, Boston, and Philadelphia. In the eighteenth century, commerce often spread disease. New Haven also offered many more distractions than Hanover, not the least of which was a surplus of young women looking for eligible mates. Finally, Samuel's resources were stretched, and he saw an opportunity to make an advantageous arrangement with Wheelock for Joel's room, board, and tuition. Wheelock needed someone to manage the kitchen that served the school and college, and Samuel agreed to hire and pay Esther's kinswoman Elizabeth Burr, a spinster, to do the job. Since the school was a charity school, many of its students worked as they studied; Joel was to wait on table and run errands for Elizabeth Burr when not pursuing his studies. Samuel and Wheelock entered into a formal agreement to this effect on September 14, 1773, several weeks after the beginning of the school year, when Joel's father brought him to Hanover.

The trip from Redding would have been Joel's first exposure, aside from occasional visits to Fairfield, to the larger world. Father and son made their way to Hartford before proceeding north along the Connecticut River to Hanover. The length and novelty of the journey must have dramatized to Joel the separation between his past and future. But as the lad parted with his father in mid-September, he could have had little inkling that he was about to experience an even greater separation. Three short months later his father died on December 20, 1773.

We know from Samuel's will, dated the same day he died, that he intended Joel's share of his estate to pay for his education. Although Samuel held almost £170 in notes and cash at his death, he owed Esther's brother-in-law, Ezekiel Burr, in partnership with Stephen Burr, £185. Samuel directed his executors to provide Joel with the necessary resources to continue his studies without interruption, even if the funds had to be borrowed. It is well he did so because Elizabeth Burr abandoned her job at the beginning of March, either because Samuel was no longer performing his part of their bargain or because he was no longer able to force her to comply with hers. Her departure threatened Joel's continuance at Moor's Charity School because he was technically a paying student.

Since Joel was still a minor, the will required him to choose a guardian to manage his share of his father's estate until he reached his majority. On March 7, 1774, Joel designated his mother, and a Connecticut probate court quickly ratified his choice after Esther posted a £300 bond to exercise her duties according to the law. Because Joel's student earnings did not cover the full costs of his education,

Esther periodically sent small sums to Hanover. The inventory of Samuel's estate mentions a debt due Wheelock for £6 17s. 8d.[7]

Samuel's total estate came to £1,060. The will provided that after Esther received her dower third for the remainder of her life, the rest was to be divided among the surviving children. Each son was allotted an equal share, but the two daughters got only one third of what the males received. The lands and other distributions Samuel had made to each child before his death—like James's Ridgefield farm—did not show up in the probate inventory of the estate, but Samuel specified that the value of gifts made prior to his death were to be deducted from each survivor's entitlement. The same provision applied to disbursements made for Joel's education. By the time the final distribution of the estate took place on March 31, 1777, Esther was also dead, thus permitting her dower third of Samuel's estate to be divided as specified in Samuel's will.

Each of Samuel's male heirs eventually received a share valued at £146 5s. 8d., while the daughters' shares were valued at £45 7s. 10d. Since the assets were by then entirely tangible and the most valuable portions were real estate, what went into constituting each share would have been the subject of negotiation among the heirs. Joel and Samuel were given one set of contiguous assets from which to take their respective shares. In Joel's case this included fractional ownership of a house and a barn in addition to several parcels of land. Jabez, Nathaniel, and Aaron divided another bundle of contiguous assets. James, who was living a few miles off in Ridgefield enjoyed a separate portion all to himself, as did Ruhamah and Huldah.

Since Joel had no means of returning to Redding, he remained in Hanover. There is no record of how Joel felt about his father's death, but he was kept busy by the school's routines, which demanded that he rise each morning at six and retire each evening at nine. His days were filled with recitations before his tutors and kitchen chores. On the Sabbath, long church services in the morning and afternoon took the place of recitations. Winter weather provided the biggest diversion with the occasional blizzard giving the youngsters a chance to engage in snowball fights.

The school and college authorities were unable to control the students' reaction to the quality of victuals Elizabeth Burr and her successor prepared for them. Complaints about the food came to the attention of the wider public and even reached the governor of New Hampshire. As a kitchen worker whose room, board, and tuition were at stake, Joel did not join in these protests. That was just as well, because in the spring of 1774, the more ungovernable students were dismissed. The charity students, comprising roughly half the total student body, were not involved, and Joel seems to have identified with them. He dutifully copied the letter a New Hampshire clergyman had addressed to the student body, reminding them of the "great things" that were expected of them because of "your present happy situation among such as are able & willing to instruct you in the Truths of the Gospel."[8] No evidence survives of how Joel regarded the thirteen Indians in the school as he concentrated on passing the examination requirements for Dartmouth.

In the eighteenth century, commencement marked the beginning of the academic year, providing the occasion on which the President and tutors examined those seeking admission to the college. In 1774, Dartmouth's commencement occurred on August 23, and Joel demonstrated enough proficiency in the classical languages to be admitted to the freshman class. He was 20, though the average age at which a freshman began college at the time was closer to 16. It is clear from a surviving evaluation of him as a "middling scholar," as well as from his need to borrow a Greek dictionary from the college library during his first college term, that there remained plenty of room for improvement. His evaluators were more appreciative of his "good Genius," by which they meant his imagination and deportment. The last won universal approval both from the college authorities and his peers.[9]

It is not clear whether mother or son initiated Joel's transfer to Yale, which took place in November 1774. Wheelock referred to Joel's "Straitned" circumstances resulting from his father's death and the "prospect of some Advantages for his releif [sic] by being Nearer Home," when he wrote acting Yale president Naphtalie Daggett about Joel's transfer. It is safe to assume that Esther and Joel had communicated with each other by letter on the subject. With Joel closer to Redding, Esther could forward money to him as required, and he would be available when she needed him. Since Yale was still struggling to get back on its feet from the disorders of the past decade, they had little reason to fear he would be refused admission. Joel would not be the only member of his class to join after the school year had begun. Nor was he the eldest member of the class of 1778, whose ages as freshmen ranged from 14 to 23.

Barlow entered the most talented class that Yale graduated in the eighteenth century. Among his forty classmates was the future lexicographer Noah Webster; a future secretary of the treasury and governor of the state, Oliver Wolcott Jr.; a future jurist and author of a classic treatise on the state's legal code, Zephaniel Swift; a future judge on Connecticut's Supreme Court, Asher Miller; a future mathematics professor and founder of the University of Georgia, Josiah Meigs; and a future U.S. senator, Uriah Tracy; as well as two future members of Vermont's Supreme Court. Most of these men would align themselves with the Federalist Party between the 1790s and the 1810s. But Abraham Bishop, Asa Spalding, and Alexander Wolcott, three leaders of what would become Connecticut's Republican opposition in the early nineteenth century, were also members of the class. Barlow did not have as much in common with his future political allies as he initially had with Webster and Oliver Wolcott.

The quality of his classmates would prove especially important because of the interruptions the Revolutionary War imposed upon Yale. On April 23, two days after reports of the clashes at Lexington and Concord arrived, the student body was sent home several weeks prior to the scheduled conclusion of term. Joel returned to Redding to help the family with its spring chores. When college reconvened at the end of May, New Haven was buzzing with excitement. Under the guidance of two "regulars," the student body formed a company that began drilling on the town green. One month later came news of a bloody engagement fought at Bunker Hill, followed by the passage of Gen. George Washington through New Haven on his way to assume command of the continental army forming around Boston. The entire town turned out to salute the new leader of the revolutionary cause, and the student company drew commendation for the skill with which it executed certain military exercises. War and revolution had its hazards, but the town's denizens preferred having Yale's undergraduates under military discipline to the riotous misbehavior that had previously emanated from the college.

At the conclusion of his freshman year, Joel's mother died on August 28, 1775. Joel probably had some warning that all was not well. A note to Esther dated July 6, the first of his letters to survive, assures her that he was ready to return home if "your circumstances [were] such as to want me."[10] Esther had barely reached 54, but she was one of many to sicken and die that summer and autumn. The war brought epidemic disease in its wake as soldiers in unsanitary camps fell ill. Since there was no hospital service, the sick were either taken in by local residents or they made their way home as best they could. Either way, they spread their afflictions among the civilian population. Camp fever—possibly typhoid fever or a virulent form of dysentery—became common among the population from which the army was drawn. Nathaniel's son Jonathan died on the same day as Esther, and grandmother and grandson were buried together. While Jonathan appears to have suffered from a chronic respiratory condition, probably tuberculosis, Esther apparently died of dysentery.

Joel was summoned to Redding shortly before his mother's death. There he joined his half-brother Jabez, his fourteen-year-old sister Huldah, and Nathaniel. His half-siblings, James and Ruhamah—still living in Redding—would also have been present for the funeral, but it is unlikely that Aaron and Samuel were able to attend, even though their company at the time was no further off than New York City. The summer's heat would have allowed little delay in arranging for Esther and Jonathan's interment.

Joel's mother had named him sole executor of her will upon his reaching 21. He had no incentive to put off settling her affairs, since he was already substantially in arrears with his college bills. Yale's schedule included a six-weeks vacation between the middle of September and the end of October, and he used the interval to probate Esther's will, getting himself empowered to administer her estate. Most of Esther's property consisted of a life interest in the dower third of Samuel's as-yet-unsettled estate. But Esther also had independent title to other assets through inheritance. She left Joel a six-acre plot of land together with all her livestock. Huldah received all of Esther's apparel and personal property, less the livestock that Joel got and a token bequest of five shillings Esther left to each of Samuel's other children.

The bequests would only take effect after settling outstanding claims against Esther's estate, including charges for administration. These came to £87 7s. 11d., three-quarters of which were debts due to members of her immediate family. Her largest creditor was Aaron, followed by Joel, and her brother Ezekiel Hull. Nathaniel was the smallest creditor among her relations, perhaps reflecting a coolness that had grown between them because of his flirtation with loyalism. Joel recorded only one debt of £0 11s. 9d. due Esther, which he conscientiously collected.[11]

Five months later, Joel's older brother Samuel died from an unspecified illness contracted during the northern campaign. Most of Captain Zalmon Read's disease-ridden company had been discharged on November 28, 1775, and Aaron and Samuel got as far as Poughkeepsie before Samuel collapsed. Despite the care he received from Aaron and Nathaniel, who joined them, Samuel slipped away at the end of January 1776. The death of the brother nearest to him in age, so soon after his mother's death, was painful for Joel. Later he romanticized this brother's memory in *The Vision of Columbus*, likening young Samuel's heroism to General Richard Montgomery's.[12]

The conceit behind the simile was extravagant. Montgomery had fallen leading a desperate New Year's Eve effort to capture Quebec in a blinding snowstorm; Samuel had perished while trying to make his way home after being discharged before his term expired. Though their heroisms hardly bore comparison, it comforted Joel to associate his brother's sacrifice with that of the preeminent hero of the first year of the war. Twenty years later he altered his treatment of Samuel's and Montgomery's deaths in *The Columbiad* to make it clear that Samuel had only aspired to Montgomery's heroism.[13]

Samuel Jr. died intestate, without wife or children. The probate court accordingly ordered that his estate, which came to £262 19s. 1d., be divided equally among the full and half brothers and sisters, who shared a father. Joel's portion of the bequest, along with the other assets he had recently acquired, insured that he would have the wherewithal to continue college. Realizing that losing three of his closest relatives also conferred upon him the opportunity to take full charge of his life, he resolved to use his new freedom to get the most out of what remained of his sojourn at Yale.[14]

There was a bright side to the disruptions that punctuated Barlow's freshman year. Upperclassmen customarily subjected first-year students to intense hazing. The school year began for freshmen when the seniors lined them up to explain their subservience to their "superiors." New students had to show "proper respect" for upperclassmen by never preceding them through an entryway. They also were at the beck and call of any upperclassman who wished to appropriate their services for menial tasks. Sophomores relished harassing freshmen with their newfound power. But any upperclassman, including MA candidates, could commandeer freshmen energies. Barlow was older than most of the sophomores when he entered Yale and found being ordered around by his juniors particularly galling. By arriving in New Haven three months into the first term and having his last two terms shortened by the beginning of the war and his mother's death, he avoided the worst hazing. When he returned to college at the end of October 1775, he was no longer vulnerable.

Barlow found Yale and Dartmouth's daily routines were very similar. One rose just as early, was exposed to as many religious harangues accompanied by prayers, spent as many hours reciting in class, and ate food almost as monotonous and unpalatable as that which had caused controversy at Dartmouth. There were differences, though, which were largely attributable to Yale's being located in the midst of a port town in direct touch with the larger Atlantic world.

Eighteenth-century New Haven's eight thousand inhabitants occupied an area that included modern East, West, and North Haven, as well as Hamden and Woodbridge. Some features of the former town have survived to the present, including one of New England's largest greens. Then, as now, this pastoral space was graced by prominent churches and bordered by academic buildings. The town also had a range of shops and a waterfront where vessels capable of overseas voyages docked at the Long Wharf. As Barlow took his daily walks through the town, there was no shortage of pretty girls wishing to be noticed or rich fragrances emanating from hogsheads full of sugar and molasses. He could enter one of the shops where fabrics imported from Europe were still available, admire elegantly decorated china plates, or peruse the latest European books. New Haven offered a range of diversions; what Samuel Barlow had feared, Joel reveled in sampling.

Yale also had a library that far surpassed the one at Dartmouth. The college Athenaeum contained four thousand volumes that provided access to most of the learning of the Western world. Not that Yale's freshman or sophomore curriculum gave Barlow much free time in which to explore these riches. He still found himself harnessed to a regime of composing in Latin and Greek, reading classical texts by Virgil and Juvenal, and digesting works on logic and rhetoric, geometry, and geography. But now that he had grown more proficient in the classical languages and no longer had to worry about passing entrance exams, he had some leisure. Because borrowing a book required him to pay a fee, Barlow devoted more of his free time to broadening his associations within the student body than to reading beyond the curriculum.[15]

At the end of his freshman year, he, along with thirty-two classmates, joined a literary and debating society known as the Brothers in Unity. It had been founded less than a decade before by David Humphreys (class of 1771) in the wake of the student protests of the 1760s. The Brothers in Unity challenged the hegemony of an older debating society that only admitted upperclassmen. Because the Brothers in Unity were inclusive, more than 80 percent of the class of 1778 joined. By 1776 the Brothers in Unity included more than half of Yale's undergraduate body. Among its prominent upperclassmen were Chauncey Goodrich (1776), a future congressional representative and senator; Nathaniel Chipman (1777), a future governor of Vermont; and Ebenezer Fitch (1777), the future founding president of Williams College. Before he graduated Barlow would also come into contact with Elizur Goodrich (1779) and Jonathan Ogden Moseley (1780), two future congressmen.[16]

The Brothers in Unity had their own library, which, though small, by 1780 surpassed the library of the rival society. Each year the Brothers held an elaborate anniversary celebration in which selected members presented orations, dialogues, and plays to the assembled membership. Barlow may have gotten a chance to recite the poem he composed about a snowball fight on the Yale campus on one of these occasions. The one line that has survived—"And Jove descends in magazines of snow"—reveals little beyond Barlow's familiarity with classical figures.

More significantly, the Brothers in Unity provided Barlow with an opportunity to measure his wits against the rest of Yale's student body. Because the membership was too numerous for everyone to perform, becoming a recitalist conferred distinction upon Barlow among his fellow students and even some alumni. David Humphreys would pen a complimentary verse about Barlow after meeting him, apparently for the first time, in 1780:

> Barlow I saw, and here began
> My friendship for that spotless man:
> Whom, though the world does not yet know it,
> Great nature form'd her loftiest poet.[17]

Supervising freshman and sophomore recitations fell to the tutors. One tutor then continued with the class during its junior year as student disputations gradually replaced required recitations. Seniors only had one recitation a day, the bulk of their instruction coming from the president and Yale's two professors. But the class tutor still served as advisor to the students, who occasionally petitioned the governing board to permit him to give them special instruction outside the standard curriculum.

Joseph Buckminster (1770) acted as tutor to Barlow's class. A grandson of Jonathan Edwards, and the son of a Congregational minister in Massachusetts, Buckminster had held the prestigious Berkeley fellowship for three years after graduating. In 1773, he joined Timothy Dwight (1769), also a grandson of Jonathan Edwards; Joseph Strong (1772); and Abraham Baldwin (1772), Barlow's future brother-in-law, as tutors. Buckminster would spend much of his life struggling with chronic depression, the early symptoms of which were already emerging during his mid-twenties. But everyone acknowledged his brilliance, and he was known for being approachable and an excellent listener. More than a disciplinarian who made sure the class kept up with their assignments, Buckminster encouraged the talented young men under his supervision. Later he would become noted for subordinating the intellect to religious emotions, a preference that would find reflection in Barlow's life-long quest to articulate the sublime in poetry.

The relationship between the two men was not without its tensions. Buckminster did not entirely trust Barlow because of a disrespectful parody Barlow wrote about acting president Daggett in January 1777.[18] Buckminster also disciplined Barlow for being absent without leave during his last year. Barlow, for his part, along with Uriah Tracy, submitted a petition to the Yale Corporation on behalf of the entire class to have Dwight rather than Buckminster instruct them during their senior year. The petition was a protest against the trustees' efforts to dismiss Dwight for insubordination rather than a slight directed at Buckminster. Barlow turned to Buckminster for guidance and advice after graduation. No one was more responsible for the distinction of the class of 1778 than Buckminster because the repeated interruptions the Revolution imposed on the operations of the college magnified his influence.

In March 1776, after the British were expelled from Boston, everyone expected the conflict to shift to New York. In April, when Americans learned that Britain was sending the largest military force ever dispatched from Europe to North America, Connecticut doubled its contingent in the continental army and mobilized its western militia. As the weather warmed, the flow of men moving toward New York led New Haven's civilian population to sicken as troops streamed through the town. By the beginning of August, camp fever had become so prevalent that the college temporarily disbanded.[19] Barlow stated in a 1781 petition to the General Assembly of Connecticut that he had marched "upon a Tour of Military Duty in the Service of the United States" during the summer of 1776. Presumably, he joined one of the militia units ordered to New York to reinforce the continental army on the eve of the climatic battle that all expected would determine the outcome of the Revolution.[20]

College students were exempt from militia service, and it is by no means clear what Barlow could have contributed to a military campaign. He would have attended very few training days before going off to Hanover, so his military skills could not have extended beyond what little he had imbibed from drilling with Yale's student company. They probably did not include loading and discharging a weapon. His academic training better suited him for clerical duties. Barlow's petition stated that upon becoming sick he was discharged by his commanding officer. The petition followed one he had filed in 1778 that has been lost. The General Assembly had then granted him compensation for his medical bills, but Barlow was forced to petition again because he had not received a warrant for the funds until after the currency collapsed in 1779. Some friends, who wrote about Barlow shortly after he died, asserted that he had been in the Battles of Long Island and White Plains.[21] But his poetic renderings of the war give little hint that he knew the face of battle at first hand. All that can be said with certainty is that it is unlikely the assembly would have passed favorably on his petition had he not had some role in the campaign of 1776.

Similarly, it is impossible to prove that he came close to harm's way when half a year later the British burned the continental army's supplies in Danbury. Twice during the early months of 1777, President Daggett sent Yale's students home because the college could not feed them. The furloughed students were expected to continue their studies, and it is not clear where Barlow went on these breaks. He could have been a guest in the household of one of his classmates. But without a tender of hospitality, he would have had little choice but to fall back upon his Redding brothers, who would surely have welcomed an extra hand for their spring chores.

Yale was in recess on April 25, 1777, when the British landed a force of 1,800 men under Gov. William Tryon's command on Compo Beach in modern Westport. In the ensuing thirty-six hours the enemy marched twenty-three miles to Danbury through Redding before making their way back via Ridgefield to where they had disembarked. On their way in, the main British column passed within three miles of the Barlow homestead. No one expected the citizens of Redding to resist the invasion. A local company that Capt. Zalmon Read had recruited for the continental army did march from its bivouac in Danbury toward the advancing British column on April 26. But when they stumbled on a flanking detachment of the British that morning to the west of what today is Connecticut Route 58, Read's company quickly dissolved and most of his men were taken prisoner. Because manpower and firepower bore a one-to-one ratio to each other, a mere handful of soldiers could expect to make little impression on superior numbers. The flanking column is thought to have passed within a mile of the Barlow homestead before turning east on an old Cross Highway to link up with the main column on Redding Ridge.[22]

The town's inhabitants were principally concerned with securing their women and children and sequestering as much of their property as possible. Before the British arrived in the late morning of the twenty-sixth, some of the children—including Gershom Barlow, one of Nathaniel's sons—with a few older women took refuge in the Devil's Den, a rocky wilderness area several miles south of the Barlow homestead. There they would remain until the enemy reembarked on the evening of the twenty-seventh. Because the weather was stormy through much of the twenty-sixth, not everyone found this option attractive. Most instead focused on figuring out where the British were going and trying to get out of their way. The invaders paused for several hours where the modern Cross Highway intersects with Black Rock Turnpike but had little incentive to wander because they still had a hard day's march ahead of them. Similarly, most of the Redding loyalists in Tryon's force under Montfort Browne's command came from East rather than West Redding, and any who were inclined to wander westward from the main body of Tryon's force would have been wary about descending the steep hill that slopes from Redding Center to the Saugatuck River.[23]

After fighting a brief engagement in Ridgefield and bivouacking overnight, the invaders marched out within walking distance of West Redding. The Barlow clan preferred observing the invaders from a distance to joining the militia trying to intercept them. That Barlow did not refer to the Danbury Raid in *The Vision of Columbus*, though he alluded to other British pillaging raids , is hardly surprising. Discretion, while the better part of valor in such situations, is not the stuff from which heroic epics are made. Twenty years later he did allude to the Raid in *The Columbiad*, after time had made the unheroic character of those three April days more acceptable.[24]

Yale's governing board directed the juniors to reassemble in Glastonbury at the end of May 1777. The students lodged in private homes, which often required four of them to share a room designed for two. However, a summer term in Glastonbury had the advantage of placing them more under Buckminster's supervision. President Daggett, who had announced his resignation in March, tried to circulate between Glastonbury, Wethersfield, and Farmington, the three towns to which the college had dispersed. But he was not as ubiquitous as he would have been in New Haven, with the result that the academic routine became less strict. Barlow took advantage of the new circumstance to experiment with writing poetry. One poem, dated July 5, 1777, was entitled "To a Friend at Cambridge." In seven stanzas it celebrated the capacity of friendship to thrive despite physical separation. The other surviving poem from that summer consisted of two stanzas addressed to "Chloe." Neither is significant beyond showing that Barlow was losing any shyness he might have had about exhibiting his verse to his classmates.

Glastonbury proved sufficiently agreeable to the class of 1778 that they petitioned the Yale Corporation in September to allow them to continue their studies there with either the junior or the freshman classes. The Corporation instead authorized Buckminster to continue with the new seniors as best he could. The advance of Burgoyne's army down the Hudson River dictated the continued dispersal of Yale. Connecticut detached two full regiments from its state brigades to join the continental army to the North, while two brigades drawn from the state's western militia saw briefer service along the lower Hudson. Maj. Gen. Oliver Wolcott, the father of Barlow's classmate, also led three hundred mounted volunteers to join Gen. Horatio Gates's army at Saratoga. Concurrently, Connecticut's Council of Safety sponsored an abortive attempt to dislodge the British from Newport, Rhode Island, while supporting Gen. Israel Putnam's misguided attempts to move against the British around New York City.

Although Yale students were missing from these detachments, no one could have been indifferent about the looming battle. The Yale Corporation awaited the results of the campaign before calling the college back to New Haven. Some of the class dutifully tarried in Glastonbury with Buckminster until mid-November 1777. By then it was apparent that the great victory won at Saratoga had again made New Haven a suitable place for instruction, despite military disappointments closer to home. But five members of the senior class—Barlow among them—had begun teaching school during the prolonged period in which the college's normal operations were in limbo. Two of the absentees did so in defiance of express instructions from college authorities. The Yale Corporation ordered them to appear before the board at its next meeting. Barlow had not defied explicit orders and won official reinstatement simply by rejoining his class in January. Uriah Tracy and Jonathan Frisbie did not fare so well and were ordered to receive a public reprimand at chapel on February 3, 1778.

Twenty-six of their classmates, including Barlow, ostentatiously walked out of this ceremonial humiliation, precipitating a fierce reaction from the college authorities. If mass expulsions were not threatened, the denial of diplomas certainly was. To win reinstatement, the rebellious students acknowledged they had acted "in Consequence of a premeditated and preconcerted Combination." Though there is no evidence that Barlow was among the organizers of the protest, the tutors suspected him of being a ringleader. He probably also had a hand in drafting the apology, which confessed that their conduct could "not be rationally viewed in any other light than that of an audacious Contempt of the Authority of the College," as well as "a practical Countenancing and Approving of the Crimes of others." The signers of this document "publicly condemn[ed]" themselves for what they had done and admitted "we justly deserve a very severe punishment on account of it." But they begged for "all that lenity . . . towards us, that is consistent with the due Government of College," promising "that we will for the future carefully avoid all such like disorderly Behavior" and observe "a decent Deportment, and a becoming dutiful obedience to all the Authority and Order of College."[25]

Students and the college authorities only narrowly avoided inflicting lasting damage on the institution. To give everyone a chance to cool off, the class of 1778 was once again dismissed from the end of February until late May. Mercifully the turmoil into which Yale had been plunged by the Corporation's attempts to run the institution without a president was about to end. In late March, Ezra Stiles (class of 1746) agreed to become the college's next leader. A native of North Haven, where his father had been the Congregational minister, Stiles had served as a tutor after graduation before accepting the pastorate of the Second Congregational Church in Newport, Rhode Island. There he officiated for twenty years until the beginning of the Revolutionary War, when the death of his wife and the exodus of many of his parishioners from Aquidneck Island induced him to follow them to Massachusetts. In April 1777, he accepted a Congregational pulpit in Portsmouth, New Hampshire, only to agree to become president of Yale less than a year later.

Stiles took his time moving to New Haven, setting aside four weeks to be inoculated with small pox now that he faced an increased risk of contracting the disease. Any excitement Barlow may have felt on learning of Stiles's appointment was tempered by the news that Buckminster would assume the pulpit Stiles had just vacated. But the new president immediately began instructing the senior class and quickly demonstrated his determination to compensate for some of what they had missed throughout their college career. The class responded by petitioning Stiles to double their number of daily recitations with him. Instead, Stiles treated them to a series of lectures in which he exposed them to the breadth of his learning. He also increased the number of disputations during their last month at Yale, enabling Barlow to catch the new president's attention during his final term.

On June 29, Stiles chose Barlow to be the sole respondent at a public disputation on the proposition *"Diluvium Noachi fuit universale"* (The flood of Noah was universal). Barlow had to challenge the proposition while everyone else in the class defended it.[26] In July, Stiles also selected Barlow to be one of five featured seniors who would perform at a ceremony scheduled for the twenty-third, following the morning examinations that concluded the term. Barlow was to recite a poem of his own composition, while Josiah Meigs would deliver a Latin oration. Three other classmates were assigned English dialogues.

Drafting a major poem lent additional excitement to Barlow's last days as an undergraduate. He chose as his theme and title *The Prospect of Peace*. During the summer of 1778, it looked as though the nation was about to emerge from the thralldom of war. Burgoyne's surrender the previous year had led France to enter into an alliance with the American republic and to dispatch a powerful expeditionary force to the western Atlantic. For the first time since the commencement of hostilities, Britain's naval dominance seemed in jeopardy. British forces in North America, confronted with the prospect of Franco-American cooperation, went on the defensive. Reflecting rising optimism, the continental currency—which had been falling steadily in value since the British had occupied New York City—briefly reversed its inexorable decline. It was still too early for Yale's student body to learn much about the combined operations that were taking shape against British-occupied Newport, but everyone expected that a decisive engagement would soon be fought. The senior class hoped to enter the larger world just as a military victory inaugurated a new era, and Barlow sought to give form to their expectations.

The Prospect of Peace, containing 234 lines in rhymed hexameter, took Barlow twelve minutes to recite.[27] It began with the claim that the revolutionaries acted as agents of divine providence.

> In this grand conflict Heaven's Eternal Sire,
> At whose dread frown the sons of guilt expire,
> Bade vengeance rise, with sacred fury driven,
> On those who war with Innocence and Heaven.   (11–14)

Most of the poem described a millennium that could be expected to emerge from the approaching peace. It foresaw material prosperity, urban development, social justice, and a general flowering of the arts and sciences as freedom fired "the genius of the rising age" (142). Even slaves would benefit from the new order:

> Afric's unhappy children, now no more
> Shall feel the cruel chains they felt before,
> But every State in this just mean agree,
> To bless mankind, and set th' oppressed free.   (81–84)

Barlow cast the poet as the herald of his imagined millennium (153–58), and his expectations about the coming peace extended beyond the United States to embrace the entire human family.

> From each far corner of th' extended earth,
> Her gathering sons shall claim their promis'd birth,
> Thro' the drear wastes, beneath the setting day,
> Where prowling natives haunt the woods for prey,
> The swarthy Millions lift their wondering eyes,
> And smile to see the Gospel morning rise:
> Those who, thro' time, in savage darkness lay,
> Wake to new light, and hail the glorious day!   (189–96)

The ensuing revelation would lead to a new birth for mankind in which "Love shall rule, and Innocence adore, / Discord shall cease, and Tyrants be no more" (225–26). After a thousand years, the crowning fulfillment of Christian history would occur when material creation would be consumed in flames. Then

> The Church elect, from smouldering ruins, rise,
> And sails triumphant thro' the yielding skies,

Hail'd by the Bridegroom! To the Father given,
The Joy of Angels, and the Queen of Heaven!   (231–34)

The poem reassured Buckminster and Stiles that Barlow was aligned with Yale's religious mission, and the publishers of the *Connecticut Journal*, Thomas and Samuel Green of New Haven, quickly printed an edition of it. Upon seeing a copy, Buckminster wrote Barlow from New Hampshire to congratulate him on his achievement, reporting that "Your Poem does you honor in this part of the Country and every person that has seen it speaks very highly of it."[28] Its popularity, as well as Buckminster's relief, derived from Barlow's success in synthesizing two basic strands of revolutionary ideology: Christianity and Republicanism. Though few clerics were oblivious of the potential for conflict between them, Barlow had managed to conceal that tension. It was an achievement that did not go unnoticed among his contemporaries, fully justifying the subsequent encouragement he received not just from the Yale community of talented classmates and teachers but from many of nation's gentry leadership.

CHAPTER TWO

Ambitious Goals

On the Sabbath following the senior ceremony, two brigades of the continental army (approximately 4,000 men) passed through New Haven on their way to rendezvous with Charles Hector, the Comte d'Estaing's expeditionary force in Narragansett Bay. Detachments of militia followed them. Ezra Stiles commented on the "amazing Spirit for rushing towards Rh. Isld. spread 100 miles around."[1] Joel Barlow could have joined as a volunteer, since the seniors were excused from any further requirements aside from attending commencement on September 9. However, he never mentioned doing so, and it seems likely that he went home to Redding instead. A week later a fleet of British vessels sailed west past New Haven after failing to reinforce their garrison at Newport. D'Estaing had gotten there first and blocked their access to the Bay. Allied strength seemed to be waxing as the enemy's strength waned.

The first hint that combined operations against the British in Rhode Island had gone awry came on August 13, 1778, when a violent northeaster struck southern New England. By then reports were circulating that a stronger British naval force under Admiral Richard Howe had arrived off Newport on August 9. d'Estaing ordered his vessels to sea on the tenth, and both fleets maneuvered for advantage. The northeaster hit just as they began to engage. The storm damaged both equally; Howe limped back to New York to refit, while the French fleet returned to Newport. Once d'Estaing realized his damaged fleet could not be readily repaired in Narragansett Bay, he retreated to Boston. A former gateway port that was emerging as the privateering capital of the revolutionary confederation, Boston had naval resources Narragansett Bay lacked. The withdrawal of the

French expeditionary force compelled abandonment of the siege of Newport and, because d'Estaing was under orders to make the conquest of British possessions in the West Indies his priority once the hurricane season passed, threatened to prolong the war indefinitely. After refitting in Boston, the French fleet would not return to the North American coast until the next hurricane season in 1779.

These developments adversely affected New England. The combined pressures of outfitting the French and feeding Burgoyne's captured army drained the region's limited resources. By winter, grain was in chronically short supply and would remain so at least until the next harvest. But more ominous than the shortage of provisions was the effect the failure of combined operations had on the continental currency. At the beginning of 1778 Congress had faced a choice between cutting back on its war effort and betting on the French alliance bringing the conflict to a speedy, triumphant conclusion. Once it became apparent that Congress had lost this bet, its currency went into a tailspin from which it never recovered. By the summer of 1779, Congress had contracted a debt of more than $200 million, which it clearly could not pay. After suspending the issuance of any more bills of credit, it became dependent for financial support on the separate states, which also had contracted large debts, or on foreign allies.

Far from taking their places in a larger world brimming with opportunities, Yale's 1778 graduates found themselves confronting seriously diminished prospects. Most had the advantage of parents who could help. A college degree prepared its recipients for the three learned professions; law and divinity were held in the greatest esteem, but medicine also qualified. Twelve of the class would eventually become lawyers, six doctors, and four ministers. Oliver Wolcott and Uriah Tracy were lucky enough to read law with Tapping Reeve, who would soon establish the nation's first law school in Litchfield. Zephaniel Swift, Josiah Meigs, and several others placed themselves under the guidance of prominent local attorneys, while the parents of the four who became clergymen made provision for their sons to read theology.

Barlow lacked a father able to ease him over difficult times. Noah Webster was equally strapped and chose to teach in Hartford while simultaneously studying law. Although only three of Barlow's Yale class would teach school after graduation, it was an acceptable, temporary expedient for a recent college graduate. Many distinguished men, including John Adams, had taught before reading law. However, Barlow felt reluctant about doing so because he was interested in none of the customary professions. Instead, the success of *The Prospect of Peace* had fired his ambition to make a name for himself as a poet.

He was not alone among his generation in assuming America needed a distinctive poetry. In 1771 Philip Freneau, James Madison's Princeton roommate, in collaboration with Hugh Brackenridge, had sown the seed of nationalistic verse in their "The Rising Glory of America." In 1775 Timothy Dwight completed his biblical epic, *The Conquest of Canaan*, though a decade would elapse before it was published. Barlow began toying with the idea of writing a heroic epic about the Revolution toward the end of 1778. But because such a work required years of labor, it seemed beyond the reach of someone without visible means of support. The failure of the campaign of 1778 also made the likelihood of having a victory to celebrate more problematic. Milton had achieved renown with a tragic epic, but Barlow had no intention of following that path. He wanted to sing a song of triumph. Balancing his hesitation was the realization that if he did not stake his claim to the enterprise soon, some one else might. Deeply perplexed and unsure of himself, Barlow turned for guidance to Joseph Buckminster.

Barlow approached his former tutor with diffidence because Buckminster had disciplined him for failing to return to college in November 1777. During the autumn of 1778, though, Buckminster reassured Barlow of his "particular tenderness for your class and for you," which was cemented by "the peculiar share of genius and merit with which as a class they were distinguished." He even flattered Barlow by confessing that he had been tempted to assume part of the credit that *The Prospect of Peace* had garnered in Portsmouth because "it grew up . . . under my Auspices." Like all great teachers, Buckminster continued to encourage Barlow to pursue his genius, reminding him that one's education should not cease upon leaving college. Instead one's degree was the foundation on which each graduate should build the best "superstructure" he could.[2]

Barlow still needed reassurance that he was not hopelessly misguided in attempting so ambitious an enterprise. Buckminster wrote reassuringly at the beginning of January 1779, "I believe you are the only person that has this scruple who has seen the *Prospect of Peace*." Buckminster declined to be more effusive because "Were I to say all I think of your abilities you would perhaps judge it flattery." But though he could offer no guarantees, he did believe that Barlow's "fondness for the great Scenes of literature . . . [could] . . . be productive of something that will here after do you honor and benefit mankind." The problem as Buckminster saw it was not Barlow's talent but how to proceed when "neither our Country nor our Country men are sufficiently inriched [*sic*] and improved to give sufficient support to works of Genius." A Pope or a Milton would "starve upon the pittance that a few Persons capable of relishing your productions would give."[3]

In the absence of rich patrons, Barlow needed a way to support himself. Buckminster would not recommend the law because lawyers inevitably found themselves sacrificing moral concerns to their clients' interests. Medicine looked as though it was compatible with poetry, but in practice it had not proven to be. Buckminster preferred divinity, arguing that the Bible furnished some of the greatest examples of poetry accessible to man, pointing specifically to the book of Job and the Eighteenth Psalm. Barlow acknowledged the natural affinity between divinity and poetry and admitted an inclination to pursue both, but he was more interested in the study of divinity than the practice of it. "The ministry is too important for my abilities and attended with too little prospect of success. If I can better serve mankind in some other way, I hope a regard to duty will direct me to it." Though he feared his "prospect of . . . proficiency" in poetry was no greater than that for divinity, he decided "to attend to the former . . . while I tarry at college."[4]

Barlow had hoped for a Yale tutorship. The position carried with it room and board, and would have provided a congenial environment in which to pursue his poetic interests. But the only opening had already been offered to his classmate, Josiah Meigs. Uncertain about what to do next, he wandered between New Haven and Redding in the first months after graduation. He even made a visit to Washington's army on the Hudson, although he never seriously considered seeking a commission. The rank of ensign carried so paltry a salary in depreciating continentals that it could not possibly support Barlow in the style to which he aspired.

Barlow's past made him hopeful despite his uncertain prospects. He had repeatedly extracted advantage from adversity. The death of his father had led to his transfer from Dartmouth to Yale, while the death of his mother had enabled him to thrive at the college despite its irregular wartime sessions. Serendipity seemed to bless him in the autumn of 1778 when he agreed to instruct the children of several prominent New Haven families. Needing room and board, he took lodgings in the house of one of them, a local blacksmith named Michael Baldwin. Barlow had known two of Michael's sons at college. The most gifted one, Abraham, was almost exactly Joel's age and had entered Yale in 1768. After Abraham graduated in 1772 and became a tutor, his older brother Dudley matriculated with the class of 1777. Both recommended Barlow to their father. Boarding with the Baldwins introduced Barlow to a family with whom he would remain close for the rest of his life.

Michael Baldwin, a native of nearby North Guilford, had married a local woman, Lucy Dudley, two years his junior, when he was 30. Their first child, a daughter named Ruth, died at the age of 4 in 1755. Four children followed in rapid succession, two boys, Dudley and Abraham, and two girls—another Ruth and finally Lucy. Mother Lucy died two weeks after giving birth to little Lucy, who died two years later. Barlow's father, Samuel, had responded to a similar misfortune by quickly remarrying, but Michael Baldwin remained a widower for a decade before taking a second, much younger wife, Theodora Wolcot, aged 22, just before he turned 50. That created a greater gulf between the children of his first and second marriages than had been the case in Samuel Barlow's family. By 1778, as Michael Baldwin approached 60, his children by the first marriage were referring to him distantly as "the old Gentleman."[5]

Michael Baldwin did one other unusual thing at the time of his second marriage. He moved his family to New Haven when Abraham, aged fourteen, entered college. Eventually, four of Michael's sons would earn Yale degrees, and three of these had distinguished public careers. Abraham would become an influential member of the Constitutional Convention at Philadelphia and a four-term senator from Georgia. Michael (class of 1795) migrated to Ohio where he was elected to the legislature, serving for a while as speaker of the state's House of Representatives. And Henry (1797) served as a congressman from western Pennsylvania before eventually being appointed a justice of the U.S. Supreme Court.

Several of Michael Baldwin's younger children were among Barlow's pupils, but the Baldwin who most attracted Barlow's attention was Ruth. Two years the junior of Abraham and Joel, Ruth was the only surviving female child of Michael's first marriage. Her stepmother's first child, another Lucy, was born when Theodora was 24 and Ruth not quite 14. Theodora naturally turned to Ruth for assistance, who gladly helped. But as Ruth grew older, tensions developed between the two women. Nor were the strains within the family confined solely to the relationship between Ruth and Theodora. The surviving three siblings from Michael's first marriage formed a special intimacy with one another. Each took a nickname they used among themselves, and together they developed a way of speaking and writing that Abraham referred to as their "antiquarian expressions."[6] Yet the bond between the older children did not create an insuperable gulf with their half-siblings. Abraham eventually put two of his half-brothers through Yale, and Ruth grew especially attached to her younger half-sister, Clara, later in life.

Barlow quickly won his way into this tight-knit circle by capturing Ruth's fancy and reciprocating her offer of love. Initially, he could only have had vague intimations of how important the three Baldwins would soon become to him. Although he was preoccupied with keeping school, before long Barlow was spending "every evening in Ladies company."[7] A circle of young women that included Ruth formed around President Stiles's oldest daughter, Betsy; they found Barlow far

more interesting than most of the other eligible men. Elizabeth Whitman became infatuated with him after a game of forfeits that required them to pretend
they were husband and wife for an evening. Elizabeth, who was keen on poetry,
found an ideal mate in Barlow, who readily matched her wit when she proposed
adopting the nine muses as their children.

Whitman had already gone through two failed engagements to Yale tutors.
The first had been terminated by death, but Elizabeth had taken the initiative in
breaking her second engagement to Buckminster, in whom she may have sensed
the seeds of chronic depression. She found being married, if only in jest, to an
aspiring poet two years her junior appealing. In her letters Whitman referred to
herself obliquely as his wife as she invited Barlow to embark on a correspondence
"in which all disguises are thrown off."[8] Barlow responded with equal playfulness
to this conceit, even as his and Ruth's attraction to each other ripened into love
and mutual commitment.

Once Michael Baldwin became aware that something was afoot, he banned
Barlow from the house and sent Ruth away to North Guilford. Elizabeth Whitman probably had a role in the banishment, since she subsequently apologized to
Barlow for his being "so ill received at Mr. B.'s . . . I cannot conceive where Mrs. B.
got her intelligence, or who gave *you* yours." Whitman promised to rectify any
misinformation the Baldwins attributed to her and thanked Joel for his understanding. "I wish I could repay you and one other friend [Abraham?] for the kind
part" he had taken in the affair.[9]

Ruth's two older brothers were not put off by Barlow's penniless condition or
his poetic ambitions. Dudley and Abraham supported their sister in her romantic
preference, and Abraham invited Barlow to move into his tutor's suite at Yale. The
invitation provided Barlow with a temporary refuge as well as with daily reports
about Ruth. But Michael Baldwin also insisted on breaking up the school Barlow
had been keeping, raising anew the problem of what he should do with himself.
In March 1779, Barlow applied for appointment as college butler, but the position
went to Dudley. This setback failed to dislodge Barlow either from New Haven or
from courting Ruth. The distance Michael had established between the young
lovers simply fueled a correspondence that flourished in the face of adversity. The
youngsters enjoyed the support of many peers, who derived satisfaction from participating peripherally, and therefore safely, in a rebellious romance. Even Elizabeth Whitman joined in, referring to Ruth as "your 'second wife.'"[10]

The romance offered their friends a welcome distraction from the dreary stale-
mate that had overtaken the war. The winter of 1779 brought the first reports that

the British meant to make good on a threat the Carlisle Commission had issued the previous autumn. Established by Parliament in an effort to abort the French alliance by conciliating America, the Commission had responded to being rebuffed with a manifesto promising a war of devastation against the former colonies. In March, Buckminster expressed concern about a published report—it proved false—that a British detachment had managed to advance up the Connecticut coast from Horseneck (modern Greenwich) as far as Milford. While it did not seem "possible that they should march . . . unchecked thro such a settled country," Buckminster wondered whether Barlow might not "be realizing those scenes that you have often described in the field of Mars."[11]

Instead of witnessing a military engagement, Barlow was busy seeking financial support from Nathaniel and Aaron. Initially, they declined, and Barlow wrote Wolcott that instead of finding "dame Fortune," he had met with "Mis[s] fortune."[12] Eventually, though, his brothers agreed to support him while he got a masters degree at Yale. They were faring far better than Barlow, and if they had purchased the livestock Esther had left him, as well as his share of the lands he had inherited —as seems likely given the tight-knit nature of the Barlow family economy—he would have had some claim on their generosity since they had received appreciating assets in exchange for depreciating currency.[13]

There was no set curriculum for a master's degree. While candidates were expected to attend prayers, lectures, and divine services, they were excused from all other requirements and had unfettered access to the library. This freed Barlow to experiment with writing poetry. One of his short productions, dated March 7, 1779, addressed to Abraham Baldwin, saluted him as "my Friend" and celebrated how "welcome your plaudits" were "to the grateful ear." In the next verse, however, Barlow worried lest Abraham "varnish weakness with the tint of Praise." He continued,

> What tho' thy willing ear be pleas'd awhile,
> This be the test: be Friendship's noblest end,
> Let partial fondness ne'er thy skill beguile,
> Nor the bold Critic soften in the Friend.[14]

At this point Barlow put more stock in Buckminster's than Baldwin's advice.

Barlow knew that fugitive bits of poetry led nowhere, and Buckminster urged him to find a subject that would serve the cause of religion as well as literature. Barlow was wary of Buckminster's specific suggestions because they all involved the Old Testament. Referring to *The Conquest of Canaan*, Barlow argued that "Mr. Dwight has been so particular in every thing that concerns the interest of that people, that he had precluded the beauty of any subject which principally concerns the Jews." Barlow did consider exploring Christian themes. The Messiah tempted him, but Milton had already demonstrated its perils with the failure of his sequel to *Paradise Lost*. *Paradise Regained* simply showed "we have no need of it." Buckminster was inclined to agree, though for a different reason: the Messiah as a subject was "too grand for mortal Eloquence."[15]

Prodding from Buckminster and Elizabeth Whitman eventually led Barlow to experiment with several elegies and to try putting a biblical story into verse. Whitman approved of his elegies, but felt Barlow's "History of Joseph" fell flat. Barlow also attempted a longer poem about Cyrus the Great but quickly abandoned the enterprise after realizing that such a subject could never establish the reputation of an American poet. The same objection lay against Buckminster's suggestions about the story of Cain and Abel and Saint Paul's trial and martyrdom. Instead, during the spring of 1779, Barlow decided to commit himself to drafting a long poem about Christopher Columbus. Barlow felt "the discovery of America [had] made an important revolution in the history of mankind," which "as much as any human transaction that ever took place" had furthered "knowledge, liberty and Religion."[16] Though Buckminster later expressed reservations about this decision, the project gathered momentum over the next several months.

However, difficulties remained to undertaking so ambitious a project, not the least of which was timing. Barlow feared that "literary accomplishments will not be so much noticed till some time after the settlement of Peace and the people are more refined. More blustering characters must bear the sway at present. [A]nd the hardy veteran must retire from the field before the philosopher can retire to the closet." The accelerating depreciation of the currency was also eating into his dwindling resources. In mid-March he reported to Oliver Wolcott Jr. that in his recent quarterly bill, board had risen to £5 9s. 7d. a week. "This makes me feelingly sensible of what I am, and leads me to some serious tho'ts about quitting my hold at N. Haven," even though the alternative "to go plowing" was incompatible either with his inclination or his artistic ambitions.[17]

During this dark period of uncertainty his principal consolation was his developing relationship with Ruth. When Ruth took up Elizabeth Whitman's game of claiming him as her husband, he experienced no difficulty in playing along. Abraham Baldwin's decision to resign his tutorship and go into the continental army as a chaplain to the Connecticut brigade, however, complicated Barlow's situation. Deprived of a close friend and confidant, Barlow looked around for a substitute and took the initiative in approaching Timothy Dwight through Elizabeth Whitman, who was Dwight's second cousin.

In May, Whitman wrote Barlow, "I heard last night from Mr. Dwight that he will soon take a journey to camp. He will certainly either go or return by way of New Haven, so you will be able to consult him yourself."[18] Dwight had already heard of Barlow's project from Baldwin and Buckminster and agreed to meet Barlow at the end of June. That led to an invitation to spend the summer in Northampton to assist at Dwight's new academy. Barlow immediately accepted but postponed joining Dwight until after paying his brothers a visit during the grain harvest that took place at the beginning of July. Barlow's presence would have significantly enhanced his brothers' and their neighbors' capacity to bring in what they had planted the previous autumn. Since they had been generous with him, it was only fitting he make himself available when they most needed him.

On July 5, 1779, a large British force under the command of William Tryon attacked New Haven. Half the student body of the college turned out to resist the enemy, fighting effectively under the leadership of President Stiles's son, Ezra Junior, a recent Harvard graduate. New Haven enjoyed an advantage in resisting the enemy because the British divided their force in approaching the town. This, in turn, helped spare it from the torch. But twenty-seven Americans died as a consequence of the raid, among them Naphtalie Daggett. The British also burned the Long Wharf together with several vessels, and while they pillaged some properties, the Baldwin household escaped unharmed.

Barlow was closer to the raid on Fairfield, which the British visited on July 8 after leaving New Haven. Because Redding's militia had responded to New Haven's summons, it failed to reach Fairfield before the British withdrew on the ninth, after burning more than two hundred structures in the center of town. The next day the British struck several miles to the west, burning the smaller, outlying community of Green Farms. The smoke from both conflagrations would have been clearly visible in Redding, but such evidence meant it was already too late to render assistance. The demands of the harvest would have deterred Barlow from viewing the extent of the destruction, especially as the tales of refugees, who sought temporary shelter in Redding, supplied him with many firsthand accounts of the attack.

Sometime around July 22, Barlow set out from Redding for Northampton via Kensington and Hartford. At the time Ruth was visiting in Kensington, and the day they spent together revived his ardor for her. Barlow subsequently wrote from Hartford that he could not take "a step farther without sending back a piece of my soul." He confessed that "ever since I set out for Redding [three weeks before] I have been unhappy." By this stage in their relationship, his "Dearest Ruthy" was making shirts for him. "I wish you to set the ruffle very full," he instructed her. But since the distance between them would increase over the next few months, he entrusted her "happiness . . . to your own care this summer."[19] Northampton was no more than two day's ride from Hartford, but a round trip would consume the better part of a week and was incompatible with his short-term commitment to Dwight's academy.

Barlow reported to Ruth that "my present retirement is much more agreeable than I expected, I have banished every uneasy tho't and live like an Arcadian." Earlier, in mid-August 1779, he had described himself to Webster as being "eagerly imployed in building poetical air-castles as ever I was when a boy in building cob-houses." But the self-disparagement that followed—"and they are about as important"—reflected the sense of inadequacy Dwight inspired in him.[20] Nonetheless, while in Northampton, Barlow succeeded in completing the first full outline of the poem that would become *The Vision of Columbus*. It called for a survey of the development of the Americas since Columbus's discovery and utilized a device employed by *Paradise Lost* where the archangel Michael explains to Adam the full consequences of his and Eve's transgression. An angel would free a defeated and imprisoned Columbus just before the end of his life so he could survey the human development that his discoveries had set in motion. The last book of the projected epic would be devoted to the "Future progress of society," leaving open the possibility that Barlow would be able to celebrate not only a victorious conclusion to the war but the many improvements he expected would flow from the Revolution.[21]

Despite what he had accomplished, three weeks after leaving Northampton, Barlow confessed to Ruth that depression had reduced him to tears. "I rose this morning about eight o'clock and all the shades of uncertainty and disappointment fell upon my mind at once and I trembled upon the borders of despair." The fruitfulness of his imagination had created a plan that would require Herculean exertions to execute while doing nothing to address the problem of where he was to find support for such an enterprise. He complained to Ruth: "I have now got to the end of my line. I am here in Hartford without a single prospect of resource of any kind. I have not a plan that will carry me an inch out of this town and know not which way to ride." His second application to be the college butler looked as though it too would fail when the position was again offered to Dudley. If he accepted, "I shall go into the army or a school or lie down and die. [A]nd I am very indifferent which I do."[22]

Until then self-pity had been absent from Barlow's correspondence. But the tension between his ambitions and the reality of his circumstances momentarily overpowered him. Ruth's reply has not survived, but she clearly was not put off by this revelation of weakness. Whitman's response was equally supportive. "Let me beg of you, dear friend, not to be discouraged with regard to your design, though it should not proceed at this time." She added, "Fortune owes you much—& she will pay you. You are placed at the bottom of the whell [sic] & every change must be for the better. You have every thing to hope and nothing to fear." Though Barlow might despise "the favors of Fortune," Whitman reminded him that all he needed was "a decent independence that will enable you to gratify your favorite inclinations." She assured him that "those gentlemen," whom his friends in Hartford had been talking to, approved of his plan. Whitman was confident "you will certainly meet with assistance. Keep up your spirits, and be certain of the constant affection of your friends."[23]

It was not like Barlow to remain down for long. Writing to Ruth from Middletown, where he had stopped to visit Josiah Meigs, he reported that "President [Stiles] and some of the principal Gentlemen in the State are endeavoring to make me happy, and I am <u>determined</u> to make you happy." Paraphrasing Whitman's letter, he voiced his confidence that "Our Good Fortune is yet to come." Barlow found it encouraging that influential people were trying to arrange a way for him to pursue his ambition, and he continued to circulate among those who were most likely to help. In early October he tarried for almost a week at General Wolcott's visiting Oliver Jr. He then moved on to Redding, where General Parsons had established his headquarters in an encampment two miles from brother Aaron's house. There Abraham and Dudley joined him. After listening to Abraham preach to Nathaniel Bartlett's "little flock," they repaired to Aaron's for dinner and a long talk about the future. Abraham and Barlow then spent a glorious autumn afternoon building imaginary "castles . . . [that] wanted nothing to support them but a little mammon of this world." Much as Barlow disliked pursuing patrons, he thought it justified by his desire "to make virtuous people happy."[24]

Finding a patron in wartime New England remained difficult. Barlow might have taken a position as tutor in a wealthy family had one been available. But Buckminster reported from Portsmouth, "the times have reduced our best characters to moderate means of subsistence, and those that are now rising are but mushroom-gentry and knowing little of learning themselves they are but little anxious that their children should know more."[25] Noah Webster suggested Barlow approach a Norwich merchant, John Perkins. Perkins advised Barlow "to go into business for a living, and . . . make poetry only an amusement for leisure hours." Barlow rejected this suggestion because he feared "leisure hours will never come to me after I am buried in business for life." He wanted "to devote the heat of my youthful imagination" to a poetical enterprise and asked Noah Atwater and William Lockwood, currently tutors at the college, to approach Stiles again about a tutorship. However, since Stiles had passed over him many times, Barlow realized "the matter is delicate," and that there was a danger of "saying too much or driving too fast." Stiles had "always been friendly," and his influence might be useful in flushing out future opportunities.[26]

Barlow's wanderings had the advantage of widely dramatizing his plight. His Hartford friends, chiefly Elizabeth Whitman and Webster, seconded by classmates Asher Miller and Josiah Meigs, talked with everyone they could about Barlow's plan. Miller brought it to the attention of Titus Hosmer, who had graduated from Yale in 1757 and settled in Middletown to practice law. A dozen years later Hosmer emerged as a local leader of the revolutionary movement and was elected to the General Assembly in 1773. After the commencement of hostilities, he joined the state's Council of Safety and in 1778 was elected an assistant or member of the upper house of the legislature as well as a member of Connecticut's delegation to the Continental Congress. Hosmer was wealthy enough to possess a private library of over two hundred books.

In the middle of December 1779, Barlow wrote Oliver Wolcott Jr. that "Mr. Hosmer has undertaken to find some Gentlemen to patronize me . . . for executing my poetical plan" and had already made some progress in finding someone "ready to assist me."[27] But the prospect failed to fit Barlow's needs. Elizabeth Whitman's attempt to interest Col. John Broom in Barlow's work also came to naught. The family was mourning the "loss of a dear sister," which deterred Whitman from pressing the matter "at present." There was another problem as well: "his children are so young. I can hardly think he wants an instructor."[28]

Barlow would spend half a year futilely searching for a way to support himself so that he could write the poem gestating in his head. During that interval he declined the opportunity to take classmate Seth Storrs's place in Timothy Dwight's Northampton academy. Instead, he moved into a vacant college room between December 16, 1779, and February 1, 1780, when Yale was in recess, using it as a base from which to explore additional opportunities. He briefly visited Hartford at the end of December to check out a prospect Hosmer had turned up, and then New London. Both sorties yielded nothing. But there were compensations amid his repeated frustrations. When Barlow wasn't in the company of the Baldwin brothers, or other friends, he caught occasional glimpses of Ruth. Sometimes, when weather permitted, she joined Barlow for an evening ride. By then Elizabeth Whitman had begun to recognize that Ruth came first in his life. In February, Whitman observed that "I hear little from you this winter, but will not complain," though "there was a time when no cares would have made you so long unmindful of your *dearest*, I mean *one of* your *dearest* 'wifes' [*sic*]." Formal acknowledgment of Ruth's primacy would not be forthcoming until more than a year later when Whitman promised "to be as generous as possible, and . . . not begrudge you to her but a little."[29]

During the winter of 1779–80 Barlow began drafting the first book of *The Vision of Columbus* to have something to show prospective patrons. His efforts at promoting his poetical ambitions sometimes yielded unexpected advantages. In the course of one excursion during the spring of 1780, probably to visit Abraham at an army encampment, he was introduced to David Humphreys. Despite the small world they inhabited, they had not formally met before. Upon learning of Barlow's dilemma, Humphreys wrote prominent friends like Jeremiah Wadsworth, who had recently resigned as commissary general, and Nathaniel Greene, the quartermaster general. Wadsworth would soon become the provisioning agent for the French expeditionary force under Gen. Rochambeau's command that arrived at Newport in July 1780, while Greene was responsible for all the army's transportation needs in the approaching campaign. Abraham Baldwin thought Barlow had three choices: to "turn parson pedagogue or pettifoger." Baldwin's advice was to become a brigade chaplain. A commission similar to his would enable Barlow to "poeticize as much as you pleased."[30]

However, Baldwin's reports about camp life during the winter of 1779–80 were far from encouraging. There was "nothing to eat or drink for men and cattle or at least not half allowance," and starved horses died for lack of forage. Baldwin complained there was "no possible excuse" for this except that public bodies would inevitably make things "turn out Bagaduce," an allusion to the disastrous expedition Massachusetts had launched during 1779 to dislodge the British from the Penobscot region. Still, Baldwin succeeded in extracting an optimistic moral: "if it is Bagaduce every where what matters that to us." Why not take life as it comes and let "the world slide"? Baldwin would repeatedly advise Barlow to "do what you can if you can't do what you would."[31]

Turning chaplain required a license from the New Haven Association of ministers, who required applicants to submit to a theological examination, make a profession of faith, and formally join a church. Making a profession of faith was a serious commitment, which Barlow had been reluctant to consider, less because his beliefs were casually held than because he, like Abraham, took such matters seriously. His religious concern is evident from the meditations and prayers that appear in a commonplace book they apparently shared.[32]

Sometime in the spring of 1780, however, Barlow decided that a chaplaincy in the army was the only occupation open to him that would allow him to write his epic. In March, Abraham Baldwin reported a vacancy was opening. As brigade chaplain, Barlow would be entitled to the pay of a colonel, which was a good deal more than he had ever dreamed of making. The salary was also to be paid in the new emission currency, designed to hold value better than the older continentals. Aside from the obligation to produce a weekly sermon, he would be free the rest of the time to write poetry. When the vacancy Abraham mentioned failed to materialize, David Humphreys started scouting around for another one.

In the meantime Barlow retired to Redding in June to study theology after briefly visiting Ruth in New Haven. Since he had reason to think he would not be the New Haven Association's first choice for an army chaplaincy, he intended to keep his plans quiet. When a new opening materialized, early in the summer, he made a profession of faith and applied to be admitted a full member of the college church. Then it was back to the books in Redding to continue his crash course in theology. In August, he was admitted as a full communicant of the college church, and the Association, after examining him, licensed Barlow as a candidate for the ministry. That was all he needed to qualify for the chaplaincy of a Massachusetts brigade, which he was formally offered in early September.

Barlow immediately accepted and joined his unit in northern New Jersey. On his arrival in camp, Barlow experienced a momentary bout of sickness that left him feeling "pretty slim for two or three days." It helped that Abraham was there to greet him and that he took the initiative in finding them a room they could share. Barlow had only partially recovered before he was required to utter his first public prayer to the brigade. In a letter to Ruth he likened his performance to emitting a "noise which the brigade received as the duty of my office." His first sermon three days later was more successful. "Will you believe Ruthy I was flattered afterwards by some of the most sensible hearers with the great merit of the performance." The disparity between the quality of his prayers and his sermons persisted. One auditor excused Barlow's "very ordinary" praying on the grounds that his training "was more calculated to attain eminence in the art of poetry, than in the clerical profession."[33]

However, Barlow quickly gained notoriety in the army for a fiery sermon he delivered on October 8, 1780, six days after witnessing the execution of Major John André, the British officer who arranged for Benedict Arnold's treason. Barlow's sermon was either listened to or read by "several gentlemen from the Other Brigades." There was even talk of publishing it. Although he was pleased with the credit it had earned him, Barlow did not want it to circulate among the larger public: "tho it would be a sweet mortification to my Revd fathers the Association . . . to see their heretic son gain such applause, yet I have no ambition of appearing to the world in the character of a <u>declaimer</u>."[34]

Camp life was filled with distractions that prevented Barlow from writing poetry. Within several days of Barlow's joining, Gen. Enoch Poor of New Hampshire, who had died in camp, was buried with full military honors. Then the army moved a short distance to a new camp, forcing Abraham and Barlow to live separately after Baldwin's commanding officer insisted he join his brigade's mess. Diversions like a general review of the army were pleasant enough, and Barlow enjoyed the sociability of the officers. Even before Barlow had delivered his "flaming political sermon," Gen. Greene had invited him to dine with a number of prominent gentlemen. After the sermon, he received a dinner invitation from the commander-in-chief and found himself seated on George Washington's right, next to Lord Sterling. The seat of honor came at the price of having to offer a blessing before the meal, but this time Barlow was able feel "perfectly easy & happy" with his performance.[35]

The distractions of camp life led him to postpone serious work on the poem until the army went into winter quarters and he could retire to Connecticut. He was also growing uneasy about Ruth, who was unhappy with her stepmother. Tension on the home front in turn led to a momentary contretemps between the lovers. We don't have Ruth's letters to Barlow, but he reacted to her unhappiness by urging her to move to Stratford, where her brother Dudley was trying to establish himself as a lawyer. In response to a verbal report, Barlow also lectured her on behaving "with dignity" in company, cautioning her to "treat my name with tenderness . . . and never give occasion to others to say you are jilting me." A subsequent letter reiterated the same exhortation, though in the context of urging her to improve herself by combining "<u>Dignity</u> and <u>ease</u>." He softened his advice by adding, "I know of no place where they make a happier concert than they do sometimes in my Ruthy." But "sometimes" was not as generous as it might have been, especially when followed by a caution against treating any "acquaintance with too much confidence."[36]

When Ruth scolded him for chastising her, Barlow replied contritely: "My dear how could you be so cruel as to mistake my meaning so entirely in my first letter—or how could I be so foolish as not to express my meaning." What he had meant was "treat my <u>name</u> with tenderness, and never give <u>people</u> occasion to say you are jilting me." This advice pertained to her "apparent <u>conduct</u> before <u>other</u> people, not for your <u>feelings</u> toward me. . . . I meant simply to convey this idea . . . that there is nothing more beautiful in any lady's external character than the

appearance of a steadiness of attachment to the man she loves." He had not offered "this as a piece of advice that I thot you absolutely needed." It was just a
"sensible observation."

Barlow's attempt to explain away what he had written was less convincing than
his determination to construe her protestations as "expressions of sweetness &
frankness" and his confidence that her love for him was so great that he was prepared to "risk any thing short of my eternal Salvation upon" it.[37] She must also
have found reassuring his concern about her "groveling . . . abject" situation in
her stepmother's house. "I never will see you many times more in that family
without a material alteration in your favor." Although Barlow didn't say so, one
course he undoubtedly considered was marrying her despite her father's objections. But three months of salary in a depreciating currency, even had he received
it, was not enough to support them both. And he had not despaired of bringing
Michael Baldwin around to accepting him as a desirable match. That ambition,
though, required him to earn his future father-in-law's esteem, and he realized
this would take time. A more available, short-term solution was for Ruth to lodge
with friends either in Hartford, Wethersfield, or Stratford, while Barlow worked
nearby on his poem, whose prospects he thought were "better now than ever."
"He was determined to "set Quamminy [his creative self] to work like a Sprite all
winter." But she would see "Cleremont" [his public self] within five weeks, and if
she lodged close to him, he would be able to pay her periodic visits.[38]

At the end of October, Barlow informed her that he would set out from camp
with Abraham in a week. Their approaching reunion promised only a fleeting
respite, but two developments during the summer of 1780 offered hope for the
future. The state governments and Congress abandoned the fiction that the nominal value of their currencies corresponded to real values. Instead they agreed to
use depreciation tables in converting nominal values into hard money values.
Then the arrival of Rochambeau's expeditionary force at Newport in July 1780
started injecting enough French specie into the economy of the northern states
to give hard money values a tangible reality.

Ever since turning 21, Barlow had watched the value of his inheritance evapo-
rate. Now it began to look as though money might become an appreciating asset,
especially if the war could be brought to a victorious conclusion. Nothing was
certain, and he would not be the only one whose confidence would be shaken by
the mutinies of the Pennsylvania and New Jersey lines in January 1781. But with
the French committed not just to help America fight its battles, but to pay for the
privilege, his concern about being repeatedly "Bagaduced" lifted. Still, Barlow
had little to offer Ruth besides promises: "My dear I shall certainly be able to

make your situation agreeable." When it came to concrete measures, he recommended that she find an agreeable situation "for a year or two, or at least till my prospects take a turn" for the better. He felt "the war and my own plans will keep me unsettled for some time."[39]

The tension between this dash of realism and his love momentarily vanished in New Haven on November 10 when the lovers were reunited. On November 13 he was inducted into Yale's new chapter of Phi Beta Kappa, and, as a candidate for the ministry, he was expected to seek guidance from the college in continuing his theological studies. While Barlow had other reasons for being in town, there was a limit to how long he could stay in New Haven without arousing Michael Baldwin's suspicions. When he finally started out for Redding, he left Ruth sobbing at the prospect of not seeing him again for a long time. Although he had the consolation of lodging first with her brother Dudley at Fairfield, and then with his brothers at Redding, he remained tormented by his recent memory of her. "My leaving you in the little chamber is the last I knew of you," he complained on December 19. He was "exceedingly anxious for your situation and your health" and decided to lodge in Hartford. There he could enjoy the support of a circle of friends centered on Webster and Elizabeth Whitman. And if Ruth could contrive to lodge in a nearby town, they could make periodic visits to one another so long as the sleighing lasted.[40]

Ruth took the hint and during January settled into the household of Benoni Upson in Kensington Parish, now part of Berlin. After graduating from Yale in 1776, Upson had remained in New Haven to study theology. A nephew of Stephen Hopkins, Jonathan Edwards's most prominent disciple, Upson was licensed to preach in September 1777. Barely a year later, after marrying his second cousin, Kensington Parish offered him a generous settlement. He was ordained in the spring of 1779. Benoni and Lydia Upson would have eight children over the course of their forty-nine-year marriage. Ruth would have been a welcome guest who could assist the young parents. Residence in the Upson household also provided a plausible cover under which Barlow and Ruth could continue their romance.

Upson's career would be a long, if sedate, one—at its end his colleagues described him as a "prudent, safe" shepherd of souls, otherwise lacking in positive qualities.[41] Yet within a month of Ruth's arrival in his household, Upson performed a singularly questionable act for a recently settled minister: He secretly married Ruth and Barlow on January 26, 1781. Upson knew that Michael Baldwin opposed the match. Parental consent was only legally required if the bride was a minor and Ruth was in her mid-twenties; nevertheless, secret marriages were viewed with suspicion as promoting bigamy. Connecticut at the time had no statute banning them, but the General Assembly subsequently passed a law imposing a £20 fine on any clergyman conducting such a ceremony. Upson must have realized that he was doing something controversial. However, Ruth's emotional distress and a pledge from the lovers that their union would remain secret until such time as Barlow wrung consent from her reluctant father seems to have prevailed over the prudence Upson was later remembered for.

Since pregnancy was inconsistent with keeping the secret and winning her father's consent, Ruth and Barlow agreed that full sexual consummation of the marriage would be postponed until Michael accepted Joel as his son-in-law. Both realized that none of the many birth control nostrums then available was reliable. On the other hand, the close relationship Barlow had established with Ruth's two older brothers argued strongly in favor of his being able to win their father's eventual consent. Barlow was confident that his completed epic would win over Michael Baldwin. Although it is possible that the newlyweds consummated their marriage, there were few places where they might retire without running the risk of discovery. Life was lived on a smaller, more intimate scale in the eighteenth century. If Barlow had to worry about the social consequences of being recognized by someone in Hartford as he passed through town at dusk, then stealing away for even the briefest tryst would have been even more difficult.[42] While the Barlows could enjoy a measure of privacy at the Upsons, neither of them had a place they could call their own.

The unconventional union Barlow and Ruth entered during the winter of 1781 addressed competing concerns. As long as Barlow was preoccupied with Ruth's unhappiness, his epic was unlikely to progress to the point of winning Michael Baldwin's approval. And as long as Ruth was left without some firmer pledge, managing the frustrations of being a grown woman with neither resources nor a household of her own threatened to overwhelm her spirits. She was not getting any younger and probably sensed that Elizabeth Whitman and Betsy Stiles, neither of whom would marry, were headed either for spinsterhood or something worse. (Indeed, Whitman would eventually die a tragic death as an unwed mother in a rural Massachusetts tavern, after delivering a stillborn child.) There was a limited supply of suitable mates for bright, young women at the time. Nor did an unconsummated marriage preclude physical intimacy. A letter from a dispirited Barlow mentions longing for "my Ruthy's bosom to lay my head upon." Their relationship was far from platonic, but it was a good deal less than they both wanted. Still, they were very much part of the revolutionary generation in accepting sacrifice as the necessary accompaniment of heroic achievement.[43]

CHAPTER THREE

Uncharted Waters

"I never was so happy . . . in my life," Barlow wrote to Ruth soon after they were married. At last he was confident that "my plans will in some measure be answered." Barlow had dropped Ruth off at a friend's house at Waterbury before heading back to Hartford and work, but their marriage now allowed him to address her with a new freedom.[1] In his letters, he referred to her as "you little rogue" and threatened to "whip you to death . . . if you don't give some account of yourself." His improved spirits also affected his capacity to work. "I make the swiftest progress. So rapturous are Love and poetry united and such mutual hand maids are they to each other."

To share his life, Ruth needed to enter a cultural world that was still largely the preserve of men: "Throw off all care but to furnish your mind for the enjoyment of your Joel," he urged.[2] He proposed to guide her reading and in the process assumed a condescending tone. That tone came naturally because women were denied the educational advantages open only to a select group of men. Barlow had lent Ruth a copy of Henry Home, Lord Kames's *Elements of Criticism.* "Some of your sage gentry will tell you that such authors were not designed for a Lady's attention. But my love you know I despise such sentiments and I never would have a lady but what despised them. [I]t is telling you that . . . you are not capable of any of the embellishments of life . . . these same gentlemen would tell you . . . that you were not made for companions but for servants." Realizing that his suggestions for study implied Ruth needed considerable improvement, he added, "tho I talk about your improvement as I do about my own, yet you sweet girl . . . possess [virtues enough?] to charm away my heart and make it forever your own."[3]

Their few surviving letters from the spring of 1781 indicate that they spent as much time together as was consistent with maintaining their marriage's secrecy. They were not averse at this point to having their friends conclude they were engaged. While the sleighing season lasted, it was easy for them to see a good deal of each other, but at the end of February the melting snow and muddy roads made travel more difficult. Both realized that the distance separating them would widen when Barlow rejoined the army for the coming campaign, and that increased the ardor of their correspondence. In mid-March, Barlow described his ecstasy upon receiving one of her letters. "Our minds are the perfect images of each other, they produce the most perfect harmony, and if they do not bestow a constant flow of happiness, it is from want of power and not from want of inclination." The next morning he added a postscript: "I am happy my dearest love, and go to my daily labor with delight knowing that I am taking the most probable method to make happiness for my Ruthy."[4]

During the winter of 1780 and spring of 1781, Barlow managed to write barely seven hundred lines of a poem that eventually would expand to 5,140 lines. Husband and wife surely realized that separation was more likely to produce the poetic achievement necessary to lift the veil of secrecy that cloaked their marriage. Knowing this may have helped reconcile them to separating in early May, almost a month before Barlow was due in camp. He took a circuitous route back to the army via New Haven and Redding. During Barlow's stay in New Haven, President Stiles invited him to deliver a poetical composition at Yale's first public commencement since the beginning of the war, scheduled to take place on September 12, 1781.[5]

Rejoining the army had its upside. There was plenty of food now that French purchasing was reviving the northern agricultural economy and Barlow could expect to be paid when he returned to camp. After the mutinies of the Pennsylvania and New Jersey lines in January 1781, Congress had realized that they could not expect to continue the war without offering the army something. Since it possessed little besides promises, Congress asked the states to raise the necessary funds. Barlow benefited from being attached to a Massachusetts brigade; that state's economy was far stronger than Connecticut's, thanks to the revival of Boston's overseas commerce.

Barlow proudly wrote Ruth from camp, "I have 400 new dollars in my pocket." To cheer her, he added, "My pay is £360 pounds per year," (the equivalent of roughly $1,200 in 1780 dollars or around $20,000 current dollars), and "my half pay [is] established for life. I am rich your Brothers are both rich & you are the happiest Girl in the state." He discouraged her from opening a school. Having his wife known as "Miss Baldwin Schoolmistress of Middletown" was incompatible with Barlow's gentry aspirations.[6]

However, Congress's new currency depreciated faster than the old continentals. Barlow told Ruth he was thinking of making a "run up to Vermont next week" to sink some of his cash in lands. His sojourn in Hanover eight years before had convinced him that investing in the future development of Vermont might be profitable. Not wishing anyone to know that he was speculating while with the army, he added: "Tell no body of it I charge you."[7]

For two weeks at the end of June, Barlow rode four hundred miles into Vermont, having a "fine tilt of it . . . both for interest and amusement." He returned on July 3 to West Point, where he intended to tarry for a couple of days to "recruit my horses and get on my baggage" before joining the main body of the army, now forty miles away in New Jersey. But on July 5 he came down with a high fever. In the course of half a day, he lost so much of his strength "that I could not walk nor scarcely raise my head." Abraham came to the rescue. He stayed with Barlow for six days: "he was Nurse & Physician, Father, Brother, and Friend, he lay on the floor by the side of my Bunks for several nights and administered every medicine." Barlow reported that "my friends were scared about me & the Doctor tells me my situation was extremely critical," but he "encountered the disorder, when I knew what it was, with as much fortitude as ever I did any important business." He assured Ruth, now that he was firmly on the road to recovery, that "I . . . had [not] . . . a single low spirited feeling thro the whole."[8]

As Barlow gradually regained strength, his mind turned to his commencement poem. He regarded the invitation as the opportunity of a lifetime and was determined that Ruth witness the occasion. "Chauncey [Goodrich] must carry you. . . . if there is no other way Dudley must go after you. I would not have you fail of being there for a thousand dollars." Lest she think attendance was an unnecessary extravagance, he added three days later, "We Massachusetts folks are going to receive 3 months pay very soon, half hard and half in new Emission. [T]his will make for me 150 dollars in hard." With the proceeds from a horse, which he had sold for $65 in a hard currency, he would soon "be rich."[9]

⚜

Barlow at first hoped to use some of the lines he had already written for his epic, but less than 15 percent of *A Poem, spoken at the Public Commencement at Yale College in New Haven, September 1[2], 1781* eventually reappeared in *The Vision of Columbus*. That left him with more to do than he had initially expected, but his illness turned out to be a blessing in disguise. Because he was too weak to visit

Ruth, he had more time for poetry. He was also too weak to join the army in New Jersey, so he enjoyed what amounted to an extended sick leave. By the end of August he felt he had the poem in hand.

Still Barlow had several reasons for worrying about how it would be received. First, he was not sure the new poem measured up to his previous performance. To avoid repeating himself, he employed the device of the muse of "Neglected Science," which articulated a utopian vision of the postwar period when the gentler virtues would again flourish. Using a transcendent messenger to portray the future was not an issue since most of his auditors were familiar with John Milton's *Paradise Lost.* The problem lay in the poem's central theme. Where *The Prospect of Peace* had simply looked forward to a flowering of the arts and sciences at the end of the war, the commencement poem identified commerce as the force behind an emerging utopia.

> Yet thro' the whole the same progressive plan,
> Which draws, for mutual succour, man to man,
> From men to tribes, from tribes to nations spreads,
> And private ties to public compact leads,
> Shall rise by slow degrees, and still extend,
> Their power and interest, their passions blend,
> Their wars grow milder, policies enlarge,
> Increasing nations feel the general charge,
> From broad alliances for mutual aid,
> Mingle their manners and extend their trade,
> Till each remotest realm, by friendship joined
> Link in the chain and harmonize mankind . . .   (159–70)

More notable was what he omitted. Barlow's only bow to Christian expectations came as an ambiguous characterization of the rapturous gratitude his utopia's beneficiaries would direct "To loves pure source . . . th' inspiring God" (370, 372). This omission is surprising because he was still a candidate for the ministry and had actually preached in the college chapel on the preceding Sabbath. The orthodox Calvinism embraced by the Yale Corporation held that only God could bridge the gap between unredeemed nature and the transcendent through the bestowal of grace. Barlow's concluding lines describing a transcendent termination for human history were not especially heterodox in themselves:

> Thro' heavens, o'er-canopy'd by heavens, they soar,
> Where floods of light in boundless beauty pour

Seraphs and system'd worlds innumerous move,
Link'd in the chain of harmonizing love;
Thence following down, th' effulgent glory trace,
Which brought salvation to their kindred race.   (373–78)

But the route to his millennium—through commerce, the arts, and the sciences—
was heterodox, since it implied the future was in the hands of man, not God.

Nonetheless, the poem was initially well received. President Stiles recorded in
his literary diary that Barlow's commencement performance was the only one
to be "clapped."[10] The response of the auditors owed something to adventitious
circumstances. On September 6, a British force under the command of Benedict
Arnold had burned New London and parts of Groton, destroying 146 structures
and slaughtering the garrison at Fort Griswold after it had surrendered. When on
September 9 the fleet carrying Arnold's raiders anchored off what is now Clinton,
it precipitated a general militia alert. Stiles recorded in his diary that they were
"ordered in along the whole Sea Coast of Connect. from N. London to Stam-
ford." Reassured by the withdrawal on the tenth of the British vessels to Long Island and the arrival of the "militia flocking into New Haven," Stiles still feared
"that Commencement will be interrupted by the Enemy."[11]

Amid a heightened sense of contingency, the ceremonies scheduled for the
twelfth began punctually at 10:00 a.m. with the procession of the entire college
body. It included more than half of Barlow's graduating class. Many of them had
felt shortchanged by the interruptions during their college years. Others were
driven to continue their education by the absence of promising opportunities. But
the primary reason for seeking an advanced degree was to avoid the militia drafts
that by 1780 had become Connecticut's principal means for filling its continental
and state regiments. What today looks like shirking was more acceptable then.
College degree holders were considered gentlemen. Because few recent graduates could expect to be elected officers in the militia, many preferred to take an
advanced degree rather than serve in the ranks. The same motives affected younger
men between the ages of 18 and 21 with gentry aspirations. They accounted for the
dramatic swelling of Yale's undergraduate enrollment in the classes of 1784–86.
By the end of the war, its student population was larger than it had ever been
before.

Barlow's moment of glory came in the afternoon, sandwiched between two
orations in English by classmates Noah Webster and Oliver Wolcott Jr. Then the
president conferred the degrees. In addition to the Yale graduates, six men received honorary degrees, including Gen. Samuel Holden Parsons. So distinguished

an assemblage, protected by a large body of the militia, highlighted the drama of the occasion, especially as everyone realized that the current campaign held the key to the outcome of the war. On September 8, Stiles had learned that Washington and Rochambeau were on their way to Virginia and on the eleventh that they had been joined by a French fleet from the Caribbean. If this concentration of military power failed to produce the desired outcome, it was unlikely that anything else would. Barlow's poem, by promising release from the grinding realities of war, gave his audience exactly what they wanted.

Two days later the corporation voted to offer Barlow a tutorship. Now that he felt financially secure, he refused the offer for the same reason Abraham Baldwin declined appointment as Yale's professor of divinity. Barlow was earning much more in the army than he ever could at Yale. Though the war would soon be over, "the numerous vacancies" that had arisen in the churches opened up the prospect of securing a handsome settlement should he become a minister.[12] In addition, being a tutor was no longer compatible with finishing his long poem as quickly as possible so that he and Ruth could live together as husband and wife. He proved more amenable to the suggestion that the commencement poem be published, as that seemed consistent with securing Michael Baldwin's consent to the marriage. However, the poem still contained "several passages taken from [the] larger work" that would become *The Vision of Columbus*. Barlow was torn between his fear that an adverse reaction from the public might keep him from completing his epic and his hope that the commencement poem would promote his epic and his marriage.

After tarrying in New Haven as long as the pretext of considering the corporation's offer would permit, Barlow made his leisurely way back to camp in New York via Redding. Since he had missed the entire campaign with his brigade, he felt obliged to contribute to the army's celebration of the anniversary of Saratoga. Barlow hurried off a poem, hardly his best, which he read at a dinner. Three of its four verses celebrated the victory of Saratoga. The last alluded to the victory everyone hoped Washington was about to win at Yorktown. Barlow's timing could not have been more opportune; Cornwallis surrendered his entire army the following day.[13] The *New-York Packet* published Barlow's celebratory poem on October 25, though without attributing it to him.

Shortly afterward, Barlow proposed to "return to Redding to spend the winter in a chamber which my Brother [Aaron] has finished on purpose."[14] But first he visited Ruth in Hartford and then proceeded to New Haven, arriving on November 29. Despite a ride on "a long frozen road well whitened with a snow storm" and a "very illnatured fall from my horse," he claimed he was "happy."[15] Happiness bred productivity, for his next letter, written in Redding, recorded dramatic progress with *The Vision of Columbus*. "I began the 3ᵈ of December. On the 3d of Jany. I had written more than a thousand lines which are uncomly [*sic*] good."

He had also completed an elegy about Titus Hosmer, who had died in August 1781, which he proposed to have printed in Hartford when he again visited Ruth there. "It is the best piece I have to brag of in the world."[16] The elegy consisted of sixty quatrains addressed to Hosmer's widow, celebrating his role as patron, patriot, and spouse, in that order. Barlow made more of a bow to Christianity here than he had in his commencement poem, but the poem served little purpose beyond advertising that Barlow's services were available to other potential patrons. He later confessed to Noah Webster to losing "half the cost & and all my labor" by the venture.[17]

Barlow continued to concentrate on his epic. In mid-January he reported, "I have now finished 1500 lines in seven weeks."[18] Despite intense preoccupation with his work, he never lost sight of what it was costing Ruth. "You are a sweet Girl to temper so much tenderness with so much resolution." Joel admired her "mixture of dignity & tenderness" and assured her that it "rivet[ed] her still closer to my heart." He was no "stranger to the heartrending conflict of love & appearance which necessity has imposed upon us." Her consolation was that he was devoting all his time "in the most laborious employment in order to lessen the . . . absence which hides him from the joys of life."[19]

Gone were the false starts that had plagued his previous efforts. At last he was experiencing a creative surge. Things were going so well that by the end of the first week in January he thought he had earned the midwinter reunion they had agreed upon for January 30. In his excitement, Barlow confessed to Abraham Baldwin that he and Ruth were formally engaged if not actually married. Baldwin was visiting with Barlow on his way to preach at Greenfield Hill and may have teased the information out of Barlow by making assertions that Barlow chose not to deny.[20] The Barlows subsequently blamed the Upsons for blowing their cover, but it is more likely that Barlow let Abraham infer the truth, perhaps as a strategy for keeping the fires of inspiration stoked.[21] On his return to Redding, after visiting with Ruth, he informed her of "a new plan . . . [t]o set eight weeks at this table from next Sunday" and "write 3600 lines from this time which will finish my poem."[22]

Abraham expressed his "surprise" to Ruth at being informed "that you had consecrated yourselves at the shrine of the Ceyprian queen" (Aphrodite or Venus). Her brother did not disapprove her choice of a mate; his comment followed a glowing report about the progress of Barlow's epic and the prediction that "he will get the palm from every one of our Geniuses." Abraham continued to feel that their connection with Barlow would do the Baldwins "more honor than they can ever do him." Abraham was surprised that neither Barlow nor Ruth had consulted him about their intentions. Still, he was the last person to stand in the way of their happiness: "if you were suited it would ill become me to grumble at anything which you supposed would be conducive to the happiness of so dear friends."[23]

Even so, Abraham's response to Barlow's revelation suggested the lovers would encounter further difficulties when Michael Baldwin found out. In early February, Ruth's two older brothers came to Hartford to confer with her about managing the situation. Ruth reported to Barlow that they stayed up talking until 1:00 a.m. When she explained the nature of her marriage, they approved of her conduct.[24] Now that everyone in Hartford thought they were engaged, though, word was bound to travel to New Haven. Somebody had to tell Michael soon. If nothing else tipped him off, Ruth would have to go to New Haven by the middle of March to "prepare her furniture" if she and Barlow were to set up their own household before he was due back in camp.

When Barlow next preached in the college chapel, he paid Michael Baldwin a visit to assess his disposition. This interview had proven so successful that Barlow told Ruth, "the old Dadda . . . feels well, & I believe is proud of me."[25] Barlow then consented to Abraham and Dudley disclosing "the whole affair & [Ruth's] reasons for not speaking to him about it." Dudley's initial conversation with his father was not encouraging. Barlow informed Ruth that Michael had received the news "we are married" with much displeasure; "says we acted without his knowledge or consent, and we may go on as we have begun, he shall give himself no trouble about us."[26] Abraham was more upbeat about his conference, reporting to Ruth that their father had said "he loves you and sincerely wishes you well, but feels injured in your treatment of him." Since Abraham also felt neglected, he agreed that Ruth should have been more sensitive to their feelings. Abraham reported that their father had then said, "you know Repentance is the only cure for a fault." Abraham recommended that Ruth approach Michael contritely: "I believe a confession of that kind in conversation with him would be proper and of service. He seems only to want some pretext to tack about and he will be good natured."[27]

Now that the secret was out, Barlow realized that "people of a tender turn" would "wonder how I can waste my life in the absence of so good a girl." It was no mystery to him, though, because their continued separation was paying off. In mid-

March, he reported to Ruth his "astonishing progress in the poem, this night finishes four weeks & four days, I have written near 2400 lines." His achievement justified a change in plans. Instead of staying in Redding until the poem was completed, he proposed "to ride over to camp after mony [sic], then to come . . . to N Haven . . . to finish [the poem] at Mr. Chauncey's, where I can see my Ruthy till the middle of May." He would have preferred to carry Ruth to New Haven "but . . . knew in that case my poem would not be finished, which [is] the great object."[28] Barlow was proud to have it known that he was married to Ruth, but the prospect of their rendezvous in New Haven continued to be soured by Michael Baldwin's disapproval.

To make it easier for Ruth to approach her father, Barlow penned a long letter to him explaining his behavior. When Barlow had first met Ruth, "she appeared to me [as] the only person that could make me happy." But "I was repeatedly told that the connection would be disagreeable to you" because "my situation in life . . . was then unpromising." Under such circumstances, "how could I enter into a conversation with you upon the subject, when I supposed my character, my person & pretensions were odious to you? To croud [sic] himself into a family is what no Gentleman of my feelings ever will do; but to take a daughter from any family upon the principle of mutual affection is a right always given by the God of nature wherever he has given that affection." Barlow had initially determined to postpone marriage until his poem was finished and he "could support her with dignity." He had only changed his mind because "an opportunity presented from which I presumed our marriage could be kept a secret from the world till we chose it should be known." Now that his "affairs are . . . in a good situation, [and] I think they will enable me to maintain a family," he was willing that "the secret should be known." He assured Michael he would have eschewed secrecy had not the revelation promised to "frustrate the whole design."[29]

This letter failed to produce the assistance the Barlows sought to help them set up in the house Ruth had found in Hartford. Instead, when Joel returned to the army in May, Ruth went along with him as far as Ridgefield and boarded at the home of Barlow's cousin, Col. Philip Bradley. Once Ruth moved in with the Bradleys, Barlow was able to spend a third of his active duty time with her. This diffused some of the ardor that had characterized their former correspondence but did little to quench his longing during their separations. "My Love I never had so fine a little visit as the last, but it only serves to make me more homesick. I shall certainly count the days till thirteen more are gone, and bring me to [your] arms." He remained reluctant, however, about "bringing you over to make a visit of a fortnight."[30] Part of his hesitancy reflected the possibility that his brigade might be ordered elsewhere, leaving Ruth stranded. But the dangers of camp life were of greater concern. Two of Barlow's most searing experiences had involved illnesses contracted in military camps, and he was reluctant to expose the love of his life to such hazards.

As his epic neared completion, Barlow sought to extract financial return from his labors. Authors at the time customarily paid printers to manufacture their work as a book or pamphlet. If a printer thought well of a piece, he might share the production costs on condition that the author shared the proceeds from the sales. Most authors preferred to retain a full interest in their literary works, however, even when this involved accepting finished sheets without a binding. The expense of printing Barlow's poem promised to be considerable because the finished product needed to be of the best possible quality to reflect positively on the character of the American Revolution. Barlow may have had more money than ever before, but he also had a wife who wanted a place of her own.

Authors often raised capital through subscriptions. Before copyright laws protected intellectual property rights, subscriptions, if sufficiently plentiful, also enabled authors to reap a return before the work could be pirated. Britain had fashioned copyright laws during the eighteenth century, but the American colonies had been reluctant to follow her example because of their dependence on British materials. Even after the states began to pass copyright laws, their statutes only had local effect. In the absence of a general copyright law, nothing stopped printers in one jurisdiction from stealing an imprint—especially a high-end one— from a printer in another state. The issuance of a knockoff would rob the author of the fruits of his industry and of his capital.

Barlow's classmate Noah Webster would have considerable success with his low-end, pedagogical books, using different printers in different states. But Webster traveled extensively and spent considerable time in places like New York and Philadelphia, protecting valuable markets. Barlow's higher-end product didn't lend itself to being issued at multiple sites. These considerations dictated a strategy of securing subscriptions in advance. Barlow accordingly started soliciting them from among the army's officers for a poem that he eventually priced at one and a third dollars (about $20 in today's money).[31] That was still an extravagance for some of his fellow officers who felt impoverished at the end of the war. But a poem celebrating the American Revolution was far more likely to appeal to the officers than any other group, and with rumors circulating that peace was in the offing, Barlow wanted to secure as many subscriptions from them as possible before "furloughs bec[a]me fashionable."[32]

As the officer corps shrank during the summer of 1782, Barlow looked for other constituencies that had a stake in the Revolution. They included the political leadership in Philadelphia and the leaders of the French expeditionary force. Persuading foreign officers to subscribe to a poem in a language many of them did not understand did not seem like a stretch to Barlow because the French officers had plenty of money and relatively few things to spend it on. Barlow's problem was getting access to these constituencies. His only entrée to the Confederation's leadership was through the continental army. In mid-August he reported to Ruth, "I am getting . . . letters to Phila.—which are absolutely necessary & must be had now or never." That endeavor required him to postpone their next planned reunion. Barlow realized that Ruth would be disappointed but assured her that "this business is infinitely more important."[33]

He linked his visiting Philadelphia to their being able to take a house in Hartford the following autumn and winter. Expecting to go south in September, Barlow urged Ruth to make arrangements with Abraham to go to New Haven for commencement, where she could stay with her family until he returned. But he quickly modified this plan upon learning that the French and American armies would join forces in New York during mid-September. The French army relied for their provisions on Jeremiah Wadsworth, Hartford's most prominent citizen. Though Barlow and Wadsworth were probably not yet acquainted, Barlow was friendly with James Watson, one of Wadsworth's agents. David Humphreys had drawn Wadsworth's attention to Barlow's epic the year before, and now Barlow had a chance to cultivate an acquaintance with Wadsworth.

Wadsworth expressed enough interest in Barlow's project—as well as the problem of expanding his subscriber base—to embolden Barlow to ask him for assistance in approaching Rochambeau's officers. Barlow hoped eventually, through Wadsworth, to gain access to the French ambassador, Anne-César, Chevelier de la Luzerne. Barlow wanted Wadsworth to persuade Luzerne to make a special appeal to the French officers on his behalf. After Barlow learned that Rochambeau's army had been ordered to Boston preparatory to leaving the continent, time became important. To strengthen Wadsworth's hand, Barlow claimed that the poem's publication depended on the support of the French. Barlow regarded Luzerne's endorsement as crucial and was prepared to give him "as much of the honor of midwifry [sic] as he pleases" in exchange.[34] It had also occurred to Barlow that Luzerne might approach Louis XVI about accepting the dedication of the poem. This was an audacious, if not presumptuous, idea for an obscure New Englander to entertain, but, as a child of the Revolution, Barlow no longer felt bound by past experience in his expectations about the future.

The urgency of obtaining subscriptions led Barlow to conclude that he and Ruth would have to postpone setting up housekeeping in Hartford until the New Year. By way of compensation, he proposed to join her at Aaron's house in Redding. The absence of a surviving letter between September 12 and October 24 suggests that they were reunited for the better part of a month. Barlow returned to camp in mid-October, refreshed by the interlude and buoyed by what had happened in his absence. "The subscription here is likely to be more extensive than I expected, I have more & better letters to carry, & indeed every wish I have formed upon the matter is likely to be more than answered."[35] Best of all, Barlow had made the acquaintance of Benjamin Lincoln, who had recently been elected secretary of war in the new Confederation government. Barlow accompanied Lincoln back to Philadelphia in November 1782 and reported to Ruth that "Gen Lincoln treats me with the greatest friendship & promises me a most favorable introduction at Phila."[36] Barlow subsequently credited Lincoln with circulating him among the Confederation's officialdom: "My reception here is quite as favorable as I . . . expected. I am treated with civility by the great, with formality by the many & with friendship by the few."

Barlow was also impressed by the town. Instead of the "haughtiness or idleness" he had been led to expect from common report and from what "we find in Boston & many places of less resort," Philadelphia's "polite circles are easy . . . & agreeable."[37] Ruth need not fear that he was enamored of city life. Instead, he longed to spend winter evenings with her at their fireside. There he imagined they would "find new arguments against the bustle, the ceremonies & the follies of the town. . . . We will look with pity upon their specious parade of happiness by contrasting it with the charming reality of our own." They would also avoid another side to urban life that was never far from Barlow's mind. "Mrs. Carter [the wife of Wadsworth's partner in provisioning Rochambeau's expeditionary force] is yet unwell, & her sister Miss Schuyle[r] who is with her is very low. It is doubtful whether she recovers."[38] Hartford at the time, with one sixth of the population of Philadelphia, was less sickly. Though a rural life was no proof against disease — half of his brother Nathaniel's brood of six children had died of consumption — the success Barlow and his wife had enjoyed so far in surviving the rigors of southern New England's climate made living there a better prospect than in a teeming cosmopolitan center lacking adequate sanitation.

When Barlow was not looking for subscribers, he busied himself buying Ruth various items not readily available in Connecticut, like satin, lace, gloves, a muff, and handkerchiefs. But extending his circle of acquaintances consumed most of his time and energy. "Many . . . of the first & greatest characters offer the warmest encouragement, & think that they & their country will be more indebted to me than I can be to them." Best of all, "Col. Wadsworth is come into town, which is one of the fortunate circumstances I have met with since I have been here."[39] Three days later Barlow reported that "the Minister of France treats me with the utmost friendship & have this day finished [m]y business with him according to my old romantic wishes which you used to laugh at. He promises to promote the subscription here, he has taken a paper to send to France & will procure permission for the Dedication according to my former scheme." The only downside was the high expectations he had raised in the course of promoting himself. He now thought the poem "very imperfect" and that the coming "winter's work will be harder than the last."[40]

Sometime before the river crossings became difficult, Barlow made his way back to Connecticut. We cannot tell exactly when, and therefore we don't know whether he remained in Philadelphia long enough to learn that his expectations of half-pay for life were in jeopardy. Because it lacked an independent source of revenue, Congress had relied for funds more on French subsidies—soon to terminate—than on the exhausted states. Amending the Articles of Confederation required the consent of all thirteen states, and every attempt to vest the central government with the power to lay a uniform impost had been rejected by one or more of them. Congress could have left the problem for the states to solve, but it would have done so at the expense of what little remained of its authority.

Superintendent of Finance Robert Morris set in motion a general settlement of accounts between the continent and the states and between the individual creditors of both. Specially appointed agents reviewed all claims and then computed the hard money value of the valid ones according to depreciation schedules. Inequalities deriving from when a credit had been created were equalized by carrying its specie value forward from the settlement date at 6 percent interest. Eventually, Morris hoped to "liquidate" three kinds of debt: the loan office debt, the certificate debt, and back pay due the army. The life pensions of Barlow and his fellow officers were on the line because the claims of the soldiers and officers of the army accounted for the largest portion of the newly consolidated debt. The officers of the army were willing to commute their half-pay pensions for life into full pay for five years. This would enable them to reestablish themselves as civilians without unduly burdening the new nation or creating a body of permanent pensioners. But until Congress possessed some funding source, the army would depend on their respective states to honor the continent's pledge. Barlow would not have been upset by the prospect of having his half-pay for life tampered with so long as he got enough to survive on until his poem was published. Then, he assumed, his fame and their fortune would be secure.

Barlow had other things on his mind as he made his way back to Hartford via camp and Redding. Brother Nathaniel, who suffered from a chronic respiratory disease, died on the day after Christmas. If Barlow had not been at the death, he may have been at the funeral, because the season of the year would have allowed for a delayed burial. He and Ruth set up housekeeping that winter in an accommodation Chauncey Goodrich found for them near the residence of the poet John Trumbull. This development deprives us of any letters they might otherwise have exchanged. We can only infer from Barlow's later correspondence that he must have worked hard during the winter on revising his epic.

Insofar as Barlow diverted his attention from the poem, he focused on securing the enactment of copyright laws. Connecticut's General Assembly passed a copyright statute in January 1783, but gaining nationwide protection proved more complicated. Since the Confederation Congress was not authorized to pass such legislation, Barlow wrote its temporary president, Elias Boudinot, whose acquaintance he had recently made in Philadelphia. He asked that Congress recommend to "the several States" the passage of laws similar to Britain's. Barlow argued that "a literary reputation is necessary in order to complete [the nation's] character," noting that "we are not to expect to see any works of considerable magnitude . . . offered to the Public till such security be given." He cited as proof Timothy Dwight's reluctance to publish his epic, *The Conquest of Canaan*, and the recent pirating of John Trumbull's *McFingal*.[41]

The efforts of Barlow and other aspiring authors proved surprisingly successful. By 1786 every state but Delaware had made some provision for protecting intellectual property rights. And when the constitutional convention assembled in Philadelphia in 1787, it bestowed upon the new federal Congress the power to "promote the Progress of Science and useful Arts, by securing for limited Times to Authors and Inventors the exclusive Right to their respective Writings and Discoveries." The first Congress passed a national copyright law on May 31, 1790, that incorporated most of the features of the British law. But neither Dwight nor Barlow waited for the protection provided by the national government. Dwight's poem appeared in 1785 and Barlow's in 1787. Barlow felt he could bring out *The Vision of Columbus* without a federal statute because he had secured enough subscribers to protect him against outright loss.

Barlow's focus on literary matters insulated him from the political ferment taking place inside Connecticut during the winter and spring of 1783. The debt Robert Morris had started consolidating led some in Congress to propose laying a continental impost despite the absence of constitutional authority to do so. Since the nation's imports were largely confined to the gateway ports and since the merchants in these ports would benefit from the revenue, these congressmen concluded that the impost would be collected even if it were not strictly legal. Because a majority in Congress remained mindful that the Revolution had originated as a tax revolt, advocates of an impost concocted a scheme for scaring some of their timid colleagues into line. While they sought to have Congress commute half-pay for life into full pay for five years on the supposition that there would be no way to deliver on the obligation except through a continental impost, their allies in the army tried to use the threat of a military rebellion to nudge reluctant congressmen in the desired direction.

In March 1783, John Armstrong—later ambassador to France and secretary of war—wrote an inflammatory address threatening that the army at Newburgh would remain under arms until Congress did it justice. Though Washington succeeded in branding the address as a betrayal of the Revolution, army unrest did persuade one recalcitrant Connecticut congressman who opposed commutation to change his vote. This enabled the measure to pass, but Congress still declined to authorize an impost. Instead of solving Congress's fiscal problems, commutation simply made them worse by creating a large, unfunded debt.

Commutation was a particularly explosive issue in Connecticut because the state was struggling with the crushing debt it had incurred defending its coastline against British and loyalist incursions. Connecticut's continental regiments had played very little role in the state's defense; aside from the occasional winter encampment, most of its troops had been deployed in New York and New Jersey. Connecticut thus had reason to feel its liberty had been purchased at an exorbitant price, and the state's system for raising revenue did little to alleviate that sense of grievance. Because Connecticut lacked a major gateway port, most of its revenue had to be raised from direct taxes on lands and polls. The enormous tax arrearages that had accumulated during the war underscored the weakness of the state's fiscal arrangements, which worsened as the desire to avoid taxation fueled a substantial migration out of the state. By further diminishing tax revenues, emigration increased the burdens facing those who remained.

Besides having to bear its additional costs, commutation infuriated many because it would make the officers a privileged caste that prospered at everyone else's expense. Such an outcome seemed directly at odds with the Revolution's goal of preventing Britain from prospering at America's expense. The Barlows' cozy circle of Hartford friends and his focus on revising his poem desensitized him to the discontent fermenting nearby. Barlow's decision to rejoin the army in early May 1783 further blinded him to the signs of an impending political explosion. Though he had previously planned to resign his commission after the campaign of 1782, when Congress made serving until the end of the war a requirement for commutation, he changed his mind.

His brigade was posted close to Newburgh, so he heard firsthand reports about the conspiracy of the previous March. Rather than drawing alarming conclusions, he wrote Ruth cheerfully that he hoped to "receive more money at camp than I expected." In the same letter he expressed confidence that "Public securities will shortly be as good as mony [sic]. My 5 years pay I believe is secure." After preaching at camp, Barlow and his Hartford neighbor John Trumbull had made a quick visit to Congress to promote copyright laws. He added, "I shall receive money enough before I return to last us one year. Providence will provide for the rest of our lives, if I am as insignificant a dog as we have reason to expect."[42]

His self-deprecation reflected the gap that had opened between his ambitions for his long poem and the difficulties he had experienced revising it during the preceding winter. It was the first time he and Ruth had spent a prolonged period of time together, and making the necessary adjustments to accommodate his writing had not been easy. Barlow had also begun to realize that five years full pay backed only by the promise of a government that lacked revenue was a dubious asset. He was not the only one coming to this conclusion during the spring of 1783, though his presence in Philadelphia in May had awakened him to the new realities he confronted. During his sojourn there he wrote, at Abraham Baldwin's request, to Benjamin Lincoln about the reception a northerner was likely to meet in the South. "Upon the prospect of a dissolution of the army a friend of mine, who has considerable knowledge of Law & is desirous of establishing himself in that Profession, wishes to obtain your sentiments upon the probability of succeeding in Charlestown."[43] Flirting with divinity before choosing another career was not that unusual, and it became especially common after the Revolution. Abraham now looked to the law, while there was little doubt that Barlow preferred literature to the ministry.

The official cessation of hostilities on April 11, 1783, led Congress to authorize a general reduction of the army. Barlow was discharged sometime in June and returned home to spend the remainder of the summer with Ruth in Hartford.

Whether he came away with any money is less clear. It is possible Barlow received a final settlement note that he succeeded in negotiating for ready money. In a letter he wrote Wadsworth on September 10, he mentioned Wadsworth's "willingness to oblige," possibly a reference to discounting a note in his favor.[44] Barlow must have come home with something, though, because there is no record of him taking any new steps to support his wife until the middle of 1784.

A full year earlier the towns of Torrington and Farmington had taken the lead in mounting a revolt against the political leadership of Connecticut, using commutation as their excuse. Seconded by Killingworth, they issued a call for a convention to meet in Middletown just before the September freemen's meetings. At these meetings the next slate of nominees for governor, lieutenant-governor, and the twelve assistants, who comprised the upper house of the legislature or council, would be chosen. The following April the freemen would make their final choice of officers for the coming year. Since each candidate who had placed twentieth or higher in the nominations was voted upon in order of their seniority in office, it took considerable coordination to dislodge any sitting member. Everyone familiar with Connecticut's political structure understood that the Middletown Convention was challenging the state's revolutionary leadership.

Neither the Middletown Convention nor the spread of a similar protest movement to portions of rural Massachusetts threatened Barlow's immediate financial interests. But discrediting the Revolution's leadership menaced the cause his epic celebrated. Nor was Barlow alone in the alarm with which he watched the convention movement gather force. His close neighbor and fellow poet John Trumbull shared Barlow's concern. So, for that matter, did almost all the officers of the continental army, who under the pressure of such ominous circumstances, banded together in a fraternal organization that came to be known as the Society of the Cincinnati. Its name derived from Cincinnatus, a Roman general who had renounced his military command at the conclusion of a successful war and by returning to his farm had preserved the republic against military usurpation.

Doubts about the republicanism of the Society of the Cincinnati quickly arose because it excluded all but officers of the French and continental armies and specified that only the eldest male heir could take the place of a deceased member. However, its stated mission was to provide for the deserving but indigent officers whom the Republic was neglecting, which seemed reasonable enough in the immediate postwar period. The society also had a compelling interest in preventing the Revolution from wrecking itself through the kind of internal discord being sponsored by the Middletown Convention. Barlow's military identity as an officer in the Massachusetts line initially compromised his eligibility for membership in

Connecticut's branch of the Cincinnati. Because he was well known to its leaders and because he identified with the plight of the officers, however, he was present at the society's first Hartford meeting on March 17, 1784.[45]

Barlow spent almost a year, between June 1783 and June 1784, putting finishing touches on the draft of his epic poem. Settling down with Ruth in a place where they were surrounded by their friends limited his correspondence. No letters written to or by Barlow from between September 10, 1783, and March 21, 1784, survive. Aside from attending the first meeting of the Society of the Cincinnati in Connecticut, the only direct evidence of his presence in Hartford is a public endorsement he, John Trumbull, and Chauncey Goodrich gave the first volume of Noah Webster's *Grammatical Institutes* published in October 1783.[46]

In late March 1784, Barlow wrote to Gen. Nathaniel Greene, prematurely announcing that the *Vision of Columbus* would "shortly be put to press." During 1782, David Humphreys had asked Greene to circulate subscription papers for the poem in the South, where Greene had exercised command over the American forces. In his letter, Barlow inquired whether there had been any takers. When the poem finally appeared in 1787, only three subscribers, apart from George Washington, were from the South, and all three came from Georgia where Greene had settled. Greene himself was absent from the list because death claimed him in 1785.

Barlow also wanted Greene's backing for a partnership he was contemplating with a kinsman of Greene named Ward in "the business of printing, bookselling & stationary in all their branches at Baltimore." Compared to Hartford, Baltimore looked like the land of opportunity. Having been spared British attack and occupation during the war, Baltimore was about to emerge as the Chesapeake Bay's first gateway port. Barlow hoped to bring out "the works of Mr. [John] Trumbull & Mr. Dwight as well as my own" on the new press. Publishing a paper on the side would provide these works with public notice. He was convinced "that a newspaper may have a large run, & perhaps [even] a magazine may be managed to advantage." Should the local gentry become interested in establishing "libraries [as] an ornamental species of furniture," bookselling and stationary would be profitable.[47]

Evidently, Greene declined because three months later in June 1784 Barlow established a printing business in partnership with Elisha Babcock at Hartford. Babcock, formerly a journeyman printer in Springfield, Massachusetts, had with Anthony Haswell started printing that town's first newspaper, the *Massachusetts Gazette*, in May 1782. A year later, Babcock became its sole publisher. When he found managing the enterprise burdensome, he sold the *Gazette* and joined Barlow in establishing the *American Mercury*. College graduates seldom aspired to editing or publishing newspapers at this time. Since the actual printing by a hand-powered press required brawn as well as brains, it was not considered a genteel occupation. The partnership contemplated with Ward probably had been based upon the understanding that Barlow would supply the brains while Ward supplied the brawn, as was initially the case with Babcock.

Ruth's health helped Barlow abandon any thought of moving to Baltimore. At the beginning of June 1784, he sent her to visit with Dudley at Greenfield on the shoreline, where it was cooler. Ruth, now in her late twenties, had been gone little more than a week before an anxious Barlow was inquiring about whether she had arrived safely, as well as about her "precious health." Dudley had promised to take good care of her, and Barlow exhorted his "lovely Girl" to "refuse no party of pleasure & amusement with moderate exercise. If you are well & tolerably happy I will not be anxious if you stay till you presently recover."[48] But from what? His concern over her "spirits . . . not get[ing] depressed" suggests that there was more to Ruth's condition than a physical ailment. Since eighteenth-century women were reticent about their health and psyches, we cannot be sure what the cause of Ruth's depression might have been, or even if what we now refer to as depression was the problem. There are hints, though inconclusive ones, that learning to live in intimate proximity with each other had not been as easy as they had initially assumed it would be. Having spent the first year and a half of their marriage apart, they had brought heightened expectations to being together. At the end of January 1785, the *American Mercury* published a poem entitled "The Bliss of Matrimony" satirizing marital tensions.[49] The poem traced the problem back to Jove and Juno but closed with lines that located it in the present. There is no proof that Barlow wrote this poem, though it seems likely he was responsible for most of the verse that appeared in the *Mercury* during its first year of publication. What is certain is that the author was no stranger to marital tensions and was attempting to come to terms with marriage's potential frustrations.

The principal frustration in the Barlows' marriage was their failure to have a child. Though for much of the three years of their union they had lived separately, they had been together through the winter of 1783 and for nine months prior to Ruth's departure in June 1784. The absence of children changed nothing in Joel's feelings for Ruth. Instead, it increased the bond between them by removing the distraction that children inevitably would have provided. Childlessness enabled them to develop an intimacy to which most of their contemporaries were strangers.

However, adjusting to a situation that few of their friends shared was trying, particularly for Ruth. In the spring of 1784, when they were facing up to their unwelcome situation, Barlow began voicing concern about Ruth's spirits. "Write me very particularly about your passage & feelings & when you wish to return & how." For the moment, though, he could only urge her to "Be happy—be happy," as he had so often done in the past.[50]

Ruth was back in Hartford before the end of July 1784 and was well enough on the twenty-seventh to accompany Noah Webster on a short ride. The next surviving communication between the Barlows was written a year later when Ruth again visited her family on the shoreline. In this letter Barlow appears much needier than he sounded during the previous year: "Thirteen days, my dearest Ruthy, are gone & your absence is more intolerable than ever." He was particularly distressed that he had not heard a word from her, though he had instructed the post rider to get an answer to a previous letter and had "been thro the mud all this rainy evening to catch him upon his arrival" so as "to learn whether you were yet alive." Not that he seriously feared she was dead. It was just that he was "raving homesick" for her. He insisted "you must positively come this week. . . . Make some body set off with you on Friday morning at all events. At farthest if you are not here by Saturday night you must not expect to find me alive." Barlow had hoped to send her something other than a lament, "But it is out of my power. I can say nothing but, come home, do Ruthy come home. . . ."[51] The plea lacked any hint of playful irony, and Ruth could not have doubted its genuineness. What was the source of Joel's urgency?

CHAPTER FOUR

Dead Ends

Joel Barlow and Elisha Babcock began their partnership in difficult times. The first issue of the four-panel *American Mercury* appeared on July 12, 1784. Though it was still a town of little more than five thousand inhabitants, Hartford already boasted a newspaper. The *Connecticut Courant* had helped define Hartford as the commercial hub of the Connecticut River Valley, circulating in all the settlements on the river and its tributaries. Hartford merchants supplied Farmington River towns as well as the river towns from Long Island Sound north to Springfield, Massachusetts—and even beyond—more effectively than could the merchants of Hartford's only potential competitor, Middletown.

The technology of newspaper publishing combined with Hartford's strategic location to provide the opportunity for another paper in the area. Because newspapers were still printed by hand, their production runs could not expand without dramatically expanding their overhead. The paper Babcock had established in Springfield continued to be published under the new title of the *Hampshire Herald*, but there would be no rival paper south of Hartford until the *Middlesex Gazette* began publication in Middletown on November 8, 1785.

Barlow behaved as though he did not believe his own claim that the *Mercury* had been launched "without the least injury to others who were established in the same business" by arranging for the *Mercury* to appear on Mondays,[1] giving it an edge over the *Courant*, which came out on Tuesdays. Initially, the *Courant* had been a Monday paper, but that often required printers to work on the Sabbath. On May 16, 1785, the *Courant* returned to a Monday schedule. That the *Courant* could afford to wait ten months to do so shows that the advantage the *Mercury* had reaped by appearing a day earlier was at best limited.

Most of a newspaper's content was copied from other papers printed in the nearby gateway ports, who in turn copied each other and the European and West Indian papers. In the absence of copyright restrictions, every printer was free to take whatever information he wanted from these publications. There was enough material that two papers situated in the same small town did not have to be identical. Though many items in the papers were the same, Barlow devoted the first issues of the *Mercury* to serializing an account of Capt. James Cook's voyages of exploration, while the *Courant* reprinted "Lectures on Modern History" from the *London Magazine*.

The commercial diversity of the regional market they both served created enough advertising demand to sustain two papers. The *Courant* enjoyed an advantage because it retained its oldest and best customers. Barlow and Babcock devoted their unused space to publishing notices about the imported books, stationary, hardware, and West India goods they offered for sale in addition to publishing the *Mercury*. They also advertised the few small publishing ventures they attempted beyond bringing out a newspaper. Among the first of these was an almanac.

Almanacs were attractive start-up ventures because they were small and quickly became obsolete. Since almost every household had one, they were in constant demand. Nor did a printer necessarily have to write the text or make the calculations they contained. Because almanacs were ubiquitous long before copyright laws became prevalent, the texts of the more popular ones were regarded as public property and knock-offs were common. Benjamin Franklin's *Poor Richard's Almanac* set the standard in the middle Atlantic region, while Isaac Bickerstaff's almanac published in Boston held sway over New England during the last thirty years of the eighteenth century.

Barlow and Babcock utilized Bickerstaff's template for the first almanac they issued for 1784. On November 9, the *Courant* printed a protest written by Nehemiah Strong, who several years before had resigned from his post as Yale's professor of mathematics. Strong criticized the Bickerstaff knock-offs circulating in the area. His principal gripe was against a Springfield version that he claimed plagiarized Bickerstaff's astronomical calculations, but he added that "excepting some Anecdotes . . . alien from the subject," the Bickerstaff issued by Barlow and Babcock was "the very copy of another Almanack . . . by one Mr. Judd . . . entirely without his consent."

Barlow immediately replied to Strong in the *Courant*, accusing him of trying to turn "the popular prejudice against the works of others in order to extend the sale of his own," alluding to an interest Strong was known to have in a competing almanac. Barlow dismissed Strong's attack as "no more than an ardent sigh for the love of other men's property."[2] However, the partners' subsequent advertising of their almanac as derived from Judd's and Bickerstaff's suggests that Strong's objection was valid. Barlow's aggressiveness toward a former Yale professor reflected a mutual dislike dating back to 1777, when Yale's class of 1778 had been under Strong's nominal supervision at Glastonbury. But Barlow ran little risk of alienating the network of Yale graduates he was trying to cultivate. Strong had been suspected of entertaining loyalist sentiments during the war and, after resigning his professorship, had criticized the college. Barlow's attack on Strong was more significant in underscoring that one printer's gain could be another's loss as the American economy entered a postwar recession during 1784.

Such recessions had plagued the colonial economy because warfare in the Atlantic basin inevitably compromised access to overseas markets. During the Revolutionary War the price of local produce had declined while the price of increasingly scarce imports had risen. Upon the cessation of hostilities, the price of domestic produce relative to foreign imports recovered as Americans regained access to distant markets. Forgone consumption during a war created pent-up demand that led many Americans to buy imports on credit, assuming the current favorable terms of trade would persist. This proved to be a serious miscalculation, because once pent-up foreign demand for American exports had been satisfied, the price of domestic produce declined. As importers realized American indebtedness was cutting into consumption, they pressed for payment, leaving many struggling to pay off the private debts they had contracted in the first flush of peace.

The adverse effect of the recession after the Revolutionary War was compounded by two other developments. The first involved the public debt that the states and nation had incurred during the course of the struggle. The second was the exclusion of U.S. shipping from the commercial empires of the European powers. Both developments combined to force the American economy into a deep recession that lasted well into 1787. Since the typical New Englander had limited involvement in the commercial economy, many succeeded in avoiding disaster. But the pressures of public and private indebtedness converged in 1786 to provoke Shays's Rebellion in Massachusetts. Despite warning signals that economic and political danger lay ahead, Barlow and Babcock continued adding to the stock of books and goods they were advertising for sale in the *Mercury*.

Because most of Barlow's experience with money had been watching it lose value to hyperinflation, he was happy to take supplies from wholesalers on credit, convinced that goods would remain more valuable than money.

The initial success of the *Mercury* helped disguise the problems that would later trouble the partners. Their principal exposure to creditors was not their press —which could be made to generate revenue by publishing other works besides the newspaper—but their stock of books, stationary, and other imported goods. This inventory, particularly of books, required the investment of considerable capital. Regardless of whether it was theirs or a creditor's, they encountered increasing difficulties in turning their investment into cash. Eventually, these difficulties contributed to defeating one of Barlow's principal motives for entering into the partnership, which was to publish the works of his friends—as well as his own—even though substantial texts were potentially the most profitable items a publisher could issue.

On August 23, the *Mercury* printed a notice that the General Association of Connecticut's Congregational Church had authorized Barlow to revise Isaac Watts's English edition of psalms and hymns. In adapting the Hebrew texts to the sensibility of an eighteenth-century British audience, Watts had introduced references to Britain and its monarchy, which now seemed incongruous to American readers. Barlow, who was still technically a candidate for the ministry, saw an easy opportunity to remedy the problem by revising Watts's psalms. To broaden the project's appeal, he decided to supply translations for the twelve psalms that Watts had neglected and five hymns. Barlow did not do all the work himself. He had the assistance of several collaborators, including Lemuel Hopkins and John Trumbull. Though Barlow made most of the changes incorporated into his version of Watts, he accepted Hopkins's changes in three psalms without formal acknowledgement. He also got the General Assembly to grant him the exclusive right to print the work, though Babcock probably expended more time and energy in running off its three hundred pages than Barlow did in making the revisions.

Doctor Watts's Imitation of the Psalms of David, corrected and enlarged. By Joel Barlow. To which is added a collection of Hymns; the whole applied to the state of the Christian church in general did not appear until March 21, 1785. It had taken so long to produce because Babcock had also been working on printing Part III of Noah Webster's *Grammatical Institutes of the English Language* since the previous December.[3] When Part III appeared on February 7, 1785, Barlow and Babcock ostentatiously announced that the volume, which came to 186 pages, was printed "under privilege of copyright." They had good reasons for putting Part III ahead of Barlow's psalms because Part I, published in 1783 by Hudson and Goodwin and which eventually became known as *The American Spelling Book*, was already in its third edition. Over the next century, it would sell in excess of 80 million copies. The publishers of the *Courant* knew a winner when they saw it and brought out Part II of the *Grammatical Institutes*, devoted to the rules of grammar, in 1784. Before the end of that year, a second edition of Part II was underway. Barlow must have known of Webster's intention to spend much of 1785 and 1786 traveling to sell his speller and grammar. Thus, by early 1785 the partners realized that one could not lose by publishing the capstone to the *Grammatical Institutes*.

The real puzzle is why Webster allowed Barlow and Babcock to publish Part III under privilege of copyright, since that prevented Hudson and Goodwin from doing so. Webster pursued this course because some of the texts in Part III, which covered "the necessary rules of reading and speaking, and a variety of essays and dialogues and declamatory pieces," were excerpts from Barlow's and Dwight's as yet unpublished epics. Webster gave Barlow and Babcock the initial, exclusive right to publish Part III to protect Barlow's and Dwight's intellectual property. The arrangement was a temporary one because on November 1, 1786, after Babcock finally issued Dwight's *The Conquest of Canaan*, Webster assigned his copyright to Part III of the *Institutes* over to Hudson and Goodwin.[4] Barlow's *The Vision of Columbus* had yet to appear, but by then the last obstacle to its doing so had been surmounted. If Barlow and Babcock were entitled to anything beyond the advantage already derived from issuing the first edition of Part III, they were more than compensated when Webster allowed the partners to republish Part II.

Barlow's version of Watts's psalms initially looked as though it might be almost as successful as the *Grammatical Institutes*. A second printing emerged from Barlow and Babcock's press a year after the first with the declaration that it too was published with "privilege of copyright," but the partners had printed it for the two other printing establishments in town. Besides Hudson and Goodwin, Nathaniel Patten owned a small press. Just prior to the appearance of Barlow's version of the *Psalms*, Patten had reprinted Watts' original *Psalms*.[5] The new arrangement, which gave everyone a stake in Barlow's version, may have been intended as a peace offering to his rivals, but it also reflected Barlow's strategy for accommodating criticism of his revision of Watts.

Members of the state's Congregational establishment viewed Barlow's work with suspicion. Ezra Stiles noted that Barlow had "left out & made anew whole Stanzas, and even Psalms." Stiles also took exception to the hymns that he felt were "an indiscriminate Mixture of his own [Barlow's] & Dr Watts." Stiles suspected many of Barlow's alterations were motivated by a desire "to assume the *Place* of the Author, as if he was the Author." In his eagerness to take credit, Barlow had "corrected too much and unnecessarily mutilated the Book & sometimes hurt the poetry." Stiles concluded that though "Mr. Barlow is an excellent Poet; yet he cannot retouch Watts to advantage."[6]

Barlow could not have been oblivious to his critics. Tradition has it that he encountered Oliver Arnold, a cousin of traitor Benedict, on the streets of Hartford around this time, who regaled him with the following verse:

Tis God's blest praise you've sought to alter,
And for your pains deserve a halter;
You have proved yourself a simple creature,
Murder'd great Watts, and ruin'd metre.[7]

But disapproval came from more visible quarters, as well. On August 8, 1785, the *Mercury* republished a short piece taken from John Mycall's *Essex Journal and Massachusetts and New-Hampshire General Advertiser* out of Newburyport, Massachusetts. The excerpt took aim at both Webster and Barlow, commenting caustically on Connecticut's efforts "towards becoming the Guide and Pattern of ALL THE States, in Learning and religious matters." Not only had Connecticut authors "already undertaken to dictate the manner of pronunciation, spelling and dividing words," but "Watts' Psalms and Hymns . . . have undergone another great change, one opposite to the opinion of their excellent author." Repeating Stiles's objection, this writer charged that, "the Doctor is made the author of many new ones, of which HE never thought," and added that "those most ingenious and learned gentlemen [Barlow and Webster] censure all attempts of that nature which have preceded theirs."

Barlow responded as defiantly as he had to Nehemiah Strong's criticism of the partners' almanac by attacking Mycall's motives. Mycall was "*said to have a large number of Dilworth's spelling books and Watts's Psalms on hand.*" Barlow also accused Mycall "of making his own alterations to Watts's psalms."[8] At the end of August, Barlow and Babcock issued a separate, fourteen-page edition of the psalms Barlow had translated, which had been added to the sixty-five done by Watts, along with five hymns of Barlow's composition. The *Mercury* additionally published a brief, anonymous essay critical of exclusionary religious creeds, before capping its campaign against Mycall with a general plea for religious toleration.[9] By inviting his readers to associate "religion" with "culture," Barlow hoped to tap the resentment many in Connecticut felt about Massachusetts's claims to cultural superiority.

During the winter of 1786, Barlow also had the *Connecticut Courant* print the endorsement of fifteen of the state's Congregational clergy and the text of a letter he had received from Joseph Huntington, the pastor of the Coventry Congregational Church, in an advertisement for the second printing of his *Psalms*. Huntington's letter praised the emendations Barlow had made and expressed his confidence that adoption of the work "will in due time become universal."[10] Barlow's spirited, multilayered response showed he was a man one could not cross with impunity, but his feistiness did little to refurbish his religious credentials because he never followed through with his candidacy for the Congregational ministry. To reconsider such a commitment was not in itself grounds for criticism. Rather, Barlow's problem stemmed from appearing to straddle the sacred and secular realms in his management of the revision of Watts. In addition to drawing the ire of those who objected to his tampering with sacred texts, his former friend Lemuel Hopkins would join Richard Alsop and Theodore Dwight in attacking him for his "ever-changing, Proteus mind" in *The Political green-house* (1799). They then pointed to "all his turns, thru' every wind" from "telling sinners where they go to / To speculations in Scioto,"[11] a reference to a land company with which Barlow had become associated. Nor did it help his religious reputation that his version of the *Psalms* did reasonably well in subsequent years. After the second edition in 1786, it was republished six more times in the United States and once in Scotland before a new version of Watts's Psalms, undertaken by Timothy Dwight at the request of the General Association of Connecticut's Congregational Churches, appeared in 1801.

By the time a second printing of the *Psalms* had been arranged, the postwar economy was in a tailspin. In October 1785, the *Mercury* announced a substantial reduction in price for the *Psalms* because of the "general scarcity of cash."[12] The same issue also contained a notice from the tax collector of the town of Stafford initiating proceedings against more than one hundred delinquents. A subsequent issue carried the resolution of the General Assembly threatening to sue all tax collectors in arrears. These signs of economic distress appeared amid a chorus of laments about merchants stripping Americans of all their cash. The complaints were coupled with repeated reports of the highhanded treatment American vessels were receiving from the British in the West Indies and Canada. As if the economy was not troubled enough, reports started appearing about the capture of American vessels by North African pirates.

A gradually worsening economy was not the only thing Barlow had to worry about. His work on the *Mercury* was neither enhancing his literary reputation nor stimulating the production of works of native genius. Between the end of January and July 1785, the *Mercury* published no poetry. Not every poem that had appeared in its pages had come from Barlow's pen. He was perfectly happy to publish the work of his friends and neighbors like John Trumbull and Hopkins. The group, which originally included Noah Webster, had formed a literary club on December 13, 1784. Their initial meetings were devoted to debating public issues such as "What are the means of improving & establishing the Union of the States?" or moral questions like "whether Polygamy is prohibited by the Law of nature?" and even religious ones like "Whether there being 3 attributes of a God are discoverable by the light of nature."[13] This club's philosophical interests may help to explain the poetic drought that was to make the *Mercury* appear to be almost as unfriendly to verse as the *Courant*. Not until the second half of 1785 did the Connecticut or Hartford Wits—as they came to be known—resume their former level of poetic output. Barlow would be very much at the center of this group for two years thereafter. But during the early months of 1785, the Wits behaved as though they had lost their artistic way, probably taking their cue from Barlow since the *Mercury* was their principal outlet.

Barlow was preoccupied with a dilemma related to the publication of his epic. During June 1785, he devoted a great deal of effort to drafting a letter to Louis XVI. It was not a letter most Americans would have dreamed of writing. European monarchs did not customarily receive letters from their own subjects let alone from the republican citizens of another country. Not only was Barlow unknown to the king of France, but the tone with which a republican should address a monarch presented a problem. Yet Barlow wrote the letter, undoubtedly with Ruth's encouragement.

The seeds of the letter had been sown in November 1782, when the French ambassador, Anne-César de la Luzerne, had agreed to approach the throne with Barlow's request that Louis XVI accept the dedication of his poem. In September 1783, before anything tangible had come from Luzerne's promise, Barlow wrote to Jeremiah Wadsworth, then in Europe. Barlow claimed that "some of my friends" had advised him to press the matter with the king, but he added hastily, "should you think it worthy of his attention & yours." If Wadsworth did not have direct access to the throne, Barlow hoped the matter could be addressed "through the channel of Doctor Franklin or some other person."[14]

It is not known whether Wadsworth exerted himself on Barlow's behalf during his sojourn in France. Wadsworth returned to Hartford from Europe on October 7, 1784. Four days later Lafayette visited and stayed with Wadsworth until the thirteenth. As the most prominent alderman in Hartford's newly constituted municipal government, Wadsworth played a key role in the civic celebration held in the French general's honor. Lafayette's arrival was announced by "a discharge of artillery," and the next day "he dined with a number of . . . gentlemen" at Bull's tavern. The dinner concluded with the presentation of an effusive address from the mayor, aldermen, and common council of the city that saluted Lafayette for risking "his life and fortune in the cause of liberty."[15]

Barlow probably used the occasion to speak directly to Lafayette himself or to have Wadsworth intercede on his behalf, or both. In any case, upon Lafayette's return to France in 1785, the general spoke to the French foreign minister, the Comte de Vergennes, several times about Barlow's poem. A letter from Lafayette to Vergennes, written on January 26, 1786, reveals the degree to which Barlow had captured the general's ear. Lafayette explained that Barlow had already delayed the publication of his poem for two years waiting for the desired permission. So long as the issue of the royal permission hung in the air, Barlow would be stymied in his efforts to bring out *The Vision of Columbus*. If he went ahead and published the poem before receiving permission, he risked giving offence by apparently ignoring the authority he had already acknowledged. He had also worked into the poem material premised on the royal dedication that would be inappropriate if that permission were denied.[16]

The problem that now confronted Barlow was whether a direct address to the throne would make matters better or worse. Considering the difficulties involved, Barlow's letter to the king performed the task of soliciting a royal favor credibly enough. He began by linking the discovery of America to the emergence of the Enlightenment in Europe, referring to Columbus's voyage as "an event which laid open all parts of the earth to the range of the liberal mind." Barlow then described Louis's "royal Ancestors" as among those who "have been conspicuous in seizing those advantages and diffusing [the] happy effects" flowing from the first contact, at least for Europeans. Barlow pointed specifically to Henry IV's proposal for a confederation of monarchies dedicated to ensuring peace. Barlow looked forward to the day when this "political system shall be realized among the nations of Europe, and extend[ed] to all mankind." He depicted France's role in establishing American independence as a "glorious" deed reflecting Louis's willingness "to accelerate the progress of society, by disregarding the temporary interests and local policies of other Monarchs." In extending "the hand of beneficence to another hemisphere," Louis had "rais[ed] an infant empire, in a few years, to a degree of importance, which several ages were scarcely thought sufficient to produce." Barlow continued: "This is the sublime of humanity, to feel for future ages and distant nations: to act those things, as a Monarch, which another can only contemplate as a philosopher, or image in flights of poetry. America acknowledges her obligations to the Guardian of her rights; mankind, who survey your conduct, and posterity, for whom you act, will see that the tribute of gratitude is paid." The best way for Louis to add to the luster already attached to his achievements was to patronize the arts "as there are none, who can feel the subject so strongly as those who are the particular objects of your royal condescension." Barlow assured Louis that granting permission to have the poem dedicated to him could only add "a new obligation to those I before felt—in common with a grateful country."[17]

It is a safe bet that Louis XVI never saw Barlow's letter, although it did end up in the archives of the French Foreign Ministry. Had Louis read it, the visionary qualities Barlow attributed to him might have led the king to doubt Barlow's sanity. Vergennes probably was aware of the letter, whose presumption would have attracted the attention of the clerks who processed it. In fact, it may well have provided the occasion for at least one of the conversations Vergennes had with Lafayette about the matter. Vergennes may also have consulted Thomas Jefferson, who at the time was U.S. ambassador to France, though there is no record of this happening and Jefferson was not yet personally acquainted with Barlow. The power of Barlow's letter derived more from the current state of Franco-American relations than it did from either Barlow's rhetoric or his connections.

By the time the letter reached France, the court was wondering why it had supported American independence. As France's fiscal system lurched toward bankruptcy brought on by the American war, much of the commerce of the United States was reverting back to Britain. Shared traditions, religion, and language had made maintaining France's influence over the young Republic an uphill battle. The rapturous receptions Lafayette met with wherever he went during his postwar tour of the United States was one of the few hopeful threads the French court could clutch. In his letter of January 26, 1786, Lafayette urged that Barlow be granted the permission he desired because the author was "a man of great spirit" whom it might be useful to encourage.[18]

Louis XVI's ministers approved Barlow's request because they hoped doing so would serve as an inexpensive symbol of France's continuing commitment to the Franco-American alliance. They subscribed for twenty-five copies of the *Vision of Columbus* in the king's name, while Lafayette took ten more copies. Assuming Barlow received the money, it would have done little to meet the expenses of the first printing. By lending the cachet of the king to Barlow's enterprise, however, the endorsement led to more subscriptions in the United States, replacing those that had been withdrawn due to death or financial distress.

The American economy continued its downhill slide for a full year after Barlow dispatched his letter to Louis XVI. Economic distress added to Barlow's anxiety about his poem, though not necessarily in ways one would have expected. At this point in his life he expressed contempt for financial gain. He was far more worried about the reception *The Vision of Columbus* was likely to meet if it appeared during the depths of a recession that was leading some to question whether the American Revolution had been a mistake. Barlow viewed the publication of Dwight's *The Conquest of Canaan* as a trial balloon for his own epic. Barlow and Babcock first advertised Dwight's epic on April 11, 1785, but the work was not released until August 15, and then it bore only Babcock's name as the publisher. Part of the delay was due to Dwight's insistence that all press errors be corrected before the final sheets were run off, but some of the delay reflected Barlow's desire to find a more propitious moment for the release of Dwight's poem. As economic prospects grew darker throughout the summer of 1785, Barlow became increasingly concerned. He certainly didn't want *The Vision of Columbus*, which strove to establish a sublime and triumphant motif, or Dwight's work—even though it was less dependent on the success of the American Revolution—to appear when everything else was going to pieces. Other sources of tension had emerged between the printing partners, and Babcock eventually lost patience and brought out *The Conquest of Canaan* on his own.

Babcock turned out be a careless printer, and Webster spent more time than he cared to supervising the work on Part III of the *Grammatical Institutes.*[19] Then Babcock twice inserted an ad for a local merchant in the *Mercury* upside down. Barlow clearly entertained higher standards for how his *Vision of Columbus* would be published or he would not have previously asked Wadsworth to procure him elegant European paper on which to print it.[20] When his epic finally appeared in May 1787, it came from Hudson and Goodwin's rather than Babcock's press.

Barlow's name remained on the masthead of the *Mercury* until the middle of November 1785, and the formal dissolution of the partnership was not announced until the beginning of December. In the interval, a veritable deluge of poetry ended the half-year drought in the *Mercury*. Five new poems graced its pages between the end of July and mid-October, though judging from their stylistic qualities most of these did not come from Barlow's pen. The *Mercury* also began serializing a long piece entitled "Yarico and Inkle, a Poetical Epistle," which did not conclude until November 7, in the last issue of the *Mercury* on which Barlow's name appeared on the masthead. Barlow had no hand in the poem's composition; it was a reprint of an anonymous production that had first appeared in London in 1736.

English readers were familiar with the story of betrayal involving the castaway Thomas Inkle and an Indian maiden, Yarico, who had saved Inkle's life when her people threatened him. She had then offered him her love and was carrying his child, when—on being rescued by a European ship—Inkle sold her and his unborn child into slavery. The English public first learned of the story from Richard Ligon's *A True and Exact History of the Islands of Barbadoes* (1657). It was subsequently popularized by Richard Steele in the March 13, 1711, issue of the *Spectator*. Its pathos inspired several poetic renditions, of which the anonymous 1736 version was the most dramatic. The story could be put to many uses, as George Coleman's *Inkle and Yarico: An Opera, in Three Acts*, first produced in 1787, in London would show. The merciless lampoon of English colonizers made this the most successful comic opera of the late eighteenth-century English stage.

Before becoming Barlow's partner, Babcock had republished the anonymous 1736 poem on his Springfield press, and the first issues of the *Mercury* advertised the back stock from that venture. Since this was the sort of poem Barlow appreciated, Babcock's willingness to print it may have served to recommend Babcock to Barlow as a partner in the first place. Its theme of betrayal, however, raises the question of whether its republication in the autumn of 1785 obliquely reflected the tension that had developed between the two men. Barlow may have regarded "Yarico and Inkle" as more effective than Dwight's poem in cultivating the taste for heroic verse in the reading public, while it gave vent to Babcock's sense of being abandoned. Printing it was the last thing the partners were able to agree on before going their separate ways.

Babcock kept the press and continued publishing the *Mercury*, while Barlow took over the store with its stock. This placed Barlow in a difficult situation as the postwar recession bottomed out in 1786. An advertisement in the December 12, 1785, *Mercury* declared that in addition to the large stock of books, he was also selling an assortment of dry goods together with the West and East Indian goods the partners had previously carried. But after the beginning of the year, there were no further notices about his inventory in the newspapers until May 22, when an ad in the *Mercury* made it clear Barlow had transformed his store into a specialty bookshop. As it grew harder to get wholesalers to supply his store on consignment, he gradually closed his shop during 1786 and turned to the law.

The usual way one became a lawyer in postrevolutionary Connecticut was to apprentice for several years with an established attorney before applying for admission to the bar. Quite a few of Barlow's classmates at Yale—including Noah Webster, Uriah Tracy, Zephaniel Swift, and Oliver Wolcott Jr.—took this route. But there was an alternative. Though the law had its own technical language and procedures, anyone could become acquainted with them by reading the standard legal treatises, of which Blackstone's *Commentaries* remained the most popular. Alexander Hamilton had studied law on his own for four scant months after leaving the army and then been admitted to the New York bar. Ruth's brother Abraham Baldwin followed a similar course and rose to the top of his profession when he moved to Georgia. Barlow chose Hamilton's and Baldwin's path.

The law was a gentlemanly profession appropriate for a Yale graduate to pursue, and legal knowledge would be useful in defending his own and his friends' intellectual property rights under the new copyright laws the states were passing. Barlow was also aware that lawyers tended to prosper during recessions. And finally, then as now, legal training provided a versatile pathway into many other fields besides drafting conveyances and wills, or pleading in court. One such ancillary occupation that had already attracted Barlow's attention was public office. In March 1786, a full month before he joined the Connecticut bar, he was elected a member of Hartford's Common Council, which enacted bylaws for the municipality.

As evidence of his suitability for admission to the bar, Barlow offered a dissertation that explored the divergence between the law of nature and common or statute law.[21] This again was not customary, and we may assume a lawyer friend vetted the composition before the court agreed to hear it. By now his reputation as a rhetorician was known, and those in attendance would have looked forward to listening to him as a welcome relief from the monotony of countless debt actions with which the courts had become clogged.

Barlow started from the premise that initially there had been little difference between the two kinds of law. They had diverged only when the common and statute law had failed to evolve in ways that corresponded to changes in society. Barlow argued that "the feudal system applied to a simple military state" had been nearly perfect. "No human institution" suited "that stage of society or was better calculated to commence that improvement which nature pointed out to the small independent jurisdictions which at that time extended over most of the countries of Europe." As proof of his contention, Barlow cited similar systems adopted by the Turks in Asia and by the Mexicans and Peruvians in the Americas. Problems only arose when feudal principles of landholding incorporated into the common law were applied to commercial society. Barlow traced to feudal times the distinction in the common law between the way real and personal property was treated in cases of debt. He argued that distinctions between kinds of property, though appropriate when real property was predominant, no longer made sense. He then cited instances in which this distinction affected Connecticut law, putting it in tension with the law of nature.

Before he was through, Barlow criticized the state laws' excessive use of capital punishment for thefts, the doctrine of acquiring a right through adverse possession, and the power of creditors to imprison their debtors, all part of the standard Enlightenment repertoire of reform. Barlow was more original when he attacked what he claimed was a European notion that subjects owed their sovereigns unqualified allegiance. This idea was inappropriate for a nation that thought of itself as a refuge for the oppressed of mankind. But Barlow's greatest originality lay in his use of history rather than reason to critique Connecticut's legal system. That approach helped him with another problem he faced in addressing practicing lawyers and sitting judges. Brash as Barlow could be, he did not presume to lecture them on how they should be conducting their business. Historical criticism of the law was far less categorical than invoking the abstract authority of natural law. The academic nature of his dissertation additionally reassured practicing attorneys that Barlow was unlikely to eclipse them in their profession. Both attorneys and judges knew that what mattered was not what the law should be but what it was.

Barlow was admitted to the bar, but he failed to attract enough clients to compensate for the loss of his book business. Hard times made those who could afford the services of an attorney prefer someone more seasoned and less theoretically oriented. It quickly became clear that Barlow would have to explore other options in achieving the genteel independence his literary ambitions required.

CHAPTER FIVE

Literary Recognition

As a childless couple the Barlows faced fewer financial demands than they would have had their marriage been fertile. But at least their unwelcome fate allowed them to serve as the social center for a circle of talented friends despite their constrained circumstances. Noah Webster recorded in his diary frequently dining with the Barlows, who also regularly entertained John Trumbull and Lemuel Hopkins with their wives. They also saw a good deal of Oliver Wolcott Jr. while he remained in Hartford trying to bring some order to Connecticut's finances.

Not surprisingly, Barlow became a spokesman for the Hartford "Wits." In a letter to William Livingston, the governor of New Jersey, Barlow claimed to speak for "several Gentlemen of taste in this part of the country" who sought to assemble an anthology of American poetry. He asked Livingston to send him such of his poems "as you are willing should be presented to the public." Barlow left no doubt about his determination to have them. "Altho' your Excellency's character can receive no advantage by being ranked among the Poets of the present age; yet the public will claim an undoubted right to those pieces they have already in possession; & would be farther obliged could you afford them more."[1] Barlow's circle of "Wits" briefly constituted the poetic vortex of the new nation. They enjoyed the support of Jeremiah Wadsworth, and because Hartford was the state's capital, talented nonresidents like David Humphreys often came to town to conduct public business.

Humphreys had been Washington's aide-de-camp during the last years of the war and had served between 1784 and 1786 as secretary of a commission—consisting of Thomas Jefferson, John Adams, and Benjamin Franklin—charged with negotiating commercial treaties in Europe. When Humphreys returned home in May 1786, he was alarmed by what he found and reported to Jefferson that "our federal concerns are not in a very promising situation. . . . Many people appear to be uneasy & to prognosticate revolutions they hardly know how or why. A scarcity of money is universally complained of" and some of the state legislatures had begun issuing paper money.[2] Compounding Humphreys's general sense of dismay was his fellow citizens' total indifference to "A Poem on the Happiness of America." He had written it during 1785 to counter hostile criticism of the new nation in Europe. Though it had been acclaimed abroad, it was being ignored in America.

Seeking wider recognition, Humphreys approached Hudson and Goodwin, publishers of the *Connecticut Courant*. Though the *Courant* had not published much poetry since 1783, Humphreys persuaded them to run his "Elegy on the Burning of Fairfield" (1779) on June 19, 1786, and to print the first American edition of "A Poem on the Happiness of America," a 176-line excerpt of which appeared in the *Courant* on June 26. Humphrey's ability to change the *Courant's* course testified to his powers of persuasion. Physically large by the standards of any age, he was used to people agreeing with him. But the *Courant's* change of heart reflected more than Humphreys' personal charisma. The *Courant's* aversion to the work of local poets had stemmed from the Wits' failure to address the issues agitating the public in the postwar period. This feature of the their work made Hudson and Goodwin content to have the *Mercury* serve as their exclusive outlet. Humphreys turned the *Courant* around by demonstrating the political potential of poetry. He then mobilized Barlow's circle of Wits to assist in countering the influence in Connecticut of Shays's Rebellion.

The Massachusetts insurgency had been ignited by the direct tax in hard money the legislature had levied in response to a congressional requisition to protect the Republic's foreign credit. During the last half of 1786, insurgents obstructed the courts from seizing property for the payment of private and public debts, protesting that forced sales were fetching only a fraction of the assets' value because of the general shortage of money. When the Massachusetts legislature authorized a military force to suppress the insurgency, the insurgents attempted to seize the federal arsenal at Springfield. Several lives were lost in the assault, after which the rebels retreated toward Peterborough. In late January 1787, an army under Benjamin Lincoln's command caught up with the rebels in the midst of a blizzard and dispersed them. But when the people of Massachusetts next went to the polls, they elected a general court sympathetic to the insurgents.

Many found this as disturbing as armed insurrection. The election following the uprising suggested that the American people were either unwilling or unable to pay their revolutionary debts. Connecticut's legislature had avoided rebellion by refusing compliance with Congress' requisitions, but Humphreys felt inaction compromised the Confederation's government as much as Shays's followers had. When Humphreys appealed to Hartford's poets for assistance, Barlow readily responded because *The Vision of Columbus* depended upon the success of the Revolution. If the nation dissolved in response to insurgencies like Shays's, the glorious future that Barlow's epic assumed would vanish.

Alexander Pope had popularized the satiric epic in Britain, and John Trumbull's "The Progress of Dullness" and *M'Fingal* naturalized it in America. *M'Fingal* alluded to James MacPherson's forgery of an ancient epic "Fingal," allegedly written by a third-century Gaelic bard named Ossian. MacPherson's forgery appeared in London and Dublin in 1762 and subsequently attracted considerable attention on the Continent, where it helped shape the sensibility of the emerging Romantic movement. Samuel Johnson eventually questioned Ossian's authenticity, setting off a prolonged controversy within British literary circles. The attention Ossian had attracted persuaded Humphreys and his collaborators in *The Anarchiad* that fictional documents purportedly from an ancient civilization would lend themselves to effective satire.

Much speculation has developed over who contributed what to *The Anarchiad*. Aside from the authorship of Number V, "The Genius of America," which Humphreys subsequently claimed, the issue of authorship cannot be resolved. The Wits could have made claims similar to Humphreys had they wished, and their reticence about authorship suggests they regarded *The Anarchiad* as a group effort. The subsequent attempt of Elihu Hubbard Smith to maximize Lemuel Hopkins's role in the enterprise at Barlow's expense occurred after Barlow's republicanism turned the state's Federalists against him.[3] No independent evidence supports Smith's attributions, and Humphreys failed even to mention Hopkins when describing the participants to Washington.

No one disputes that Humphreys acted as the impresario of the project. After being elected to the autumn general assembly, he visited Hartford before the legislature met and subsequently carried the first number of the *Anarchiad* back to New Haven. It appeared in the *New Haven Gazette* of October 26, 1786, under the title of "American Antiquities." During the next four months, Humphreys returned to Hartford several times on official business, on each occasion reenergizing the Wits to continue their project.

This first number of *The Anarchiad* contained more prose than verse to explain

the poem's controlling conceit. An antiquarian had discovered an ancient manuscript of a twenty-four-book epic entitled "THE ANARCHIAD, A Poem on the Restoration of Chaos and substantial Night" while excavating a ruin "in the Western
country." The antiquarian was so struck by the "sublimity of [its] sentiments" that
he concluded it "ha[d] been the model of all subsequent epic productions." By
way of proof, he offered a sample from Book Eight that was entitled the "Book of
Vision." This selection also demonstrated the ancient bard's prophetic powers. It
was as if the poet had "taken for the point of vision one of the lofty mountains of
America" and caused "the years of futurity to pass before him." There "the scenes
of fate unroll, / And Massachusetts opens on my soul; / There Chaos, Anarch old,
asserts his sway; / And mobs in myriads blacken all the way."[4]

The next week a second number, dealing with Connecticut, appeared. It consisted of an excerpt from a speech delivered by Anarch to Beelzebub, "for the
purpose of persuading him to come over and help his faithful friends in our
Macedonia [Connecticut], since his affairs were in so thriving a posture in Massachusetts and Rhode Island." The speech referred in code to members of the
Connecticut legislature who had opposed "a compliance with the *requisitions of
Congress.*" They were accused of favoring a resolution "that we will not pay interest on our foreign or domestic debts—that we should furnish nothing for the
support of the federal government—*that we should withdraw ourselves from the
Union*—that all government should be prostrated in the dust—that *mobs, conventions,* and *anarchy* should prevail," or in other words, "that THE GLORIOUS
TEMPLE OF LIBERTY and happiness which had been erected in these ends of the
earth, for an asylum to suffering humanity, should soon be dissolved."[5] In this way
the Wits equated the Shaysites and their allies with the repudiation of everything
the Revolution stood for.

Number III of *The Anarchiad*, appearing at the end of December, took aim at
the misdeeds of Rhode Island. The state had recently issued paper money and had
passed a law that allowed debtors to retire their obligations to creditors in depreciated bills simply by depositing the nominal value of the debt with a justice of the
peace. Debtors had only to publish the creditor's name and a notice that the debt
had been paid to extinguish it legally. The antiquarian thought the *Anarchiad*'s
treatment of paper money a "very poetical digression" because "in an unfunded
and depreciating condition, [it] is happily calculated to introduce the long expected scenes of misrule, dishonesty, and perdition."[6] As Anarch concluded,

Each weekly print new lists of cheats proclaims,
Proud to enroll their knav'ries and their names;

The wiser race, the shares of law to shun,
Like Lot from Sodom, from Rhode Island run.

The antiquarian promised to collect the names of all those who had taken advantage of the Rhode Island law so that "whenever the army shall be raised for the support of anarchy, or whenever that new state . . . *the State of Confusion* shall be properly organized, and admitted into the confederacy," people would know to whom they were indebted for their blessings.[7]

By the time Number IV came out in January 1787, the public had become sufficiently familiar with *The Anarchiad's* controlling conceit so that nothing more than the heading "Extract from the Anarchiad, Book xxxiii" introduced eighty-five lines of verse. They invidiously compared the "Western world" with Britain, so far as honoring national debts went, and lamented that Washington's retirement and Nathaniel Greene's recent death had left the Anarch in undisputed control until challenged by "Great Hesper." A figure in Greek mythology who achieved apotheosis as the evening star, Hesper would figure prominently in Barlow's *The Columbiad*, which appeared twenty years after *The Vision of Columbus*. Barlow may not have been personally responsible for inserting Hesper in *The Anarchiad*. But having employed the poetic device of a supernatural agent in *The Vision of Columbus*, he would have approved the use of the same device in *The Anarchiad*.

Number V of *The Anarchiad* consisted of Humphreys's six-stanza hymn entitled "The Genius of America." Its appearance coincided with the repulse of Shays's followers at the Springfield arsenal and the arrival of Lincoln at the head of an army of 2,500. Humphreys was the officer commanding the Connecticut troops that Congress had requisitioned to help suppress the rebellion, so he had designated Hartford as their rendezvous. Though he did not receive marching orders until the middle of February, he probably regarded this contribution to *The Anarchiad* as a farewell to the project. When it resumed in the last week of February, the rebels had been routed and the worst of the crisis had passed.

Still, Shays's followers presented a political threat within Massachusetts and in its neighboring states, where they had many sympathizers. That is why successive numbers of *The Anarchiad* ridiculed the Connecticut politicians, whom the Wits claimed were of the same ilk as Shays and his followers, for resisting efforts to strengthen the federal government. Thus Number VI assaulted "Wronghead" (James Wadsworth of Durham), who was made to lament that:

Those congregated sages, who, ere now,
Had I my wish, were doom'd to guide the plow,

Are planning, still, to build a fed'ral name,
And blast my laurels with eternal shame.[8]

Anarch urges Wronghead on but has to confess that all his plans for sowing chaos
and injustice "can scarce survive the year" unless

The lamp of science [has been] quench'd in night,
Till none, or next to none, can read or write;
The press, anon, in brazen chains must groan,
First watch'd and guarded by our saints alone;
The numerous schools that live along the shore,
Must fall, successive, and must rise no more;
The wits be hang'd; the Congress forc'd to flee
To western wilds, or headlong to the sea.[9]

Wronghead was again the butt of Number VII, which was cast as a eulogium
delivered by Tweedle, a fictional protégé of Copper (Joseph Hopkins), to celebrate Wronghead's ability to "see farthest into total darkness." Anarch rewards
Wronghead with "a pair of spectacles, which showed every object inverted, and
wrapped in a mist of darkness."[10] In a similar vein, Number VIII purported to be
a eulogy at the execution of "William Wimble" (William Williams), who advocated sacrificing federal creditors to the interests of the state's creditors. Number
XI, which appeared on August 16 after a twelve-week interval, parodied Dante's
Divine Comedy, its hell being populated by all the leaders of Connecticut's anti-
federal opposition. By the time the last number of *The Anarchiad* appeared in
mid-September, those who favored strengthening the federal government in Connecticut were sufficiently in the ascendant so that the Wits could turn to a new
subject, America's cultural adequacy.

Sometime during the late autumn of 1786 Barlow learned that the King of France
had consented to having *The Vision of Columbus* dedicated to him. With the final
obstacle to publication removed, Hudson and Goodwin started advertising for
additional subscribers on January 1, 1787: "It will be bound, gilt, and lettered by
an Artist equal to any in America, and perhaps not inferior to any workman in
London," while the price would not "be higher than imported Books of this size
have commonly borne in America." The poem was printed in March, and Barlow
started distributing it in April. But most of the 750 subscribers received their copies in May as the constitutional convention, representing every state in the Confederation but Rhode Island, assembled in Philadelphia. At the end of October,

Hudson and Goodwin advertised a second printing. When it appeared, it listed an additional 177 subscribers, together with 37 who had subscribed to the first edition too late to have their names appear in it.

Anyone confronting the poem's 2,570 rhymed couplets knew that fortitude would be required to get through the work, especially as the early portions offered little encouragement to the faint-hearted. But Barlow's introductory essay on the life of Columbus was engagingly written. While he admitted that the poem contained a minor anachronism in having Isabelle die before Columbus returned from his fourth voyage, Barlow failed to acknowledge how the controlling conceit of the poem, which has Columbus liberated from a prison in which he has been unjustly placed by an ungrateful Ferdinand, distorted the record. The anguish of Columbus's last years derived from his failure to secure the extravagant credit he thought his due. Barlow sacrificed accuracy to create a contrast between an undeserved neglect and the glorious results of Columbus's discoveries.

Barlow almost forfeited the benefit of this contrast by devoting so much of Books I and II to a description of the American continent and its inhabitants prior to the "discovery." Since Barlow had little firsthand knowledge of most of the geography and limited access to accounts of the first encounters between the Europeans and Amerindians, his descriptions are impressionistic at best and resemble a geography lesson more than a drama. Barlow does not get around to engaging the interest of ordinary readers until almost the end of Book II, when he has Columbus ask his angelic escort about the origins of the physical and cultural differences in the human family. Are the obvious divergences between Europeans and American Indians to be attributed to separate creations or some other cause?

The angel replies that there are many reasons for the differences, including climate, physical environment, and local, historically specific circumstances, but that the human family still derives from one source. To the question of how the Americas became populated, the angel answers that it happened by seaborne migrations from Europe and Asia. This explanation diminishes Columbus's role as "discoverer," but the explorer doesn't seem to mind because the angel beguiles him with the achievements of two native cultures, the Aztecs and the Incas. The Aztecs, as personified by Montezuma, are portrayed as the tragic victims of Spanish aggression. Though Columbus is saddened upon learning of the sufferings of the Mexican people, the angel bids Columbus not to despond:

> Enough for man, with persevering mind,
> To act his part and strive to bless mankind;
>
> . . . .

> Nor think no blessings shall thy toils attend,
> Or these fell tyrants can defeat their end.
> Such impious deeds, in Heaven's all-ruling plan,
> Lead in disguise the noblest bliss of man.   (II, 355–56, 363–66)

The angel then invites Columbus to contemplate the Inca Empire as exemplifying a society built on human creativity comparable to Columbus's.

Book III tells the story of the legendary founders of that empire, Capac and Oella. Epics customarily contain a long digression, and Barlow prefaces this Book with a fifteen-page prose "Dissertation On the Genius and Institutions of Manco Capac." The dissertation claims that "the [constitutional] system of Capac" is "the most surprising exertion of human genius to be found in the history of mankind."[11] Barlow supports his contention by comparing the establishment of the Inca Empire with the achievements of Moses, Lycurgus, Mahomet, and Peter the Great, all of whom had introduced hitherto barbarous peoples to civilization. Barlow measures the achievements of each against three criteria: "*First*, that his system be such as is capable of reducing the greatest number of men under one jurisdiction. *Secondly*, that it apply to such principles of human nature for its support, as are universal and permanent." And "[*t*]*hirdly*, that it admit of improvements correspondent to any advancement in knowledge or variation of circumstances, that may happen to its subjects."[12] Capac won the competition because of his success in "drawing together" a barbarous, savage people and developing a "plan of policy, capable of founding and regulating an extensive empire; wisely calculated for perpetual duration; and expressly designed to improve the knowledge, peace and happiness of a considerable portion of mankind."[13]

Capac's "humane ideas of religion" also impressed Barlow. He marvels that "a savage native of the southern wilds of America . . . void of every trace of learning and refinement, . . . [had] acquir[ed] by the mere efforts of reason, a sublime and rational idea of the Parent of the universe!" He credits Capac with instituting an injunction against human sacrifice and a prohibition against beginning "an offensive war with their savage neighbours." Barlow thought the Inca had made war with the sole objective of civilizing rather than extirpating their adversaries. "The conquered tribes and those taken captive were adopted into the nation; and, by blending with the conquerors, forgot their former rage and ferocity."[14] Barlow covers himself against being charged with Deism by noting that Capac's "just ideas" about religion had come only as close as "the unenlightened efforts of human wisdom" could in perceiving "the nature and attributes of the Deity."[15]

Inserting a fifteen-page dissertation at the beginning of Book III provided readers with a contrast between Barlow's prose and his poetry. Modern readers will be tempted to ignore the problem and dismiss the dissertation because of the dubious quality of Barlow's history. His image of the Inca empire is rosier than any modern scholar would paint and is derived largely from Paul Rycaut's translation of Garcilaso de la Vega's *Royal Commentaries of the Inca* (London, 1688), which Barlow had seen in Yale's library.[16] The accuracy of the information, however, is less important than what Barlow's dissertation purports to accomplish. As an essay in comparative civilizations, it develops a well-argued thesis in fifteen pages that the succeeding thirty-one pages of verse fail to match.

Not that Book III lacks drama. It tells of Capac's son, Rocha, being taken captive by fierce savages on the fringe of the Inca Empire, to whom Rocha was bringing peace and civilization. They want to sacrifice Rocha to placate their gods. The savages almost succeed because the Sun withdraws its power from Capac and his followers until they seek guidance in the Sun's temple. Barlow's fantastic account resembles Homer's epics where heroes like Achilles and Odysseus are temporal pawns of the gods on Mount Olympus. Relying on the conventions of the Greek epics addressed another problem upon which Barlow felt the reputation of his poem depended. He wanted to be taken seriously in Europe and hoped to encourage the idea that an American epic could be as good as a European one. In the same vein he sought to present Capac as the superior of his Old World counterparts. In his victory speech Capac addresses the dying leader of the savages, Zamor, "with soft pity":

> Too long, dread prince, thy raging arms withstood
> The hosts of heaven, and braved the avenging God;
> His sovereign will commands all strife to cease,
> His realm is concord, and his pleasure peace;
> This copious carnage, spreading all the plain,
> Insults his bounties, but confirms his reign.   (III, 823–28)

Barlow hoped a European audience would find moral qualities in this speech that would compel their respect if not emulation.

Books IV, V, and VI of *The Vision of Columbus* abandon historical fantasy for a panoramic view of Europe's development before the American Revolution. The trajectory traced by Columbus's angelic guide is not devoid of horrors, but they prove to be transitory obstructions on the road to enlightenment. Thus the greed that the discovery of gold in the New World spawned among the first Europeans eventually serves as a liberating agent. The new prosperity it generates leads to the Renaissance and Reformation, whose great deeds were "Call'd into life and first inspired by" Columbus (IV, 259).

Barlow's focus on Europe's subsequent relationship to the New World, particularly North America, leads him to celebrate the achievements of the early English colonizers. He argues that North America was blessed by the absence of precious metals because that enabled it to avoid the crimes against the native inhabitants that Latin America witnessed. In a convenient fit of historical amnesia, he has the angel declare:

> Nor think the native tribes, these wilds that trace,
> A foe shall find in this exalted race;
> In souls like theirs, no mean, no ungenerous aim
> Can shade their glories with the deeds of shame.   (IV, 407–10)

North America, peopled by Europeans fleeing "eastern tyrants," offered the natives "leagues of peace" (IV, 415, 417) and would

> Pay the just purchase for the uncultured shore,
> Diffuse their arts and share the friendly power:
> While the dark tribes in social aid combine,
> Exchange their treasures and their joys refine.   (IV, 419–22)

A glorious destiny awaited "the western shore" (IV, 445) that eventually would lead to the political redemption of mankind when the "arts and laws, in one great system bind, / By leagues of peace, the labours of mankind" (IV, 471–72).

Such a view of the colonization of North America today seems preposterous. Nor does it help the modern reader that the panorama the angel presents to Columbus fails to observe the chronology of the events mentioned. But Barlow was more interested in presenting the American people with a vision of what he hoped their destiny would be than with an accurate description of the past. And he does not entirely exclude the struggle that took place for North America between the Europeans and the Indians. Book V treats "the savage tribes of foes" (48) that the English confronted. But there was never a doubt about how this contest would be resolved nor about whether, once the Indian threat had been subdued, the culture of the European settlers would prosper and expand.

The struggle between France and Britain commanded more of Barlow's attention because the Seven Years War allowed him to introduce the other great hero of his poem, George Washington.

Thy greatest son, in that young martial frame,
From yon lost field begins a life of fame.
Tis he, in future strife and darker days,
Desponding states to sovereign rule shall raise,
When weak empire, in his arm, shall find
The sword, the shield, the bulwark of mankind.   (V, 249–54)

Barlow makes no attempt to explain the issues that lay behind the Revolution. However, he leaves the reader in no doubt that more was at stake than the defense of the colonists' property and their families from the ravages of the enemy. He assumes that his audience is so familiar with what had driven the revolutionary crisis that there is no need to describe it.

The same approach governs his handling of the events of the Revolutionary War. It is rendered as a spectacle in which most of the defeats are passed over, unless they serve—as in Richard Montgomery's case or in Lincoln's surrender of Charleston—to define a hero's fame. The most distinctive aspect of Barlow's account is Louis XVI's place in it. The "Great Louis" (V, 5) acts like a Greek god whose attention is caught by what is happening in North America:

Each virtuous deed, each new illustrious name,
Wakes in his soul the living light of fame.
He sees the liberal, universal cause,
That wondering worlds in still attention draws.   (VI, 9–12)

After deciding to intervene in the American war, Louis proclaims France's disinterest in American possessions. He acts instead in response to

. . . Virtue struggling with the vengeful Power,
That stains yon fields and desolates that shore,
With nature's foe bids former compacts cease:
We war reluctant, and our wish is peace;
To suffering nations be the succour given,
The cause of nations is the cause of Heaven.   (VI, 59–64)

To which the rest of Europe, with the exception of Britain, responds:

                        . . . in glad amaze,
Gaze on the scene and brighten as they gaze;
Wake to new life, assume a borrow'd name,
Enlarge the luster and partake the fame.   (VI, 129–34)

That no European state ever did or ever would act in such a fashion bothered Barlow not at all. His quest was for the sublime rather than the realistic, and he made Washington into the embodiment of that sublime. Barlow has Columbus witness Washington at Yorktown acting the same way that Capac had previously acted towards his vanquished enemy, Zacor.

The conclusion of the war provided Barlow with the chance to present a glorious view of the future that the American Revolution had made possible. America was to emerge as the granary of the world, and a newly prosperous land would provide the arts and sciences with a chance to flourish as never before. These were themes Barlow had developed in *The Prospect of Peace* and in his 1781 commencement poem. But in this iteration, Barlow could not resist enumerating the cultural contributions America had already made. After noting the new nation's one scientific luminary, Benjamin Franklin, however, Barlow was left looking at a largely empty cupboard. He had more material to work with in the arts, but the best American painters of his generation, Benjamin West and John Singleton Copley, had both pursued careers in Britain. Barlow showed some critical awareness of their significance, but the only painter with an American career he might have heard of at this point was Charles Willson Peale. He is not mentioned, though Gilbert Stuart—yet to return from studying in Britain—is. Poetry offered a richer field, but only John Trumbull, Timothy Dwight, and Humphreys are mentioned.

Barlow's catalogue of American luminaries is followed by a digression on the nation's religion in which the diversity of sects is represented as an unqualified asset. Nonetheless, he realized that if he did not acknowledge that their "sacred task" had something to do with human salvation, he risked giving the impression that he valued religion only for its social instrumentality. He solved the problem by treating Columbus to an audience with the deity in which "the Lord of Life" (VII, 193) explains his creation and his promise of redemption:

> . . . hear, ye sons of earth,
> Rise into life, behold the promised birth;
> From pain to joy, from guilt to glory rise,
> Be babes on earth, be seraphs in the skies.
> Lo, to the cries of grief mild mercy bends,
> Stern vengeance softens and the God descends,
> The atoning God, the pardoning grace to seal,
> The dead to quicken and the sick to heal.   (VII, 213–20)

While the view of salvation presented to Columbus may not be that of orthodox Congregationalism, it is recognizably Christian. By bestowing divine sanction on the drama of history, Barlow prepares the way for the even more glorious future outlined in Book IX of the epic.

Before pursuing that lead, Barlow, tackles another problem implicit in his fusion of the sacred and profane. Columbus asks his "Kind messenger of Heaven . . . Why this progressive labouring search of man?" (VIII, 11–12)

> Why did not Heaven, with one unclouded ray,
> All human arts and reason's powers display?
> That mad opinions, sects and party strife
> Might find no place t'imbitter human life.   (VIII, 17–20)

The angel replies that "the counsels of th' unchanging Mind, / Thro' nature's range, progressive paths design'd" (VIII, 25–26). Did not progress govern the creation as well as the early prophetic hints about the "filial Godhead" (VIII, 48) assuming human form? It also governed the development of the "fair Science, of celestial birth" (theology, VIII, 53) in its attempt "By gradual steps to mark the extended road, / That leads mankind to reason and to God" (VIII, 55–56). Similarly, progress has described the evolution of human society from savagery to civilization, from civilization to empire—including feudalism, and from feudalism to the Renaissance. "Blest Science," until then confined by conquest and enslavement, now "Taught milder arts the peaceful prize to yield" (VIII, 207). As a consequence, "A happier morn now brightens in the skies, / Superior arts, in peaceful glory, rise" (VIII, 215–16).

The angel promises Columbus that this new state of affairs will lead to the progressive expansion of the human mind and a new order where "Contending kings their views harmonious blend, / With temper'd force their arts and arms extend" (VIII, 235–36). Columbus is not entirely convinced, given what he knows about human nature, and asks the angel for reassurance: "Say, what connecting chain, in endless line, / Links earth to heaven, and mortal with divine?" (VIII, 293–94). While the angel acknowledges that reason by itself can be perverted in the service of passion, it argues that God has endowed man with resources to find his way out of the potential morass:

> Of human powers, the Senses always chief,
> Produce instruction or inforce belief;
> Reason, as next in sway, the balance bears,

Receives their tidings, and with skill compares,
Restrains wild fancy, calms the impassion'd soul,
Illumes the judgment and refines the whole.   (VIII, 403–08)

Since "all nations" (VIII, 426) and all languages refer to God, "What cause mysterious could the thought impart, / Not taught by nature nor acquired by art?" (VIII, 429–30). Though heaven and earth may have to wait, eventually they will be reconciled. This was the answer Augustine had given to a similar question twelve centuries before, and with it Barlow planted himself firmly in the mainstream of the Christian tradition.

Having charted his philosophical course, Barlow turns to a vision of a future that embraces the whole world. The engine driving "the same progressive plan, / That draws, for mutual succor, man to man" (IX, 45–46) is the same one behind his commencement poem of 1781: commerce. Cooperation and brotherhood will take the place formerly occupied by competition and strife among nations and in the process improve human nature. Similarly, diversity will lead to universal harmony, and "the tongues of nations, here, harmonious blend, / Till one pure language thro' the earth extend" (IX, 253–54). Barlow even sees a divine plan working through "the unconscious steps of human kind" (IX, 276) to construct one earthly government "To hear and give the counsels of mankind" (IX, 428).

Line 68 of Book IX refers the reader to a three-page footnote, which argues that events since the conclusion of the Revolutionary War have confirmed his optimistic predictions. Barlow asserts that the "state of peace and happiness as is foretold in scripture and commonly called the millennial period, may be rationally expected to be introduced without a miracle." He acknowledges that the course of improvement in history to date has "been slow and often interrupted." But he is encouraged because "the causes of these interruptions" appear to be "designed" by "Providence" to be "accelerating the same events, which they seemed for awhile to retard." Barlow argues that mankind had been closer to achieving "universal civilization" at the time of Charlemagne than at the time of Augustus because by then Europe was divided into enough states to prevent tyrants like Caesar or Alexander from emerging.[17]

Barlow thought three preconditions were necessary for "civilizing the world." First, all its parts had to be inhabited. Second, the different nations had to be aware of each other. Third, they had to trade with each other. "The spirit of commerce is happily calculated by the Author of wisdom to open an amicable intercourse between all countries, to soften the horrors of war, to enlarge the field of science and speculation, and to assimilate the manners, feelings and languages of all nations." Thus the key to the general improvement of mankind lay in "Geography, Navigation and Commerce," but the most important of these was commerce. It would "produce a thousand advantages in . . . government and legislation, give Patriotism the air of Philanthropy, induce all men to regard each other as brethren and friends, eradicate all kinds of literary, religious, and political superstition, prepare the minds of all mankind for the rational reception of moral and religious truth, and finally evince that such a system of Providence, as appears in the unfolding of these events, is the best possible system to produce the happiness of creatures."[18] A footnote in prose says what was on his mind better than 460 lines of his verse.

The Vision of Columbus received only passing notice in the American press and then not until more than a year after its publication. It was first referenced in other literary works. One of the characters in William Hill Brown's *The Power of Sympathy* (1789), which is credited with being the first American novel, reported having read Barlow's poem. It also drew some hostile comments. Peter Markoe alluded to *The Vision of Columbus* in his doggerel *The Times* (Philadelphia, 1788), describing Barlow as a poet "Who drowsily pursues his drowsy theme, / And to the gallant chief ascribes his dream, / Thick mists of dullness on his readers fall, / Who sleep so soundly—they ne'er dream at all."[19] But none of the limited commentary took notice of Barlow's potentially contentious footnote in Book IX.

The most extensive and judicious assessment of *The Vision of Columbus* appeared in an essay published by the *Mercury* comparing Barlow's epic with Dwight's. While the author of this piece thought "both excellent," he was harder on Barlow than Dwight. Nonetheless, he acknowledged "that the deficiencies in Mr. *Barlow's* poem, if deficiencies there are any, are [not] to be imputed to any want of genius, or poetical powers, but rather to the nature of his subject." He also felt Barlow had "discovered such a fund of taste; invention and poetical enthusiasm" in *The Vision of Columbus* "as gives us reason to expect . . . if he continues to cultivate and improve his poetical talents, [he will] be able to produce something equal, if not superior, to anything written in the *English language*." Finally, after favorably noting Trumbull's *M'Fingal*, this critic concluded that "I think there ought not and cannot be any rivalship between three *American poets*; because they all have their *peculiar* excellencies, such as do not eclipse the excellencies of each other."[20]

The Vision of Columbus drew more attention from critics in Britain. Barlow had sent Richard Price a copy of his poem in 1786 with a letter requesting his advice about publishing it in England. The passages lauding Louis XVI and condemning Britain led Price to counsel against the attempt. But Barlow revised the poem shortly after it was published in America, and an English edition appeared in October 1787, inspiring an unnamed writer in the *Critical Review* to complement Barlow on his choice of subject and design. He congratulated Barlow on abstaining "from all illiberal abuse of the British army" and favorably noted the "many philosophical disquisitions" contained in the poem on such a variety of subjects as "the dissimilarities among nations . . . the peopling of America . . . the progress of the arts and sciences." Still, his praise was guarded. "So daring a muse as his must sometimes be expected to veil her head in the clouds." He went on to say "that subjects so extensive and arduous should not always be accurately investigated, that several faulty passages might be selected from a poem of such magnitude . . . ought not to detract from its general merit. Mr. Barlow thinks with freedom and expresses himself with spirit."[21] The two other London reviews were shorter and less effusive, but assuming Barlow's objective was to be taken seriously in Europe, there can be no doubt that he had succeeded.

On the strength of his *Vision of Columbus* and his role in coauthoring *The Anarchiad*, Barlow was invited to give the July Fourth oration to the Connecticut chapter of the Cincinnati at Hartford. He used the occasion to promote the Federalist program of strengthening the central government. Like many during the summer of 1787, he hoped that major changes would issue from the constitutional convention meeting in Philadelphia and the *Oration* articulated the same visionary republicanism that infused *The Vision of Columbus*.[22] The American Revolution was the product of "reason" and "clear understanding," albeit assisted by the favorable circumstance that Americans were "habituated to liberty," living as they did in a thinly settled "extensive territory" and possessed of "a mild and benevolent religion" (4–5). These ingredients had contributed to the emergence of a society able to react to the threat of British tyranny and oppression before feeling its full force. "It was not the quantity of the tax, it was not the mode of appropriation, but it was the *right of the demand*, which was called in question." Even then the continent had spent a decade debating the matter "before they assumed the sword." The "peculiar glory" of the American Revolution lay in "sober reason and reflection" rather than blind enthusiasm. "What other age or nation has *reasoned* before they *felt*, and from the dictates of duty and conscience, encountered dangers, distress and poverty, for the sake of securing to posterity a government of independence and peace?" Thus had Americans set a liberating example for millions in "unborn nations" (5–6).

However, the Revolution was only "half completed. *Independence* and *Government* were the two objects contended for, and but one is yet obtained. . . . Could the same generous principles, the same wisdom and unanimity be exerted in effecting the establishment of a permanent foederal system, what an additional lustre would it pour upon the present age!" Barlow warned that "without an efficient government our Independence will cease to be a blessing," negating the sacrifices that all had made, but especially those of the Revolution's fallen heroes (8). The current "crisis" was "the most alarming that America ever saw." Though Americans had "contended with the most powerful nation and subdued the bravest and best appointed armies," they had now "to contend with [*themselves*], and encounter passions and prejudices more powerful than armies and more dangerous to our peace" (11). Barlow saw the Philadelphia convention as holding the key to the future. "If there were ever a time, in any age or nation, when the fate of millions depended upon the voice of one, it is in the present period of these states. Every free citizen of the American Empire ought now to conduct himself as the legislator of half mankind." How Americans responded to the crisis would "entail happiness or misery upon a larger portion of human beings, than could be affected by the conduct of all the nations of Europe united" (12, 13).

Barlow did not assume all voices should be equal in producing the happy result he sought. Instead, he celebrated the patriotic examples set by prominent Cincinnati members who had recently died, especially Nathaniel Greene, and called on his fellow countrymen to give those lives additional meaning by supporting the work of the federal convention. At this point Barlow would go no further in the direction of democracy than to assert that "the majority of a great people, on a subject which they understand, will never act wrong" (12). Americans when properly informed would understand that "the present is an age of philosophy; and America, the empire of reason," and that "our duty calls us to act worthy of the age and the country which gave us birth" (19). "Under the idea of a permanent and happy government," which he expected the federal convention to propose, Barlow predicted the advent of a boundless prosperity coupled with a "rapid improvement in all the arts that embellish human nature." He was confident that "the example of political wisdom and felicity here to be displayed will excite emulation through the kingdoms of the earth, and meliorate the condition of the human race." Though Barlow did not quite promise the redemption of mankind, he saw a chance for America to become the agent that would promote "peace . . . through the extended world" (19, 20). His Fourth of July oration presented as sublime a vision as any he had described in the 5,140 lines of *The Vision of Columbus* and was considerably more accessible.

CHAPTER SIX

Land Fever

The literary recognition Barlow received during 1787 still left him unable to make a living by his poetry. Nor was he tempted to embark on another heroic epic as a friendly critic had suggested. Instead, the appearance of *The Vision of Columbus* raised with new urgency questions about the course he and Ruth should take. Though Barlow continued to do some legal work, it did not suit his temperament. He might have dabbled in the law longer, however, had not another enterprise attracted him that was more compatible with his visionary nature — the settlement and development of the western territory to which the United States had won title in the Peace of Paris.

In 1783 Britain, France, and Spain had recognized the new nation's claim to lands extending to the Mississippi River. Though they disagreed about where on the river the new nation's title terminated, no one disputed that the United States had ended the war with considerably more territory than its citizens currently occupied. This circumstance caught the attention of people on both sides of the Atlantic. In *Common Sense* (1776), Thomas Paine had suggested that western lands could be used to pay for the Revolution, and after 1783 the West seemed to be the nation's principal asset. Congress's failure to acquire revenue powers under the Articles of Confederation made exchanging that debt for land its most eligible option. Several southern states with undisputed claims to western lands were using them to honor the bounties they had offered soldiers during the war. If Congress could persuade the states with conflicting claims over lands north of the Ohio River to cede them, the national government would be able to follow the example of the southern states.

Middlemen entrepreneurs were eager to help governments wishing to dispose of their lands and pioneers wishing to settle them. Settlement required more than the acquisition of secure title, though that was the principal benefit purchasers expected from speculators. Settlers also needed supplies to tide them over until they became self-sufficient. Speculators were willing to provide these services because they expected to purchase large tracts of land more cheaply than an individual could buy a plot. They could do so because governments preferred receiving lump sums for their lands to retailing them to individuals. State and national governments alike sought to promote settlement because they knew eventually it would produce additional revenue. The federal government had an added stake in the rapid settlement of its western domain lest this vast expanse slip from the nation's grasp. The pressure to settle the area in turn made the government willing to shoulder the expense of negotiating the removal of Native Americans and protecting settlers.

Speculators were willing to offer governments large, lump sums because they expected the value of virgin lands to appreciate as they were settled. This appreciation would help to offset losses that might otherwise have been incurred after the first settlers claimed the best land in an unsettled region.[1] Limitless profits seemed to be in store for anyone who could draw emigrants from overpopulated Europe to America's undeveloped lands, but expectations of profit did not depend only on foreign immigration. Barlow understood the difficulties the rising price of Fairfield lands had created for his father in providing for his numerous sons. The western territories promised liberation to American patriarchs burdened by their fertility as well as to those seeking to escape the oppressive sway of European monarchies. Thus the disposal of these lands conformed to Barlow's expectations about the liberating potential of the American Revolution at home and abroad.

New lands were of particular interest to Connecticut because after 1750 the colony had started exporting its people. Connecticut's initial commitment to the Revolution owed much to its desire to solidify a claim to the Susquehanna lands in north central Pennsylvania. In 1769 Connecticut had begun issuing title to petitioners settling those lands. When in 1774 the Susquehannah Company claimed that five thousand people had moved to Pennsylvania's Wyoming Valley, Connecticut organized them into Westmoreland County, entitled to representation in the General Assembly. Westmoreland County fared badly during the Revolutionary War after British-sponsored Indian raids seriously weakened Connecticut's foothold in northern Pennsylvania. By the end of the war only two thousand settlers remained, many of them widows and children. Congress's December 1782 decision in favor of Pennsylvania's claim to the land further dimmed their prospects.

Almost immediately, Pennsylvania began despoiling Connecticut settlers of their titles to the soil and their improvements. During 1783 and 1784 the clash between Connecticut settlers and Pennsylvanians led to occasional skirmishing between them. Barlow identified with the Connecticut settlers, and in early 1785 the *Mercury* serialized a long essay entitled, "The CLAIMS of *Connecticut* to Lands west of the *Delaware,* deduced from authentic records and fairly stated," that highlighted Pennsylvania's mistreatment of the settlers.[2] After losing the dispute over the Susquehanna lands, the best hope for Connecticut's veterans lay in the creation of a national domain north of the Ohio River. The author of the essay on Connecticut's western claims argued that such a domain could not only sink the revolutionary debt but also provide a "perpetual patrimonial estate to defray the necessary expenses of the united states. Additionally it would form a strong and permanent band of union, because it would be equally the property of every citizen of the united States."[3]

Most of the states with western claims agreed, and beginning in 1782 New York ceded all of its claims to lands west of its border with Pennsylvania. Virginia, which claimed all of the Old Northwest, followed suit in 1784, with most of its claims north of the Ohio. But Virginia acted on condition the other states with overlapping claims make similar cessions. Massachusetts, whose original charter resembled Connecticut's in extending to the "South Sea," complied in 1785, relinquishing its right to portions of modern Michigan and Wisconsin. In May 1785, Congress provided for the survey of this emerging national domain into townships six miles square, setting a minimum purchase price of $1 per acre and a minimum land purchase of 640 acres. Connecticut's legislature exempted a 120-mile stretch of land in Ohio, usually referred to as the Western Reserve, from its 1784 cession of the state's western claims as compensation for its recent losses in northern Pennsylvania.

Because accepting Connecticut's cession threatened to nullify Virginia's conditional cession, Congress initially refused Connecticut's offer. That refusal fueled sentiment among the settlers and their backers in the Susquehannah Company to continue resisting Pennsylvania. Despite the efforts of moderates in both states to quiet the controversy, an unwelcome impasse persisted in northern Pennsylvania. Congress found it alarming because as the postwar recession deepened, the West came to look like its only asset in providing for the Revolutionary War debt. At the same time, the British refusal to surrender the posts in the Northwest portions of the territory it had ceded under the Peace of Paris reminded Congress that title without occupation was meaningless. Low-intensity civil wars on the frontier —like that in Pennsylvania's Wyoming Valley—discouraged westward migration and distracted attention from more pressing priorities.

Settlement of the Susquehanna dispute thus became linked with a compromise worked out in Congress during 1786 whereby the Connecticut cession was eventually accepted, even though it involved recognizing the state's claim to the Western Reserve. In exchange, Connecticut's delegates backed away from insisting that Congress rather than Pennsylvania determine the rights of Connecticut settlers to the Susquehanna lands and accepted Pennsylvania's pledge to treat Connecticut settlers justly. Extremists in the company sought to sabotage this understanding by sending more settlers to contest Pennsylvania's jurisdiction. They even toyed with forming a new state around the nucleus of the Connecticut settlements on lands that extended into southern New York, where Massachusetts had a competing claim.

Barlow let himself become associated with the extremists during a Susquehannah Company meeting at Hartford on December 26 and 27, 1786, for which he served as "Clerk Pro Tem." The meeting ended by naming him one of twenty-one commissioners with authority to confirm titles granted by the company to proprietors and settlers, to order surveys, and to grant title to squatters settling on vacant lands. The company also empowered its commissioners to create new townships within the area of the company's original purchase from the Indians. Any five of their number could form a court to settle all disputes among those claiming company lands in direct violation of Pennsylvania's sovereignty. Barlow's minutes of the Hartford meeting drew the condemnation of a Pennsylvania legislative committee charged with investigating the Connecticut settlements. It accused the company of trying to revive "the pretended title to a large territory within this state" and to erect "it into a separate government independent of" Pennsylvania.[4]

When Barlow realized that the company's actions were working at cross purposes with the efforts of Connecticut's representatives in Congress to trade the state's claims to the Susquehanna lands for congressional recognition of the Western Reserve, he distanced himself from the company's activities. But he had not done so before May 17, 1787, when—in the capacity of secretary—he authorized John Franklin to represent the interests of the Susquehannah Company settlers before Congress. Franklin had petitioned that the Connecticut legislature become involved in the Company's dispute and was known to favor the formation of a new state between New York and Pennsylvania. Though the wording of Franklin's

commission—bearing Barlow's signature—specified that his mission was to persuade Congress to establish the Connecticut settlers' "private right of soil and
property to the lands," Franklin was given authority to do anything "you may
judge necessary" on behalf of the Susquehannah Company, provided it was legal.
That was giving Franklin a lot of discretion, which in the past he had not used to
quiet the controversy.[5]

Fortunately for Barlow, another, less controversial land venture materialized during 1787. The Ohio Company was formed by two Massachusetts generals, Rufus
Putnam and Benjamin Tupper. Early in 1786 they had invited former members
of the Massachusetts line with continental bounty rights to join in an association
to buy some of Congress's lands bordering the Ohio River. The Company had its
eye on a specific stretch of territory in what today is southeastern Ohio. It purposely eschewed northern Ohio because the organizers did not wish to become
parties to a conflict over the Western Reserve. Though Congress had accepted
Connecticut's cession, Virginia had yet to confirm its conditional cession of the
area. At the time, Massachusetts was involved in a controversy with New York
about each state's competing claims to western New York, which would be resolved by a compromise arrived at in Hartford on September 16, 1786. The compromise traded the recognition of New York's jurisdiction for the validation of
Massachusetts' title to the land, but it failed to induce the Ohio Company to shift
its focus to western New York for another reason.

The October 22, 1784, Treaty of Fort Stanwix entered into between Congress
and the Six Nations had specifically recognized the Indians' title to a major portion of those lands. The remainder were proximate to Fort Niagara, which the
British still occupied. The lingering British presence threatened to slow, if not totally obstruct, efforts to extinguish Indian title in the area. By contrast, the Indians
in the January 21, 1785, Treaty of Fort McIntosh explicitly renounced title to all
lands the Ohio Company wanted. The military leaders of the Ohio Company
also preferred federal lands in the West to lands in New York or Pennsylvania because they expected to get a better bargain from an impoverished Congress than
they were likely to get from a large, relatively prosperous state. Army officers
would attract veteran soldiers whose familiarity with the hardships of camp life
ideally qualified them to become settlers. The Ohio Company thought its ability
to settle the country quickly with men committed to the union and capable of
defending themselves would enhance its bargaining power with Congress.

Putnam and Tupper enlisted the Rev. Manasseh Cutler to join them in leading
the company. A native of Connecticut, Cutler had graduated from Yale a decade

before Barlow and had served as chaplain in the Massachusetts line between 1776 and 1778. In addition to presiding over a Massachusetts parish, Cutler was a polymath with wide-ranging interests in science and medicine and connections to match those interests. What he lacked in wealth he made up for in influence. One authority speculates that Cutler was responsible for the exclusion of slavery from federal territory north of the Ohio River, which Congress wrote into its Northwest Ordinance in 1787.[6]

However, Cutler's influence failed to solve the difficulties the Ohio Company encountered in raising capital. After a year in which only a quarter of the $1 million in depreciated certificates it sought had been subscribed, it decided to recruit subscribers from other states. Connecticut was the logical place to turn because of its proximity and the state's fiscal problems, which disposed its continental veterans to expect better treatment from a private company than from their own legislature. Samuel Holden Parsons, who saw in the unsettled West his best opportunity to reconstitute a shattered fortune, was ripe for cooption. As Connecticut's highest ranking continental officer at the end of the war, his example could be determinative.

The postwar depression enhanced the Ohio Company's appeal to Congress by making the exchange of public land for depreciated certificates look more feasible than raising money through taxation. Even after it seemed as though the Philadelphia convention would have a happy issue, supporters of the new government believed its chances of succeeding would be directly proportional to the amount of debt that could be extinguished in exchange for federal lands. The smaller the debt the new government faced, the more likely it would be to establish its credit and authority now that Shays's Rebellion in Massachusetts had made clear the consequences of resorting to heroic taxation. If the new government fell into a similar trap, its enlarged powers would prove meaningless.

The principal sticking point for Congress was the land the Ohio Company wanted to purchase. The company's tract was bounded by the Scioto River to the west and watered by the Muskingum River flowing through its eastern portion. The Ohio River that constituted its southern boundary also intersected with two major Kentucky rivers, the Great Kawanha and the Little Kawanha. Finally, a large military reserve that Virginia had exempted from its cession of 1784 lay directly to the northwest along the Scioto River. The company knew what to ask for because Benjamin Tupper had recently surveyed the region.

In January 1787, Congress rebuffed Manasseh Cutler, whom the company had deputed to negotiate the purchase of the lands.[7] Congress was more receptive when Parsons approached it on May 9. However, some still questioned whether the Ohio Company's offer was in the best interests of the United States since it required Congress to grant more acreage than the company initially had money to pay for.[8] Congress was also busy with providing for the government of this territory and was hobbled by the departure of some of its members for the constitutional convention at Philadelphia. Lack of a congressional quorum led Parsons to return to Connecticut empty-handed at the beginning of June.

Cutler replaced him on July 9, but it still looked as though no bargain could be struck because of Congress' continued dissatisfaction with the company's offer. Cutler in all likelihood would have again been rebuffed had not William Duer intervened. As secretary to the board of treasury, Duer was in a strategic position to tailor the proposal in a way that would overcome the reluctance of at least some congressmen. He advised Cutler to enlarge the company's proposed purchase from 1.5 million acres to 5 million acres and suggested that a second company, known as the Scioto Company, take responsibility for the additional acreage. The Scioto Company would not start paying for its additional lands until the Ohio Company completed its purchase. Duer expected Congress to warm to a proposal that retired a larger portion of the debt. At the same time, Duer hoped to benefit from acquiring a major stake in the speculation. Since the additional grant from Congress increased the burdens its backers were assuming, Duer promised to provide the New England investors with reinforcements from New York.

On July 29, 1787, Manasseh Cutler and Winthrop Sargent entered into two separate contracts with the treasury board, both largely fashioned by Duer. Under the first contract, the Ohio Company purchased outright 1.5 million acres for $1 million. Half was to be paid up front, and the remaining $500,000 was due upon the completion of a land survey. Half a million acres were set aside to pay for the survey or were assumed to be waste. A second contract granted Cutler, Sargent, and their associates the 3.5 million additional acres on the same terms as in the first contract. But title for this tract would only pass after the associates, subsequently known as the Scioto associates, completed the $3 million payment in six equal installments over a three-year period.[9]

Congress does not seem to have been aware that the two contracts involved distinct entities. The Scioto associates—including Cutler, Sargent, and Duer—counted on the Ohio Company rapidly settling and developing its lands to make the Scioto lands more saleable. At the same time, the second company would benefit the first because, according to an internal agreement between the two, the Scioto lands would wrap around the north and west of the Ohio Company settlements. All the Scioto associates had to do was find the capital Congress required to complete the purchase within the time frame specified in its contract.

⚜

Though Cutler and Duer struck their bargains with Congress in late July 1787, Cutler did not present the first contract to the Ohio Company until it met on August 29. The news spread quickly to Connecticut. In September, Barlow wrote Noah Webster: "We have contracted for a quantity of lands near the mouth of the Muskingum equal to what a million of dollars will pay for at 2/3 of a dollar pr acre in contil securities." One share in the venture required only an investment of $1,000 in paper certificates and $10 in specie.[10] Barlow reported to Abraham Baldwin that he had collected $12,000 in certificates, which he intended to subscribe for twelve shares. The Ohio Company succeeded in making its initial payment of $500,000 on October 27, to which Duer contributed $143,000 in depreciated certificates.[11] By that time Barlow had acquired rights to eighteen additional shares despite a company bylaw that no individual should hold more than five of its shares.

The limitation could easily be bypassed by distributing the excess shares among kin. An account book reflecting Barlow's activities after he had become an agent of the company shows Aaron holding five shares and Jabez holding one, while Joel held four.[12] By the company's articles of agreement each "division" of twenty shareholders was supposed to have an agent. But thirteen of the sixteen agents at the Ohio Company's November 10 meeting each assumed responsibility for collecting subscriptions from more than twenty people. Only Sargent's and Cutler's 146 and 167 shares respectively exceeded Barlow's 140 shares.[13]

The Ohio Company quickly came to regard Barlow as their chief point man for recruiting Connecticut subscribers. From the company's perspective, Barlow's war record as a continental officer in the Massachusetts line, together with his experience gathering subscriptions for his epic poem, perfectly qualified him for the task. Many of his former friends from the officer corps of the army were prominent in the Ohio Company, but Barlow's contacts reached well beyond Massachusetts veterans. Of the subscribers to the first edition of The Vision of Columbus, 394, or slightly more than half the total, were Connecticut residents. The advantage of having a widely known agent could not have escaped the attention of the Ohio Company's leaders. Barlow, for his part, didn't need prodding to exert himself on the Ohio Company's behalf because its affairs seemed much less messy than those of the Susquehannah Company.

Barlow's willingness to take a prominent role in the Ohio Company soon led to his involvement with the Scioto Company. The sponsors of the latter company had divided its domain into thirty shares, each representing roughly one hundred thousand acres. Duer was given thirteen shares to dispose of, while Cutler and

Sargent retained control over another thirteen shares. The remaining four shares were reserved for disposal in Europe under Duer's direction, either by sale of the preemption right or mortgage. To broaden the base of the Scioto Company, Cutler and Sargent distributed fractional shares to Samuel Holden Parsons, Benjamin Tupper, Rufus Putnam, and Return Jonathan Meigs. Duer employed the same technique but with an eye to expanding the company's access to capital. He gave the largest portion of shares to Andrew Craigie, a Massachusetts native who had settled in New York after serving as apothecary-general of the continental army. Since the end of the war, Craigie had participated in a transatlantic consortium of investors interested in the depreciated American debt.[14]

The most significant figure in Craigie's network was Daniel Parker, who hailed from Craigie's hometown. Parker had emerged in the early 1780s as a supplier of New York flour to Wadsworth and Carter, the contractors responsible for provisioning Rochambeau's expeditionary force. In 1782 Parker joined William Duer in the contracts Robert Morris let for provisioning the continental army. With the peace, Parker invested as did Craigie and Morris in a series of ventures that included the first American entry into the China trade. Parker was not alone in overextending himself in the postwar period, but at the onset of the recession in 1784 he pursued the novel route of moving to Europe to avoid his American creditors. Though these included his former partners, they proved forgiving once he began including them in the syndicates he started organizing among Dutch and French investors to speculate in the U.S. debt. In 1786, Craigie visited Europe to sound out Parker about participating in speculative ventures like the Ohio and Scioto Companies and returned with the information that Parker was willing "to enter into an engagement with you as will be satisfactory to you"—an oblique reference to his past debts—by promoting a land scheme among European investors.[15]

Both land companies assumed that the depreciated federal securities issued during the final liquidation of accounts at the war's termination would constitute most of their capital. By 1786 these securities were selling at 20 percent of their face value, opening the prospect of the promoters acquiring a substantial quantity of land at a dramatic discount. To avoid competition the two companies agreed to focus on different constituencies in their search for capital. The Ohio Company would concentrate on domestic sources, while the Scioto associates turned to Europe. Because of Europe's superior capital resources, the speculators assumed a substantial portion of the American debt had found its way there.

Duer originally hoped to send Royal Flint to Europe as the Scioto associates' agent. But when Flint fell ill, the leaders of the enterprise turned to Barlow, who was Manasseh Cutler's first choice. As a former chaplain in the Massachusetts line, Cutler was aware of Barlow's reputation and Parsons's approval of him. Barlow's literary reputation might be less useful in promoting an ambitious land speculation in Europe than it was in America, but Cutler still felt Barlow would confer on the enterprise a respectability that would otherwise be lacking. James Watson, a 1776 Yale graduate and Barlow's Hartford friend, also vouched for him. Beyond these endorsements, Barlow had several undeniable assets: he was available; he was already deeply concerned in the Ohio Company lands; and—according to Cutler—he was prepared to leave almost immediately.

Speed was of the essence if the Scioto associates were to make their payments at bargain rates because the prospect of the Philadelphia convention was already raising the price of federal securities in America. Duer remained unenthusiastic about Barlow, sensing his visionary disposition and fearing his lack of business experience. Duer also realized one had to give a European agent a free hand to benefit from his agency. Finally, Barlow was not the sort of person the Duers normally associated with. Duer had inherited a British fortune and his wife—often referred to as "Lady Kitty"—was the daughter of Lord Sterling, a Revolutionary War general who claimed a disputed Scottish title. The Duers' home in New York City resembled a nobleman's establishment, and Barlow was never socially at ease with Duer.[16]

Duer eventually bowed to the pressure exerted by his other partners. He certainly could not question Barlow's intelligence and cultural competence, qualities that might be critical in attracting the right sort of backers in Europe. Barlow knew hardly any French, but there was a sizable English-speaking community in France, composed predominantly of merchants. During February 1788, Duer summoned Barlow to New York City to discuss the agency, but he delayed making a final commitment until he heard further from his European contacts about the prospects of the speculation. In the interim, Barlow traveled to Boston to confer with Flint, stopping in Providence to meet with Sargent. These conversations were designed to familiarize Barlow with the details of the speculation and to acculturate him to the ways of the partners. Barlow appears to have satisfied them, and eventually Duer acquiesced as well, after concluding that the only alternative was to abandon the speculation.

Barlow for his part saw the agency as a way to put his and Ruth's fortunes on a more secure footing. Half-brother Jabez's fate served as a warning. He had not prospered in Connecticut and was among the forty-eight men sent out by the Ohio Company to attend the surveyors, whose work had to be completed before settlement could proceed. Barlow had no intention of following in his brother's footsteps. Barlow's literary interests led him to prefer contact with an advanced culture to life on the primitive frontier. He also had trouble imagining Ruth, who continued to suffer ill health, as a pioneer woman. The West for him would remain an object of speculation, and the Scioto Company's European strategy looked as though it was more likely to hold the key to future riches than the Ohio Company.

In addition to his expenses, the associates offered Barlow a substantial stake in the venture. Cutler and Sargent had already conveyed to him roughly four thousand acres of Scioto lands in recognition of his active promotion of the Ohio Company in addition to one-sixtieth of their Ohio Company lands. Flint also had acquired a substantial interest in the Ohio and Scioto Company lands, which — together with fifty thousand acres of lands on the Wabash River and 7,500 acres of lands on the Mississippi associated with another speculation — he transferred to Barlow, probably as a form of life insurance for Ruth should Barlow die during his agency. Shortly before Barlow sailed for Europe, Duer added to Barlow's stake by conveying one-sixtieth of his Scioto lands to him.[17] With so much riding on Barlow's management, Duer wanted to be sure that Barlow realized he stood to profit handsomely from his efforts.

Having been a landless farm boy, Barlow was undoubtedly dazzled by the prospect of becoming proprietor of a vast inland empire. However, that did not make it any easier for him to leave Ruth for what they both realized would be at least a year. Circumstances did not allow time for indecision. Both companies were aware of the effect a new federal government was already having on the price of the securities with which they hoped to pay Congress for their Ohio lands. While it was still not clear that the new government would be ratified — and if ratified whether it could be successfully implemented — the process had progressed far enough to make it imperative that Barlow leave immediately, which somewhat eased his pain at parting with Ruth. Since they had not acquired a house of their own and had been unable to start a family, Ruth could spend the interval visiting family and friends. The probability that Ruth, now in her early thirties, and Joel would not have children was verging on certainty. And if Joel managed his mission successfully, he would return to the United States comfortable, if not rich. Barlow sought financial independence primarily as a means of pursuing his literary ambitions. His mission could also lead to literary contacts in Europe where poets like Alexander Pope and James Thomson not only enjoyed national renown but had achieved financial independence as writers. Barlow had more curiosity about Europe than most provincial Americans and was eager to drink at the fountain of an older, more developed culture.

An Atlantic crossing in the eighteenth century required considerable preparation. For the better part of a month, Barlow busied himself making the necessary arrangements. He would not go completely alone, as Nathaniel Greene's widow asked him to escort her son George Washington Greene to Paris, where Jefferson and Lafayette had promised to supervise his education. Barlow met with all the principals in the Scioto speculation, who agreed to advance monies to cover his expenses in Europe, though "with all Regard & Attention to the most rigid Economy."[18] On May 4, Duer gave Barlow his full power of attorney to act for the Scioto associates, though the document bore the date of May 16, 1788, when he was initially scheduled to depart. Contrary winds delayed him for nine days. Ruth did not tarry to see his vessel sail because she had found a convenient means of getting back to brother Dudley's place in Greenfield, Connecticut, more than a week before.

On a brilliant Sunday morning, Barlow boarded the British-built packet vessel of little more than 400 tons that the French had captured during the Revolutionary War. After passing through the Narrows, it set course for Le Havre. At this time Atlantic crossings undertaken from west to east in the late spring were more uncomfortable than they were dangerous. Because the vessel that carried Barlow was not a fast sailor, he could expect to be at sea for about six weeks. Due to the prevailing winds and currents, this particular crossing took just over four weeks. Barlow suffered miserably from seasickness despite encountering only one storm as they entered the English Channel. His problems began almost from the moment he boarded the vessel in New York. Most people adjust to a vessel's motion with time. That Barlow failed to do so suggests that he was suffering from an inner-ear disorder, a hypothesis supported by the relief he derived from closing his eyes and lying on his back and from his ability later in life to make such ocean crossings with far less distress.[19] His misery was heightened by the cramped, dirty quarters and foul food available.

While the disagreeableness of the ocean crossing engrossed Barlow's attention, events in America were further compromising his mission. Just before he landed in Le Havre, New Hampshire ratified the new Constitution, thus insuring that it would go into effect. New Hampshire's action brought in Virginia and New York later that summer because neither state wanted their voices to be ignored in shaping the new government. As these developments became known in Europe, American securities rose. Daniel Parker would respond to the news by authorizing Andrew Craigie to acquire any amount of the American debt at double the price he had been prepared to give earlier in the year.[20] That meant that the European capital Barlow sought was much more likely to be interested in speculating in the rising value of American securities than in the settlement and development of the American West.

In a letter to Duer, Barlow described his physical condition on arrival in France as one in which "my brain vibrates like a pendulum & my eye will scarcely follow my pen."[21] The first weeks of his stay in Europe were devoted to recovering his balance and strength. Had he fully understood the implications of developments back home and in Europe, his recovery might have been even slower. As Barlow was in the process of exchanging the New World for the Old, both were being transformed in ways that exceeded the powers even of his visionary imagination.

Barlow found fascinating the many differences between the Old and New Worlds that daily came to his notice. Much as he marveled at the sophistication of his new surroundings, however, the responsibility he bore to his American partners was never far from his mind. As soon as he was able, he set out for Paris with the young George Washington Greene in tow. Two Swedish merchants, who happened to be fluent in English and French, assisted them on their journey. Barlow delivered young Greene into Lafayette's care, taking the occasion to renew his acquaintance with the man who had proved so crucial in securing Louis XVI's patronage for Barlow's epic. The American also carried official dispatches as well as letters of introduction to Jefferson. The year before, Barlow had sent him a copy of *The Vision of Columbus*. Jefferson now invited Lafayette and Barlow to join him, along with a protégé of his own, William Short, in planning young Greene's education.

Of more immediate import, however, was Barlow's meeting with Daniel Parker, the American in Europe best situated to introduce Barlow to investors with the kind of money the Scioto associates needed. Significantly, Parker did not choose to have Barlow remain long in Paris. On July 12, just nine days after Barlow's arrival in the French capital, the two men set out for London. During the course of the previous year, it had become clear that the French state could no longer meet its financial obligations. The most obvious means to redress the budgetary imbalance would have been for the propertied classes to have shouldered their share of the public burdens. However, they, together with many of the clergy, proved more interested in defending their privileges. The crisis had ripened as first one and then another financial minister failed to extract the concessions that would have restored the solvency of the French state. With no one prepared to compromise, the Crown's only option narrowed to summoning the Estates-

General—which had last met in 1614. Louis XVI resorted to this expedient after interest payments on France's public debt were suspended on August 16, 1788.

Well before the summoning of the Estates-General, it was obvious where events were headed. Though Parker used the looming bankruptcy of France to justify going to London, he also realized that French capital might be turned more advantageously to other speculative ventures and wanted to avoid tapping the local capital market for speculation in American lands. Barlow lacked the knowledge to understand the situation. His first impressions of France were of an advanced society where poverty was less evident than he had expected. He had little inkling that the political options for avoiding a violent revolution were vanishing, though hints that revolutionary change was imminent did not alarm him. Like most Americans, Barlow distrusted centralized power and welcomed the summoning of the Estates-General. He remained optimistic about the tendency of events in France, declaring that "the Patriots have seen too much the example of liberty in America" to submit to anything short of a constitution on the American model.[22]

Despite the loss of its colonies in the American war, Britain's finances were healthier than France's. Other factors, however, made Britain's capital market unreceptive to American land speculations. Though Anglo-American trade was beginning to revive, the British government and much of the British public had yet to warm to American independence. After the Peace of 1783, Parliament had vested the Privy Council with the authority to regulate trade between the two nations. It excluded American vessels from Britain's colonial trade and only allowed them to carry U.S. products directly to Britain. America had friends in Britain's mercantile circles, but the capital of those trading with the new nation was already tied up in commercial ventures.

Although Barlow contracted a severe respiratory virus then raging in London, he nevertheless managed to make the rounds, meeting Americans with business interests like the brothers John and Nathaniel Cutting and the painter John Trumbull. Trumbull, one of the few Connecticut graduates of Harvard in Barlow's generation, was a man with whom he remained on civil though distant terms for the rest of his life.[23] He also widened his circle of acquaintances to include several English radicals like Horne Tooke and Thomas Paine. Audiences were even arranged for him with the Marquis of Lansdowne and Sir Joseph Banks, the president of the Royal Society, but none of these contacts were serious prospects as investors.[24] Barlow realized that dining out six days a week with a widening circle of acquaintances was "bad oeconomy" for a man of business, but he justified it on the grounds that he was collecting valuable information.[25]

When Barlow learned that every state but North Carolina and Rhode Island had ratified the new constitution, he welcomed the development as "surprising the world more . . . than in any of their former atchievements" [*sic*].[26] He was slow in realizing how the resulting rise in the value of the American debt, in conjunction with the French government's desperate need for funds, would affect the availability of capital in Europe. Speculators had begun to see opportunity for trading France's American debt at a steep discount for ready cash. When Britain turned out to be a dry well for the Scioto Company, Parker steered Barlow toward the Low Countries. This course allowed Parker to test how intense the competition to acquire France's American debt had become among the continent's capitalists.

Since 1782, Low Country bankers had shown much more interest than the rest of Europe in betting on America's future. Two Dutch banking houses, the Amsterdam firms of Wilhem and Jan Willink and of Jacob and Nicholas Van Staphorst, served as commissioners of the U.S. loans in the Netherlands and paid most of the nation's bills in Europe, including the annual interest on the outstanding Dutch loans. The Van Staphorst brothers were known to be interested in American lands, and Parker thought their response to the Scioto speculation would probably prove decisive.[27] At the end of the first week in September, Barlow and Parker left London for Brussels, via Dover and Calais, to meet with them.

The Van Staphorsts proved unwilling to commit themselves. Parker and Barlow lingered in Brussels because the Van Staphorsts had shown enough interest to suggest that they might change their minds. Before the two men headed back to Paris, Barlow tried a one-day excursion on his own to Antwerp, where he had trouble finding anyone who could speak English. This inability to communicate helped reconcile him to returning to Paris. Not the least of its many delights would be the repeated invitations from Jefferson and Lafayette to dine, chiefly in the company of Americans with whom the French patriot often surrounded himself. Parker and Barlow had been back in Paris for less than a week when they received a new summons from the Van Staphorsts to return to Brussels. They set out on October 5 only to find after their arrival that the Van Staphorsts were in Antwerp. An interview there ended as inconclusively as their first one had, leading Parker to turn to schemes for providing the bankrupt French state with cash in exchange for its American debt at a steep discount.

Proposals for transferring France's American debt to private hands had been circulating in Europe since 1786. In June 1788, Parker had provided Jacques-Pierre Brissot de Warville, who represented a syndicate of European investors, with a letter of introduction to Andrew Craigie in New York pursuant to such a scheme.[28] Barlow was unaware that Brissot's mission in America paralleled his in France. Nor did Parker yet know that Brissot had concluded an agreement by which Duer, Craigie, and Parker became equal partners with Brissot's European sponsors in an enterprise.[29] The promoters of the scheme wanted to borrow enough money to pay interest on the American debt's face value, which would have appreciated it to par. They then hoped to use the appreciated securities to purchase other assets at bargain prices. Barlow, as the hired agent of a competing enterprise and without resources of his own, had nothing to contribute to such undertakings. As the scramble for funds intensified among Duer's speculating friends, Barlow would find himself progressively more isolated.[30]

Documentation concerning Barlow's life between October 1788 and July 1789 has largely disappeared, but it isn't difficult to image how he spent his days. Learning French would have consumed a good deal of his time. Then there were multiple invitations to dine in the company of a growing circle of French and American friends. Everyone in Paris was debating the political pros and cons of various constitutional proposals for France. As an American, Barlow's opinion was in demand, though not nearly as much as Jefferson's before he returned to the United States in the autumn of 1789 to become secretary of state. We do know from Barlow's reaction to criticisms of the new U.S. Constitution that he felt most Frenchmen were ignorant of the true nature of liberty. But he was not yet in a position to contribute directly to the debate over what would be the best constitution for France. When not otherwise occupied, he could sample the many cultural delights of Paris, including the public baths, the opera, the theater, and the perpetual carnival at the Palais Royal.[31]

Barlow's routine in the French capital contrasted with that of Gouverneur Morris, who arrived in January 1789. As the member of the Philadelphia convention principally responsible for the final wording of the U.S. Constitution and the agent of Robert Morris, Gouverneur Morris had access to Parisian circles that Barlow was denied. Fluent in French, Morris also came equipped with a shrewdness that enabled him to make the most of his entrée to official circles. Despite being encumbered with a wooden leg—the result of a 1778 carriage accident—his tall, imposing figure caught the attention of the women who presided over society. He fell in love, as much as a man of his cynical temperament was capable of falling in love, with the beautiful young Countess de Flahaut. She was married to someone twice her age, and Morris ended up competing successfully with the Bishop of Autun, later known as Talleyrand, for her attention and sexual favors.

Just before the meeting of the Estates-General, Morris was invited to join the prestigious Club de Valois. In addition to Lafayette and Talleyrand, it included such luminaries as the Abbé Sieyès, the marquis de Condorcet, and the explorer and naval officer, Louis-Antoine Bougainville. Barlow realized he would never be included among Morris's circle of friends and connections. He had to settle for the café society of the Palais Royal, where Morris also cut a much larger figure than Barlow.[32] It took more than a year before Barlow became acquainted with some of the new men who would shape France's revolution. The most important of these would be Brissot, whose mission to America with Parker's endorsement undercut Barlow's mission in Europe.

Before Parker learned of Brissot's agreement with Duer and Craigie, he approached Morris about joining the group of investors he was assembling to purchase the American debt held by the French government. If Barlow had known of Parker's overtures to Morris, it would have enhanced Barlow's growing sense of powerlessness and irrelevance. In time, however, the comparative influence of Barlow and Morris would be reversed. Barlow and Brissot eventually became friends and political allies, incurring Morris's hostility.[33] Morris thought the French ought to retain the monarchy and aristocracy, while Barlow and Brissot wanted France to become a republic. But during the interval in which everyone was waiting for the Estates-General to meet, Barlow was little more than an isolated spectator.

Many men, confronting the situation Barlow faced at the beginning of 1789, would have retired to America. Paris was certainly expensive, and returning home would have cut his losses. At first Barlow had not felt threatened by the high cost of living because he expected his expenses to be covered by the Scioto associates. He later complained that he had been provided with less than half of what he had been promised, which forced him to borrow on the assumption that he would eventually be compensated. Only belatedly did Barlow recognize that the "persons in France and Holland to whom I was recommended [Parker and Van Staphorst] and ordered to apply . . . were amusing me with false hopes." It took him three-quarters of a year to grasp that "their interest as dealers in the American funds rendered them enemies to the sale of any lands which were to be paid for to the united states in those funds."[34] Still, Barlow rejected the idea of immediately returning to America, even though he complained to Winthrop Sargent about his personal poverty.[35]

His fear of undertaking another Atlantic crossing was probably the primary reason. He felt he had only narrowly survived the west-east transit undertaken in the late spring, which had the reputation of being shorter and easier than the return journey. What would be the effect of an east-west crossing, where one could expect to encounter head winds? The best time to make the latter crossing was in April or May as the winter westerlies abated. If he were going to return to the United States, he should have begun planning his trip in March 1789. But, as Barlow later admitted, that was the month in which he decided to stay in France.

His decision also reflected a reluctance to return without anything to show for a year's effort, yet his conviction that something positive could still be extracted from his mission owed more to his past than present prospects. Barlow had grown used to extracting advantage from unpromising circumstances. Michael Baldwin's expulsion of him from the family had led the older Baldwin children to adopt him first as a sibling and then as husband and brother-in-law. Where others had suffered economically from joining the army, Barlow had managed to improve his fortunes. He had then staked his future on writing an ambitious epic poem that he knew would be a hard sell in America. Nonetheless, his army connections and stubborn persistence enabled him to get the king of France to accept its dedication and to extract a modest profit from its publication. Barlow was used to the unexpected. Change seemed in the cards during the autumn of 1788 and winter of 1789, and Barlow assumed the advantages associated with unprecedented circumstances would outweigh the dangers.

During 1789 there was no better place from which to view the growing political excitement than Paris. Barlow witnessed at close quarters the first meeting of the Estates-General. When the three Estates became deadlocked in controversy, the Third Estate, joined by some of the nobility and clergy, proclaimed themselves the representatives of the nation. The deputies then took an oath not to disband until they had given France a constitution. The Estates-General thus transformed itself into the National Assembly. Within weeks it had adopted sweeping social reforms, including the abolition of feudal privileges and the church's tithe, as well as the Declaration of the Rights of Man and Citizen.

Not all of these events took place peacefully. The meeting of the Estates-General at the beginning of May was preceded by the Réveillon riots, which took twenty-five lives. Louis XVI's dismissal of his finance minister, Jacques Necker, on July 11 led to the storming of the Bastille on July 14. Barlow's later claim that no one had died as a result of the Revolution was willfully inaccurate because the Parisian mob displayed the heads of the more prominent men they had killed outside the Hôtel de Ville. Barlow had more reason to be disillusioned by the irresolute, spoiling role Louis XVI played in the unfolding drama, since Barlow's dedication of *The Vision of Columbus* had painted the King in entirely different hues.

Barlow's decision to remain in France meant that his separation from Ruth would last longer than both had expected. Some Americans visiting Europe took advantage of the availability of women and the anonymity that a large city afforded to cultivate new intimacies. Despite Gouverneur Morris's observation that Barlow was improperly flirting with Col. Samuel Blackden's wife at one of Jefferson's dinners, Barlow appears to have remained faithful. The absence of letters from Ruth made him extremely anxious. Knowing that her health had not always been the best, he often assumed the worst. His devotion is also evident from the dozens of letters he wrote Ruth during his first year and a half abroad. Though most of them have been lost, the twenty-nine that survive bear witness to his continuing need for her approval and affection. This need would lead him to urge her to do what he was reluctant to undertake himself. Toward the end of 1789 he suggested she cross the ocean to join him.[36]

Barlow assumed that the meeting of the Estates-General would result in France's peaceful evolution from a centralized monarchy checked only by public opinion to a monarchy limited by a constitution. He was confident that the major strides toward liberty he expected France to make would improve the human race. Barlow accepted uncritically France's claim to be the leading civilized nation of the world, and he continued to dismiss as lies—motivated either by British envy or aristocratic intransigence—any reports of violence. Two weeks after the storming of the Bastille, he wrote Ruth that "it is really no small gratification to me to have seen two complete revolutions in favor of liberty" at first hand. Barlow remained confident that France would settle its affairs upon a "rational & lasting foundation."[37]

Gouverneur Morris, by contrast, was struck by the savagery of the Paris mob. Some of its ferocity can be attributed to a bread shortage that persisted throughout much of 1789. Barlow's experience during the American Revolution made such privations seem routine, and, with regular access to the dinner tables of others, he ran little risk of experiencing hunger himself. Nor did he construe the continued signs of financial disarray as an indication that the Revolution was in trouble. Such an inference would have been equivalent to concluding that the collapse of the continental currency would derail the American Revolution.

Revolutions in their initial stages attract a wide range of adventurers, often men of considerable talent though not necessarily with characters to match. It was Barlow's fate to encounter one such individual during this period. William Playfair (1759–1823) was the son of a Scotch parson without social or political connections. Playfair had apprenticed as an industrial metal worker and worked afterward for the inventor James Watt, preparing drawings of some of his steam engines. In 1786 Playfair invented the line series graph for displaying statistical information, but this innovation, as well as his subsequent development of bar and pie charts, was greeted with indifference, and his early writings on economic subjects were similarly ignored. A sense that his ingenuity was being discounted—and his chronic need for money—led Playfair into questionable business practices. In 1787 he moved to Paris where he hoped to make his fortune transferring Britain's new industrial technology to France. He seemed on the verge of winning the king's patronage until the financial crisis of 1788 doomed his prospects.

Sometime in late 1788 or early 1789, Barlow and Playfair met through Col. Samuel Blackden, a Massachusetts native who had come to Paris to sell his Kentucky lands. Barlow and Playfair turned out to have a lot in common. In addition to resenting their exclusion from the best opportunities, they both wanted to profit from the Revolution that was unfolding before their eyes. Barlow was especially impressed by Playfair's knowledge of French and France. In 1789 Playfair published a tract about his statistical innovations under the title of *Tableaux d'arithmétique linéaire* and sent Jefferson a copy. Two pamphlets in French about paper money would follow in 1790. Playfair looked as though he knew what he was doing and was capable of influencing events.

During the summer of 1789, Barlow and Playfair joined forces to save the Scioto enterprise by finding new ways to raise the large capital due Congress.[38] Their partnership would gradually transform the Scioto Company from an enterprise trying to sell its preemptive right to large investors to one that sold lands directly to individuals. From Barlow's perspective, there may not have seemed to be that much difference between the two ventures so long as the capital needed to purchase the preemptive right from Congress could be assembled. It is not clear whether Barlow or Playfair first conceived of changing Barlow's Scioto agency into a colonizing venture. Barlow later said the scheme had begun taking shape in April 1789. As the French Revolution took a more violent, uncertain turn, both realized that a rupture of such magnitude would lead people of substance to seek refuge from the upheaval engulfing France. What better refuge was there than North America?

In July 1789, probably shortly after the storming of the Bastille, Barlow gave Playfair a one-thirtieth interest in the Scioto Company in exchange for "rendering such services as might be in his power."[39] Playfair successfully recruited a group of French investors to form a company to buy the preemption right from the Scioto associates. On August 3 this group signed an Acte de Formation before a notary of the Crown, constituting itself into the Compagnie du Scioto. The Acte de Formation stated that the company was issuing eight thousand shares of stock each priced at one thousand livres. In this manner, the company hoped to raise the 8 million livres, or roughly $1.5 million, either from their own resources or by selling shares to third parties. Since the sum was not large enough to pay for all of the preemption right to the Scioto associates' 3.5 million acres of Ohio lands, it seems probable that all the parties involved saw this as a trial balloon. If success-ful, the Compagnie du Scioto could issue another eight thousand shares. If un-successful, it would transform itself into a colonizing venture.[40] It also seems probable from Barlow's repeated and bitter complaints about Duer's failure to communicate that Barlow had written home proposing the new direction that was eventually taken, but such a letter has not survived.

Playfair had succeeded in recruiting French investors who looked as though they had the wherewithal to make the Compagnie du Scioto a success. Leading the list both officially and socially was Louis Marthe, the marquis of Guoy D'Arsy, who was High Bailiff of the Sword, a lieutenant general, and a member of the Constituent Assembly, which had recently evolved out of the Estates-General. The group also included the comptroller of the pay office of the domain of the king, Jean François Noël Maheas; Guillaume Louis Joseph, the chevalier de Coquelin; and the Parisian merchant, Antoine St. Didier. At the end of August, Barlow wrote Winthrop Sargent that he expected a contract with the Compagnie du Scioto to be consummated within ten days time and that the deal would en-able the Scioto associates in America to honor their Congressional contract.[41]

Playfair's recruits turned out to be disappointments. None were from the front rank of the nobility with whom Gouverneur Morris routinely associated, and before the end of the year the most prominent of the eight, Maheas, had been forced to flee France. A less prominent associate absconded with fifty shares of the new company and a power to sell the company's lands. These misfortunes only partially explain why the new company was no more able to raise the capital re-quired to pay for the preemption than Barlow had been. More important was France's deepening political crisis. In early October, a Parisian crowd marched to Versailles, led by an angry mob of women, and their success in bringing both the king and the National Assembly back to Paris, pointed strongly towards events taking a more radical course. Money went into hiding, making it increasingly difficult for the new company's members to borrow on their own accounts.[42]

Barlow undoubtedly hoped to keep the Compagnie du Scioto from abandon-ing its identity as an enterprise that recruited capital from French men of sub-stance, at least until his American associates agreed to a change of plan. But as land came to be regarded as the only safe investment, it wasn't long before the members insisted on selling Scioto lands and recruiting settlers. They did so even though neither the Compagnie du Scioto nor the Scioto associates would legally own the land until all of it had been paid for. They simply assumed that once a beachhead of settlers was established, a land rush to America would ensue. They gambled on assembling one-quarter of the funds needed to complete the Scioto associates' contract with Congress before the first settlers arrived and assumed that demonstrating the potential of the course they had adopted would be sufficient to persuade Congress to confer title. Having yoked himself to a group of Frenchmen and to Playfair, all of whom had other priorities, Barlow proved unable to resist his partners' insistence that direct sales and settlement was the only route to success.[43]

Barlow remained troubled, since neither the Compagnie du Scioto nor the Scioto associates had title to the lands involved. At the beginning of November, he attempted to relieve the Scioto associates of responsibility for selling what they did not own by transferring the full preemption right to the Compagnie du Scioto. For six livres per acre, Barlow—acting as agent for Cutler, Sargent, and Duer—promised to deed over to the Compagnie du Scioto the entire 3 million acres of land. The sale price of 18 million livres would be payable in eight installments in cash or in American securities at 90 percent of their face value. The first payment of 1.5 million livres was to be made in December 1789, followed by additional payments at the end of April and December for three years. Beginning in April 1792, the payments would rise to 3 million livres annually through 1794, when the purchase would be completed. In return Barlow bound himself to deliver title to the lands as the Scioto Company received payment for them. Playfair, Barlow, and the Parisian attorney, Jean Chais Soisson, were to act as agents for the Compagnie du Scioto in selling the land at the best price that could be obtained.[44] As the Scioto associates received payments, they would redeem the preemption from Congress and issue valid title to the lands that had been purchased. The principal problem that this contract failed to address was that the Compagnie's schedule of payments was not in synch with those the Scioto Company was obliged to make to the U.S. Treasury.

Barlow accepted the idea that once the Compagnie demonstrated its commercial viability, the Scioto associates in America would have little difficulty persuading Congress to adjust its contract. Such a painless way of reducing the Revolutionary War debt by $3 million—not to mention settling the western country —was unlikely to be rejected by a government that had yet to make any progress in either enterprise. If the government proved inflexible, Barlow assumed that his American associates could borrow the sums needed to get title because "the

sacrifice is small, & the object infinite." If all went well with his plan, the Scioto
associates stood to make a profit that Barlow estimated would come to over $1 mil-
lion.[45] Barlow thought he had not only saved the venture but made the fortunes
of the participants, his own included. His calculations were based on a confluence
of developments in the first part of November 1789, which led him to assume the
Scioto lands would all be sold in a matter of months. He expected the intensifying
revolutionary upheaval to initiate a mass migration of twenty thousand Frenchmen, many of substantial property.

As France was absorbing the implications of the autumn's events, the Compagnie du Scioto issued a pamphlet under the title *Prospectus pour l'establisement sur
les rivières d'Ohio et de Scioto en Amérique* that provided a glowing description of
the lands involved. It claimed that the Scioto River offered access to the Ohio
River and Lake Erie and that the Ohio Company had managed to settle one thousand persons on neighboring lands in the previous year, leading to a 50 to 400
percent rise in land values. The *Prospectus* argued that the Compagnie du Scioto
would keep in France the profits derived from settling the American wilderness.
Once the enterprise was launched, American funds would be available to complete the purchase agreement that stretched out until 1794. The rising payment
schedule was presented not as a weakness but as an indication of the increasing
profits the Compagnie would reap as settlement progressed. Since the market
price of the American debt was currently no higher than 70 percent of face value,
the Compagnie's offer to accept them at 90 percent of face value gave purchasers
paying in such instruments a 20 percent discount. Finally, the *Prospectus* announced that purchasers would only be required to pay half the price up front.
The other half was due within two years, payable in crops like tobacco and wheat,
in livestock, or by the sale of a portion of the lands the settlers had improved.[46]

Only the urgency of the Compagnie to come up with their first payment of
1.5 million livres by the end of December 1789 can explain the terms of purchase
outlined by the *Prospectus*. Barlow can be excused from direct responsibility for
most of its hyperboles for two reasons: his French still was not up to writing such
a document, and the terms outlined were totally incompatible with a timely honoring of the Scioto contract in which he had a major stake. Nonetheless, he probably had a hand in two of the more realistic passages in the *Prospectus*. The first
dealt with the difficulty American farmers experienced in establishing contact
with distant markets; the second, an addenda entitled "Avis," estimated the actual
cost of moving from France to America and settling there to be between 1,320 and
3,120 livres. The "Avis" assumed that most of the French emigrants would be men

of substance, while the *Prospectus* tried to reassure them that they would retain access to European markets.

Barlow went along with the claims made in the *Prospectus* because the Compagnie still seemed like the only way of saving the Scioto venture. At the same time, Gouverneur Morris began quietly discouraging any Frenchmen who enquired about the Compagnie. His opposition did little initially to diminish the enthusiasm for investing in American lands, and the rage to purchase the Scioto lands continued. During the last two months of 1789 and January 1790, more than seventy-five thousand acres were sold.[47] Barlow certainly was not prepared to take responsibility for puncturing the ballooning expectations of the French public. He was also aware of the effect his prolonged stay in Europe was having on expectations in America. On December 9, 1789, his Hartford friend John Trumbull had written Barlow's Yale classmate Oliver Wolcott, expressing bewilderment at what had kept Barlow in Europe for eighteen months. "If he should not effect something soon, I would advise him to write 'the Vision of Barlow' as a sequel to those of Columbus & McFingal."[48]

Both considerations pushed Barlow into predicting that events in France would permit the United States to extinguish its entire Revolutionary War debt in the course of a few short years. Barlow wrote several letters to Alexander Hamilton drawing attention to this possibility, but Hamilton probably did not receive them until after he had committed himself to the policies outlined in his January 1790 Report on Public Credit. The letters have not survived. We only know about them because Abraham Baldwin mentioned that Hamilton had received them when Baldwin wrote Barlow during the spring of 1790.[49] Though Hamilton refused to commit himself, Barlow's proposal still looked like a live option to Baldwin well into the summer of 1790 because of the difficulties the secretary of the treasury was encountering in getting Congress to agree to an assumption of the state debts.

CHAPTER SEVEN

Disgrace

Even as Barlow embraced a wildly optimistic vision for the outcome of the Scioto venture, he remained aware of the risks. He imagined that his "careless & insensible associates at home conceive me to be rioting in the luxuries of Europe." But he confided a very different reality to his wife: "I should be infinitely more happy to be locked in a prison in America, where I might hear the cheering voice of my Ruthy thro' the grate, saying good morning . . . my love."[1] That fantasy revealed the darker implications of transforming the Compagnie du Scioto into a colonizing venture. The Compagnie's success in collecting five hundred French settlers by December, while reassuring in one sense, alerted him to a new peril. They could depart as early as January 1790, possibly arriving in Alexandria, Virginia, by the end of February. Though it was too late to have reservations about selling lands directly to settlers, settling families on company lands forced Barlow to confront the scheme's weaknesses.

One difficulty arose from not knowing whether the land involved had been surveyed. The Scioto associates' preemption began at the eighteenth survey range, and if the line setting it off from the seventeenth range had yet to be established, it would be impossible for the settlers to locate their lands. A more troubling difficulty was that in selling Ohio lands to settlers who meant to take immediate possession of them, the future of the Scioto speculation was placed entirely in their hands. If they came to grief or were disappointed in significant ways, the whole scheme might collapse. If, on the other hand, they were well provided for, sales in France might continue at a brisk pace. Naturally, Barlow was anxious about the settlers' reception in America.

Barlow advised his American associates to have someone who knew French meet the first party of emigrants in Alexandria and escort them to Ohio. He also wanted twenty-five to fifty workmen hired to build huts for the accommodation of the newcomers and to show them how to clear and plant the land. Hunters ought to be engaged to procure meat until the settlers were able to buy livestock. Finally, Barlow thought the settlers should be provided with tools and provisions, as well as some money with which to purchase supplies outside the local market. Even if all these details were attended to, however, Barlow recognized that the venture would still be vulnerable to the settlers' "first impressions." He knew enough from the hardscrabble nature of his time at Dartmouth to realize that these would not always be positive. For French immigrants coming from a sophisticated, urban culture, he knew the "customs, manners, face of the Country, language, mode of cultivation, and almost every other circumstance will be new and strange to them." He also felt personally responsible to them, realizing that by "leaving their country" the emigrants were "absolutely sinking their lives and fortunes on the representation of a stranger."[2] However, that didn't stop him from jollying them along by offering the first wave of settlers a two-acre town lot, lest the whole enterprise collapse.[3]

Though he was uneasy, there were enough positive developments associated with the French emigration to keep Barlow from despairing. In January 1790, twenty-three prominent Frenchmen joined with Barlow in forming a "Company of Twenty-Four," known as the *Vingt-quatre*. Each member either had purchased or committed himself to purchasing a minimum of one thousand acres of the Compagnie's lands and settling four laborers in America after first transporting them to the embarkation point at Le Havre. The *Vingt-quatre* in return got the privilege of choosing the location of their settlements. Duval d'Eprémesnil, a member of the Parlement of Paris who had been elected as a representative of the nobility in the Estates-General, was the *Vingt-quatre's* most prominent member. He had opposed the unification of the three estates and—in the wake of their consolidation into the National Assembly—had purchased ten thousand acres of the Compagnie's lands with a view to establishing a refuge.[4]

Louis Le Bègue de Presle Duportail, whom Barlow learned was considering settling on the Scioto Company's lands, was almost as prominent as d'Eprémesnil. In 1777 Benjamin Franklin had dispatched Duportail to the United States, where he had served as an engineer for the remainder of the war and was awarded the rank of major-general for his service at the siege of Yorktown. Though Duportail would postpone emigrating, Maj. Stephen Rochefontaine, who had served with distinction under Duportail and was also one of the *Vingt-quatre*, looked as though he would be among the first wave of settlers.[5] The presence of a military man familiar with the American environment augured well for the enterprise, though Rochefontaine would also postpone his departure.

Other prominent members of the *Vingt-quatre*, like Claude-François-Adrien, Marquis de Lezay-Marnésia, did join the first wave of emigrants. Lezay-Marnésia had been a member of the Estates-General, had supported the renunciation of the nobility's privileges, and enjoyed a reputation in France as a man of letters. His embittered son later claimed he had recruited one hundred colonists to settle on his land.[6] John Joseph de Barthe, sometimes referred to as the Comte or Chevalier de Barthe, was also a *Vingt-quatre* and part of the first wave. Before departing for the United States, de Barthe was careful to solicit letters of introduction from Gouverneur Morris, among them one to Alexander Hamilton.[7]

Hamilton confessed to being impressed by the credentials of the *Vingt-quatre*. In a letter to Arthur St. Clair, then governor of the new territory created by the Northwest Ordinance, he described the "leaders . . . and their associates" as "persons of considerable consequence who are on that account entitled to regard." "If these emigrants render a favourable account of their situation to the country from which they come, there is no saying in what numbers they may be followed." In other words, Hamilton himself was prepared to buy into Barlow's claims about the significance of the Compagnie's Ohio settlement. Since the land needed to be occupied, Hamilton felt it was "best that it should be in great measure settled from abroad rather than at the entire expence of the Atlantic population [of the United States]."[8] Barlow may have been naive in his choice of business partners, and he may have allowed them to push him toward expedients he knew were risky and for which he lacked authorization, but the participation of the *Vingt-quatre* in the project suggested that the Compagnie could actually succeed.

Barlow's effort to make the Compagnie du Scioto serve the interests of his American principals began collapsing after the Compagnie failed to make its first payment at the end of December 1789. The failure did not become public knowledge until sometime later, and it had no immediate effect on land sales, which during January 1790 exceeded the combined sales of the two previous months.[9] Scarcely more noticeable was the flight of several associates. That a few aristocrats joined the émigrés in Europe rather than migrating to the United States hardly seemed important. Of far more significance was the delayed departure of the first emigrants. Barlow knew enough about pioneering to realize that the settlers needed to reach Ohio early enough to plant a crop that could tide them over through the following winter. He had hoped the first emigrants would arrive in the Chesapeake before the end of March. Though he expected the settlers to venture on a winter voyage such as he was not prepared to undertake himself, the need to get them to their lands during the spring took precedence over their comfort and even their safety.

As it transpired, none of the settlers—a small group of servants excepted—left Europe before mid-February, and the first vessels bearing the bulk of them did not limp into Alexandria until early May. No one was there to meet them despite Barlow's warning of their impending arrival. Duer had dispatched Col. David Franks to Virginia in April, but after waiting the better part of a month, Franks decided that they had made for a different port and returned to New York. That proved to be a good guess because a British vessel deposited ninety settlers there after they had been forced to abandon their sinking ship in the middle of the Atlantic. Abraham Baldwin noted that the misfortune provided an inauspicious beginning for the Scioto Company, but the New York investors kept the matter quiet, and Baldwin was confident "true colons" would not be deterred.[10] The New Yorkers also provided for the unfortunates, and within two weeks they were ready to set off overland to join their compatriots in Virginia.

The bulk of the immigrants arriving in Alexandria felt less well cared for, though not because of any neglect by Duer. Once he learned of their arrival, he dispatched Maj. Isaac Guion, a French veteran of the continental army, to make arrangements for their transit to Ohio. Nonetheless, they did not start until the end of July because of a grain shortage in the Ohio Valley, and they did not arrive at their destination until the following October. Those sponsored by the *Vingt-quatre* were well equipped to cope with the reverses all the immigrants encountered and generally refrained from denouncing the Compagnie. But Barlow and William Playfair had recruited some indentured servants with the promise of receiving lands in exchange for several years of service. The less affluent settlers—including the small group who had arrived in Philadelphia during February—complained bitterly about their treatment. Their grumblings started filtering back to France in mid-May, followed by a few disillusioned returnees.[11]

Long before that, the Compagnie's reputation in Paris had collapsed. Its fall from grace took Barlow very much by surprise. Toward the end of 1789 he had thought the Compagnie's affairs sufficiently promising to authorize Duer to draw on him for 220,000 livres; 100,000 livres immediately, another at ninety days if necessary, and an additional 20,000 livres to assist in persuading Alexander Hamilton that the Scioto Company held the key to retiring the nation's debt.[12] All these authorizations were made before the Compagnie failed to meet its first payment. Still, the strength of the January sales led Barlow to reiterate the first authorization because he realized his American partners were entitled to compensation for having to help so many French settlers.[13] Playfair later claimed Barlow had grossly exaggerated the amount of land that had been sold and that most of the purchasers had paid only half the purchase price. Some larger purchasers like Lezay-Marnésia did pay up front, but he paid with thirty thousand bottles of champagne, which left the Compagnie having to turn wine into money.[14]

Nevertheless, there should have been enough in the Compagnie's coffers to pay Duer's first bill, which came to less than $20,000, assuming that the land was fetching $1 per acre. Barlow may have hoped to use Duer's bills to pry the funds out of Playfair and Jean Soisson. Until then they had claimed that the down payments were being held in escrow pending the purchaser's receipt of title. It had undoubtedly crossed Barlow's mind that something might be amiss, but he was reluctant to risk deflating the boom in land sales. He did not know that out of the 127,000 livres Playfair would eventually admit to receiving, roughly a third was in bills that would be protested.[15] Nor would Barlow ever have authorized Duer to draw for 220,000 livres, or even 100,000 livres, had he realized that the Compagnie du Scioto was about to be denounced as a scam.

Though the Compagnie shared in the general loss of faith in all institutions that accompanied the collapse of the ancien régime, the Parisian press was principally responsible for turning the public against the Scioto enterprise. Toward the end of January 1790, Le Spectateur National published a four-part series entitled "Observations relative au plan de l'établisment d'une colonie sur les bords de l'Ohio et du Scioto, dans l'Amérique septentrionale," warning that the Compagnie was misleading the public. This series acknowledged that southern Ohio would someday be prosperous and that one could flourish in the New World. Readers were only cautioned against assuming prosperity and happiness would be easy or automatic.[16] The author's point was that upheaval at home did not by itself justify emigrating to America.

Reason and restraint vanished in early March when the Moniteur and the Chronique de Paris published articles accusing the Compagnie du Scioto of two crimes.[17] First, they claimed it was deceiving the public about what it had to sell; second, they charged it with trying to entice men of substance, who were needed at home, into leaving their country. In mid-March a pamphlet entitled Le Nouveau Mississippi attacked the company and the United States. It argued that the price of $1 per acre was too high in view of the Indian threat, a claim that seemed confirmed by the option Hamilton had inserted in his funding proposal to redeem public securities with lands at the rate of twenty cents per acre. Le Nouveau Mis-

sissippi maintained that indentured servants were really slaves and that most American lands were of inferior quality. American agriculture suffered from a harsh climate and the low value of its crops, which necessitated assembling several cargoes of American produce to buy a return cargo of European goods. This pamphlet signaled the opening of a campaign against the Compagnie that resulted in a dramatic decline in its land sales.[18]

Gouverneur Morris contributed, possibly critically, to the transition from measured to unrestrained criticism of the Scioto enterprise during the spring of 1790. Aside from being temperamentally Barlow's opposite and moving in different social circles, Morris's interests clashed with those of the Compagnie du Scioto. Morris advised prospective emigrants against joining the Compagnie's colonization project, recommending instead moving to lands he was trying to sell for Robert Morris in western New York. Additionally, Gouverneur Morris was interested in several ventures that competed for capital with the Scioto enterprise: one involved feeding the Parisian populace; the other, more important one, speculating in France's American debt.

By this time such speculative ventures had to address the growing reluctance of French officials to accept cash in exchange for an appreciating American asset. When Morris realized that the French were holding back because they thought the longer they waited the better the terms might be, he and Daniel Parker organized a consortium, in which Duer was involved. The consortium offered to exchange the entire American debt owed France at par with interest for an equivalent amount of depreciated French debt owed to Holland. Since the sums involved ran into the millions and the French authorities wanted guarantees, the proposal got bogged down in complex negotiations. The Compagnie du Scioto's offer to accept the American debt at a 20 percent premium posed little threat to Morris's attempt to make a deal with the French government. But a subsequent proposal by the Compagnie to exchange the French public debt held by individuals at par with interest for equal portions of the America debt at par with interest was a different matter.[19] By harnessing American lands to retire the French debt on such advantageous terms, it trumped the proposal Morris and Parker were pushing.

When Morris found out about the scheme from de Barthe in early February, he was not pleased.[20] He resolved to do all he could to undermine Barlow and the Compagnie. His most effective strategy was to publicize that the Scioto Company did not yet have title to the lands it was selling. Morris later tried to justify his actions by claiming that the reputation of the United States and his personal honor were at stake. "When it became a Subject of Conversation in Society," he wrote Jefferson, "I thought it incumbent on me to undeceive those who imagined the Government of the United States was concerned, and those who supposed that I might be interested." He acknowledged that his "necessary conduct has given offence" and suspected it had "occasioned Misrepresentations."[21] Morris wrote Jefferson in this vein because his hostility to the Scioto enterprise had become common knowledge. As the trusted associate of Robert Morris — next to Franklin and Washington — the best known and admired American in France, Gouverneur Morris had more influence than any other American in Paris. At one point he was even approached about joining a French government. When Morris criticized the Scioto project, his disapproval carried weight with precisely the class of Parisians whose opinions most mattered.

The attacks that began in March proved decisive in bringing about the Compagnie's eventual demise. Barlow had no choice but to release the Compagnie from honoring its contract once sales started slipping, but he postponed formally abandoning the contract until July for two reasons. First, he feared the enemies of the enterprise would construe a public dissolution as confirmation of their charges, and second, he had nothing to put in its place. Morris's disclaimer that he acted against the Compagnie only to protect his and the government's honor and innocent victims failed to convince even those closest to Morris. A year later Daniel Parker complained to Andrew Craigie about an unequal settlement Morris had forced him to accept in a related matter. "G. Morris was very violent, & my apprehension of his injuring me in france, induced me to" accept his proposal.[22] Parker did not scare easily, and his avowal stemmed at least in part from the damage Morris had managed to inflict on the Scioto enterprise.

As the Compagnie's affairs disintegrated around him, Barlow was cheered to learn that Ruth was willing to join him. What sealed Ruth's fate, though, was less Barlow's invitation of the year before than her brother Abraham's endorsement of the plan. As a senator from a southern state in the first Congress, Baldwin spent more time in New York than in Georgia, often visiting Dudley in Greenfield when Congress was not in session. Abraham concluded toward the end of 1789 that Ruth would be better off with Joel in Europe than continuing to wander from household to household in America.

Abraham agreed to help Ruth find a suitable vessel and to make the other necessary arrangements. On May 1 he reported, "The girl is in very high spirits on the subject of the voyage." Her friends in Greenfield advised her to take passage with Captain Woolsey, who was scheduled to sail for London at the end of

May.[23] Woolsey was the half-brother of Mary Dwight, Timothy Dwight's wife, whose husband now presided over Greenfield's Congregational Church. Woolsey proved to be a wise choice. During the initial two weeks of Ruth's voyage, when she suffered acutely, he treated her as tenderly as he would have a member of his own family.

Barlow responded to the first hint that Ruth might join him by supplying her with a long list of things to take on board. They included "woolen stockings to keep your feet warm, don't object that it is summer," as well as "oat meal & Indian meal to make grewel, rice, chocolate—oil of peppermint & some stomack medicines—rhubarb or sals." Barlow also advised her to find "a good maid who is used to the sea" in New York, "unless you find a female companion, that you like, in which case you may do without the maid. . . . I would gladly pay the expence." Finally, Barlow wanted her to "give the captain a good price, even double the price & bargain with him to see you lodged at the place I shall mention." That was with a Mrs. Rogers at No. 18 Kingstreet, Cheapside. Barlow did not want her to come straight to France; he wished to shield her from the difficulties the Scioto Company was experiencing, and he thought adjusting to London would be challenge enough without the additional burden of an unfamiliar language. He relished the idea of a summer vacation in England and hoped to be waiting for her there when she arrived.

Should he not be able to get away, he instructed her to contact John Paradise at 15 Margaret Street, Cavendish Square, who would take care of her until he arrived. Paradise was one of many American adventurers who had come to Europe to improve their fortunes. He had married into the prominent Virginia family of the Ludwells, and Barlow hoped Ruth would find Paradise as "intimate & dear" a friend as Lemuel Hopkins had been in Hartford.[24] Barlow failed to add that Paradise's wife, Lucy, had become estranged from her husband and was behaving as if she were mad. If Barlow expected the Paradises to be as good friends with Ruth as the Hopkinses, he was dreaming.

Barlow's immediate problems in Paris were compounded by the presentation of Duer's first bill for 100,000 livres and a notice to expect an additional one for 20,000 livres.[25] The receipt of the first reports of neglect and misfortune from the less privileged "colons" limited Barlow's options in dealing with these drafts. The larger one hundred thousand livre bill in favor of William Constable Co. of New York had been sent to the firm of Phyn, Ellices, and Inglis, with branches in London and Paris.[26] Normally, one either accepted or protested a bill on presentation. Acceptance did not require one to pay immediately; one simply promised to pay at the interval specified by the drawer, usually within thirty to ninety days. The holder of the bill could then get it discounted. Though Barlow had nothing with which to pay Duer's first bill, he took the less usual course of leaving open the possibility that he would pay sometime soon without specifying exactly when.

Barlow still hoped that Playfair and Soisson could be prevailed upon to release the money from the sale of land, which had continued, though on a decreasing scale. He knew that Phyn, Ellices, and Inglis would prefer waiting to going to the trouble and expense—not to mention delay—of a suit at law. Since the presentation of the bill coincided with Ruth's expected arrival in London, Barlow dashed off a letter on June 20 informing her he could not join her for another fortnight. During the interval, she could recover from the ocean crossing. For the first time he confessed to having had "many fears for your safety." He anticipated her provincial sensibilities would make "dress & appearance" a major concern in London. But he urged her to "give yourself no trouble about" them until he arrived.[27]

Nine days later Barlow wrote Ruth that he was unlikely to leave Paris for at least another week. In the meantime, Col. Samuel Blackden's wife, originally from Connecticut, was going to London and planned to lodge with Mrs. Rogers. Barlow assumed the two women would keep each other company until he arrived. He also had sent his agent Henry Bromfield, the scion of a Boston mercantile family who specialized in handling the affairs of Americans in Europe, a bill to supply Ruth with money. Barlow was still in Paris ten days later when Paradise delivered a note from Ruth announcing her safe arrival in London. While Barlow expressed delight at the news, he was no closer to joining her than before. Since the bill he had sent Bromfield had been endorsed to a Mr. Broome, Ruth was only entitled to the portion beyond what was due Broome. No matter—Barlow was sure Mrs. Paradise would provide for Ruth's needs until he arrived.[28]

Barlow had another diversion from his troubles with Duer, besides Ruth— participating in the pageantry of revolutionary politics. The difficulties that had plagued the Scioto enterprise since the end of 1789 had narrowed his social options, and he had welcomed the chance to join a group of Americans, led by Capt. John Paul Jones and including Samuel Blackden, James Swan, Thomas Appleton, William Vernon, Benjamin Jarvis, and George Washington Greene, in presenting an address to the Constituent Assembly on July 10. The preceding summer four of them had collaborated in signing a July 4 address Barlow had drafted congratulating Jefferson on his contributions to promoting liberty and establishing closer ties with France.[29] Gouverneur Morris had pointedly refused to take part in the 1789 testimonial and was in London during July 1790.

If Barlow was not the sole author of the address to the Constituent Assembly, he had a major hand in it, for its rhetorical extravagance bore the unmistakable marks of his imagination. It rejoiced that "the rays of the western star, diffused from a distant portion of the globe, are now met, and reverberated by that rising sun of glory, which floods with light the dominion of France, and begins to illuminate the world." It gave uncritical endorsement to the progress that had been made in reforming the corruptions of the ancien régime. Lavish praise for the Constituent Assembly and Louis XVI accompanied a request for "the honor of assisting at the august ceremony which promises to perpetuate the future happiness of France."[30] According to Barlow, the address was greeted with "such thunderclaps of applause [as] never were heard,"[31] leading the president of the Constituent Assembly to reply in kind and the assembly to order both the address and the president's reply be published. Barlow sent his address to America, hoping it would meet with as much applause at home as it had in the French assembly.

The ceremony in question was the Fête de fédération scheduled to take place four days later on the Champs de Mars to mark the initial anniversary of the fall of the Bastille. This was the first of the great public festivals accompanying the French Revolution. It celebrated the remaking of France's administrative institutions and was supposed to symbolize the French people coming together with Louis XVI to affirm a new order. Pressure for the Fête de fédération had originated in the provinces. As the ancien régime disintegrated, provincial fêtes had become common rituals, reflecting the need for continuity and community in the face of radical change. The central government had first opposed the idea but eventually bowed to popular demand. An estimated one-quarter of the population of Paris, including respectable women, turned out to transform the Champs de Mars into a vast stadium. The actual celebration, however, was confined to a select sample of national guardsmen from the provinces, known as *fédérés*, joined by certain line units of the army and the Paris militia. Barlow and his compatriots had to ask permission to attend the ceremony because all who would have liked to attend could not be accommodated.

The celebration began with an elaborate parade on a cold, windy day marked by intermittent rain. After the king reviewed the procession, he was supposed to take his seat on a throne that had been erected in the middle of the stadium. But he arrived late for this part of the ceremony, allowed someone else to take his place on the throne, and generally remained aloof from the proceedings. Politicians like the marquis de Mirabeau, who specialized in grand gestures, were profoundly disappointed with the ceremony.[32] Though the Fête de fédération was revolutionary theater on an unprecedented scale, Mirabeau understood immediately that it had contributed little toward legitimizing the new order. Barlow by contrast thought the event "the sublimest that was ever exhibited to [?] man."[33]

A letter from London, dated July 13, reported that Ruth was unwell. On the nineteenth he replied, "My love, I am killed a thousand deaths that I cannot set out today—My business has been vexatious beyond all description." Barlow realized that if he abruptly departed for London, he could trigger a suit by Phyn, Ellices, and Inglis and possibly be imprisoned for debt. In his desperation, he clutched at the one straw available to him. Since the fundamental conditions for selling American lands to Frenchmen eager to flee revolutionary upheaval were still favorable, he sought and found a new set of investors who were willing to take the place of the Compagnie du Scioto and enable him to pay Duer's bill. "I have been almost sure every day of bringing it [the negotiation with new investors] to such a close in four or five days as to leave it [the enterprise] cleverly for a month," he wrote Ruth.[34]

On July 22 the parties finally reached an agreement, though the terms were far less favorable to the Scioto associates than the first contract with the Compagnie had been. In exchange for promising to pay Barlow 150,000 livres, a new company known as de Barthe and Coquet acquired the right to the Scioto preemption free of most other obligations to the American principals. De Barthe's father was already in America as one of the *Vingt-quatre*, and his son saw the new company as a means of supporting a branch of the family as well as an investment. The de Barthes, father and son, took half the shares, while Marc Anthony Coquet and Louis Philippe Douvalette each took 10 percent, and the ubiquitous William Playfair held the remaining 30 percent.[35] Though Barlow had begun to suspect Playfair, at this point it was too late to get rid of him.

There is a tantalizing reference in a document in the Cincinnati Historical Society to Playfair discharging Barlow from all previous engagements, and especially one entered into on March 8, when Barlow publicly released the Compagnie du Scioto from its contract at the end of July.[36] I have been unable to clarify what these engagements were, but Barlow seems previously to have made commitments to Playfair which he later regretted. In any case, retaining Playfair in the new company enhanced the likelihood that the proceeds from the sales made by the Compagnie du Scioto would be turned over to it, as the July 22 contract specified.

Covering Barlow's expenses in Europe and paying Duer's larger bill would cost 150,000 livres, thus compensating the investors for some of their expenses in settling the French immigrants. But since Barlow had no way of knowing how large those expenses would become, the July 22 agreement also made provision for de Barthe and Coquet eventually to assume them once the amount was ascertained. Beyond reimbursing the American investors for their costs, the contract also made a gesture at giving them a stake in the future profits of de Barthe and Coquet by allowing them fifteen sous for every acre of Scioto land sold. Barlow's American principals objected to such a radical reduction of their stake in the speculation. When Rufus Putnam learned of it, he assumed that Barlow meant to pocket the 150,000 livres himself and share with the French partners and Playfair all but a microscopic fraction of the revenues derived from future land sales.[37] Putnam was encouraged to assume the worst by Major Rochefontaine's objections to the new contract.

Rochefontaine wrote Duer shortly after the formation of the new company, objecting to the abandonment of the former Compagnie. Rochefontaine believed Barlow had only agreed to the new contract because de Barthe and Coquet had paid him off. He claimed that he and Duportail could have borrowed the money needed to cover Duer's bill had the Compagnie's contract been retained. Rochefontaine also alleged that Barlow and his new associates intended to sell off the best lands and then abandon the enterprise.[38] Here Rochefontaine touched on a nerve, since interior lands were far less valuable than those fronting rivers. Over an extended period of time, as the choice lands were developed, the value of inferior lands could be expected to rise, but Putnam feared that process would take a century. He had become suspicious "the moment I found he [Barlow] had begun to retale [sic] lands in small quantities," but he had hoped this would last no longer than necessary to prime a mass migration.[39]

In claiming he and Duportail had access to a more promising set of French backers than Barlow, Rochefontaine spoke as an interested party. However, he made the mistake of adding that he wanted to retain Playfair's services because under their employ he could become a valuable man. Duer had received reports accusing Playfair and Soisson of misrepresentation and subjecting the immigrants to double charges; thus, Rochefontaine's endorsement of Playfair backfired.[40] Barlow enjoyed a better reputation among the immigrants because of his efforts to warn them about the challenges they would face in the American wilderness.[41] But Putnam continued to assume the worst, concluding that "if the facts are truly stated Mr. Barlow must be a consummate villain or greatly wanting in sagacity not to see the fatal consequences" of his actions.[42]

Barlow's new contract enabled him to persuade Phyn, Ellices, and Inglis that he would soon have the money to honor Duer's two bills. That prospect allowed him finally to join Ruth in London. The contract also enabled him to provide for her, since by this time current expenses had become a problem for Barlow.[43] The same note that informed him of Ruth's ill health also said that Broome had failed to provide her with any of the money Barlow had sent. Barlow dispatched another bill to London for £36 6 s. 6d. drawn at seven days sight.[44] Once de Barthe and Coquet paid the 150,000 livres, Barlow's immediate financial worries would lift.

Sometime around August 1, the Barlows reunited in London. Ruth had been sick for six weeks, probably experiencing the "seasoning" common during the eighteenth century when one entered a new disease environment. When her husband arrived, she must also have learned of the troubles plaguing him. The knowledge could not have contributed to her sense of well-being, but the support and good advice she offered him was doubtless what he had in mind in 1796 when he attributed "the acquisition of the competency which we seem at last to have secured . . . more to your energy, than mine." She provided "consolation and even happiness under circumstances, wherein, if I had been alone, or with a partner no better than myself, I should have sunk."[45]

Despite poor health and anxiety about financial difficulties, the Barlows enjoyed their time in England so much that they would have stayed indefinitely had London offered a refuge from the pressures of the Scioto business. But a letter Andrew Craigie had entrusted to Ruth reminded Barlow of his jeopardy. Craigie complained of having to cover the initial advances for the "colons" because Duer had encountered difficulties in selling his bills on Barlow. While Craigie expressed confidence in Barlow, he gave notice that he was sending him yet another bill in favor of Brissot de Warville. Craigie was certain Barlow would honor it since "a demur would ruin the whole Business," and this could not happen "unless you have trusted others to [sic] much & they should betray the confidence you have placed in them."[46]

Craigie's message forced the Barlows to return to Paris in mid-August, when Barlow executed an agreement with a French surveyor to ascertain the boundaries of the plots to which the Scioto settlers were entitled.[47] There he found that de Barthe and Coquet had yet to pay any of the 150,000 livres due under their contract. He also learned that Rochefontaine was attacking him and that François de Moustier, France's former ambassador to the United States, had sent a letter to the Constituent Assembly warning against "the devices employed by the Compagnie de Scioto to entice citizens into a disastrous emigration."[48]

De Barthe and Coquet's default meant Barlow's best chance of avoiding imprisonment was to protest Duer's bill, which would also put a stop to additional bills arriving from America. Morris, ever ready to compromise Barlow, may have had a hand in precipitating the protest because on September 3 he urged Phyn, Ellices, and Inglis to sue over their bill. Their counsel advised that while Duer alone had the right to initiate such a suit, the firm could attach Barlow's property as a precaution.[49] Barlow had no tangibles except his person for creditors to lay their hands on, and we can infer that he reluctantly made his decision to protest the bill in early September from Duer's angry letter written in New York on November 4 about the protest.[50]

Shortly after receiving news of the July 22 contract and Rochefontaine's letter condemning it, the American partners in the Scioto enterprise dispatched Benjamin Walker to Paris to investigate Barlow's management of their affairs. Along with David Humphreys, Walker was one of Washington's closest aides at the end of the Revolutionary War and in 1790 was the federal naval officer at New York. Since he had business in Britain that needed attention, he was easily persuaded to undertake this additional mission. Walker did not arrive in Paris until the end of the year, and in the meantime Barlow had to contend with Morris's continuing enmity.

Morris used Barlow's protest of Duer's bill to attack the new company's attempts to sell Ohio lands. When Barlow sought a personal interview in mid-November, hoping to arrive at an understanding with his adversary, Morris proved unyielding. He recorded in his diary that in the course of "a lame stammering Conversation I find he [Barlow] has no means to retire the Bill [probably Duer's second draft] upon him." The only thing Barlow had to offer was the prospect of future sales. Morris then indulged himself with a prediction that was no less satisfying because of his determination to make it self-fulfilling: "this Scioto Business will turn out very badly."[51]

Barlow later claimed that he had become so unpopular in Paris that his French friends felt he was in personal danger. The return of a few discouraged Scioto immigrants fueled public hostility against him. "The cries of many people who believed or affected to believe their children and other friends devoured by the American savages were on the point of collecting the mob of Paris," threatening him with the kind of vigilante violence that was becoming routine.[52] De Barthe and Coquet's failure to make their payment of 150,000 livres also forced the Barlows to skimp, and Ruth made much of their "disagreeable" circumstances. She complained about being "pent up in a narrow dirty street surrounded by . . . noise folly & filth." This was not living but "only existing. I have not an hour I can call my own but when I sleep, but must at all times be draped & see company." Ruth was filled with homesick longings for Connecticut. "O! how ardently do I wish to return to America & my Dear friends there, to Greenfield that dear delightful Village, where I passed so many pleasant hours in that friendly and agreeable little circle" that included the Dwights, her brother Dudley, and his family.

Not only was Ruth offended by the "strange extremes" of "extravagance & luxury folly wickedness & wretchedness" that differentiated the Europe she saw from North America, but she had also to contend with a foreign language.[53] Moreover, the Barlows' circumstances were such that they could only afford an apartment on the top floor of the Palais Royal. Samuel Breck's account of visiting them there in February 1791 suggests that the accommodation left much to be desired. "In order to reach the apartment of Mr. Barlow, I was obliged to pass through the door of a great gambling establishment that occupied the floor immediately below his." Breck concluded that "the poet's poverty consented [to such quarters] rather than his will." The only bright spot during that autumn and ensuing winter was that Ruth finally regained her health.[54]

Under these circumstances, they regarded Benjamin Walker's arrival at year's end as a blessing. He came equipped with three separate commissions from the Scioto associates. The first appointed him joint agent with Barlow in managing the concern's European business. The second empowered him to examine its "accounts and proceedings" in Europe, and the last appointed him sole agent. These commissions were drafted before Duer learned of his first protested bill. Walker was cautioned to "act with all delicacy, and discretion, which our esteem for Mr. Barlow, and the nature of the case requires," indicating that Barlow had yet to forfeit all his credit with his principals. The Scioto associates remained mindful that the fundamentals still favored settling large numbers of French refugees in America, but they "wanted solid security for the funds received on account of the sales." Walker was only to make use of his third commission "if the state of the company's affairs and the conduct of the parties, who have been entrusted with their management, should in your judgment render it advisable."[55]

Walker at first assumed that Barlow was at fault and communicated this judgment to Morris. By then Morris had concluded that Walker would administer the coup de grace to Barlow, so Morris declined to comment on the basis of insufficient information, though he thought that Walker appeared to be ignorant of "some of the most important" facts pertaining to the company.[56] As Walker became better informed, he increasingly held Playfair rather than Barlow responsible for the Scioto fiasco. Barlow was not alone in refusing to accept bills drawn on him from America. Late in 1790, Playfair refused to accept two bills from de Barthe in favor of Duer for 1,800 livres each.[57] This refusal may have been the

information Morris declined to share with Walker, but Walker found more compelling evidence about who was behind the company's troubles.

Barlow cooperated with Walker as much as possible, leaving Playfair with little
option but to appear equally accommodating. At the same time, however, he
wrote Duer a long letter blaming Barlow for all the company's troubles.[58] Walker
was not aware of this letter, but several other considerations turned Walker against
Playfair. First, he found out that Barlow had not prospered at the company's expense, while Playfair had. Then, despite an ingenious arsenal of excuses, there
were features of the enterprise Playfair couldn't explain. His claim that he had
had no hand in the contract of July 22, 1790, was belied by his 30 percent stake in
the new firm of de Barthe and Coquet. And he could not give a satisfactory account of several unauthorized bills he had drawn on Duer in favor of the immigrants. But Playfair's biggest problem arose from his refusal to come to a financial
settlement with Walker. Playfair later claimed that Walker had lacked proper
authority to make such a settlement,[59] but Walker could find no evidence that
either the Compagnie du Scioto or de Barthe and Coquet had ever paid a penny
to the Scioto Company.

Though Walker continued to judge Barlow's management of the company's
affairs deficient, he ended up buying into Barlow's vision of France's potential for
supplying the United States with useful citizens. Walker wrote Hamilton that the
venture remained promising enough to justify prolonging his stay in France.
Since Walker felt that the interests and reputation of the United States were involved in rescuing the company's fortunes, he recommended that Congress permit the land to be sold directly to individuals instead of requiring the company
to make large advances independent of its receipts.[60] To further the movement
of French immigrants to America, Walker reached out to Duportail and Rochefontaine. At this point Duportail's star was rising in France—he had just become
minister of war—so it seemed he had much to contribute to the enterprise. Rochefontaine's harsh criticism of Barlow the previous August might have posed a problem, but Barlow was more than happy to retire from the venture after Walker
exonerated him from all malfeasance.

Playfair, by contrast, approached both Duer and Hamilton with proposals for
continuing to sell American lands. "If things are well Managed America will gain
More in Population and Imported Wealth in the three years to come than She
would otherwise in thirty."[61] Walker and Playfair's enthusiasm about the struc-
tural underpinnings of the speculation led an unidentified associate, probably
Royal Flint, to assume in March 1791 that the Scioto Company could still be

salvaged.[62] But Walker and Playfair quarreled about who was authorized to sell the Ohio lands, and just before returning to Britain in April, Walker placed an announcement in a Parisian newspaper and had broadsides posted throughout the city warning people against buying from Playfair. Playfair responded by claiming an exclusive power to sell the Scioto lands. Barlow had not seen a counter from Rochefontaine to Playfair's claim, but he thought Walker's "publication must answer all the purpose that was expected from it."[63] Not much was required since by then Playfair was too controversial for anyone to trust.

The Scioto enterprise staggered along despite Walker's efforts. Duportail's duties distracted him from the company's concerns, while Rochefontaine was unable to undo the damage Playfair had inflicted on it, despite a glowing notice in the *Moniteur* about the support French settlers were receiving in America from the Scioto associates.[64] Eventually, Playfair, Rochefontaine, and Duportail would all be driven from France, though only the latter two came to America— Rochefontaine in 1792, Duportail in 1794. However, neither Frenchmen inspired many others to follow their example. Though the Terror led to a sizable migration of French aristocrats to the United States, most of them eventually returned home. The wars of the French Revolution that began in 1792 would divert the less affluent into France's armies for the next twenty years. The Frenchmen who had come to America under the Scioto Company's aegis would be exceptions rather than the rule.

Though the settlers ended up having to pay twice for their lands, the price was not an exorbitant one. In many ways they fared better than native migrants. The Scioto Associates provided supplies and escorts to guide them to Ohio. They secured horses and carts to transport women and children, as well as boats to float the entire company down the Ohio. Finally, they hired more than thirty-five men to build huts for the small settlement that would be known as Gallipolis, while hunters provided meat for the settlers over the winter.[65] No one died as a direct consequence of the company's failures, and after the Battle of Fallen Timbers (1794) the settlers had little to fear from the hostility of the Indians. Their dissatisfaction stemmed more from the primitive conditions in which they found themselves than from anything else.[66]

Barlow's legacy from the debacle was as enduring and almost as agonizing as the hardships of the settlers. After learning from Walker that Duer had disbursed 220,000 livres in supporting the immigrants, Barlow had reason to fear Duer, and that anxiety increased after Duer was forced into debtors prison in 1792. Though

Barlow was directly responsible for less than 2 percent of Duer's total indebtedness, protesting Duer's bill had damaged Duer's credit just as the immigrants had increased his burdens. The threat Duer posed would persist until he died in 1799.[67] Barlow blamed the collapse of the enterprise on "delays & inattention in America." Though he was unwilling to accept responsibility for the debacle, two things continued to haunt him. He worried about the settlers who had ventured forth on his representations, asking Baldwin "whether the colons are on their lands & what you learn of their situation." Since he was debating whether he should return to the United States, he also wanted to know what his former associates "say of my conduct." He needed reassurance "before I determine positively on sailing for America" that he would not fall victim to Duer's or anyone else's enmity.[68]

He also needed something to do. His options seemed limited to practicing law in Hartford, settling in Ohio or Georgia, or securing a public appointment. There was little left for him in France except to wind up loose ends, though even here he encountered difficulties. He lamented to Walker that "an American friend" had negotiated a 6,300 livre note for him at a 23 percent discount and then had his pocket picked clean of the remaining 4,800 livres of depreciating *assignats*. Barlow remained on good enough terms with Walker to ask him to tend to minor matters in Britain for him, offering in return to do "anything in which it is in my power to serve you in this country or elsewhere."[69] Walker for his part portrayed Barlow's services to the Scioto enterprise with sufficient sympathy that Craigie sent him a draft for one hundred guineas to cover his expenses in returning to America. That was a generous gesture, given Barlow's handling of Craigie's bill in Brissot's favor, but Barlow couldn't be sure that it wasn't too generous and therefore designed to entrap him.[70]

During the spring of 1791 Barlow tried to make amends for failing to honor Craigie's bill by beginning a translation of Brissot's *Nouveau Voyage dans les États-Unis*, which had just appeared. The precise understanding between the two men has not survived, but Barlow behaved as though he had a proprietary interest in the work because he had two copies made of his translation. It seems probable that one was intended for the English market, from which Brissot would receive the royalties, while Barlow was to make what he could of the other copy in America. According to Durand Echeverria, who edited the most recent English version of the *New Travels*, Barlow was unfaithful to the text, deleting all criticism of the new nation and eliminating half of the original. Barlow also failed to reap any reward from an American printing because someone pirated the first English edition before he could get his duplicate manuscript to a printer. Nonetheless, the connection he established with Brissot during the first half of 1791 would later become important.

The other thing holding Barlow's attention that spring was the unfolding drama of the French Revolution. Here he began to enjoy an advantage over Gouverneur Morris, who had hitched his expectations to the survival of the French monarchy. The reorganization of the church had made all clerics employees of the state who were required to acknowledge their loyalty to their employer. Louis XVI's insistence upon celebrating Easter Mass with priests who had refused to take the Constituent Assembly's Civil Oath signaled that the monarch opposed the new reforms. Barlow still expressed optimism about France's future. "Though affairs . . . go on their slow train, I am as sure as ever they will come out right."[71] He was one of the few to entertain such optimism because most sensed that the alternative to preserving the monarchy was civil war.

During the remainder of the spring, the monarchy's prestige deteriorated. Shortly after Easter, Louis XVI and his family were prevented from going to St. Cloud by elements of the national guard who suspected that the king wanted to join the army of émigrés collecting on the frontiers. Louis dealt the monarchy a further blow on the night of June 21, 1791, when the royal family was caught at Varennes, more than one hundred miles from Paris, trying to escape France disguised as commoners. The king's actions struck at the heart of the Constituent Assembly's constitutional design by depriving it of a credible monarch. Reluctant to admit failure after more than a year of effort, the assembly pretended the king had been kidnapped. Thomas Paine, in conjunction with a French noble who had served in the American war, Achille du Chastelet, construed Louis's actions as an abdication and drafted a manifesto calling for the establishment of a republic.

On July 1, as the Barlows were preparing to leave for England, Paine and du Chastelet posted their broadside manifesto throughout Paris. It set off a lively debate in the Parisian papers between the supporters of limited monarchy and those who would be satisfied by nothing less than its total abolition. Several of the more radical political clubs, including the Cordeliers and Cercle Social, weighed in on the side of the republicans and started agitating for Louis's removal. The Cordeliers subsequently summoned the people of Paris to assemble on the Champs de Mars to sign a petition for a republic. Despite the mayor's warning against assembling, fifty thousand responded to the Cordeliers' summons. They were greeted by units of the national guard under Lafayette's command. After the crowd refused to disperse, the guardsmen opened fire, killing as many as fifty and wounding one hundred before the assemblage broke up. The violence forced the republicans to retreat and paved the way for the Constituent Assembly to accept a final draft of the Constitution with enhanced powers for the monarch on September 3.

These events had little effect on the Barlows who in July were about to depart Paris for Lille.[72] At the time, Lille was a thriving center for the production of linen and woolen goods in French Flanders. Barlow seems to have been more preoccupied with exploring economic opportunities than observing the revolutionary drama playing out in Paris. Not long after, the Barlows arrived in London. The English poet William Hayley wrote on August 7 inviting them to visit him at his country retreat. Hayley assumed they would find this invitation a relief "after what you have witnessed in Paris."[73]

CHAPTER EIGHT

Revolutionary Adventurer

At the end of July 1791, the Barlows took up residence at No. 18, Great Titchfield Street. Though London was just as odiferous and dirty as Paris, they were surely glad to be living in a more familiar, stable society. The occasional incidents of criminal violence bore no comparison to the revolutionary *journées* of Paris, while the countryside surrounding London was bucolically serene and prosperous. Nor were the Barlows distracted by the daily doings of Parliament, as they had been by the activities of the Constituent Assembly. London lacked the pretentious civic festivals with which Parisians attempted to come to terms with revolutionary change. Finally, a subdued privacy—in which the Barlows controlled their sociability—replaced the incessant carnival of the Palais Royal.

Barlow had adjusted to Paris better than Ruth, whose initial contacts were confined to the few Americans residing there, supplemented by an occasional Briton. Barlow's growing facility with the French language gave him access to the cafés of Paris, where "playful irreverence and utopian speculation were preferred to pedestrian practicality."[1] Though this discourse left its mark on Barlow, he fared better in London's coffee houses, where he had nothing to live down. Because specific coffee houses attracted like-minded clients, Barlow found congenial company almost immediately. During his first weeks in Britain he became acquainted with a network of English radicals that had formed around the publisher Joseph Johnson. Barlow moved quickly from the periphery of Parisian society into the center of a London subculture whose values he prized.

Developments in France had changed Britain dramatically since Barlow's last visit. A civic sermon Richard Price preached to the Revolution Society in November 1789 initiated the alteration. Price praised France for "spurning . . . slavery, and demanding liberty with an irresistible voice." He hoped its spirit of liberty would lead to "the dominion of kings [being] changed for the dominion of laws, and the dominion of priests giving way to the dominion of reason and conscience." Price's *Discourse* concluded with a rousing warning to the "oppressors of the world." He urged them to "restore to mankind their rights; and consent to the correction of abuses, before they and you are destroyed together."[2]

Price was not alone in hoping the spirit of liberation would spread from France to Britain. Thomas Paine pressed similar views on Edmund Burke. Because Burke had been friendly to the American Revolution, Paine assumed he would remain a political ally. Burke's February 9, 1790, speech to Parliament criticizing events in France caught Paine by surprise. A week later Burke announced he was undertaking an extended critique of the French Revolution. His *Reflections on the Revolution in France* appeared the following November, when he took issue with Price as well as with the events in France. Burke's *Reflections* ran through eight editions before Paine's response, Part I of *The Rights of Man*, appeared in March 1791.

By then Catherine Macauley, James Mackintosh, and Mary Wollstonecraft had protested Burke's assessment of the French Revolution. Of the three, Wollstonecraft's *A Vindication of the Rights of Man* (1790) was the most powerful, assaulting Burke's political morality and accusing him of obfuscation. Mackintosh's *Vindiciae gallicae: defense of the French Revolution and its English admirers against the Rt. Hon. Edmund Burke* (1791), on the other hand, showed that one could still endorse France's quest for liberty without advocating that Britain follow her example. Part I of Paine's *The Rights of Man* rejected the notion that revolutionary developments in France had no implications for Britain. In doing so it ignited an intense debate about the merits of what France had accomplished and the applicability of the example of the French Revolution to Britain. Throughout the remainder of 1791 and into 1792, this discussion took place free of the immediate threat of war.

Nonetheless, Louis XVI's attempted flight transformed the political landscape of Britain as much as it did that of France. After June 1791, endorsing the principles of the French Revolution no longer seemed consistent with maintaining Britain's status quo. The French king's actions polarized English society in ways not seen since the American war. It inspired the revival of the extraparliamentary associations in Britain that had emerged in the 1770s and 1780s to promote parliamentary reform, as well as angry responses such as that of a Birmingham mob in July 1791.

A handbill announcing an anniversary celebration of the fall of the Bastille set off four days of rioting culminating in the destruction of the distinguished British scientist Joseph Priestley's home and papers.

The Barlows saw in these developments the seeds of yet another revolution. The associations resembled the town meetings in New England and the political clubs of Paris, while the problem of taxation provided an additional parallel between Britain's political landscape and the American and French Revolutions. The British taxpayer still staggered under enormous burdens. Since taxation had precipitated the American Revolution and a fiscal crisis had triggered the disintegration of the old order in France, it seemed as though Britain was on the verge of succumbing to a similar fate.

While Barlow found the rising political tensions in Britain exciting, he still needed to find a means of supporting himself. The funds Andrew Craigie had made available were for the specific purpose of coming home and, even if diverted to another end, would not have tided them over for long. Barlow was never at a loss for words, and his coffee house exchanges quickly suggested he might capitalize on his modest literary reputation in Britain by turning to political authorship. The avalanche of pamphlets issuing from British presses in response to Burke's *Reflections* only served as a momentary deterrent because English supporters of the French Revolution were by no means united about its implications for Britain. While some like Paine called for a republic, others valued Britain's existing political institutions and thought they could be improved through reform. Barlow identified with those who urged radical change and was eager to help them triumph over the more conservative reformers.

Barlow claimed that he and Ruth had lingered in Europe for the remainder of 1791 to wrap up his affairs in France.[3] However, it seems unlikely that their brief sojourn in Lille could have led to enough business to detain him. It is more probable that he did not want to make a late summer departure, which meant sailing into the western Atlantic at the height of the hurricane season. He was also worried about how the Scioto fiasco had damaged his reputation in America. Barlow expected "no great difficulty in convincing . . . [his acquaintances] of the rational combination of the plan" on which he had tried to conduct the Scioto business. But "how far others will trouble themselves to judge of it, I cannot tell." He now acknowledged that "mismanagement & misfortune" had dogged the affair in France and predicted that both Duer and he would "be losers by the job." But Barlow still felt "the delay of six months in getting [the French settlers] to the land" was "the sole cause of the failure of the whole project. All the difficulties in Europe had their origin in that."

Pecuniary loss was the least of Barlow's concerns. Of far greater consequence was having "half wore out my life in two years' constant anxiety labor & exertion" and having "raised the expectations of my friends and my own" without "having accomplished a thing that I thought proper." He had squandered precious time that "I might have employed in putting myself forward in my own country." He was unwilling to accept being consigned to oblivion. Instead, he wanted compensation for the years he had squandered on the Scioto Company. Appointment to a federal office that could support his literary ambitions would have been welcome. Barlow thought his experience qualified him to head up a federal land office. "I'll be hanged if they will find a better fellow to put at the head of it, & perhaps they may be brought to think so." But appointment to a state office might do just as well or, short of that, the patronage of someone like Jefferson, who had already suggested that Barlow write the history of the American Revolution.

Barlow did not have extravagant expectations and advised his brother-in-law Abraham to remember the "kind of an animal you are planning for—one that has no offspring, & is not anxious for any great estate." He described himself as a "phlegmatic, irritable fellow" who expected "the means of a comfortable subsistence . . . [to] be reconciled with as much laziness as is convenient." Yet in this same letter he outlined an ambitious literary project entitled *"The renovation of Society, or an Essay on the necessity & propriety of a revolution in the governments of Europe."*[4]

Barlow's rapidly expanding circle of friends among Britain's radical intelligentsia, which eventually included Wollstonecraft, John Horne Tooke, and William Godwin, encouraged him to undertake the project.[5] But Paine remained Barlow's most important and enduring inspiration during this heady period. Shortly after the Barlows arrived in London, a group of 250 radicals meeting at the Thatched House Tavern adopted Paine's "Address and Declaration of the Friends of Universal Peace and Liberty." During the remainder of 1791, Paine withdrew from public view, living with the family of Thomas Rickman to flesh out his "Address" into what became Part II of *The Rights of Man.*[6] Though he confined himself to socializing with a select group of radical friends that came to include Barlow, Paine reemerged briefly on November 4 to be feted by the Revolution Society at what had become an annual occasion. Priestley and a delegation of four Frenchmen headed by Jérôme Pétion, who had ridden in the coach with the king and queen upon their return from Varennes and who would soon be elected mayor of Paris, were also present. The Constituent Assembly had suspended the king's powers until he swore to observe the Constitution of 1791. Louis did not comply until September 28, 1791. Even then, no one believed he could be trusted, which created considerable uncertainty surrounding the future of France and Europe. Paine took advantage of that uncertainty to propose a toast to "The Revolution of the World."

Barlow's *Advice to the Privileged Orders, in the several states of Europe, resulting from the Necessity and Propriety of a General Revolution in the Principle of Government* seemed to follow Paine's cue, though it appeared on February 6, 1792, ten days before Part II of *The Rights of Man.* Both works were printed by Joseph Johnson after Paine concluded that his initial publisher, Thomas Chapman, was being paid by the government to suppress his work. Paine had circulated the proof sheets of Part II, which Chapman did produce, among his inner circle, allowing Barlow to keep abreast of Paine's work as it developed and to design his own essay to complement Paine's. Some overlap, of course, was to be expected. Thus, both works stressed the peaceful nature of the French Revolution, which suggested that a liberating future was within the grasp of all nations. And both assumed that the example of France would inevitably be followed by all of Europe. While Paine outlined a political program for the British people, however, Barlow addressed a wider world.[7] He sought to persuade the privileged orders to eschew the example of France's émigrés by demonstrating that the "establishment of general liberty" would not be "injurious to those who now live by abuses." Why? Because the new republican order would "produce effects far more astonishing than have ever been calculated" and "the increase of enjoyments will be such, as to ameliorate the condition of every human creature" by sweeping away all vestiges of feudalism (97).

Barlow singled out primogeniture and entail as embodying feudalism's unnatural social order, where superiors commanded and inferiors obeyed. The focus seemed natural to someone who as the youngest son of his father's second wife had not been as favored as the first born of each of his father's marriages had. Barlow's claim that there was "nothing more difficult in the management of the affairs of the nation, than the affairs of a family" revealed the connection he assumed existed between public and private spheres. He expected that once "the mysticism of inequality" was banished from both, "almost all the evils attendant on human nature" would vanish with it (116). Whatever difficulties might arise from empowering the ill informed and illiterate would be overcome through their representatives, and the people could be "*safely armed*" since they could never threaten "*society*" but only "*government*" (117). The experience of the American Revolution had demonstrated that "where the people at large feel and know that they *can do every thing* by themselves personally, they really do nothing by themselves personally," and instead defer to their chosen leaders (120).

Most of Barlow's *Advice* attacked the institutions he held responsible for "conceal[ing] the strength of the many, and magnifying that of the few" (129). Among them the church enjoyed preeminence because the first objective of every priest "is to establish a belief in the minds of the people, that *he himself is possest of supernatural powers*" (136). Such notions not only encouraged "inequalities" but also made "men cruel and savage" because whoever felt he was "doing the immediate work of God . . . divests himself of the feelings of a man" (138). He argued that the alliance between church and state made them "factious and turbulent" because they were likely to use their power to revenge injuries instead of preventing them (139). Barlow concluded, *"The existence of any kind of liberty is incompatible with the existence of any kind of church"* (135).

The military systems of monarchies were not far behind established churches by encouraging pernicious values like honor. Princes pronounced what they wanted to be honorable with confidence that their pronouncements would be sufficient to make it so. Barlow thought this explained why the slaughter of human beings had come to be regarded as "honorable" (150), while productive activities like agriculture, commerce, and everything that improved the human species was viewed as dishonorable. He was confident a government based on the equal representation of an armed populace would reverse such a perverse inversion of values by dissolving the distinction between noble and commoner that Barlow believed lay at the root of offensive warfare. Republics were incapable of offensive operations, though their defensive capabilities were "infallible," because everyone in a republic had a stake in it (165). Barlow invoked the example of the separate American states to support the claim that republics would not quarrel about their boundaries because their citizens had no reason for preferring one state to another.

Barlow's final target in the *Advice* was "the administration of justice" (170). Here he followed Paine in arguing that governments instead of *"compelling justice,"* should remove "the physical [causes of crime through] distributive justice" (180). He assumed the "common stock of society" was sufficient to render "all its members happy in every respect, except the removal of bodily disease." By "common stock" Barlow meant knowledge "of the improvements which men have made in the means of acquiring a support" rather than "the *contributions* . . . collected from individuals" for the state (183). No person who was properly instructed about his rights and duties would knowingly commit a crime where "the government is his own" and "the officers of the state are the servants of the people." Instead, lawful redress should be available in all circumstances but those of immediate necessity, which it was the duty of government to prevent (186).

Barlow complained that the English and French judicial systems had inverted "every thing [he considered] . . . right and reasonable" (187). English subjects neither knew what the laws were nor, given the complexity of legal processes, enjoyed the remotest chance of winning justice from the courts. Justice in France was an even greater mockery since, in addition to the formalities, it was up for sale. Justice didn't have to be prostituted because it was available to all at affordable cost in Connecticut, where the state also made public provision for educating its citizens in knowledge of the laws.

⚜

Part I of the *Advice* concluded without addressing several subjects Barlow had mentioned in his introduction. Later he attributed the interruption to "his attention [being] called to other objects" (214). One of these was composing a verse sequel to the *Advice* titled *The Conspiracy of Kings*. His introduction to the *Advice* had noted that republican revolutions in Europe depended "on a class of men . . . that cannot write; and in a great measure... cannot read" (107). Early in 1792, he ·decided it was time to appeal to the feelings of men as well as to their reason and that the best means of reaching the illiterate was through a political poem.

The Conspiracy of Kings,[8] which appeared on March 20, 1792, begins with Barlow's defiant declaration that his is "Th' unwonted voice, that no dissuasion awes, / That fears no frown, and seeks no blind applause" (5–6). The "Drones of the Church and harpies of the State" (10) that support monarchies are the targets of Barlow's defiance. Of the two, Barlow again singles out for special condemnation the "dark host" who claims to possess "The lamp of life, the mystic keys of heaven" (15, 16). Barlow's song instead celebrates

> Men, roused from sloth, by indignation stung,
> Their strong hands loos'd, and found their fearless tongue,
> Whose voice of fire, whose deep descending steel
> Shall speak to souls, and teach dull nerves to feel.   (35–38)

Monarchical parasites should not imagine "That nations, rising in the light of truth, / Strong with new life and pure regenerate youth," would "Betray the trust by Heav'n's own hand consign'd, / The great concentred stake, the interest of mankind" (43, 47–48). Nor can Burke "by thy infuriate quill" resist "Th' eternal Word, which gave, in spite of thee, / Reason to man, that bids the man be free" (129, 139–40).

Barlow invites the tyrants of the world to face their inevitable eclipse:

> The hour is come, the world's unclosing eyes
> Discern with rapture where its wisdom lies;

From western heav'ns th' inverted Orient springs,
The morn of man, the dreadful night of kings.   (159–62)

While he offers monarchs and their supporters a form of redemption, it is one they are unlikely to relish:

Driv'n to your last retreat of shame and fear,
One counsel waits you, one relief is near:
By worth internal, rise to self-wrought fame,
Your equal rank, your human kindred claim;
'Tis Reason's choice, 'tis Wisdom's final plan,
To drop the monarch and assume the man.   (171–76)

The *Conspiracy of Kings* then poses the question, "from what source the dire delusion rose, / That souls like ours were ever made for foes?" (189–90). Anyone familiar with his *Advice* would have known the answer, but Barlow proceeds to phrase it in vivid contrasts.

Not seas, nor climes, nor wild ambition's fire
In nations' minds could e'er the wish inspire;
Where equal rights each sober voice should guide,
No blood would stain them, and no war divide.   (201–4)

Instead, it is "Rank, Distinction, all the hell that springs / From those prolific monsters, Courts and Kings" (207–8).

They bid wild slaughter spread the gory plains,
The life-blood gushing from a thousand veins,
Erect their thrones amid the sanguine flood,
And dip their purple in the nation's blood.   (215–18)

France was the vanguard of a new European order: "On equal rights their base of empire lies, / On walls of wisdom see the structure rise" (255–56). France would

Renounce the wish of war, bid conquest cease,
Invite all men to happiness and peace,
To faith and justice rear the youthful race,
With strength exalt them and with science grace,
Till Truth's blest banners, o'er the regions hurl'd,
Shake tyrants from their thrones, and cheer the waking
                    World.   (261–66)

And standing behind France as the guarantor of a republican future for mankind was the United States.

Barlow referred disparagingly to *The Conspiracy of Kings* as a "mad Poem" because he feared with some reason that on this occasion his verse was superior to the prose of the *Advice*.[9] Nonetheless, he remained proud of *The Conspiracy of Kings* and felt no compunction about sending it, along with what became known as Part I of the *Advice*, to be republished in the United States.

In Europe, the *Advice* and the *Conspiracy of Kings* brought Barlow the official recognition from English radicals that until then had been only informally his. On March 9, 1792, Horne Tooke proposed him for membership in the Society for Constitutional Information (SCI), and Barlow was unanimously accorded honorary membership a week later. The next day, Barlow's translation of Brissot de Warville's *New Travels* became available. The appearance in little more than a fortnight of three Barlow productions made a considerable splash in Britain's radical culture.

Emblematic of Barlow's new status, he was appointed one of the stewards for a large celebration the SCI organized on April 13, at which Paine was the guest of honor. After Paine left the meeting, Barlow and Tooke were toasted by the assembly.[10] Barlow's credentials as a republican possessed of a fluent pen had won him admission to the inner circle of a leading radical organization at a time when it appeared to hold the key to the future. He probably also had a hand in the London Corresponding Society, which was trying to coordinate the activities of the separate associations and societies. After almost four years as outsider, Barlow had found an improbable home for himself as republican spokesman in a foreign monarchy.

Two courses of action seemed to be open to him that spring: to return home or stay in England to help transform the kingdom into a republic. There was talk of calling a convention that would, like France's National Convention, revise the British Constitution. Ruth also liked London more than Paris, primarily as a consequence of meeting Mary Wollstonecraft, who was in the process of putting the finishing touches on her *Vindication of the Rights of Woman*. She persuaded Ruth to take temporary charge of a seven-year-old Irish orphan named Ann, the niece of a friend, whom Wollstonecraft was considering adopting. Ruth had to put up with the child's chronic bad behavior, but she didn't mind because she at last felt useful.[11]

Going home would have required the Barlows to have arranged passage sometime in April or May if they were to minimize the discomforts of the voyage. Barlow instead chose to visit the continent, ostensibly for business reasons but also as a precaution against the British authorities persecuting him. The radicals suspected that repression was imminent, and Barlow's journey began around April 15, just before the royal proclamation against seditious writings and publications. Barlow set out for Ghent to consult with the American merchant James Swan, who had immigrated as a penniless, young Scot to Boston before the American Revolution. There he had risen to prominence as a merchant and a patriot, joining the "Mohawks" who had destroyed the East India Company's tea in December 1773. During the war, he prospered provisioning the army but afterward followed Daniel Parker to Europe to avoid bankruptcy and rebuild his fortunes. Swan saw opportunity in supplying the French army, navy, and the city of Paris with American produce and had unsuccessfully tried to interest Gouverneur Morris in such ventures.[12] Unlike Morris, Swan had signed Barlow's testimonial praising Jefferson before Jefferson returned to the United States in 1789, as well as the address to the Constituent Assembly before the Fête de féderation in 1790. Swan shared Barlow's vision of a pan-European revolution and had no scruples about associating with someone of modest means.

Upon his arrival in Ghent, Barlow wrote Ruth that his "bird [Swan] had flown" to Aix-la Chapelle where he "has promised to meet me." By the time Barlow arrived there, Swan was in Coblentz, a city on the Rhine roughly equidistant between Cologne and Frankfurt. Barlow was "vexed" by Swan's unpredictable movements but continued to heed his summons. The Duke of Brunswick—commanding Austria's Imperial forces numbering over one hundred thousand and including roughly twenty thousand French émigrés—had made Coblentz his headquarters after the Girondin government of France declared war on Austro-Hungary on April 20. Swan wanted to inspect the command center of the counterrevolution.[13] Francis I of Austria and his allies assumed that France had fallen into such disorder that a monarchical restoration would be a relatively simple matter. Swan wanted to see for himself whether by backing France he and Barlow would be choosing the winning side.

Barlow thought the declaration of war had given the French in Austrian Flanders "infinite pleasure—they see in it the prospect of returning in triumph to their country." Enough people in what is today Belgium spoke French for the Girondins to assume that the inhabitants of Austrian Flanders would rise against the Austrian king. Though the Girondins deceived themselves, Swan and Barlow nonetheless concocted a scheme for supplying the French forces with American provisions. Barlow's role hinged on his relationship with Lafayette, who had assumed overall command of the French armies, and, to a lesser extent, on Brissot de Warville. Brissot's *Patriote français* vigorously supported the war, and he was a close friend and adviser to the minister of finance, Étienne Clavière.

Reaching Lafayette proved difficult. Barlow was "taken up by the Austrians and sent back to Luxembourg" when only a mile from the frontier. Repeated attempts to cross further to the west met with the same fate, and he spent almost two weeks traversing the two hundred miles from Luxembourg to Ostend. There he boarded a Dutch vessel for the thirty-mile water passage to Dunkirk. As luck had it, his ship was first becalmed and then encountered a violent storm, which kept her three full days beating against a gale "within plain sight of" its destination. When Barlow eventually landed, he felt "as . . . exhausted . . . as on first arrival in Europe." By then it was May 20, and he was afraid "these delays . . . will be the ruin of every thing" because someone else would have arranged a contract.[14]

Barlow's arrival in France yielded little advantage since Lafayette was out of sympathy with the war as well as with the politicians responsible for initiating it. He sent Barlow back to Paris to confer with the appropriate ministries, aware that they were no more than window dressing for the committees of the Legislative Assembly, where connections were everything. By the time Barlow arrived in Paris at the end of May, he had grown pessimistic about his chances for success.[15] Both the politics of the capital and the armies on the frontier seemed chaotic. Gouverneur Morris likened the French nation to "Cattle before a Thunder Storm. And as to the Government, every Member of it is engag'd in the Defence of himself or the Attack of his Neighbor."[16]

Though the prospect for securing provisioning contracts was unpromising, Barlow still felt obliged to go through the motions. The forced resignation of three key Girondin officials on June 12 did not help. The resignations weakened what there was of the government and emboldened the radicals to fill the vacuum by petitioning the Legislative Assembly to suspend the king. On June 20 a mob invaded the Tuileries, where the king and queen were lodged, demanding that Louis choose between Coblentz and Paris and forcing him to put on a liberty cap and drink with them. Morris again captured the mood of the moment: "a great Part of the Nation is desirous of overturning the present Government in order to restore the antient Form . . . while another Part still more dangerous from Position and Numbers are desirous of introducing . . . a federal Republic," while "moderate men, attack'd on all Sides" were left isolated without allies.[17]

Though frustrated about the provisioning contract, Barlow remained optimistic about the prospects of the revolution. He assured Ruth that everything "was going better than you might think." While the enemies of liberty may have been heartened, the effect on France was "as reassuring as it was extraordinary. All France breathes only liberty, courage, unshakable resolve to vindicate the cause at any price."[18] Barlow never doubted France could defend itself against all of Europe. On June 18 he assured Ruth that the recent turnover of ministers was irrelevant since "bad ministers could not ruin France. The people are too aroused, and the army too well organized."[19]

The *journée* of June 20 proved harder to dismiss, but Barlow construed it as an armed citizenry responding to a higher law rather than a *coup manqué*: when "the people feel the truth, they must express it in their own way, & they always will express it by like irregular movements til they shall have wit enough to settle the matter according to the laws of nature, which admit of no king."[20] He did realize that Paris was on the brink of chaos, though, because he took steps to move George Washington Greene to London. However, Gouverneur Morris intervened at the behest of the boy's preceptor and while agreeing young Greene would be better off elsewhere, removed him from Barlow's "too negligent" supervision, arranging for Greene to return directly to the United States via Le Havre.[21]

Barlow abandoned his plan with Swan and left Paris well before the end of June, missing a showdown between Lafayette and the Legislative Assembly. Exasperated by the interference with his attempts to whip his army into fighting shape, Lafayette wrote a letter that was made public on June 18 denouncing those who represented "love of the laws [as] aristocracy, and their infraction patriotic."[22] That served as prelude for his appearance before the Legislative Assembly on June 28 to demand that the radicals be restrained. Morris wanted Lafayette to free Louis XVI from the control of the Parisian mob, but Lafayette had neither the will nor the force to do so, and he was actively blocked from attempting such a measure by the queen, to whom any fate seemed preferable to being saved by Lafayette.

The Britain to which Barlow returned in July 1792 was even more polarized than the one he had left three months before. Edmund Burke's *Reflections on the Revolution in France* now looked more prescient, while the expanding British associations continued to draw inspiration from France's quest for liberty. As the French monarchy reeled from the *journée* of June 20, many Englishmen who had previously been sympathetic to developments in France rallied to defend Britain's political system against a similar upheaval. They did so just as radical reformers sought to use the same events to increase the pace of change at home. Barlow knew that the British government had begun sedition proceedings against Paine, serving notice that future criticism would not be tolerated. Nothing compelled Barlow to remain in Europe to share its woes. If George Washington Greene could take ship in mid-July from Le Havre, it was certainly not too late for the Barlows to attempt the passage with a good chance of making it across the Atlantic before the equinoctial storms set in.

But Barlow's recent publications had begun to make him a little money. The first five-hundred-copy edition of his *Advice to the Privileged Orders* sold well enough to justify the appearance of a second edition in July.[23] *The Conspiracy of Kings* was also doing well, though its targeted audience promised less than the *Advice*. And then there was the translation of Brissot de Warville's *Nouveau Voyage*, which, even though Barlow wasn't reaping a pecuniary reward, was doing his reputation no harm. Though Barlow had initiated several small commercial ventures with other Americans living abroad, political pamphleteering offered a solution to his immediate economic problems. Writing to further the new order he saw emerging in Europe while increasing his income proved irresistible. At this time Barlow wrote an antimonarchical introduction and notes for a European edition of John Trumbull's *M'Fingal* that appeared later in the year and again in 1793.[24]

Mary Wollstonecraft saw Barlow as someone "devoured by ambition." She had grown up protecting her mother against the abuse of a drunken father and had stepped into the breach after an older brother abdicated responsibility for their siblings. She was drawn to the Barlows by their interest in having her younger brother Charles accompany them on their return to the United States. Barlow had encouraged her hope that they might even adopt him by clapping Charles on the knee in Wollstonecraft's presence and declaring that "as his wife and he could never contrive to make boys they must try what they could do with [one] ready brought up to their hands." Though Wollstonecraft suspected Barlow's "great mildness of temper" was more artificial than the expression of a "natural good humor," she went out of her way to cultivate Ruth because the Barlows offered a better prospect for Charles than she could.

Wollstonecraft grew genuinely fond of Ruth, but her estimate of Barlow never caught up with her esteem for his wife. When Ruth showed her some of the letters Barlow had written from the continent during the spring of 1792, Wollstonecraft confided to another friend that she was "disgusted with the *tender* passages . . . because . . . they looked more like the cold ingenuity of the head than the warm overflowing of the heart." Wollstonecraft also blamed Barlow for the couple's failure to depart for America. In mid-September she observed, his "thoughts are turned towards France and till the present commotions are over, I am much mistaken if he do not find some excuse every month to make to *himself* for staying in Europe." She sensed Barlow's adventurous streak would prefer the "alarms" of the old World to "the peaceable shades of America."[25]

Though Barlow had assumed the French monarchy was on its last legs when he left Paris in late June, it endured until the *journée* of August 10 brought it down. From his perspective, that event seemed like a reasonable response to the manifesto the Duke of Brunswick issued on July 25 announcing that Austria and Prussia intended to restore Louis's former powers. The manifesto also threatened Paris if any member of the royal family was harmed. The threat was construed as proof that the titular head of the nation was leagued with its enemies. On August 4, forty-seven of the Paris's forty-eight sections petitioned the Legislative Assembly to remove the king from his throne. When the legislature hesitated, an armed mob assaulted the Tuileries and took Louis and his family prisoners. Only then did the legislature proclaim his suspension. With the Constitution of 1791 clearly in ruins, the legislature called for the election of another convention to frame an entirely new form of government.

Barlow welcomed the Legislative Assembly's action because it provided an opening for another project that would be less vulnerable to English prosecution. This was a *Letter . . . on the Defects of the Constitution of* 1791 . . . (1792),[26] which he hastily addressed to the new National Convention, managing to complete it before the convention assembled. Though some might have considered it presumptuous for a foreigner to advise a proud nation on the design of its political institutions, Barlow "demand[ed] to be heard" (24) because "the French nation at this moment" had "stepped forward . . . to an enterprise which involves the interests of every surrounding nation." Barlow called upon the France "to finish as duty to the human race" "what you began as justice to yourselves" (25). Barlow felt the Constituent Assembly had neglected to resolve the basic contradiction between the "*equality of rights* promised in the Declaration of the Rights of Man" and monarchy. The only excuse for not abolishing the monarchy was the notion "that a people under certain circumstances are unfit for liberty" (35). Barlow countered that "any people, whether virtuous or vitious [*sic*], wise or ignorant, numerous or few, rich or poor" (39) would always take better care of their own interests than an aristocracy would.

Barlow focused on the "many vices" in the Constitution of 1791, "which . . . had their origin in regal ideas" (43). He assumed that once the mind was liberated from "the shackles of royalty," it would "assume a new and more elevated shape" and display "many moral features, which from having been always disguised, were not known to exist" (44). Purging the body politic of the last vestiges of monarchy would demonstrate that a government reduced to simplicity would not only promote human happiness but also regenerate mankind. The most important remnant of royalty Barlow wanted the National Convention to remove was the national church. He assumed burying the church would not harm true religion because belief in God was as "natural [a] propensity of the mind, as respiration is of the lungs." Laws "regulat[ing] the impression of the Deity upon the soul" made no more sense than laws "to regulate the action of light upon the eye, or of air upon the lungs" (47).

Next to failing to abolish the church, the Constituent Assembly's biggest mistake had been to "prevent the people from exercising the irresistible right of innovation" when "experience" had "discover[ed] the defects of the system. It is as much to these barriers" in the Constitution of 1791, "as to . . . [its] inherent vices . . . that we are to attribute the late insurrections of Paris" (49). While Barlow did not repudiate the distinction his fellow Americans made between ordinary and fundamental law, he felt no "constitutional code" (50) should preclude improvement. Instead he suggested that each legislature have the right to propose constitutional amendments, which its successor could then either accept or reject.

Barlow's *Letter* also recommended apportioning representation to population rather than to territory or property, universal suffrage for males over the age of twenty-one, and the elimination of the distinction in the Constitution of 1791 between active and passive citizens. Additionally, he wanted citizenship separated from allegiance, suggesting it instead be tied to residence. He argued for frequent elections to all offices and term limits to minimize the separation of interests between governors and governed. And he felt *"no more* [salary should] *be given for the performance of any public function"* beyond what *"shall be sufficient to induce such men to undertake it whose abilities are equal to the task"* (66). Representatives were not independent of their constituents once they had been elected, but they were also not legally bound to follow the misguided or ill-informed instructions from their constituents.

Barlow advocated several substantive changes in the laws as well. The most important was abolishing imprisonment for debt, but he also wanted the criminal code ameliorated and the death sentence eliminated. Finally, he recommended the abolition of public lotteries and standing armies and the liberation of all of France's colonies. Many of Barlow's recommendations went further than the American Revolution had, though not further than his radical friends in Britain. But there was one conspicuous omission. He failed to call for the abolition of racial slavery in the French West Indies. The omission is puzzling because he was

familiar with the antislavery movement in western Europe spearheaded by Brissot, who had been instrumental in founding the *Amis des Noirs* that had agitated
against slavery and the slave trade since 1789.

Unfortunately, abolition could not be separated from the governance of France's
colonial possessions and the rights of mulattoes in the West Indies. Brissot and his
allies had passed a law establishing mulatto rights just before the slave insurrection began in Sainte Domingue, allowing their enemies to hold them responsible
for ruining France's most important colonial possession. Barlow was reluctant to
enter that fray, particularly in view of the political difficulties Brissot had created
for himself by hesitating to condemn Lafayette's recent desertion of his command. Like Morris, Lafayette thought the future of France depended on preserving a limited monarchy, but instead of resigning his commission in the wake of
August 10, Lafayette had surrendered himself to the Austrians. After being offered
and refusing command of the counterrevolutionary army, he was imprisoned.
Brissot's response to Lafayette's conduct drew sharp criticism from the Jacobins.
Though they had not yet formally expelled Brissot, he realized that he would have
to seek election to the new convention from a provincial constituency.

While Barlow worked on his *Letter* in Britain, momentous events were transpir-
ing on the continent. The Duke of Brunswick's forces won victories first at
Longwy on August 23 and then a week later, in the wake of Lafayette's defection,
at Verdun. Paris now lay directly in the path of the invading army, and its citizenry
responded by inflicting summary "justice" on more than one thousand prisoners
incarcerated in the city's jails. No one then or since has succeeded in justifying
the mass lynching known as the September massacres. Among the victims was
the queen's closest confidant, the Princess Lamballe. The story that her body was
stripped, dismembered, disemboweled, and that her headless torso—wrapped in
her entrails—was dragged through the streets has been discredited. But she was
savagely murdered, a fate she shared with over a thousand others, and her head
was placed on the end of a pike to be paraded in public.[27] Barlow could not dismiss these reports, but he argued that the injustices of despotic governments
rather than the natural depravity of the people were responsible for crimes committed during the September massacres.

Any doubts these events raised about republicanism winning out over monarchy quickly vanished a month later when the National Convention proclaimed
a republic and French forces under Charles Dumouriez defeated the invaders at
Valmy. Though this was not a big battle by Napoleonic-era standards, it was as
significant in restoring the French nation's confidence in their revolution as

Washington's victory at Trenton had been in America's revolution. Barlow finished his *Letter* shortly after Valmy, when France's republican future no longer seemed in doubt. On October 4, 1792, he presented a copy of his handiwork to the Society for Constitutional Information, which subsequently published it. They also placed Barlow on a committee to address the National Convention, as many other British reform associations were doing. The SCI adopted the committee's work on November 9. Its extravagant metaphors bore the unmistakable mark of Barlow's influence if not his pen.

The SCI address hailed the National Convention as "SERVANTS of a Sovereign people, and Benefactors of mankind," congratulating them that the path now lay open for framing a constitution on "the basis of reason." The SCI claimed to "speak the sentiments of a great majority of the English nation." It invoked the myth that Britain had kept alive the sparks of liberty until "the American republic, like an effulgent morning, arose with increasing vigour." The United States had been "too distant to enlighten our hemisphere, till the splendor of the French revolution burst forth upon the nations in the full fervour of a meridian sun, and displayed in the midst of the European [continent] the practical result of principles, which philosophy had taught in the shade of speculation, and which experience must everywhere confirm."[28] The meeting that endorsed this text deputized Barlow and John Frost to deliver it to the National Convention in Paris.

Frost—an attorney of some means— had recently assisted Paine in fleeing to France to avoid arrest. In the process, he had made the acquaintance of several prominent members in the new government, though he spoke little French. Barlow was a natural choice as Frost's co-delegate for several reasons. The *Advice*, which Paine had delivered to the new National Convention a month before, had led to Barlow being proposed for French citizenship. Members of the SCI were also aware that Barlow was busy translating his *Letter* from English into French. It would appear in Paris as *Lettre à la Convention de France* before the end of the year. Finally, placing Barlow and Frost together underscored the fraternal connection between peoples of different nations. Matching Frost with Barlow may also have been necessary because Barlow was still not in a position to pay his own bills.

The two deputies departed for the continent on November 16 with a manuscript of the *Lettre à la Convention* and the SRI's address. The journey took a fortnight, ten days of which were spent at sea. Writing Ruth in Italian to avoid British surveillance, Barlow referred to "his customary torment from seasickness."[29] On November 28, Barlow and Frost appeared before the convention to announce they had brought to Calais one thousand pairs of shoes for the French army and that six thousand more would soon follow. However, the tender of supplies was not as controversial as the impromptu speech Barlow delivered to the National Convention. He claimed that reform societies were "now forming in every part of England, Scotland, and Ireland" and predicted that similar "addresses of felicitation" from France would soon to be sent to a *national convention in England*."[30]

The immediate effect of Barlow's rhetoric, which echoed the sentiments contained in a November 24 address framed by the British Club of Radicals in Paris, was applause from the French delegates. But his timing could not have been worse for the impact his words would have on British politics. The September massacres made all who thought the British Constitution still possessed admirable features tremble at the thought of revolution. The declaration of the National Convention on November 19 offering fraternal assistance to peoples seeking to escape the chains of despotism, following as it did upon France's advance into Flanders and her opening of the Scheldt estuary contrary to treaty, galvanized defenders of Britain's status quo. In the middle of November, the government ordered the Lords Lieutenant of the counties to have their grand juries proceed against seditious writings and began mobilizing a popular movement directed at checking the reformers.[31]

On November 20, an "Association for preserving Liberty and Property against Republicans and Levellers" met at the Crown and Anchor Tavern in London. The meeting adopted a series of resolutions that accused the reformers of seeking to "overthrow . . . the present system of government."[32] The resolutions claimed there was no country in the world that offered more opportunity to improve one's lot than Britain. If the nation followed the example of France by putting its "wild plan" of equality into effect, universal plunder would ensue, ending in "widespread poverty" from which there would be no recovery. The address accused France's "pretended philosophers" of murder and assassination. Britons should be content with the "liberty and equality" they already enjoyed rather than risk everything in pursuit of a chimera. Those present then resolved to foster the development of "similar societies" throughout the kingdom.[33]

The strategy of turning the reformers' techniques against them succeeded. Patriotic societies appeared in the major towns, passing resolutions and addressing the crown in ways that testified to their loyalty. Coffee houses that had previously served as safe havens for unrestrained political discourse suddenly became sites of vigilante surveillance. An indiscreet comment by John Frost on November 6, 1792, would later form the basis for a successful sedition prosecution the government launched against him. The counterrevolutionary movement also received encouragement from a royal proclamation issued December 1 embodying a portion of the militia to reinforce the authority of the civil magistrates against "riot and insurrection." Finally, Parliament was called into special session to protect the constitution.[34]

Barlow's unrealistic picture of a Britain ready to follow France's revolutionary lead contributed to the forces of reaction in Britain, but the government and its supporters hardly needed Barlow's extravagant language to elicit the loyalty of the average Briton. The authorities could exploit traditional prejudices against France and Catholicism to portray Britain's radicals as traitors.[35] Government repression—combined with the fear that they were sitting on the edge of a volcano of reaction—put moderate reformers on the defensive. Ruth advised Barlow on New Year's Day, 1793, that "everything evil is said of you, & I am obliged to avoid company not to hear you abused." Ruth was feeling lonely, vulnerable, and increasingly isolated. Her "prospect [was so] gloomy" that she wished she had returned to America the previous summer. Eight days later Ruth reported that Barlow was being attacked publicly in the papers and Parliament. Edmund Burke referred sarcastically to "the prophet Joel," accusing him and others of corresponding "with certain societies in France for the express purpose of altering the constitution of this country."

Ruth noted that a recently passed "alien bill would prevent you if nothing more" from returning to Britain. Not that Ruth seriously believed this likely since the English newspapers carried reports that Barlow had been "appointed member of the Convention for Savoy." She realized by now that his fascination with the revolution would make it impossible for him to leave the excitement behind, but the growing prospect of war with France distressed her. It was an open secret that after the conquest of Flanders, French forces under Dumouriez were preparing to invade Holland, a British ally. If war broke out, "what will you do with me?" she asked. Paris held less attraction for her than it did for her friend Wollstonecraft, who had crossed the channel to witness the revolution at first hand. Since Ruth had not enjoyed herself in France during peacetime, she could hardly expect to relish it during a war. A conflict would also make it impossible to return "to America with safety."[36]

The National Convention had been in the process of constituting a commission to incorporate the Duchy of Savoy, recently separated from Piedmont, as the eighty-fourth department of France, when Barlow presented the address of the Society for Constitutional Information. Bishop Henri Grégoire, a leading advocate of Savoy's annexation and the commission's most prominent member, invited Barlow to join it. The commissioners "are going to organize the internal government, & teach them how to act in forming themselves & choosing their deputies to the National Convention," Barlow told Ruth. The commissioners also talked about having the Savoyards elect Barlow to the National Convention. He was skeptical from the beginning about this happening, but he had no objection to seeing "much of the south of France, the city of Lyons, the Alps &c. . . . at the expence of the republic."[37]

Instead of campaigning for election, Barlow undertook another task for the commission. On Christmas day, 1792, he wrote Ruth from Chambery that he had been working night and day "to complete a pamphlet on the Piedmontese political situation."[38] His *Lettre addressée aux habitants du Piémont*, which was nearing completion and would be published in Grenoble early in 1793, was originally written in French—probably with Grégoire's assistance. It went beyond defending France's recent acquisition of Savoy to justifying bringing revolution to Piedmont.[39]

Barlow assumed that everyone would embrace revolution once they understood that all men had equal rights. Until then the Piedmontese had not been able to do as they wished because "the tyrants in your neighbourhood would have brought forward their armies of slaves to crush the rebellion" (319). But after France had become free and demonstrated her power by advancing "the standard of liberty" not just to the Rhine but to Piedmont's doors, things had changed (322). The issue now was not whether the Piedmontese could effect a revolution but whether they could afford to resist one. The court of Turin had to be overturned "and its powers restored to you, to whom they naturally belong" because the court had opposed France since the beginning of the revolution (323–24).

Barlow could not avoid the question of "*whether you will be benefited by a revolution in your government*" (324). He responded with a prolonged defense of the French Revolution, which put a far rosier gloss on developments than the facts warranted. Though he admitted that the reports of violence were "unfortunately true," Barlow blamed the acts on "royalty, the adherents of royalty, and the refractory priests" (333). The French Court had trained "in all parts of the kingdom a numerous class of men versed in every art of treachery and perfidy." Was it not understandable that "surrounded by traitors, and not knowing whom to trust even with the execution of their own vengeance . . . sometimes [an injured people] should assume the terrible task upon themselves" (334)? Barlow admitted that there had been cases where the innocent had been victimized but maintained that "these instances are rare" and were "chargeable upon [the Revolution's] enemies, and not upon its friends" (335).

Barlow was as much concerned with the defense of Savoy as the liberation of the Piedmont. His *Lettre* warned the Piedmontese that your "tyrants will represent

[Savoy's freedom] as a crime" (336) and try to conscript the common people . . . into the cause of defending tyranny against liberation by France. The Piedmontese should ask whether they "ought . . . to be the instrument of [Savoy's] destruction and your own" (337)? A Piedmontese revolution did not have to be violent. Savoy had completed its revolution without shedding "a single drop of blood" by employing the "force of reason." In doing so, they had tapped into "the sacred energy of liberty," which guaranteed "the moral attributes" of people who relied upon it (345). The Savoyards and the French would always be "the friend[s] of all people. . . . in [their] neighbourhood, whose peace and happiness" was "necessary to [their] own" (339–40). The choice the Peidmontese confronted was between continuing with present injustices or reaching for "great benefits." Whatever they chose, it would not "long impede the progress of liberty. Her cause is that of reason and God; she will not listen to any capitulation with despotism" (346). "What people can resist the hand that comes to break their chains?" (349).

Barlow admitted that the Piedmont would probably be invaded by Austrian troops under the pretense of defending them "against the French," but assured them that these forces would "flee . . . the moment you manifest your intention of doing your own business in a peaceable way." That was because the French army "is an army of freemen, the other [the Austrians] a horde of slaves" (350–51, 352). Barlow warned if "you . . . regard the French people as your enemies, and . . . meet their armies in the field, I shall tremble for the consequences" (351). For this reason no people had more at stake in introducing the new "pacific system" of liberty championed by France than those of Piedmont (357). He wrote this propaganda without any sense of irony because he believed it, to judge from his subsequent willingness to become associated with a scheme for France to acquire Louisiana.

Nonetheless, the disconnect between this *Lettre* and his next writing project suggests Barlow felt uneasy as political propagandist. Instead of campaigning for the upcoming election, he wrote a mock heroic epic of 369 lines entitled *The Hasty Pudding, in three cantos*, self-consciously separating himself from the tumultuous politics of the revolution, which he had just learned had culminated in the execution of Louis XVI.[40]

> Ye Alps audacious, thro' the Heavens that rise,
> To cramp the day and hide me from the skies;
> Ye Gallic flags, that o'er their heights unfurl'd,
> Bear death to king, and freedom to the world,
> I sing not you . . .   (1–5)

Rather than celebrate "the epic field" (10) of battle, the joys of a pastoral existence, or an unrequited love, Barlow sang the "sweets of Hasty-Pudding" (17) from whose "genial juices" (24) he claimed "All Bards should catch it, and all realms revere!" (30).

After reviewing the many ways in which Indian corn could enter one's diet, the poem traced its cultivation from planting through harvesting. The ripening corn encouraged another kind of fertility:

> High as hop-field waves the silent grove,
> A safe retreat for little thefts of love,
> When the pledg'd roasting ears invite the maid,
> To meet her swain beneath the new-form'd shade;
> His generous hand unloads the cumbrous hill,
> And the green spoils her ready basket fill;
> Small compensation for the two-fold bliss,
> The promis'd wedding and the present kiss.   (232–39)

Harvested corn promoted human fertility in still another way. Because it had to be husked before being ground into "powder'd gold" (260) and husking was a tedious task, young adults relieved the monotony by doing it together.

> Brown corn-fed nymphs, and strong hard-handed
>   beaux,
> Alternate rang'd, extend in circling rows,
> Assume their seats, the solid mass attack;
> The dry husks rustle, the corn cobs crack;
> The song, the laugh, alternate notes resound,
> And the sweet cider trips in silence round.   (272–77)

The setting provided the occasion for a game.

> The laws of Husking ev'ry wight can tell;
> And sure no laws he ever keeps so well:
> For each red ear a general kiss he gains,
> With each smut ear she smuts the luckless swains;
> But when to some sweet maid a prize is cast,
> Red as her lips, and taper as her waist,
> She walks the round, and culls one favor'd beau,
> Who leaps, the luscious tribute to bestow.   (278–85)

The husking ended with the farmer's wife making the huskers a feast of hasty pudding served in milk.

Barlow didn't write to Ruth about *The Hasty Pudding*, perhaps because he regarded it as a frivolous diversion. The poem first appeared in the *New York Magazine* of January 1796. Later that year a New Haven printer brought out a stand-alone edition. As Barlow's most successful poem, it was republished countless times during his lifetime and has been in print ever since, most recently in verse anthologies. Students of Barlow's life and work have judged it his best poem, but it was hardly Barlow's intention that a personal diversion from the pressures of revolutionary politics should become his principal claim to poetic fame.

Ruth was on Barlow's mind during that alpine winter. On January 26, 1793, their twelfth wedding anniversary, he reaffirmed his love for her in verse.

> Those charms that still, with ever new delight,
> Assuage & feed the flame of young desire,
> Whose magic powers can temper & unite
> The husband's friendship with the lover's fire.[41]

Barlow had recently received her letters, written at the beginning of January, about returning to America, and he warmed to the idea after receiving a communication from James Watson authorizing him "to draw on me for one thousand dollars at short sight . . . [unless] fortune have enrolled you in the list of worthies too dignified with intellectual riches to possess those of a humbler nature."[42] While Barlow had no intention of cashing that bizarre check, the offer conveyed "the reassuring idea" that his prominence as a republican ideologue in Europe had begun to refurbish his reputation in America. Four months later Ezra Stiles wrote to congratulate Barlow "upon the . . . Fame which your poetical and political Writings have justly merited."[43] Barlow's revolutionary reputation in Europe would lead his fellow Americans increasingly to refer to him as "our celebrated countryman," making returning home a serious possibility.[44]

CHAPTER NINE

The Terror

The National Convention began debating Louis XVI's fate before Barlow and Frost delivered the address of the Society for Constitutional Information but did not try the king and sentence him to death until January 16 and 17, 1793. His execution took place on January 21, initiating the judicial bloodletting for political crimes for which the French Revolution became notorious. According to Gouverneur Morris, Parisians had such mixed feelings about the king's execution that a large detachment of troops was required to insure it took place. Morris thought "the great Mass of the parisian Citizens mourn'd the Fate of their unhappy Prince."[1] But it was not clear whether they wept for the king or for the dangerous future his execution promised. A declaration of war by France against Britain and Holland followed on February 1. With Girondin backing, Charles Dumouriez invaded the Netherlands, initiating a war with Britain that would last for the next twenty-two years with only one interruption.

A worried Ruth wrote Barlow from London on January 28, 1793 to report that his affairs with Johnson "are all a wreck" due to governmental repression and popular intimidation. She was more anxious than ever to return home and announced her intention to take ship for America in the spring.[2] Barlow replied, "Leave before me to return to our homeland! No, never." He did not usually address her so emphatically and took the trouble of sending this letter in duplicate to make sure she received it. If he won election, which was unlikely, she would join him in France. Otherwise, they would sail together from Le Havre for America in the early spring.[3]

When he returned to Paris at the beginning of March, he learned that the National Convention had conferred French citizenship upon him. Barlow was one of three foreigners honored with formal naturalization (as opposed to honorary citizenship), just as foreigners in general became the objects of xenophobic suspicion.[4] He celebrated this distinction by becoming involved in a Girondin scheme for reacquiring Louisiana from Spain.[5] Barlow hailed France's declaration of war against Spain on March 7, 1793, as an auspicious preliminary to "the liberation of the Spanish Colonies." He saw the French acquisition of Louisiana, like that of Savoy, as furthering the cause of liberty. Now that France was a republic, a French Louisiana would secure "peace with our neighbours."[6] His enthusiasm for the United States and France sharing a frontier revealed how uncritically he viewed the Girondins. In Barlow's estimate their attempts to expand the dimensions of France promised to reinforce the nation's republicanism by diminishing the power of Paris.

Barlow's initial introduction to the Louisiana scheme was through two American adventurers, Stephen Sayre and Gilbert Imlay, who used the clichés of revolutionary republicanism to promote their own interests. In conception, the scheme owed much more to the Latin American visionary Francisco de Miranda. A Venezuelan Creole by birth, Miranda had been radicalized while serving with the Spanish army during the American Revolutionary War. He emerged from that struggle determined to replace Spain's Latin American empire with a continental republic. During the 1780s Miranda wandered, first to the United States and then all over Europe, looking for allies to promote his dream. After Louis XVI's unsuccessful attempt to flee his kingdom, France's political instability drew Miranda there. When, with the fall of the monarchy, defending the republic took precedence over everything else, Miranda volunteered to serve with Dumouriez. There he remained until Sayre, whom he had previously met, recommended the Girondins consult him about destroying Spain's power in America.[7]

Miranda's charisma and his view of the Spanish empire as a house of cards led the French government to instruct Edmund Genêt, the new ambassador to the United States, to promote such an enterprise. The impending French declaration of war against Spain led to further elaborations on the Louisiana scheme after Genêt's departure. On March 4, 1793, Sayre, with two French partners, proposed raising a Franco-American force in the Ohio Valley that would descend the Mississippi to seize New Orleans. They expected Spain's hold on Louisiana, Florida, and Mexico to quickly crumble in response. George Rogers Clark, who during the American Revolution had managed to wage wilderness warfare across daunting distances, had already been approached about leading such a force. Sayre's job was to arrange for the provisions Clark's army would consume, while Barlow would recruit French settlers in the West.[8]

On March 5, Barlow wrote Ruth enthusiastically about the new venture, assuring her it would "suit you my love much better & me too, because it will carry us both home."[9] But a Frenchman from New Orleans named Pierre Lyonnet, who had the ear of the government, questioned Barlow's knowledge of the Mississippi region and pointed to his controversial standing among those he was supposed to recruit. Barlow was not especially disappointed to be excused from participating in the plan because he was still uncertain about returning to America after the Scioto fiasco. In any case, Ruth's health proved too problematic that spring to make definite commitments and hampered her efforts to wind up Barlow's affairs in Britain.

Barlow was particularly concerned about a manuscript, which would evolve into Part II of *Advice to the Privileged Orders*, that had been left in Joseph Johnson's possession. He described it "as a work of great labour & of particular value to me" and wanted Johnson to have the manuscript copied so that the Barlows could take one copy home with them without risking its total loss. There were several other business matters needing closure, including a bond for three hundred livres "in French" and "endorsed on the back—William Playfair." His former nemesis, sensing advantage, had joined the bandwagon of English reaction in warning of the dangers the French Revolution posed, and Barlow relished the possibility of putting the bond into suit. Ruth was also to pack up all their possessions and deliver them to a fellow Yale graduate, Mark Leavenworth, for shipment to America.[10]

Leavenworth had been six years ahead of Barlow at Yale; his younger brother, Nathan, had been Barlow's classmate. Despite the heady idealism pervading revolutionary France, Barlow could not forget he was far from rich, and Leavenworth assumed increasing importance as his business partner. The letters Barlow wrote to Ruth during the winter and spring of 1793 repeatedly mention Leavenworth, with whom he shared the hope of profiting from the war between France and Britain. Barlow's straitened circumstances led him to nurture this relationship, which would remain important to him in the years ahead.

Fortunately for the United States, France's attempt to reacquire Louisiana never got off the ground. Its best chance lay in the Girondins' continued dominance of the National Convention. However, an internal crisis that began with a revolt in the Vendée and eventually spread to seven western departments eroded the Girondins' political base in the provinces. By posing a choice between chaos and the power of the central government, the crisis weakened those who represented the periphery while strengthening the Montagnards. The Girondins' first response to the revolt in the Vendée was to bring suspected traitors before a revolutionary tribunal that the National Convention established on March 10, 1793, but their timing could not have been worse. On March 18, Dumouriez, to whom they had entrusted the defense of the Republic, was imprisoned by the Austrians in the wake of a decisive defeat at Neewinden. After failing to persuade his army to turn on France, Dumouriez joined the allied cause.

These developments played into the hands of the Montagnards. On April 5, 1793, they proposed that the National Convention endow a committee of public safety with extraordinary powers to oversee the executive and thereby defend the revolution. When the Convention accepted the proposal, control of the French government began to slip from the hands of Brissot de Warville and his allies. In a desperate attempt to recoup lost ground, the Girondins had the demagogue Jean-Paul Marat, who had just become president of the Jacobin Club, arrested for trial before the revolutionary tribunal. Thirty-five of the city's forty-eight sections responded by petitioning the Convention to proscribe twenty-two Girondin leaders, including Brissot. When the revolutionary tribunal acquitted Marat, buckling to the pressure of eight thousand sansculottes surrounding the Convention as much as to the flimsiness of the charges against him, Girondin influence in the Convention declined further.

Realizing that a fault line was opening between the sansculottes of Paris and the rest of the nation, the Girondins tried to strike at the Montagnards' base by creating a Committee of Twelve to investigate the activities of the Commune. Their initiative backfired, however, when the Committee of Twelve was forced to release Jacques-René Hébert and Jean-François Varlet, whose arrest it had ordered, to head off a citywide insurrection. An uprising of the Paris sections at the end of May compelled the Convention to expel twenty-nine Girondins, thereby assuring Montagnard ascendancy. In the midst of such turmoil, the project of reacquiring Louisiana from Spain was forgotten. The Montagnards control of the National Convention increased markedly in response to revolts at Caen, Lyon, Marseilles, Toulon, and Bordeaux and was further confirmed by the assassination of Marat in July 1793. They were more than happy to comply with Washington's request that Genêt be recalled after his aggressive attempts to promote the reacquisition of Louisiana had compromised U.S. neutrality.

Barlow's reputation as a poet and ideologue had begun to win him entry into the cosmopolitan community drawn to Paris as the center of international republicanism. He became a welcome guest in the salon of Helen Maria Williams. Though initially it differed from the great Parisian salons by catering to a clientele largely composed of radicals known as the British Club,[11] Girondin leaders were soon frequenting it as a refuge from the rising pressure of their Jacobin opponents.[12] Barlow was now at the center of a world to which he had previously been marginal, though he could not forget this milieu presumed an independent living he still lacked.[13] A childless marriage diminished the demands on his resources, but the Barlows still had no regular income.

His new circumstances required him increasingly to choose between his former friends and the revolution. During the spring of 1793 he made a serious effort to return home, but obstacles besides Ruth's health intervened. Beginning in April the expanding war temporarily cut off communication between Britain and the continent. That raised questions about whether proceeding together across the Atlantic was possible. "If you cannot come soon, we must submit to the cruel necessity of going in different ships to America," he wrote on April 5, urging her to exert herself to the utmost. Shortly afterward he received Ruth's letter of March 26. It has not survived, but Barlow described it as containing a "refusal to come to me." From his response, it would appear she was worried about the disorders in Paris, the revolt in the Vendée, and the widening European war. Barlow claimed that "you would have been perfectly safe here" had "the passage [not] been shut." He also stressed how disappointed Mary Wollstonecraft was that Ruth had remained in Britain. Now that the Barlows were again contemplating returning to the United States, Wollstonecraft hoped they would assist her brother Charles, who had gone to Ohio.[14]

Before agreeing to return home separately, Barlow sent Col. Benjamin Hichborn to London to confer with Ruth. A native of Massachusetts and Harvard graduate, Hichborn had taken a prominent role in revolutionary Massachusetts. Subsequently, he became interested in a canal scheme to connect the Connecticut River with Massachusetts Bay and in 1792 undertook a tour of Britain and France to inspect the latest canal technology. Barlow predicted that Hichborn "will be one of the tenderest friends you ever had" and "will tell you precisely what is best to be done, & will bring you here if you think it best."[15] In other words, Barlow was sending Hichborn to fetch her. Ruth's consolation was that Barlow unambiguously wanted her to join him. His frequent references to Mary Wollstonecraft's disappointment over Ruth's continued absence were simply bait to which Barlow added a bit of gossip: "Between you & me—you must not hint it to her nor to J[ohnso]n nor to any one else—I believe she has got a sweet heart—and that she will finish by going with him to A[meric]a as a wife." Two weeks later

Barlow reported that Mary wanted Ruth to "take lodgings with her at Meudon 5 miles from town." Neither Barlow realized that they were witnessing the beginning of Wollstonecraft's doomed involvement with Gilbert Imlay.[16]

Ruth was right to sense that she was being summoned to France at an inauspicious time. Not only was the economy in crisis, but, as the Republic's military fortunes worsened, France grew more intolerant of the foreigners in her midst. On March 21, 1793, responding to a general scare about the presence of British spies in the capital, the National Convention ordered the sections to elect committees to place aliens under surveillance. This failed to deter Barlow from joining nineteen others associated with the British Club in supporting the effort to identify antirepublican suspects in Paris.[17] Barlow felt protected by his French citizenship, and his subsequent role in Francisco de Miranda's treason trial strengthened his conviction that his republicanism would defend him against the growing xenophobia.

Miranda had risen rapidly to the rank of general, but he had proven singularly inept in the field, twice ordering retreats that resulted in major French defeats. Before defecting to the Austrians, Dumouriez had ordered Miranda prosecuted for incompetence, cowardice, and treason. Miranda's trial took place in April prior to the launching of the Terror. Being found guilty on any of these charges would have led to his execution. Instead, he was acquitted by the new revolutionary tribunal at Paris. Ignoring the influence Dumouriez's disgrace had on the outcome, he credited Barlow with being one of his more effective defenders.

Barlow's defense stressed Miranda's renown as a republican revolutionary, claiming he had become widely known in the United States after the war. In addition, Barlow's republican friends in Britain had spoken approvingly of him. Barlow focused exclusively on Miranda's ideological credentials. He even invoked Washington and Franklin, assuring the tribunal that if they were present, they would give the same testimony about Miranda as they were getting from Barlow.[18] Thomas Paine joined Barlow in defending Miranda, but because he could not speak fluent French, his testimony failed to have the same influence. By focusing narrowly on Miranda's ideological credentials, Barlow seemed to extricate himself from the maelstrom into which French politics was descending.

Miranda's acquittal occurred after Barlow had reassured Ruth that "there is no apprehension of personal danger to any peaceable person here." Gouverneur Morris felt anyone who spoke against the revolution risked being lynched. Without a document issued by one's section committee certifying one's republicanism, a foreigner could not pass the customs barriers demarcating the city of Paris from its suburbs. Barlow put a deceptively positive gloss on events. Though the outcome of the struggle between the Montagnards and Girondins remained uncertain until the beginning of June, he must have been aware of the effect Dumouriez's treason and the turmoil in the provinces were having on the politics and economy of France. Under the continuing threat of foreign invasion and increasing economic shortages, the sansculottes emerged as the engine of radical revolution. On May 4 the National Convention attempted to control the price of provisions in the metropolis with the Maximum. This first step toward a command economy simply exacerbated the spring shortages, lending further support to Ruth's trepidations about joining him in France.[19]

Barlow's strongest card turned out to be the increasing repression of their friends in Britain. Paine's conviction in absentia for seditious libel in mid-December 1792 initiated a wave of judicial prosecutions. Frost, who had accompanied Barlow in presenting the Society for Constitutional Information's address to the National Convention, was tried upon his return to England. He was convicted, sentenced to six months in Newgate, and was barred from acting as an attorney. The loyalist Associations enhanced the effect of official prosecution with boycotts. Having to watch helplessly as many of their friends were harassed and prosecuted lent compelling force to Wollstonecraft's repeated entreaties that Ruth join her.

Though critical of what she considered Barlow's manipulative style, Wollstonecraft had her own agenda in summoning Ruth, of which Ruth had little inkling. Wollstonecraft was rapidly losing all capacity for self-restraint in her relationship with Gilbert Imlay. She may have sensed that her best chance of avoiding complete surrender lay in having someone like Ruth as a companion. Once she realized that the Barlows were not about to sail for America, she barraged Ruth with letters urging her to cross the channel. Ruth left London in June, presumably escorted either by Hichborn or Leavenworth. The surviving evidence fails to tell us exactly when she finally joined Barlow, but it was too late to rescue Wollstonecraft from her infatuation with Imlay.[20]

We know virtually nothing about Barlow's activities in Paris during the remainder of 1793 beyond occasional references to him in the correspondence of the expatriate Americans resident there. The most revealing of these is a letter James Swan wrote to Secretary of War Henry Knox at the end of 1793 after the National Convention had requested Gouverneur Morris's recall. Swan then described Barlow as someone "who in the highest degree has the esteem of all" and for that reason "possesses every quality that could render an agent useful to the United States at this Republic."[21] Swan's claim is backed up by the two likenesses of Barlow done

Joel Barlow (1793), by Louis C. Ruotte. In dress, hair styling, and pose, Barlow is represented as looking like any other republican zealot during the radical phase of the French Revolution. Courtesy National Portrait Gallery, Smithsonian Institution.

by French artists at this time.[22] But Swan offered no explanation of how Barlow had managed to win favor after the Terror had commenced in earnest and the xenophobic fear of foreigners had risen to the point where being an alien was as dangerous as being politically significant.

The most plausible explanation is that Barlow's growing prominence as a republican ideologue, though one detached from the more mundane issues of the moment, enhanced his stature. As early as May he had assured Ruth, "I meddle with no politics."[23] But during the last half of 1793, Barlow supplanted Thomas Paine as the leading republican author writing in English. After squandering most of his political capital in the controversy over sparing the life of Louis XVI, Paine turned to religion. The change in focus would flower into a deistic tract entitled *The Age of Reason*, part one of which appeared in 1794. Barlow still had political ideas he wanted to develop; in addition to two works published in the autumn of 1793, he wrote a revealing unpublished memo.

The first published work was a new edition of Barlow's *The Vision of Columbus*. In the preface Barlow claimed it was the fifth edition, though in fact it was the fourth. Why did Barlow go to the trouble of producing another version of a poem that very few people in France would read? An "Advertisement" dated July 12, 1793, stated that Barlow was offering a new version of the epic "for the sake of preserving the numerous corrections" which he had been making.[24] Tumultuous times placed one's papers at risk, but a couple of handwritten copies could have been equally effective if stored in a safe place Though Barlow had already deleted the dedication and more flattering references to Louis XVI from the London edition that had appeared six years earlier, after the king's execution he needed to deprive Louis XVI of all agency in the success of the American Revolution to protect himself against anyone using previous versions of *The Vision* to impugn his republicanism. In place of Louis XVI making an enlightened decision to nourish liberty in the western world, the 1793 edition pictures him as duped into committing France to the struggle by "Gallic sages" (VI, 29) who employed "honest guile the royal ear to bend, /And lure him on fair freedom to defend" (VI, 39–40), Barlow included *The Conspiracy of Kings* in the Paris edition of *The Vision* to underline his antimonarchical identity. Such a precaution seemed prudent as heads began to roll.

The Paris edition of *The Vision of Columbus* was notable in several other respects. As a reflection of Barlow's growing cosmopolitanism, France now shared credit for the success of the American Revolution with Spain, Holland, and even Russia because of Catherine the Great's sponsorship of armed neutrality. Barlow also acted upon the recommendation of James Stanier Clarke and William Hayley to shorten his poem.[25] All but one of the new edition's books was reduced in size, but because Barlow expanded his treatment of France's involvement in the American Revolution, the Paris edition shrank by only 406 lines (to 4,776), which the addition of twenty-seven notes largely offset. Many of these changes would later be incorporated into *The Columbiad* (1807).

Barlow's other publication that autumn was Part II of his *Advice to the Privileged Orders*. In the preface Barlow claimed that he had drafted the text prior to his departure from Britain in November 1792. That is probably only half the truth. Part II went well beyond the theme of Part I—that the collapse of the old order was both desirable and inevitable—to advocate a universalistic program for the regeneration of mankind through fiscal reform of the European states. This was the kind of proposal one was more likely to hear in the Palais Royal than in London's coffee houses. The basic structure of Barlow's argument may have been sketched out in Britain during 1792, but its utopian claims, together with some references to contemporary events, suggest that Barlow added portions to his earlier work at least through the late summer.

In his introduction to Part II of the *Advice*, Barlow claimed that Joseph Johnson had abandoned printing it in response to "the violent attacks on the Liberty of the Press . . . which took place about that time" (214).[26] One doesn't have to read very far to see why Johnson hesitated. The first page posited "a perpetual warfare" between governors and governed and declared "the real occupation of the governors is either to plunder or to steal, as will best answer their purpose" (215). Barlow distinguished between governments "which are called despotic, [and] deal more in open plunder" and those "that call themselves free and act under the cloak of what they teach the people to reverence as a constitution." The British government came properly under the latter rubric because it had "succeeded better by theft than the others have by plunder" (216). That was because her "people are more industrious, and create property faster; [and] because they are not sensible in what manner and in what quantities it is taken from them" (217). While Paine had argued the same point, he focused his critique on Britain while Barlow's generalities applied equally to all Europe's monarchies, whose extortions depended on foreign wars.

Barlow argued that Europe's revenue systems were intentionally enveloped in obscurity and would continue that way as long as "society remains divided into two parties" (240). The governing few would always seek to deceive the many because otherwise the many would consider "defrauding the revenue . . . not only as justice to themselves, but as a duty to their children" (241). Barlow argued that hidden taxes imposed on consumption provided the best means of perpetuating the fraud, noting that six-tenths of Britain's revenues and two-thirds of the revenue of ancien régime France had been raised this way. He maintained that such covert oppression would not be necessary if society were organized so that "there will be no aid or duty that the general interest can require from individuals, but what every individual will understand." Then voluntary compliance could be relied upon because each individual would have "a greater personal interest in the performance than he would in the violation" (246–47).

Paine was more interested in redistribution than regeneration.[27] But his distinction between "state" and "society" helped Barlow envision a stateless society that would function like a company of merchants where "every partner . . . expects advantage from the enterprise" once agreed to (248). Barlow gave this idea an additional utopian spin: "If the state consisted of nothing more than one great society composed of all the people, if the government was their will, and its object their happiness, the reasons for secrecy would cease, the intestine war [between governors and governed] would cease," and "an open generosity of conduct" might prevail (251–52). Only "the *improvident* temper of one class of men, and the unreasonable *selfishness* of others" stood in the way of regenerating the social order (260). Barlow attributed the improvidence of urban workers "in a great measure . . . to the government" (261), but he did not pin responsibility for changing the situation exclusively on rulers. Instead, he argued that the oppressor and oppressed were each other's victims and that it was the duty of the "middle classes. . . . to bring the men, who now fill the two extremes . . . to a proper view of their new station of citizens" (263–64).

Barlow's utopian proclivities had a distinctively Christian cast. Salvation was available to everyone because those crushed "under the weight of privilege and pride, or of misery and despair" were not beyond the reach of reason. They could be "brought back by degrees to be useful members of the state; [so that] there would soon be no individual, but would find himself happier for the change" (264). Barlow disposed of the problem of human selfishness with a secular version of grace. Current opinions had "been formed under the disguise of impressions which do not belong to its [the heart's] nature" (267). Past governments required the support of "imposition" because they had been established through violence (270). After bodily strength ceased to be relevant to war, other "fallacious signs of merit" had been attached to individuals to awe the common people. The two most common were "hereditary titles of honour" and "excessive attachment to property" (271). Barlow was confident "these things *will* be changed" (274) because "the universal habit with respect to" honor and property "has arisen out of unnatural and degrading systems of government" (275). "Establish government universally on the individual wishes and collected wisdom of the people, and it will give a spring to the moral faculties of every human creature, because every human creature must find an interest in its welfare" (276).

Barlow dismissed objections that his expectations were unrealistic by pointing to the example of France. Five years earlier no nation had been more obsessed with rank and wealth, but now both were of no account. Barlow was confident that the "same effect will be produced in other countries, by placing the government on the solid basis of reason, instead of propping it up on the tottering foot-stool of imposition" (281). Of course, he could not deny his argument was speculative and that many of his claims would have to wait upon experience for confirmation. But he was more interested in exploring "the *effects* that a general revolution will produce on the affairs of nations" than in precise predictions. He sought to alert people to "the corresponding change that will necessarily be wrought on the character of man; in order that, being prepared for the event, [one] may think of such arrangements as shall be likely to prevent [one's] relapsing into the errors that have caused so much misery" (286–87).

Barlow objected to funding systems because they "converted commerce," which naturally persuaded separate peoples of their mutual dependency and shared interests, "into a weapon of war" (289). Barlow admitted funding systems enhanced the ability of governments to pursue their political and military ambitions, but enabling "governments to hire men to slaughter each other with more than their own swords" was hardly meritorious, especially when "they wring out of the hard earnings of future generations the means of destroying the present" (294–95). Barlow argued that wars over commerce had replaced "religious enthusiasm" (298) in hurrying men to their destruction because high taxes rendered part of the population so "wretched" that "they are glad to engage as soldiers," while those who stood to make a profit from war could silence the rest of the community with the illusion that the losses involved could be paid for later (299). Thus commerce became perverted into an engine of destruction. So long as trade between different peoples was beneficial to both, no two nations were natural enemies. Only governments possessed of funding systems could "offer us more money for destroying our neighbours than we can get by . . . business" (302), and through "fatal deception" (303) make "enemies of our best friends" (302).

Arguments such as these did nothing to enhance Barlow's reputation among America's Federalists. Alexander Hamilton's fiscal policy depended on an impost supplemented by an excise. The latter, in the form of a whiskey tax, would set off a tax rebellion in western Pennsylvania, which the Washington administration repressed with overwhelming force to convince the British government that it was master in its own house. The impost had a more fortunate career. As the expanding European war made the United States the world's principal neutral carrier, the revenues it raised transformed the nation's war debt into a valuable asset, while the burden of funding that debt was scarcely felt. That would undercut

Barlow's claim that mankind would be better off if states foreswore public credit entirely. He did not deny either the existence or legitimacy of defensive wars that incurred debts, but he remained confident there were other ways to dispose of them that were more consistent with justice and equal rights. A footnote he had supplied for the London edition of John Trumbull's *M'Fingal* celebrated the role the depreciating continental currency had played in equalizing the burdens of America's Revolutionary War.[28]

Whether one approved of Hamilton's program or objected to it, no one in the United States wanted to go back to the economic difficulties that had afflicted the nation between 1784 and 1788. However, Barlow's critique of European public finance reinforced Republican ideological reservations about the route the nation had taken to consolidate the American Revolution. When Part II of Barlow's *Advice* appeared in the United States during 1796, it contributed to the widening gulf between the Federalists and the Republican followers of Jefferson and Madison.

Sometime during 1793 Barlow wrote a memo entitled "On the prospect of a war with England" that addressed the question of which European powers were the natural friends or enemies of the United States.[29] Since the memo opens with a reference to "the present coalition against France" and treats Britain as the leader of that coalition, the earliest it could have been written is the spring of 1793. The subsequent statement that "experience proves that a safe & honorable neutrality on the part of America can no longer exist" (1) probably references two British orders-in-council. The first dated June 8, 1793, authorized bringing American merchantmen bound for France into British ports, where their cargoes were to be sold to English buyers. The other, on November 6, permitted the seizure of any American vessel trading with the French West Indies. These actions led to a heated reaction in the United States that threatened to embroil the nation in another war. Washington only succeeded in heading off belligerent pressures in Congress by sending John Jay to negotiate with the British government in 1794. It seems likely that Barlow wrote his memo in the autumn of 1793 before learning of further depredations by the Barbary states against American shipping, which are not mentioned.

The other development dating the memo is a French controversy between the free traders—the position of the Girondins—and the mercantilists.[30] In theory, both French camps favored free trade, but the mercantilists wanted to use commerce as a weapon against Britain and to enlist the United States in that enterprise. Barlow's recommendation that all articles of "British manufacture" be banned from the United States (1) and that all debts due Britain and her subjects be "held as an indemnity for unjust captures made by the British on American property" (2) aligned him squarely with the mercantilists. He calculated the out-standing debt of America to Britons to be £3 million sterling. If the United States withheld that sum, "the stoppage" would "take out of circulation at least forty times the amount" and "overset" the English funds, whose credit was already shaky. In that eventuality, he expected "a revolution in the government would take place, and peace would be the consequence" (2). The memo also proposed a general embargo on all imports and exports similar to the one Jefferson and his followers would institute in 1807. Barlow acknowledged it would severely affect America's agricultural interests but argued that the harm would only be tem-porary and that the measure could provide a great spur to manufacturing and privateering.

In contrast to Barlow's later hostility to warfare in any form, in this memo he suggested that government insure privateers "for a moderate premium" so that "the successful enterprises would pay for the unsuccessful ones" (2–3). Under his plan he estimated that the government could have five hundred armed vessels fitted out within four months. "These privateers, aided by 12 or 15 French frigates, might ruin the trade of England, Holland, & Spain & Portugal, to the west Indies & to South America, in a very short time." Since Americans were especially skilled in naval affairs, their force of privateers "would be equal to four times that force sent against them" owing to "the immense coast not having any port open" (3) to the British. Finally, though the nation had no interest in possessing either "Canada or Nova Scotia," Barlow speculated that "both might be taken in a short campaigne" (3–4).

These ideas became the staples of Republican thinkers in the United States during the next twenty years. They assumed Britain was the nation's principal enemy and France its natural friend because Britain obstructed the free com-merce of the rest of the world. Barlow also saw Britain as ripe for a revolution, which he was more than ready to have the United States help precipitate. France as a republic was by definition stable and peaceful because its government rested on the consent of the people. Barlow was not dissuaded by the spectacle of civil war and the Terror because France was being attacked by most of Europe's mon-archies. The only obstacle to internal and external peace was the natural antago-nism monarchies bore to each other and republics. Order would be restored soon enough after the enemies of the revolution had been brought under control and no longer threatened the Republic.

The Terror only began in earnest after the Convention voted on October 10, 1793, to set aside the new constitution and institute revolutionary government until there was peace. That decision paved the way for Marie Antoinette's execution on October 16.[31] Two weeks later Brissot de Warville and twenty-one of his associates followed her to the guillotine. Barlow later gave a detailed description of Brissot's execution in an introduction he supplied for the second volume of the 1794 London edition of *New Travels*. Brissot said nothing on the scaffold, though he looked steadfastly at the other condemned deputies before he "submitted his head" to the "engine of death." Despite the detailed nature of his account, Barlow probably had not witnessed the event. Had he been present, one suspects he would have experienced difficulty in writing so dispassionately about it. Wollstonecraft narrowly escaped getting into serious trouble when she exploded in anger after stumbling into the bloody aftermath of some executions about this time.[32]

Though Barlow accepted the death of his former friends as collateral damage, no one felt safe as the Terror gained momentum. English subjects were especially exposed after the National Convention ordered their wholesale arrest in early October. The Barlows found especially disturbing the detention of John Hurford Stone—who had established an English language press in Paris that published the latest version of *The Vision of Columbus*—and his wife, Rachel Coope. Stone was a London coal merchant who had been part of Richard Price's congregation. Like many English radicals at the time, the Stones were drawn to France by the revolution and settled there in February 1793. In the early autumn, Coope had temporarily moved in with Ruth, who in turn was living with Mrs. Blackden. The Terror led women to congregate while the men moved around because it was assumed that "a family of women" would be in less danger than the men.[33] Though the arrest of Helen Maria Williams with her sister and mother on October 9 shattered that illusion, Barlow briefly found it easier to conclude that theirs was a special case than to face up to the growing danger affecting everyone.

The executions of Olympe de Gouges and Madame Roland in early November demonstrated one didn't have to be a murderer like Charlotte Corday, or a deposed queen, to be guillotined. English subjects ran a greater risk than Americans, but the execution of Brissot and his followers on October 31 made the close ties that had developed between the Girondins and people like Barlow and Paine seem like a liability. The arrest of Thomas Griffith on October 17 revealed that the French had difficulty distinguishing between Americans and Englishmen. Barlow signed a petition for Griffith's release, but initially it only succeeded in transferring him to a less crowded prison.[34] This may explain why, on November 23,

Barlow and Mark Leavenworth proposed to the Committee of Public Safety a variation of the original Girondin plan to acquire Louisiana for France.[35] Their proposal differed from its previous incarnations by offering to undertake the operation entirely at the proposers' expense. All they asked in return was the movable property of the Spanish Crown.

Had their proposal been accepted and the scheme succeeded, Barlow and Leavenworth might have been known in history for perpetrating a grand, strategic error. The last thing the United States needed was for a powerful European nation to secure a foothold in Louisiana. It would be a mistake, however, to describe their proposal as a plot against the United States, even though some in France like G. J. A. Ducher used such terms.[36] Barlow continued to view France's expansion into Latin America as consistent with the security of the United States because Britain, currently in alliance with Spain, was suspected of wanting to take over her Latin American empire. Reviving a Girondin proposal after the execution of the party's principal leaders suggests that Barlow and Leavenworth wished to signal their willingness to cooperate with anyone promoting interests they thought the two republics shared.

A month later, on December 20, Barlow and Leavenworth joined James Swan and Colonel Blackden in presenting an address to the assembly of the Réunion section of Paris that again affirmed the unity of interests between the two republics.[37] Réunion was one of the more radical of the forty-eight sections into which Paris had been divided in 1790. At the end of 1792 it had assumed this name as an expression of solidarity with the perpetrators of the September massacres. A year later the section adopted a patriotic address "to their United States brothers," to which the four Americans now replied. They implicitly endorsed the Terror when they declared that those "who had sprinkled the tree of liberty, which they had planted in America, with their blood" knew that the blessings of liberty could not be bought at too dear a price. "It was necessary for us, as for you, to endure the horrors of war; we too have seen our houses burned, our wandering families reduced to poverty, our fathers and mothers, our children and our friends have also been slaughtered to break our fetters." Now the United States was free. France likewise had succeeded in overthrowing tyranny and defeating conspiracies motivated by fanaticism and cupidity. The only task that remained for the French people was to frame a republican constitution. Once that was accomplished, the two nations would be bound in a perpetual alliance based on virtue against a coalition of tyrants dependent on crime and avarice.

When read to the section assembly, the Americans' address met with "resounding applause," and the meeting ordered five hundred impressions printed for circulation among the other sections of the city and the popular societies. This publication insured that its signers received the favorable publicity that was increasingly useful to residents of Paris now that the Law of the Suspects (September 17) officially subjected everyone's ideological identity to the scrutiny of the section committees.[38] How much foreigners remained in danger was dramatized on December 28, when Thomas Paine, Barlow's close friend and ideological associate, was arrested, along with the Prussian, Anacharsis Cloots, on an order of the Committee of General Surety and Surveillance.

Paine and Cloots proved to be more vulnerable than Barlow because, in addition to being French citizens, they were members of the National Convention. After his Girondin associates were driven from the convention in June, Paine had stayed clear of the body, though he cooperated with the foreign ministry's efforts to arrange closer relations between France and the United States. The man on the Committee of Public Safety most responsible for foreign affairs, Bertrand Barère, credited Paine with making commercial arrangements during the autumn of 1793 that would lead to significant shipments of American food the following spring during the period of acute shortages. Paine had been denounced when the National Convention voted to place the expelled Girondins on trial but then was ignored until December 25, when Robespierre demanded that the National Convention purge itself of foreigners. The convention responded by revoking Paine's and Cloots's immunity from arrest.

At the time, Paine's Part I of *The Age of Reason*, was being set into print by Stone's press near the Hôtel Grande Bretagne, in which Barlow had taken up temporary residence. Paine had asked Barlow to pick up the proof sheets from the printer as they became available, and Barlow had retrieved the first signature for Paine to correct. On the night of his arrest, Paine was at White's Hotel rather than his residence at St. Denis. Upon being asked for his papers, Paine claimed Barlow had them. When a sleepy Barlow pleaded ignorance as to their whereabouts, the commissioners repaired to Paine's residence outside the city walls, accompanied by Barlow.

Paine's arrest took place during the period of extreme de-Christianization. In this context, nothing in Part I of *The Age of Reason* struck the police examiners as particularly incriminating, and Paine was allowed to hand Barlow the remainder of the manuscript before being carried off to the Luxembourg Prison. Barlow subsequently helped see the rest of Part I through the press. Five editions of the tract would appear in Paris during 1794, but Barlow did not attempt to translate the work into French. Instead, he concentrated on trying to get Paine out of the

Luxembourg because by then the Terror had progressed to the point where the prison had become a holding pen for those awaiting execution.

Barlow helped draft an appeal to the National Convention for Paine's release, to which eighteen Americans in Paris subscribed their names. More than half the petitioners were merchants and captains who had recently come to Paris to free their property from commercial restrictions in the out ports. Neither Swan nor Blackden joined Leavenworth and Barlow in having their names affixed to this petition. On January 20, 1794, the National Convention granted them an audience to present their plea. They emphasized the role Paine had played in securing America's independence and expressed the hope "that you will not keep longer in the bonds of painful captivity, the man whose courageous and energetic pen did so much to free the Americans and whose intentions . . . were to render the same services to the French Republic." After giving them a frosty reception, the Convention referred the petitioners to the Committee of Public Surety. It would not get around to considering their petition until the beginning of March, sometime after the authorities cut off the visits Barlow had been making to Paine every few days. By then, Gouverneur Morris's inaction made it almost certain that the committee would dismiss the petition.[39]

Morris still officially represented the U.S. government, though he had retired to Seine-Porte, twenty miles outside the city, making only occasional visits to the capital. He responded lethargically to Paine's appeals for help. Even after Morris realized he risked being held responsible for Paine's death, he still did little. Paine remained incarcerated until James Monroe, Morris's replacement, secured his release in November 1794. By then Paine was so sick that it took him more than a year to recover. Since Morris had no more regard for Barlow than Paine, Barlow must have counted his failure to be elected to the National Convention as good fortune.

Everyone living in Paris during the spring of 1794 would be marked by the Terror, but not everyone bowed to its escalating violence. Henri Grégoire managed to defend his religious faith in the face of the powerful pressures brought against him during the height of the de-Christianization campaign. Unlike four bishops who renounced their ordinations, Grégoire refused to abandon his religious functions. Pleading freedom of conscience, he denied the National Convention jurisdiction over the matter. Though taunted in public and threatened in private, he remained firm. Grégoire had been appointed to the Committee of Public Instruction, where he busied himself reforming the educational system and refining France's cultural standards. In the areas of linguistics, iconography, and educational reform, Grégoire's high republican idealism could express itself with less danger of incurring the wrath of the Montagnards. Eventually, his reports about the dangers of cultural "vandalism" contributed to ending the Terror.[40]

Barlow pursued a less courageous strategy, but even it drained his creative energies. After doing all he felt he could do for Paine, Barlow announced to Abraham Baldwin that he was abandoning his literary endeavors.[41] Since the war precluded a safe passage home during the spring of 1794 and moving to England was not an option, Barlow refashioned himself into a man of business in Germany. This was quite a shift for someone who had made his name as an author and an ideologue, but Barlow could not afford to be idle, and the intensification of the Terror left no alternative.

CHAPTER TEN

Commercial Interlude

By temperament Barlow preferred literary to commercial pursuits, but in 1793 the commercial possibilities of France at war with most of the rest of Europe could not be ignored. Amid civil disorder and an economy on the verge of collapse, Americans in Europe saw opportunities for profit. They were already familiar with what the average Frenchman was just confronting. Americans had lived through scarcity and the political responses to shortages that made matters worse. Though most of the leaders of the National Convention realized that price regulations would enhance rather than alleviate commodity shortages, such knowledge was beside the point when the people of Paris were hungry and a swelling army had to be provisioned. Barlow's circle of American friends understood the connection between the politics of the revolution and the hunger of Paris's working population. Both profiting from and stabilizing the revolution added luster to a commercial venture that Benjamin Hichborn had invited Barlow to join during the second week in April 1793.

At the time, the National Convention had embargoed all English, Dutch, Russian, Prussian, and Austrian vessels in French ports, conferring an informal monopoly of France's carrying trade on American shipping.[1] The National Convention further enhanced the demand for American ships by opening the nation's colonial trade to them. U.S. consuls in western European ports trumpeted these developments, and Hichborn was not the only one to respond. Because American vessels were priced at the top of the market, Hichborn sought a British vessel — the *Cumberland* — that he chartered through Henry Bromfield. Changing the flag on the *Cumberland* was cheaper than chartering an American ship.

The *Cumberland*, loaded with rice and flour procured in England, was cleared for Bilboa in northwestern Spain, though its intended destination was Bordeaux. Hichborn assumed the captain would have no difficulty slipping into the French port since the British did not yet have the French coast fully blockaded. Hichborn's official partners were Mark Leavenworth and Daniel Parker. Nowhere was Barlow mentioned in the charter party.[2] Nonetheless, Barlow's participation in the venture was important because the investors needed someone capable of protecting vessel and cargo from greedy French officials.

The *Cumberland* arrived in Bordeaux before the displacement of the Girondins from power and the implementation of a command economy diminished Barlow's influence. It also arrived before the general embargo the National Convention imposed on all foreign ships wishing to clear French ports in August 1793. This embargo was inspired by a fear that Britain's increasing naval surveillance placed neutral vessels clearing French ports at the mercy of the British navy. James Anderson, the U.S. consul at Nantes, reported that the charters of vessels like the *Cumberland*, arriving during the spring and summer of 1793 could not be executed within their prescribed time limits. Embargoing foreign vessels brought trade to an abrupt halt at precisely the time when France seemed most in need of imports. Anderson speculated that the situation could have been avoided had the United States been represented in Paris by a minister more capable of dealing with the Committee of Public Safety than Gouverneur Morris.[3]

Local developments, however, shaped the National Convention's treatment of Nantes and Bordeaux during 1793, creating a situation that was beyond the power of diplomacy to remedy. Bordeaux protested the purge of the Girondin deputies representing the port and its environs and raised an armed force against the National Convention, provoking a military response that ruthlessly suppressed local dissidents. The situation in Nantes was more complicated because of the revolt in the neighboring Vendée. Nantes remained loyal to the central government but not without a struggle, and all the municipalities and port towns of the Loire-Inférieure suffered from the devastation of their hinterlands accompanying a widespread peasant uprising. Nantes and Bordeaux continued to be regarded with suspicion by the central authorities despite repeated protestations of loyalty to the revolution.[4] The American consul in Bordeaux, Joseph Fenwick, reported that the National Convention's deputies on mission had "very little knowledge of trade, [and] . . . all that has the name of commerce seems to be regarded as suspicious & selfish."[5] The merchants in Nantes proposed sending a delegation to Paris to appeal directly to the Convention, but Anderson doubted such a strategy would work because the merchants were regarded as counterrevolutionary sympathizers.[6]

In contrast to the previous spring, the fall and winter of 1793 through 1794 did not look like a promising time for undertaking commercial ventures. On September 29 the Convention expanded the Maximum and on October 20 created the Commission des subsistances to administer a command economy that would supply France's armies despite the growing shortages. Control of the nation's foreign trade inevitably devolved upon this Commission. Though the Convention amended the Maximum in November to exclude most international trade, the embargo on foreign shipping continued until March 1794. Ninety-two American vessels were immobilized in Bordeaux. While the Convention set aside 30,000 livres to indemnify the sufferers, that hardly covered their losses, especially after the deputies on mission insisted American vessels unload at enormous expense.[7]

Just as the commercial optimism of early 1793 turned to despair, Barlow offered to supply "potash"—probably not the potassium carbonate used in fertilizer and soap but rather potassium nitrate or saltpeter, of which there was an acute shortage—to the Commission des subsistances at Le Havre. The timing and nature of Barlow's proposal reflect his need to find other means of support now that political writing was becoming so palpably dangerous. In addition to the twin pressures of danger and need, he was drawn to commerce by James Swan's recent success.

During 1793 Swan emerged as one of France's principal importers. On September 19, 1793, he was paid 160,000 livres for thirty thousand barrels of South American salt pork.[8] Subsequently, he provided the Commission with a wide assortment of provisions, including wheat, rye, various meats, and vegetables like peas and beans, in addition to nitrates and hides needed for shoes and the equipages of horses.[9] The Commission turned to Swan because of his ability to procure large quantities of these commodities from Europe and the Americas. Through partnership with the nobleman Pierre-Gilbert Leroy D'allarde, Swan acquired connections with houses throughout Europe that were beyond the reach of other Americans in Paris.[10]

Barlow's initial proposal to import four thousand quintals of "potash" for the Commission was modest compared with the more than thirty-five thousand quintals Swan and D'allarde had already imported. As a bit player, Barlow met with less indulgence from the Commission than Swan did. It flatly rejected Barlow's initial bid on the grounds that he was asking too high a price. Barlow then accepted the lower price the Commission suggested on condition he be allowed to import additional items not covered by their regulations together with the privilege of exporting those goods should they fail to find a French market.[11] To pay for strategic imports, particularly scarce grain and nitrates, the Commission requisitioned wines, brandy, and textiles like silk. One might have assumed that its operations left little room for foreigners since it quickly established a network of agents abroad, but as domestic supplies failed, the Commission needed help. It eventually accepted Barlow's terms. Though small by Swan's standards, Barlow still had bargaining power.[12]

Contracting with the Commission not only helped Barlow launch a commercial career, it also gave him an official reason to leave Paris, a move that was crucial during the spring of 1794 as xenophobia reached new heights. On March 13, Saint-Just exposed a foreign plot to destroy the revolution by corrupting the National Convention and starving Paris. Two weeks later the alleged plot became the pretext for arresting members of the Hébertist faction on the extreme left and, shortly thereafter, Georges Jacques Danton, an influential member of the Convention who had grown critical of the Terror. A cowed Convention now fell under the Committee of Public Safety's full control, allowing Robespierre and his closest allies to streamline the revolutionary tribunal's procedures and to initiate the orgy of bloodletting that preceded his downfall.

Barlow was close enough to these events to realize it was time to leave. His contract with the Commission des subsistances together with the address to the Réunion section the previous December provided him with the papers he needed to leave the city without applying to Gouverneur Morris for a passport. In early April, the Barlows journeyed to Le Havre, where they visited Mary Wollstonecraft and Gilbert Imlay, who had moved there some months before. Though Le Havre provided the ideal location and spring the best season to embark for America, once again Barlow did not do so. This time, there was good reason for his decision besides the dread of seasickness.

France had succeeded in persuading the U.S. government to pay in grain the remainder of its debt. At the end of the winter, a fleet of 117 merchant vessels, filled with provisions, assembled in the Chesapeake under convoy of a French squadron that included two ships of the line. The fleet cleared the Virginia Capes for Europe during the first week of April, hours before Washington proclaimed a thirty-day general embargo. British intelligence sources in France picked up reports that as many as 350 vessels were involved.[13] An operation of such magnitude quickly became an open secret, and the British had no difficulty guessing where along France's Atlantic coast these vessels would head. The Atlantic ports in the Bay of Biscay provided the safest entry, but the political ill favor into which they had fallen and their remoteness from Paris pointed to a more northerly destination.

The British home fleet resolved to intercept the convoy as it approached Europe, and the French navy responded by pouring all its remaining Atlantic resources into insuring the convoy's safe arrival.

Both countries sent thirty line-of-battle ships to sea in the middle of May. Two weeks later they stumbled on each other four hundred miles west of Ushant, where between May 28 and June 1, 1794, they fought a prolonged sea engagement. The British claimed victory after capturing or destroying nearly a quarter of the French naval force. But the British failed to intercept the grain convoy, which arrived in Brest on June 12, having lost only one vessel to the perils of the sea.[14] The Barlows would have learned of the grain convoy from Swan in Paris and from Imlay in Le Havre. Outfitting France's Atlantic fleet had required such elaborate preparations that everyone in the outports was aware of what was afoot.

Barlow had good reasons for avoiding this naval maelstrom. If captured by the British, he could expect to be treated harshly by a government that was trying his radical friends for treason.[15] Nor would his French citizenship be much of an asset. At the same time, the grain convoy promised to create commercial opportunities in Europe because most of its vessels were chartered American merchantmen. The resulting shipping glut in the ports of entry was bound to complicate the procurement of return freights. American captains would need intermediaries who had commercial contacts, knew their way around France, and were familiar with Europe's markets. If the intermediaries also possessed reputations as committed republicans, they would be in a better position to reassure French officials that the ventures they were promoting served French instead of British or émigré interests.

Barlow was admirably qualified to become a charter broker. From the disgruntled American captains he had come to know in Paris, he was well informed about their needs. And no one was better equipped than Barlow to provide French officials with reassurance and to circumvent the bureaucratic administration of their regulations. However, the situation in France was too dangerous and the restrictions on commerce too onerous to remain in Le Havre. He did embark upon at least one business venture with Imlay, which involved exporting confiscated treasure and importing provisions. Because secrecy surrounded the venture, it is impossible to ascertain the extent or even the full nature of Barlow and Imlay's business dealings. But secrecy does not mean that their activities lacked official sanction.

Barlow's move to Hamburg was part of the venture. A letter Wollstonecraft wrote Ruth on April 27, 1794, shortly after the Barlows' departure for north Germany, refers elliptically to "some plague about the shipping of the goods . . . but the delay is not of much consequence as I hope to hear that Mr. B.[arlow] enters fully into the whole interest." This suggests that Barlow was to take the consignment of a cargo from Imlay in Hamburg. A month later, Wollstonecraft reported continued difficulties, describing Imlay as being "rendered impatient by the continual hinderances which circumstances and the mismanagement of some of the people entrusted with the concerns of the party—not to talk of the constant embarrassments occasioned by those whipping embargoes, that slip off and on, before you know where you are."[16]

After the Barlows moved to Hamburg, they lost contact with Wollstonecraft. A recent biographer of Imlay points to Barlow as possibly being a betrayer mentioned by Imlay in his correspondence with Wollstonecraft.[17] But suspicions based on Imlay's insinuations are suspect; at the time, he was in the process of betraying Wollstonecraft's love. It is worth noting that after Imlay's betrayal became known, Barlow urged Ruth to make provision for Wollstonecraft out of his estate should she be widowed.[18]

London and Amsterdam were the only cities in northern Europe that rivaled Hamburg as entrepôts. Amsterdam was closer to Paris and still comparable to London as a commercial and banking center, but it was threatened by the war. After taking over Flanders, France tried to conquer Holland. The effort had not succeeded, but as long as Britain and France remained at war, the Netherlands would be vulnerable to military incursions. Hamburg, as an independent city state, looked as though it was secure because all the belligerent powers benefited from its neutrality. American vessels bound for Hamburg did not fear being detained by British cruisers as they did on their voyages to France.

Hamburg had emerged as a commercial center because of its location at the head of the Elbe, the principal river draining the north German plain. Barlow understood the power of an entrepôt to attract local surpluses at the lowest prices because of the opportunity provided for exchanging those surpluses for imports. Additionally, the cost of outfits, insurance, exchange, and anything that a merchant needed to further his business would be lower in Hamburg than anywhere else nearby. For that reason Hamburg was an advantageous place for American vessels in the eastern Atlantic without return freights to make for and for Barlow to broker charters that could serve the French Republic. Large cargoes could be sent in neutral vessels ostensibly bound for Spain, though they—like the *Cumberland*—would make for one of France's Atlantic ports when the coast was clear. Smaller cargoes could go by coasters to a friendly port in the Scheldt Estuary or to Dunkirk. Or they could be shipped up the Elbe and then moved overland by canal and cart to France. Barlow expected France would soon abandon its command economy for the same reason America had during 1780 and that the relaxation of restrictions would enhance his ability to forward vital supplies to France.

Barlow's calculations proved correct. Though the machinery of the French procurement services momentarily tightened before Robespierre's fall, after Thermidor the government gradually relaxed its grip on the economy. Market forces progressively supplanted the threats, restrictions, and endless red tape that accompanied an administrated economy. The relaxation had mixed results. In the long run it generated new surpluses as producers responded to incentives to increase production. But in the short term it accelerated the depreciation of the *assignats*, leading to widespread suffering among the sansculottes. By late 1794, however, they were no longer in a position to topple any government that displeased them. Robespierre's demise in August 1793 had led to the banning of the Jacobin societies, followed by a dissolution of the section assemblies. Both developments deprived urban radicals of the power to do much about their growing privations.

The Barlows took an apartment in the Danish suburb of Altona during their stay in Hamburg. Ruth was depressed about being detained in Europe for yet another year "against my inclination." She described herself as ardently wishing "to return to my country & friends," but she had "nearly learned not to expect anything. I sometimes think my ashes will rest on this side of the water."[19] Her disappointment led Barlow to send her off to see Amsterdam without him. Before she had been traveling a full day, he teasingly wrote her on August 12, 1794, that he had "not yet found that schöne mädchen, which I promised myself" upon her departure. But Ruth was not to worry since the Dedes, an Altona merchant family with whom they had become friendly, were taking such good care of him that "I shall not be in a hurry to find the mädchen."[20]

Barlow's next letter to Ruth, on August 22, expressed alarm at a report she had become ill. He was worried about not receiving a letter from her, especially after Mrs. Dede and several others of their new circle had sickened. When Barlow wrote again on the 29, he knew she was making plans to return to Hamburg, which she did before the summer ended. Their reunion coincided with receipt of a letter from Abraham informing them of the deaths of two Baldwin siblings in New Haven half a year before. Lucy, Ruth's oldest half-sister, had been the first to sicken with a "putrid malignant soar throat [scarlet fever?], which for several months had proved very contagious and mortal." Her condition had not been considered serious until four days later when Dudley was summoned from Fairfield. He arrived the next day and because he assumed she was dying, he sat up with her all night. Two days later Dudley came down with a terrible headache. At first he "had no apprehension of his case being in the least critical," but three days later, "the doctors declared to his friends . . . that he was past all hope of recovery." Upon learning of "his situation," Dudley responded with extraordinary "calmness," dictating his will and a long farewell letter to Abraham. Immediately after completing the letter, Dudley expired, about three hours after Lucy had died.[21]

The news provided a depressing beginning to an extremely severe winter. The port of Hamburg closed for several months, cutting off all communication with America. Barlow, who seldom expressed reservations about any decision he made, wrote Abraham in February 1795, "I sometimes regret that I had not gone home a year ago."[22] He could not have been cheered by the arrival in Hamburg of the royalist refugees who had been chased out of the Low Countries by France's winter conquest of Holland. Many—whether former aristocrats or the surviving members of families which had been prominent during the early phases of the Revolution—were destitute. Counterrevolutionaries, who had managed to retain a portion of their wealth, spent the winter hobnobbing with Barlow's old nemesis, Gouverneur Morris.

Nothing dimmed Barlow's optimism for long, though, and the prolonged cold carried with it the blessing of good health for both of them. Shortly after learning of Dudley's and Lucy's deaths, Barlow received a long letter from Oliver Wolcott Jr. that gave an upbeat assessment of the progress the United States had made since 1788. "The speculative opinions which were maintained by most of your friends, when you left the country, have received additional confirmation" by the actualization in fact of the "most sanguine expectations" entertained about the new government.[23] Barlow replied that "men of information in all places that I have visited consider . . . [the United States] as the happiest [country] in the world." Both men hoped that the success of the American experiment would have a positive effect on the rest of the world, but Barlow added that he did not "doubt that the event of the French revolution will be such as to offer us much for imitation in our turn." "Many principles for the general diffusion of information, the preservation & improvement of morals, & the encouragement of such a degree of equality in the condition of men as tends to their dignity & happiness will certainly be established by them and will be equally necessary for us." Realizing that, given the excesses of the Terror, his American friends might "consider my head as turned with ideas," he acknowledged that "perhaps it is, and . . . it will be set right when I come among you."[24] Still, he continued to view France as the leader of a worldwide movement.

Barlow later claimed he missed having friends with whom he could discuss intellectual topics in Hamburg.[25] His disappointment was due more to his and Ruth's deficiencies with the German language than Hamburg's cultural resources. Hamburg had a brilliant musical culture, which Barlow failed to comment on. It also was home to many German literati. Early on Barlow met the German poet, Friedrich Gottlieb Klopstock. Barlow characterized Klopstock as someone "whom the Germans think as much superior to Milton, as we think Milton superior to him. The difference of opinion is doubtless owing to the badness of the translations in which we read the *Messiah*, and they, the *Paradise Lost*."[26] But neither man pursued further acquaintance. Instead, Christoph Daniel Ebeling, who knew far more English than Barlow did German, was the closest he came to finding an intellectual companion.

A kindred republican, Ebeling taught Greek and history at a Hamburg gymnasium, but his real passion was working on a multivolume *History and Geography of the United States*, and he was overjoyed to discover an authority on America so conveniently available. During the fourteen months that Barlow tarried in Hamburg, he spent many evenings conversing in English with Ebeling about the United States. In addition to answering Ebeling's questions, Barlow acted as cultural broker, advising him about whom to contact in the United States for assistance in completing his opus. Barlow wrote Ezra Stiles on May 28, 1794, about reviewing Ebeling's proof sheets in German, assuming that Stiles could find someone to translate them if the language posed a problem. But Stiles died in March 1795, and William Bentley, a Jeffersonian clergyman in Massachusetts, subsequently became Ebeling's principal American correspondent.

Few German intellectuals besides Ebeling were either able to or interested in conversing with Barlow, and Barlow had no desire to communicate with royalist refugees in French. He did become acquainted with an English political refugee named Joseph Gales, who had been the editor and publisher of a radical Sheffield newspaper. During the winter of 1795, Gales and his family fled to Hamburg to escape prosecution for treason and popular violence, intending to immigrate to the United States later in the year. The two families became sufficiently familiar for the childless Barlows to offer to take a Gales daughter into their care. However, the offer was refused. Though the Barlows and Galeses would encounter each other again in Washington after Joseph Gales Jr. became a partner in publishing the *National Intelligencer*, the relationship between the two families failed to ripen for the same reason that the Barlows never grew especially close to the Babcocks in Hartford. Newspaper editors were working men, while, despite all his rhapsodies about equality, Barlow saw himself as gentry. Nor was the intellectual stimulation provided by an English editor, no matter how ingenious, a sufficient substitute for what the Barlows had become accustomed to in Paris.[27]

Instead, they were forced back on themselves. Ruth complained, "I have not one rational female acquaintance here." Unlike Holland and France, where "in genteel societies they speak mostly French & some can speak English," in Hamburg and Altona one's linguistic choices were "high & low German." Language was not the only problem. Ruth thought the people, though friendly, were "overly fond of amusements. . . . they think every hour lost that is not passed in them." During the winter these included "lighting large fires, eating, dancing, skating, and roasting oxen whole on the ice."[28] Later Barlow would tell Ruth that their German sojourn had made him very happy, but he was speaking of the time they had spent together more than the place itself.[29]

Despite the forced inactivity of that winter, Barlow began to prosper. Starting with more knowledge than capital, he brokered ventures rather than directly investing in them. In addition to finding American vessels cargoes, he reflagged European merchantmen congregating in Hamburg, as his role in the voyage of the brig *Sally* (Captain Newsted) illustrates. Early in 1795 a British subject, Thomas Ashmore, purchased the *Sally* from a French owner, Jacques de Chapcaurouge. To protect the vessel from capture, Ashmore arranged for a fictitious sale between Chapcaurouge and Barlow. According to an affidavit filed eighteen years later, Barlow had been paid a commission at the time for both the vessel and its cargo. When the vessel was captured shortly thereafter, Barlow furnished Ashmore, whom he made sole agent in the affair, with the bogus bill of sale to protect it against condemnation in a British vice-admiralty court.[30]

Wartime conditions enhanced the value of a neutral flag by diminishing the risk of transporting belligerent property to otherwise dangerous destinations. By 1795, U.S. flagged vessels had largely engrossed France's colonial trade. There is no evidence to suggest that Barlow directly participated in that commerce. But with wartime freights running as high as half the value of the cargo, helping to raise the commissions and brokerage fees he could charge, it did not take long for Barlow to establish himself as an independent merchant in his own right. Before long he was loading American vessels seeking new voyages on his own account.[31] The only surviving business document from this period in Barlow's hand is addressed to Capt. Benjamin Parks, dated November 12, 1794, instructing him about whom to contact in case of detention by either British or French cruisers.[32]

Barlow was especially well positioned to take advantage of the waning of France's command economy. After the abolition of the Maximum in December 1794, the authority of the Commission des subsistances progressively declined. At the same time, the new U.S. minister, James Monroe, succeeded in getting France to grant Americans all the commercial privileges enjoyed by Frenchmen in supplying the country's needs. That gave Barlow more options in directly addressing the shortages in Paris that began to be felt in March 1795, in the wake of the severe winter. A few timely grain arrivals from Hamburg, taking advantage of the spring easterlies before the British resumed detaining American vessels carrying grain to France, as they did later in the year, would have laid the cornerstone of Barlow's improving fortunes if the cargoes had been paid for in hard money. He was also involved in shipping munitions into France.[33] James Monroe described his countrymen residing in Europe at the time as making profits "great beyond example."[34]

Despite his "pecuniaries . . . [being] bettered by coming to this place [Hamburg]," Barlow declared to Abraham Baldwin in February that he meant to "adhere to the resolution of winding up my affairs here very soon" and to resume his literary career in America. At this point he was toying with Baldwin's and Wolcott's suggestion that he turn his unusual experience to account by writing a history of the French Revolution. Barlow found the idea intriguing because it was "an event of such an extraordinary nature as scarcely to stand a chance of being treated impartially by its friends or enemies." He realized that while others might record its history "in a manner more agreeable to the generality of readers than that in which I should treat it," he "might perhaps be able to trace the causes of things with more coolness than some others who have attempted or will attempt it." One thing was certain, though. "I have done with poetry, since you have flattered & satirized me so much on other subjects I will try what can be done with them."[35]

A year later he attributed his and Ruth's failure to return home to his working "on the history of the French Revolution."[36] Barlow had started outlining the project during the spring of 1795. What is notable about the brief sketch he developed on this occasion is his celebration of the revolution's successes rather than its failures. He described the year 1793 as being "remarkable for astonishing exertions, & great disasters." The disasters he had in mind were the "great divisions in the country," compounded by the "proscriptions & massacres in the Convention itself," which alienated "the affections of one third of the country." What most attracted his attention about "this accumulated weight of calamities" was "the violence of the revolutionary measures." But Barlow marveled at them less because of their extraordinary severity than because of their success in mobilizing the "men & materials" needed for two great victories against the British: the recovery of Toulon and the defeat of an allied army under the Duke of York in Flanders.[37] In

America, the attempt of popular committees to mount a command economy had ended in economic prostration and military paralysis. In retrospect, Barlow judged the French Revolution less by the Terror than by France's ability to keep the standard of revolutionary republicanism afloat amid the chaos surrounding it.

The history Barlow pretended he was working on was more the excuse than the cause of his return to Paris during the summer of 1795. He was curious to see how France's revolution would end. Shortly after Robespierre's execution, the National Convention had begun dismantling the machinery of the Terror. In early December it pardoned the surviving Girondins—expelled from the National Convention since June 1793—and readmitted them. In February 1795, it took a step especially welcome to Barlow of making religion a completely private matter. No longer would the state prosecute someone on the grounds of what he did or did not believe. These developments could be construed as evidence that moderation was winning over extremism. As confirmation of that trend, the Convention appointed an eleven-man committee to consider alterations in the suspended Constitution of 1793. It looked as though France was at last following the American example of moving from revolutionary disorder to constitutional liberty.

Not everyone in France welcomed the prospect of increased stability. In addition to a royalist backlash that followed the relaxation of the Terror, radical elements in Paris yearned for a return to the revolutionary measures of the year II (September 22, 1793, to September 21, 1794, in the revolutionary calendar), especially during the perennial spring bread shortages. The National Convention had postponed trying some of Robespierre's prominent allies out of a desire to bring the bloodshed to a halt. When it finally addressed the matter in the spring of 1795, bread shortages were again affecting the city's poor as harshly as before. At the beginning of April 1795, a mob disrupted the National Convention during the prosecution of three of Robespierre's former colleagues, but no blood was shed. Rather than risk a trial, the Convention simply exiled the three.

The respite from executions was broken in early May 1795, when Fouquier-Tinville, the prosecutor who had sent so many to their deaths, along with nine members of the revolutionary tribunal, was sentenced to the guillotine. Two weeks later, at the height of the annual bread shortage, a riotous mob called for the Constitution of 1793—a code for resuming the Terror—and invaded the Convention. One of its deputies, who tried to resist the intrusion, was beheaded, and his severed head was placed on a pike and paraded through the meeting hall. Still, most of the deputies stood their ground, especially those who identified with the Montagnards, until a body of armed men arrived many hours later to expel the intruders. Even then the Convention was not secure from the sansculottes for several more days.[38] But Ambassador Monroe interpreted this outcome as indicating that when required to choose who should rule France, the National Convention or the city's radical sections, even former monarchists were prepared to support the Convention. Monroe concluded that the republican character of the Revolution was no longer in danger. Barlow agreed and welcomed the development.

Monroe wanted to enlist France's aid to secure free navigation of the Mississippi and a right of deposit at New Orleans from Spain. However, the treaty John Jay had negotiated with Great Britain at the end of 1794 cast a pall over Franco-American relations after news of Jay's "success" traveled across the English Channel. It did not help matters that Jay refused to disclose the text of the treaty to Monroe beyond assuring him that it was compatible with the nation's other treaties. John Trumbull, Jay's secretary, came to Paris and offered to recite the treaty's provisions from memory provided that Monroe promise not to disclose them to the French authorities. That condition was unacceptable to Monroe, who concluded the only way he could preserve his credibility was to be completely open with the French government. Monroe certainly suspected the worst long before he learned the treaty's exact terms from a Philadelphia newspaper in August 1795.[39]

Monroe thought Jay's timing in striking a deal with Britain especially unfortunate. It took place just as France had at last begun triumphing in the European war. By the spring of 1795 most of the monarchies in the First Coalition were suing France for peace. Barlow was as perplexed as Monroe to see the United States aligning itself with the British monarchy just as France was gaining the upper hand in the European war. Barlow's perception that a critical moment had arrived in the relationship between the two republics supplied another compelling reason for returning to France.

Though Barlow was not in a position to be a major player in the unfolding drama between Philadelphia and Paris, he certainly had no desire to remain on the sidelines in Hamburg, no matter how profitable his business dealings had recently become. He much preferred returning to the French capital where he might be of some assistance to Monroe in preserving the Franco-American relationship. Though Barlow and Monroe were not yet acquainted, Monroe had arrived in France the year before with a letter from Abraham Baldwin expressing confidence that Barlow and Monroe would cooperate in improving Franco-American relations.[40]

It is significant that the two men ended up sharing the same perspective about the strategic value of an alliance with France. Part of their preference for the

Franco-American relationship derived from the expectation that Britain was on the verge of bankruptcy and revolution. Both regarded Britain as weaker than the Washington administration did. Both believed forceful action by the United States, instead of producing a war, would lead to an accommodation. While Barlow advocated having American privateers join French naval forces to choke Britain's commerce, Monroe suggested seizing the Northwest posts that Britain had formally surrendered in the Peace of 1783 and even invading Canada. Monroe assumed the constitution adopted by the National Convention on August 22, 1795, would pose a more substantial threat to Britain—by example—than all France's armies. Removed from America, they were unimpressed with the way the new prosperity of the United States contrasted with its past difficulties and were far more prepared to risk another conflict with Great Britain than Washington, Hamilton, and their fellow Federalists were.

Barlow in particular had become so used to revolutions, having spent most of his adult life in the midst of them, that he discounted the value of stability. Instead, he was well on his way to concluding that revolutions were both desirable and normal. Short of living in the midst of an ongoing revolution, the next best thing was to observe one coming to a successful conclusion.

CHAPTER ELEVEN

Mission to Algiers

North African piracy had been a fact of life in the Mediterranean since the end of the Middle Ages. During the eighteenth century, the Turkish rulers of the Barbary Coast were constantly at war with at least one European nation. But the seizure of American vessels only began in 1785 after the dey of Algiers learned that the United States was no longer protected by his treaty with Britain. The seizures dramatically increased after a British-sponsored truce between Portugal and Algeria in 1793 gave the latter's armed vessels access to the Atlantic. In addition, the widening European conflict led a growing number of American captains to take their vessels into the Mediterranean on charters. By 1794, more than a dozen vessels flying the American flag had been seized and their crews enslaved. U.S. vessels presented a tempting target because the United States had no navy. At the same time, the detention of American seamen posed a serious challenge for the new U.S. government bent on establishing its authority at home and abroad.

On becoming secretary of state, Jefferson had hoped to solve the Barbary problem for less than $50,000. But the first two envoys he sent to Algiers died before they could accomplish anything. Responsibility for freeing the Americans then devolved on David Humphreys, minister-in-residence to Portugal. He failed to act before the Portuguese truce compounded the problem. When Humphreys sought a passport from a newly installed dey, Hasan Pasha, he was refused, creating a diplomatic impasse that led Humphreys to return to the United States in 1794 to brief the government on the situation. Congress responded by taking the first steps toward constructing a navy and authorizing the borrowing in Europe of $800,000. The money was to be used in freeing the captives and for treaties that would prevent a recurrence of the problem. Humphreys returned to Europe in the spring of 1795 accompanied by Joseph Donaldson, a native Philadelphian, who had been appointed consul for Tunis and Tripoli. Since the Treaty of 1778 obliged France to intervene on behalf of the United States, Humphreys journeyed to Paris after giving Donaldson authority to negotiate for the American seamen's liberty.

Neither Humphreys nor James Monroe expected Donaldson to be successful. Instead, they sought an American who enjoyed the confidence of the French government to act as consul general to the most powerful of the North African subdivisions of the Ottoman Empire, which at the time was Algeria. Humphreys's first choice for the job was Benjamin Hichborn. When he declined, Humphreys approached his former collaborator in *The Anarchiad*, Joel Barlow. Barlow quickly consented to undertake what he assumed would be a temporary assignment of a few months. Taking on the mission would allow him to see an exotic part of the world at someone else's expense, and while there he could assess the commercial potential of the Levant, an area few Americans knew much about. But Barlow might not have been swayed either by Humphrey or by the commercial potential of the mission had he not assumed that the French Revolution was entering a new phase of consolidation.

On August 22, 1795, the National Convention formally replaced the Constitution of 1793, whose implementation had been pushed aside by the "revolutionary government" of the Convention's committees, with a new form of government. Monroe thought ratification of the Constitution of 1795 by primary assemblies of the people and the army augured well for the future of French liberty. Presumably Barlow agreed, since by then he had joined the circle of Americans that formed around Monroe. France's improved strategic situation also pointed toward a more stable future. After Prussia and Spain abandoned the First Coalition, only Britain remained able to harm France. Britain would continue to pose a counterrevolutionary threat, but the decisive defeat in July 1795 of the large French émigré force the British navy landed at Quiberon Bay on the Bay of Biscay coast underscored the limits of British power. Her only continental ally of note, Austria, had fared badly during three years of hostilities, losing Flanders and having her armies pushed east of the Rhine. Nor was Britain likely to recover her former influence in the Low Countries after a revolution in Holland installed a regime beholden to France. Everything seemed to suggest that France would stabilize her republican government.

Throughout the autumn of 1795 Barlow spent 162,570 livres, or about thirty thousand 1795 dollars, purchasing presents that were considered indispensable when dealing with the North African potentates.[1] To judge from references in his subsequent correspondence, several trading ventures that he had initiated in Hamburg also commanded his attention. His history of the French Revolution would probably have taken a back seat to commerce even if diplomacy had not intruded.

Though the excitement Barlow had been used to in Paris was visibly on the wane—he had missed the most intense phase of the white terror during the first half of 1795—France's transition from a revolutionary to a constitutional government still faced significant hurdles. One problem was the constitutional requirement that two-thirds of the members of the new bicameral legislature come from the expiring National Convention. Reactionary elements in and around Paris used this requirement to stir up riots in early October just before the legislative elections were scheduled to begin, but Napoleon Bonaparte successfully defended the Convention with his artillery, and the elections proceeded without difficulty.

After the elections, the National Convention adjourned at the end of October, leaving France without any national government for the better part of a week. But no one tried to take advantage of the interregnum before the five-man executive known as the Directory convened for the first time on November 3. The smoothness of the transition signaled that the new regime would manage the challenges it faced more effectively than had the revolutionary government of the past three years. One such challenge was the continued depreciation of the *assignats*. On December 10, 1795, the Directory opened a 600-million livre "hard money" loan subscribable in either silver, gold, grain, or *assignats* valued at 100:1 at the discretion of the lender. Since the new government lacked any solid resources with which to fund such a debt, it became a forced loan levied on the wealthy, which ultimately failed.[2]

Initially, as Barlow was preparing to depart for Marseilles, the loan briefly revived confidence in the finances of the Republic and impelled him to register as a creditor of the state by acquiring what were referred to as "inscriptions" to the consolidated debt of France. Because they were negotiable, a market for "inscriptions" developed almost immediately. But since the government still had nothing with which to pay interest on their face value, they passed well below par. Only in 1797, after the government began to go through the motions of paying interest on this debt, would the market for "inscriptions" become active enough to make the pages of the *Moniteur*. Barlow was not especially worried about his "inscriptions" during 1796 because, having ventured little of real value, little would be lost. But he continued to believe that someday they would appreciate as the American revolutionary debt had appreciated between 1787 and 1792.[3]

Barlow also purchased two income-producing properties in Paris at this time. The confiscated estates of émigrés and the church constituted over ten percent of the city's real property, and once the government started selling these assets, they depressed the price of Parisian real estate. A government experiment in May 1795, which dispensed with auctions and disposed of national properties for overvalued *assignats* at four times the property's annual earnings, had stimulated a frenzy of buying. Barlow had not been around to capitalize on this brief give-away. However, the anemic real estate market still made his purchases good investments despite Ruth's refusal to live in either of them. She did not enjoy domestic duties and preferred to occupy rooms in a pension inhabited by other Americans. The rent from the investment properties, which the banker Jacques Récamier was directed to collect, would provide a steady though modest income that supported Ruth in the manner she preferred during Barlow's absence.[4] The optimistic claims Barlow made in 1796 about his wealth were based largely on his assumption that the inscriptions and his real estate would appreciate in value.

Shortly after Barlow agreed to go to Algiers, Humphreys and Monroe learned that Donaldson had negotiated a treaty with Hasan Pasha for freeing the enslaved Americans in exchange for a $642,000 ransom and the commitment to pay an annual tribute of slightly more than $20,000 in naval stores. Donaldson's unexpected success raised questions about Barlow's mission. But the progress Barlow had made with purchasing presents and Humphreys's skepticism about whether Donaldson had fully solved the problem led Barlow to continue his purchases. Someone would still be needed in Algiers after Donaldson moved on to Tunis and Tripoli. When the purchases were completed, Barlow agreed to go to Alicente in Spain to await further instructions from Humphreys. Alicente was the nearest port to Algiers on the European coast, as well as the best place for Barlow to receive communications from Humphreys, who had departed for Madrid.

Barlow did not succeed in moving himself and the gifts to Marseilles until the beginning of 1796. Part of the delay was attributable to the damage the Revolution had inflicted upon France's transportation system. The system of public stages that would have allowed Barlow to maintain a constant speed over good roads had collapsed as a consequence of six years of neglected maintenance. Added to that were the complications of traveling in the winter with the presents. Most of them were packed in a large, locked trunk that Barlow referred to as "a cow." That was his way of saying the trunk would slow his progress as much as a milk cow attached

to a horse-drawn cart would. The presents made the special carriage he had purchased to transport them top heavy, which precluded proceeding at more than a
walk. In addition, the threat of brigandage required an armed escort. Barlow set
out from Paris for Lyons, less than two hundred miles distant, on Christmas Day
1795, but did not arrive there until the thirty-first. In other words, he made less
than thirty miles each day. Barlow's repeated references to the "cow" in his letters
to Ruth were intended to distract her from the possibility that his journey could
be interrupted by highwaymen or guerrilla bands hostile to the Directory more
than to explain his rate of progress.

The least secure portion of his route that winter was the road from Lyon to
Marseilles.[5] Barlow finessed the hazard by putting his carriage and "cow" on a
"barque de poste" to descend the Rhône to Avignon. He covered three-quarters of
the remaining distance to Marseilles by water. Traveling by water only shaved a
day off the journey, but floating down a major river was safer and gave him a
chance to view the Roman ruins along the way. Barlow was especially impressed
with the Roman wall surrounding Avignon, but he also enjoyed the vistas of the
snow-covered Alps to the east. From Avignon he proceeded by land over the remaining forty miles via Aix-en-Provence, arriving in Marseilles on January 3.

Barlow expected to find a letter from Ruth waiting for him because the mail
still moved faster than he could. Though a letter Robert Lyle wrote in Paris on the
twenty-ninth had arrived, he found no word from Ruth, despite his request that
she write him each day. This turned out to be his fault because he had forgotten
to tell her how to address her letters. He had also left behind the keys to the "cow."
When she finally received his first letter from Lyons on January 6, she dashed off
a quick note enclosing the keys in a packet.[6] She worried lest they fail to arrive in
Marseilles before Barlow departed for Alicante. She need not have fretted; it took
Barlow eighteen days to find a suitable American vessel to charter for the voyage.

Barlow did not waste the time spent in Marseilles. He was fascinated by the
history of the port, whose Phoenician antiquity trumped the Roman ruins he had
recently seen. He also used the delay to interview Algerians he encountered there,
even visiting the lazaretto where the crews of vessels arriving from North Africa
were quarantined for forty days to make sure they were free of contagious diseases.
Marseilles was a principal port of entry for the North African trade and, after losing
forty thousand inhabitants to a plague in 1720, it had constructed what was considered the finest lazaretto in Europe. Its multiple structures could accommodate
as many as five hundred detainees within a walled enclosure roughly a quarter-
mile on each side, situated just beyond the city boundaries. It also was accessible
from the sea so that both crews and cargoes could be easily quarantined.[7]

Barlow thought the Algerians he met frank and likable, but they supplied him with misleading reports about Hasan Pasha, whom they described as "a most kindly, affable man, upright in his behavior to perfection."[8] One cannot help suspecting that Barlow's informants were indulging in ironies that were lost on him and that he fell prey to the kind of joke he so often liked to play on others. When he finally got to Algiers, Barlow found Hasan to be a capricious tyrant drunk with power and greed, and given to sexually exploiting young male captives.[9] Though Barlow's French was certainly up to detecting nuances, his innocent friendliness may have invited the deception, or he may simply have misunderstood the sailor's lingua franca, which was then the common tongue of the Mediterranean.

Barlow also used his time in Marseilles to explore business prospects in North Africa.[10] He made inquiries about trading in military stores, only to find this line of commerce was already engrossed by the Bacri Brothers. Joseph Coen Bacri, who represented the house in Marseilles, said he wanted to help Barlow establish himself in the Algerian trade, but Barlow suspected the Bacris really meant to exclude him from it. Their house later became a major trading partner of Barlow's, and Micayo Bacri, the head of the house in Algiers and the dey's most important adviser, provided assistance of incalculable value during Barlow's residence there. Barlow's initial suspicions about the Jewish Bacris, on whom he would come to depend, contrasts strongly with his naiveté about Algerians. What looks like religious prejudice may instead have reflected an ideological bias in favor of the opinions of common people. Still, allowing American assumptions to influence his attempt to understand an alien culture was not useful. During his stay in Marseilles, Barlow only initiated one small venture with Stephen Cathalan, a Frenchman serving as U.S. consul there.

The absence of any letters from Ruth made Barlow's time weigh heavily on him. What made her silence especially puzzling was the mail he was getting from his other friends in Paris. One of these correspondents, Konrad Oelsner, reported that Ruth felt abandoned. Barlow responded by supplying Ruth with elaborate explanations about why he had not brought her along. These ranged from not wanting to give the Algerians the impression that he intended to stay for any length of time, to the difficulties of winter travel, where bad roads were made worse by the weather and forage was expensive and difficult to find. But her continued silence unnerved him. Eventually, he suggested that when the roads improved and forage became more plentiful, she might join him in Marseilles. He had raised that possibility before he departed, and Humphreys had yet to signal that he should proceed to Algiers.[11] She could make the journey south in the spring after the Directory brought order to the countryside. Short of that contingency, he discouraged her from following him by stressing the difficulties he had just encountered.

When the vessel he had chartered finally departed Marseilles at the end of January, it encountered severe headwinds as it approached the coast of Spain. Barlow managed to disembark, "fortunately for my poor stomach," and to proceed the rest of the way by land.[12] The Spanish roads could only be negotiated by mules, as the weather turned them into mud tracks. It took him thirteen days to complete his journey, during which time he had to seek accommodation in flea-ridden hostels. Still, he reached Alicante well before the vessel carrying the "cow" arrived.

Philip Sloan, an American who had been held in Algerian captivity since 1791, was waiting for him there. The previous November, Hasan Pasha had dispatched another veteran captive, Capt. Richard O'Brien, to Lisbon with a copy of the treaty Donaldson had signed. O'Brien was supposed to return with the ransom money, and when he failed to do so, the dey had sent Sloan to Alicante to find out what had happened. Sloan told Barlow that though the agreement specified no date by which its terms were to be fulfilled, an informal understanding existed that the money would be paid within three months. Sloan also reported that when he left Algiers at the beginning of January, the dey was so irritated by delays that Sloan felt it was unwise for any American to go to Algiers without the ransom.

The best hope for assembling the required sums was Humphreys, who had authority to draw on British bankers for the full amount. However, no one in Lisbon was interested in exchanging $650,000 in specie for bills on London. Humphreys had to send O'Brien directly to London for the money. After he arrived, contrary winds cut off all communication between Portugal and Britain for the remainder of the winter. Barlow remained unaware of the difficulties with which Humphreys and O'Brien were struggling.

Barlow was much better informed about developments in North Africa. A report that Britain and Hasan Pasha had come to a new understanding made Barlow fear for the consequences if Donaldson's treaty came apart because he suspected the dey had only made peace with Donaldson to spite Britain. Barlow's anxiety increased when he learned of the dey's insistence that the British consul, who had arranged the truce between Portugal and Algeria in 1793, return to Algiers. Simultaneously, an American vessel from Boston arrived at Alicente on the strength of a report that a peace with Algeria had been concluded. That suggested the Mediterranean would soon be flooded with American vessels, making them tempting targets for the dey to prey on and compounding the problems the United States faced in redeeming its captive seamen.

Barlow now made the first of several unauthorized decisions that were to become routine during his Algerian mission. He decided that Donaldson's treaty was in danger of failing and that it was in the nation's interest to save it. Since the dey considered the absence of a treaty the equivalent of war, Barlow chose to proceed to Algiers. The decision entailed another sea passage, during which he met with the same misfortune that had dogged most of his maritime excursions. Though the passage began with a favorable breeze that should have brought him quickly to Algiers, the wind changed during the first night into "a terrible storm" that carried away one of the ship's masts with its sails. Only after being tossed about for three days did the vessel finally make Algiers on March 3.[13]

Barlow was too weak to disembark. It took him twenty-four hours to recover from the most violent seasickness he had ever experienced, and he did not set foot on North African soil until the fifth. Then he learned that Hasan Pasha would not receive him. Donaldson explained that since Sloan had been ordered to bring back the ransom money, the dey declined to deal with anyone else. Barlow also learned that the captive Americans—whose condition had temporarily improved after Donaldson had negotiated his treaty—would be plunged back into degrading servitude if the treaty's terms were not soon fulfilled.

Sloan proved reluctant to return to Algiers, despite repeated summons by Barlow and Donaldson. Only at the end of March did he at last obey despite being empty-handed. When on April 3, 1796, Barlow, accompanied by Donaldson, finally got an interview with Hasan Pasha, they confronted an enraged despot who informed them that they had only eight days in which to produce the money before they would be dismissed, followed by war after a customary thirty-day interval. Barlow felt especially vulnerable because it was clear the other European powers represented in Algiers would be pleased to have the United States become the dey's next victim. In his desperation to save Donaldson's treaty, Barlow offered Hasan a twenty-gun American-built frigate. That again exposed him to having his actions repudiated because he had acted without authorization. His only consolation was that the dey responded positively to the idea, though he raised the ante by insisting on a frigate of thirty-six guns.

Since Hasan Pasha routinely threatened anyone who crossed him with being placed in chains and a declaration of war against the country he represented, it must have crossed Barlow's mind that he might fare here about as well as his Girondin friends had in France. During the previous century, several European consuls had been murdered by the Algerians.[14] He did not enjoy having placed himself at the mercy of both the dey and the American government in trying to bridge the gap between them. Of the two, his own government was more amenable to persuasion, which is why Barlow labored so hard in the following month to justify to Secretary of State Timothy Pickering, to Monroe, and to Humphreys the offer he had made to Hasan Pasha.

To justify his decision, for which he assumed full responsibility, Barlow invoked the prospect of the captive American sailors being subjected to further disgrace and cruelty. He also employed a cost-benefit analysis to show that the benefits of complying with the dey's demands were far greater than the costs the nation would incur if peace were not secured. Barlow did not feel entirely happy about paying tribute. But while the war in Europe persisted, there was little chance the European nations could form the united front necessary to control the Algerians, and the United States was certainly not in a position to do so by itself.

In stressing the potential of the Mediterranean trade, Barlow inflated his estimate of the benefits of peace. Freights constituted the largest component in his carefully itemized memo at $1.2 million, "of which one half [is] clear profits" at $600,000. To this sum he added 15 percent of $3 million, which he estimated as the profit from the United States acting as it own carrier into the Mediterranean, bringing the total benefit to $1,050,000. From that sum he subtracted the estimated $60,000 annual cost of maintaining the peace with the three Barbary potentates, leaving a net advantage of $990,000. His accounting ignored the $642,000 Donaldson had agreed to pay as ransom and the cost of the frigate, which Barlow hoped could be built in the United States for as little as $40,000. All these expenses came to less than the $990,000 worth of advantages, but consumed most of the $800,000 that had been authorized for redeeming the captives and peace with *all* of the Barbary states, not just one.[15]

Barlow assumed Congress would increase its appropriation once it understood the situation, but to protect himself against charges of extravagance, he pursued a variety of strategies for cutting costs. Thus he recommended money be transferred from western Europe to Algiers by bills of exchange to avoid transportation charges. Some of his economies, however, were ridiculous. He insisted that James Cathcart, an American who had been a captive since 1786 and had become a prominent servant of the dey, undertake a voyage to Philadelphia to expedite payment of the ransom money at his own expense. Cathcart did benefit from being released from captivity earlier than he otherwise would have been, but Barlow might have shown more generosity to an American, who had played a crucial role in getting the dey to accept the treaty in the first place. Barlow also claimed, upon its release, as U.S. property a vessel captured by Tunis on the grounds that since the vessel had been restored to a public agent it was public property. Though that was strictly in accordance with the law, the capture had taken place just hours before a peace with Tunis had gone into effect, so some indulgence might have been shown. At least he did not charge the liberated crew for their freedom and their passage home, but his petty economies reflected uneasiness about having overstepped his powers in dealing with Hasan Pasha.

Justifying a purchased peace constituted Barlow's biggest difficulty, since he admitted that no permanent solution was available. His strongest argument proved to be the fate of Danish shipping in the Mediterranean during the spring of 1796 after the dey declared war on Denmark. Barlow reported that in the first eight days of hostilities the Algerians had brought in eight Danish prizes. The numbers rose as time progressed. Had Hasan Pasha chosen to prey on American rather than Danish shipping, the problem facing the United States would have quickly expanded to unmanageable proportions. Barlow had been advised by Micayo Barci that the rulers of North Africa were reluctant to go to war with those to whom they were indebted. Barlow construed this as a friendly hint that the United States should stay ahead of its scheduled tribute payments, and he reciprocated by passing $18,000 to Barci to be distributed among the dey's cronies, among whom Barci was invited to include himself.

Still, Barlow had not addressed the underlying problem that every successful extortion constituted an incentive for raising the ante in the future. Though his analysis of Algerian society linked its predatory behavior to the unrepublican domination of a Moorish majority by an alien, military caste, explaining the problem did not solve it. What eventually got Barlow off the hook was his success in delivering results. Results did not come easily, however, and cost him countless moments of anxiety in isolation from Ruth, his friends, and even his fellow countrymen after he sent Donaldson off to Leghorn (modern Livorno on the Tuscany coast) to look for ransom money.

Between February 20 and June 12, 1796, Barlow heard nothing from Humphreys in response to his pleas for the timely delivery of funds. The prolonged silence led him to suspect that the government disapproved his attempts to preserve the peace treaty. His anxiety increased when he learned that the dey's war with the Danes was coming to a conclusion, again raising the possibility that the United States would be next. Weeks of frustration gave rise to irritation with Humphreys. In a letter to Ruth, Barlow described a man he used to admire as having "too much beef in his head to be a good manager of such affairs. The most conspicuous talent that I can discover in him hitherto is that of keeping a secret, & keeping it from those whose knowledge of [it] is absolutely necessary to his own success. His eternal mystery & silence (I will not say inattention and folly) will probably lose us this treaty yet."[16]

The outbreak of the bubonic plague at the end of May simply made matters worse. Barlow's efforts to get the American prisoners removed to a safer location came to naught. Before long, six of the seven Americans who contracted the disease died. But spring did bring one positive development in the form of a new French consul, Allois d'Herculais. His predecessor had declined to cooperate in any way with the Americans. Barlow suspected the former French consul of being disloyal to the French republic, largely on the basis of a report that his brother-in-law had betrayed Toulon to the British in the spring of 1793.[17] It was a welcome relief to have a friendly replacement who gave Barlow valuable advice about managing U.S. interests in North Africa.

In addition to Algeria, Barlow was also responsible for Tunis and Tripoli, now that Donaldson was in Leghorn. Acting on the advice of d'Herculais, Barlow approached a French merchant in Tunis named Joseph Famin, who succeeded in liberating a recently captured American vessel and its crew. Barlow worked well with d'Herculais until the French consul received instructions in July to refrain from helping the Americans. This was Barlow's first exposure to the cooling of the Franco-American relationship as a consequence of the Jay Treaty, but by then he had heard from Humphreys and learned that instead of repudiating Barlow, the government stood behind him. Humphreys put a $200,000 credit at Barlow's disposal in Lisbon, while sending instructions to Donaldson in Leghorn authorizing him to draw for an additional $200,000.

The Lisbon credit had little value since there was no trade between Lisbon and Algiers and therefore no demand for bills on Lisbon. The only chance of getting money seemed to be through Leghorn until Barlow learned that d'Herculais had recently borrowed $200,000 from the dey's treasury, which he had used to pay a previous French debt due the House of Bacri. That development enabled Barlow to take advantage of an offer Micayo Bacri had previously made to supply Barlow with the ransom money if Bacri could be supplied with a corresponding amount of specie in Leghorn. The offer had been "safe" when initially made because Bacri thought Barlow lacked the means, but now Barlow was able to offer him $200,000 in bills on Leghorn in exchange for an equivalent amount of cash in Algiers.

The offer was attractive to Bacri because the British had responded to the recent French capture of Leghorn by blockading it, making bills the only way of safely transporting money there. Bacri's agreement enabled Barlow to advance a first payment toward ransoming the American seamen. Though the money had originally come from the dey's treasury, Hasan was impressed enough to free all the American seamen on the basis of it. Barlow lost no time in packing them off in a vessel he had acquired, the *Fortune*, which was instructed first to touch at Leghorn to return some captive Neapolitans before proceeding to America. The arrangement allowed Barlow to inform Donaldson of his success and to order him to pay Bacri's bills with drafts on Madrid, Lisbon, and London. Barlow later claimed—with some justification—that he had succeeded in realizing his government's principal objective before receiving a penny of specie.

However, this success failed to solve the other problems the United States faced in the Mediterranean. Though Joseph Famin managed to negotiate an initial peace with the bey of Tunis, Tripoli presented a more daunting challenge. It rivaled Algeria in naval power and had begun seizing American vessels just as Barlow settled outstanding differences with the other two Barbary states. Barlow had no access to anyone with influence in Tripoli besides Hasan and was reluctant to appeal to him for fear of disturbing their fragile understanding. That understanding involved sending James Cathcart back to America to speed up the delivery of the frigate. Since it would take a minimum of six months before Cathcart returned, Barlow did not want to introduce any further complications into the Algerian relationship. But Barlow did not have much choice while Donaldson remained tied down in Leghorn by the British blockade and by the need to pay Bacri's bills.

Barlow's only alternative was to work through the French government. He asked Monroe to see what he could do in Paris, but there was little hope of success, given the chill the Jay Treaty was creating.[18] Barlow was unaware that the Washington administration was in the process of replacing Monroe as ambassador because of his alleged partiality to France. Nor had Barlow received the secretary of state's endorsement of his efforts to protect the increasing number of American vessels in the Mediterranean. As he ruefully commented to Monroe, "They would sail into hell if the Devil was to turn Catholic so as to make a good market for codfish."[19] In addition, the tightness of the British blockade prevented Barlow's bills in Bacri's favor from reaching Leghorn.

To reassure Hasan that the rest of the ransom was on its way, Barlow shared with him information from Humphreys that O'Brien had left Lisbon for Algiers with $220,000 on August 4. O'Brien's failure to appear after an appropriate interval made the dey suspicious, leading Barlow to fear that all would be lost. Eventually, he learned that O'Brien's vessel had been seized by an English renegade, Peter Lyle, sailing under the flag of Tripoli.[20] One would not have expected

$220,000 in specie to fare well in the hands of pirates, but O'Brien had sailed with the dey's passport and Tripoli paid annual tribute to Algeria. When Barlow informed Hasan about what had happened and the report was confirmed, Hasan took the side of the Americans against Tripoli. Of course, if he had not done so, the bey of Tripoli would have made off with money intended for the dey. But Hasan not only menaced the bey with Algeria's superior power on land, he also threatened to get the grand signor in Istanbul to force the bey into a truce with the United States without any tribute if the bey did not accept the terms he had recently rejected in the hope of extracting more.

Why did the United States find so much favor with Hasan Pasha? Barlow was modest about claiming personal credit for his achievement, not wishing to convey the impression that he thought himself indispensable in North Africa. Instead, he stressed a number of factors that reflected his growing sensitivity to Islamic culture. These included the absence of a cross in the American flag, the fact that the United States had very few Roman Catholics, and the nation's commitment to a religious toleration that extended to Muslims. Barlow also thought it important that the United States was honoring all its agreements, even though the nation was taking much longer to do so than initially expected. Finally, the United States had never contested the Turks' sovereignty over the seas near North Africa, as many of the European powers had. All these theories reflected Barlow's growing understanding of an alien culture.[21]

Barlow's first impressions of Algeria had been distinctly negative. Unlike European cities, Algiers lacked well-built, well-ventilated houses or even proper streets. The city was a maze of twisting alleys, too narrow to permit the passage of a cart and sometimes even a horse. It was controlled by a military minority, which treated the Moors worse than its Christians and Jews. Slaves usually fared better than free people, whatever their religious identity. The punishments for certain crimes also struck Barlow as barbaric. The husband of a woman accused of adultery could take the law into his own hands and act as judge and executioner against his wife. He could even have her tied into a sack with stones and thrown into the sea. The same punishment was inflicted upon Muslim women "having relations with an infidel," though Barlow commented ironically they were at least spared the punishment meted out to the offending infidel, who was beaten to death.[22]

As Barlow grew more familiar with the country, he found its customs less shocking. Nonetheless, his increasing familiarity with Algiers gave him no more than a limited understanding of why Hasan was well disposed to the Americans. One can't help wondering if two other factors were not at work.

One was Barlow's personality. He possessed a charm that was hard to resist. That trait enabled him to make friends among a wide range of acquaintances with whom he had little in common. They included Micayo Bacri, whom Barlow now realized had saved the Americans countless times from disaster, and the French, Swedish, Spanish, and British consuls. In tight situations Barlow could even turn his charm on the dey. Such a moment had arisen when Hasan had summoned Barlow into his presence to complain of the delay in delivering the ransom while his cruisers were busy fitting out in the port of Algiers. Barlow feared that the cruisers would be instructed to seize American vessels as security for the United States fulfilling its part of a bargain. Instead of responding cravenly, Barlow looked Hasan in the eye and asserted that "the severity of your face is but the mask of an excellent heart," claiming that the dey really liked Americans. Hasan, not used to being addressed by consuls in this way, softened.[23]

Barlow would not have been so persuasive, though, had it not been for another, more important consideration. The United States offered a reliable source of supply that could buttress the dey's position against the European naval powers simply because it was so far away. What kept Algeria in business was choosing victims from among the less powerful European states. Going to war with a major naval power like Britain, France, or Spain was only possible when extraordinary circumstances put them on the defensive. Hasan realized he could never take— or extort—a frigate from them. When, unexpectedly, U.S. vessels began appearing in the Mediterranean, their coming from such a great distance seemed proof in itself of the nation's maritime resources. Barlow's offering a frigate as garnish to the demand for ransom was just what the dey needed to maintain his depredations against more customary prey.

It did not hurt the American relationship with Algiers that most of the other powers in the Mediterranean were hostile to the Americans. When O'Brien's vessel carrying the ransom money from Portugal to Algiers was seized by Tripoli, O'Brien and his crew were stripped of most of their personal property. But Barlow experienced no difficulty in getting Hasan to demand his ransom money from those who paid him tribute. When the bey of Tunis balked at abiding by the terms of the first treaty that Barlow had negotiated with him, the dey eventually declared war on him, though he conducted it in a half-hearted manner. Barlow may have been a bit naive in thinking he had done so simply out of friendship for the United States. Hasan instead was defending his parasitical claim to a new and promising host. He didn't want the bey of Tunis poaching on his turf.

Barlow was also naive to imagine that the annual tribute he had arranged constituted dependable protection against future captures. As the United States grew richer, the price was bound to rise. Jefferson recognized this during his presidency and attempted a military solution, which proved elusive and had to be abandoned after Britain and France started pressuring the United States in 1806. Only upon the conclusion of the Napoleonic Wars in 1815 did the major naval powers of Europe take concerted action against the Barbary states and the United States follow their example. Soon after the conclusion of the War of 1812, James Madison dispatched a large naval squadron under Stephen Decatur that successfully brought to heel the rulers of North Africa. Barlow's diplomatic triumph was less the permanency of the arrangements he negotiated than his success in freeing the American captives before another visitation of the plague.

⚜

Barlow proved better at liberating his fellow countrymen than freeing himself. Possibly encouraged by Famin, the bey of Tunis took infinite delight in quibbling over the terms of the agreement negotiated under Barlow's direction. Another problem was the delay in getting the money, naval supplies, and promised frigate to Algiers. In February 1797, the U.S.-built frigate—with a large consignment of naval supplies on board—fell prey to a Spanish privateer off the coast of Spain. It had been in captivity four months before Barlow found out what had happened. The delay placed everything Barlow had been at such pains to establish in jeopardy. On May 20, 1797, he wrote Humphreys that the dey was threatening to seize American shipping and place Barlow in chains in the plague-ridden city. Barlow bought time by hiring a vessel to go to Alicante to see what was causing the delay. Just before it departed, Humphreys's letters arrived informing Barlow of the frigate's fate, and Barlow was able to direct the dey's wrath against Spain rather than the United States.[24]

Barlow remained in North Africa well into the summer of 1797. As long as he stayed outside the most dangerous parts of the city, he ran little personal risk from sickness. Still, he longed to return to Ruth and Paris. Stretching a two-month separation into a year-and-a-half absence took its toll on both of them. The customary joke with which they reaffirmed their intimacy when they were apart—in this case Barlow's taking an exotic North African mistress—became something he had to deny after he declined to ask her to join him. Barlow kept up the rich flow of endearments in French to reassure her that nothing had changed between them. To cheer her, he portrayed Hasan as grown so fond of him that he had proposed sending a special vessel to bring Ruth to Algiers rather than part with Barlow.[25] He also occasionally dangled before her the idea of the two of them touring the cities of the Levant and returning through Italy when his mission was completed. He thought his first reports to Timothy Pickering, about the importance of the Mediterranean trade, might lead to a commission for making a commercial survey until he concluded that Pickering was ignoring him.

Barlow knew Pickering by reputation from the continental army, where he had been quartermaster general, and concluded that the secretary of state entertained the same opinion of him as Gouverneur Morris did. He consoled himself with the idea that he was acting in the best interests of his country and of humanity.[26] Instead of sinking into victimized self pity during his forced sojourn in Algiers, he made the most of various local opportunities. Barlow used a horse that Hasan put at his disposal to explore the surrounding countryside. This deepened his knowledge of a culture that observed few of the norms of western society and whose social organization seemed oblivious to the Enlightenment. He also broadened his contacts among the local diplomatic corps, participating actively in the sociability of the dey's court.

One such occasion occurred toward the end of 1796, when the dey's minister of marine invited Barlow and the consuls of England and Sweden on a three-day hunting expedition. The foreigners were only expected to observe the skill of mounted hunters, who killed fourteen boars and one hyena with lances. Barlow reported to Ruth that the boars were capable of turning on their pursuers and killing the people who hunted them. Three of their party, along with their horses, had been wounded in the hunt. As for the hyena, Barlow thought that animal capable of killing the entire troop of hunters.[27]

Barlow spent relatively little time in such recreations. Instead, he used his contacts with his fellow consuls to launch commercial ventures. He did so despite the official hostility of their governments toward the U.S. presence in the Mediterranean. The large supply of captured shipping, some of it of excellent quality, made vessels comparatively cheap in Algiers. The supply didn't entirely depend on piracy, though, as some Europeans found it convenient to send their prizes into Algiers for adjudication. All the European consuls were in a position to benefit, and Barlow had no trouble finding partners. He joined d'Herculais in purchasing a vessel equipped with a three-year protection issued by the dey. Barlow instructed William Little in Boston to receive the vessel's freight money in the United States and invest it in the deferred stock of the United States, half in d'Herculais's name and half in Ruth's name.[28] In exchange, d'Herculais continued to assist Barlow in managing U.S. relations with Tunis and Tripoli until he was assigned elsewhere.

Barlow's biggest commercial partner, though, was Bacri. Together they conducted a successful joint venture in Algerian wheat, which they sent from Bona to Malaga in a 250-ton Venetian barque Barlow had purchased. It came to such a good market that Barlow was able to load the vessel with a cargo for America with his half of the proceeds.[29] High wartime freights and the low cost of shipping along the Barbary coast enabled Barlow to become the owner of two other vessels during the fifteen months he spent in Algiers. He had little trouble manning them because of the availability of former captives, who had acquired the linguistic and cultural skills for conducting trade in the Mediterranean. Barlow put Philip Sloan in charge of one. The other captain came with his former ship, the *Rachel*.

There were some bad apples as well as deserving victims among the Americans. One was Samuel Graves, the captain of the American schooner *Eliza* taken by Tunisian cruisers just before Barlow had arranged a treaty with the bey. The capture of the *Eliza* added to the obstacles Barlow had to surmount in securing a peace, but he acted quickly in freeing vessel and crew. Barlow ordered them first to go to Leghorn, to check if there were any more ransomed seamen who needed a ride home, and then to Algiers in hope of using the *Eliza* as a courier for his dispatches. This was the vessel that Barlow claimed had reverted to the United States upon its release, and he thought he had done the captain and crew favor enough by buying their freedom and sending them back to America. Graves disagreed, however, and instead made for Palermo, supposedly after encountering bad weather. There he sold the cargo he had loaded in Tunis, which by Barlow's reckoning was not his, though Graves alleged Barlow had given him "discretionary" orders as his justification. Graves then took a freight for England, where he hoped to pick up another freight for Boston. When last heard of, he had sold both cargo and vessel in Spain and vanished.

Graves had taken as passenger from Tunis a Jewish merchant, whom he later robbed and allegedly tortured. Since Barlow's North African diplomacy hinged on a close working relationship with the Bacris, Graves's actions were especially detrimental. Mercantile Jews constituted a significant subculture in the Mediterranean, and the misfortunes of one were bound to come to the attention of others. To preserve his good standing with Hasan, Barlow admitted that the Jewish merchant had been wronged before receiving the sworn testimony of the victim about the extent of his losses. When that was finally forthcoming, the figure came to thirty thousand Algerian sequins. Barlow suspected the real loss was more like five thousand, but since he had promised restitution for all the property that had been taken, he had no choice but to pass the claim on to the U.S. government. He had also guaranteed a cargo Bacri had placed in Barlow's ship, the *Fortune*, to protect it from seizure by Britain. When the British seized the *Fortune* and its cargo anyway, the dey made Barlow cover Bacri's losses. Barlow, however, was reasonably confident British courts would eventually honor the neutral status of the goods involved.

The longer Barlow tarried in Algiers, the more likely it was that new problems would arise. In March 1797, Jean Bon St. André, arrived as d'Herculais's unwelcome replacement. St. André had been one of Robespierre's lieutenants, and he came instructed in the new hard line the Directory was adopting towards the United States. Barlow suspected he wanted to provoke a rupture between the two republics. St. André soon commissioned a privateer and instructed it to bring in neutral Swedish and Danish vessels. Two had been apprehended, when St. André caused something of a diplomatic crisis by trying to have the vessels condemned in an Algerian court. His actions threatened to subvert the principal that a vessel's neutral flag protected any goods in it. Barlow felt that it was very much to France's interest to uphold this principle, but St. André would hear none of that. Fortunately, the dey was offended by St. André's arrogance, and the Danish and Swedish consuls, supported by Barlow, were able to persuade Hasan to order the two prizes to depart. But that was unlikely to curb St. André's mischievous inclinations for long.[30]

If Barlow had waited until all the problems facing the United States in the Mediterranean were resolved, he would never have left Algiers. Once he had persuaded Hasan that the United States had done all it could toward implementing the treaty, Barlow started planning his exit. On May 22, 1797, one of Barlow's vessels arrived in Algiers with a cargo of salt. The vessel also brought news of the Spanish seizure of the promised frigate. Invoking an ancient custom, the dey seized the vessel's cargo at a dictated price. Barlow acquiesced in return for Hasan directing his wrath about the frigate against Spain. Now all Barlow had to do was find an American to take his place, since only then would the dey permit Barlow to depart. Even though most of the actual business of the United States would be left in the hands of Micayo Bacri, Hasan wanted an American hostage.

Barlow recruited a young American named James Clarke, who was the nephew of the U.S. consul in Malaga. Getting Clarke to Algiers during the spring and early summer proved difficult because no one wanted to visit during the plague season. Sending one of Barlow's own vessels ran the risk of having it tied up for weeks in Spanish quarantine. Barlow managed to have a vessel pick Clarke up offshore without entering Malaga, enabling Clarke to arrive in Algiers on July 17 just after the plague abated. Once Clarke was in place, it took only two nights and one full day of furious activity for Barlow to wind up his affairs.

When he presented Clarke to Hasan and Micayo Bacri, the occasion doubled as a formal leave-taking at which Hasan and Bacri gave Barlow customary parting presents. Hasan broke precedent by also giving Barlow a special present for Ruth. Barlow took the precaution of getting the Spanish, French, and British consuls to provide him with passes so that he would not be captured or detained in transit to Marseilles. Finally, there were last minute instructions that had to be sent to Famin at Tunis and to Joseph Ingraham, whom Barlow had persuaded to act as consul in Tripoli. No fear of a sea passage deterred Barlow from sailing as early as he could on the morning of July 19, 1797, and rejoicing at his liberation. After a year and a quarter of countless cares, not to mention threats and humiliations, he was at last free and returning to Paris.

CHAPTER TWELVE

Franco-American Crisis

The voyage from Algiers to Marseilles was one of Barlow's few happy experiences under sail. Aside from a brief bout of sickness on the first day out, he arrived, after a leisurely twelve-day passage, on July 30, 1797. It undoubtedly helped to be traveling on his own vessel, the *Rachel*, with his own captain, Philip Sloan. Even the forty-day quarantine in the Marseilles lazaretto failed to dampen his spirits, as he was reentering a world where he felt much more at home. A letter from Ruth awaited him there. Written on June 26, it reminded him that now the distance between them had narrowed, their exchanges should take about two weeks rather than two months. Though it was agonizing to be so close and yet so far away, he considered his circumstances vastly improved. As his spirits lifted, he ruminated on the word *Marseilles*, whose combination of vowels and consonants struck him as having peculiar beauty.[1]

The forty-day quarantine gave him time to catch up on his business and tend to some of the loose ends remaining from his mission. Fifty thousand dollars in tribute money was due in Tunis in two months, along with $10,000 in presents. His first letter on August 1, to Stephen Cathalan, addressed the Tunisian problem. Cathalan was to inquire whether anyone in Marseilles would exchange bills on Tunis for bills on Philadelphia. Barlow wanted to bypass the Bacris, who he thought were unduly profiting from serving as bankers to the United States. But there was no way around them in handling the nation's business in Algiers, and Barlow remained mindful that the United States was still deeply indebted to their house. Getting money into the Mediterranean continued to be a major problem, and Barlow urged David Humphreys to solicit Lisbon and London merchants for credits in Leghorn in exchange for drafts on Philadelphia.[2]

Barlow also wrote a final report about his mission for Secretary of State Timothy Pickering. He was reasonably satisfied with everything but the Tunisian negotiation. In retrospect, he felt the United States should have dealt directly with the bey instead of relying on Hasan Pasha to bring Tunis to terms. Barlow suspected Algeria and Tunis of coming to an understanding behind his back, possibly through the agency of Joseph Famin, whose loyalties Barlow now questioned. Barlow couldn't help contrasting the frankness of Allois D'Herculais with Famin's deviousness. He suspected Famin had aspired to dominate U.S. trade with the Levant but that the French government had pressured him into sabotaging American interests there instead. Barlow suggested a strategy for getting rid of Famin. If American consuls were forbidden to engage in trade, he expected Famin would resign.[3]

Barlow assumed that Britain and Spain felt the same way about American commerce in the Mediterranean as did France, requiring good men on the Barbary Coast to protect the nation's interests. He took a generally dim view of the North African states and was especially critical of the tyranny Hasan Pasha, supported by the Bacris, exercised over Algeria. He thought, however, the United States had no choice but to work with the dey until he was overthrown. The minute that happened, he predicted, the Bacris would become irrelevant.

Barlow did not neglect his own affairs. One matter of special concern was the settlement of his official accounts. Barlow remained nervous about the initiatives he had taken without explicit authorization, especially since he had gone to Algiers without a compensation agreement. An initial letter to Humphreys suggested he be paid $200 per month for twenty-five months, plus expenses. If that was unacceptable he would make a present of his services—though presumably not of his expenses—to the government.[4] Judging from the way he subsequently pursued the matter, the suggestion that he receive nothing for his services was either a lame gesture of gentility or a misconceived defense against being accused of extravagance. Other uncertainties remained, like the guarantee he had given the Bacris of their cargo in the *Fortune* being immune to capture by the British. Because Hasan Pasha had insisted, Barlow believed he had to make that promise to free himself from the tyrant's clutches.

The administration liberally compensated Barlow for his efforts. He requested $5,974.52 and asked Humphreys to provide him with a credit for that amount in Europe. Humphreys had anticipated Barlow's needs by sending him an authorization to draw on Baring Brothers in London for $5,000. Left almost $1,000 short,

Barlow wrote several letters to Rufus King, the new U.S. minister to Britain, as well as to Humphreys in an attempt to collect the difference. Humphreys eventually authorized Baring Brothers to pay Barlow's additional requisition, but getting the message from Lisbon to London and the money to Paris took time. Transferring funds from Britain to France during wartime required Baring Brothers to send £1,125 in sterling bills to the U.S. consul in Hamburg, Samuel Williams, who then bought livre bills on Paris. Williams purchased three such bills, which came close to making up the full amount, and for the small remainder drew on Robert Lyle in Barlow's favor. Lyle, a native of New Jersey, had been Barlow's partner in an earlier Hamburg-based venture whose modest profits Lyle had received while Barlow was in Algiers. The larger bills were all paid by the end of December, and Barlow was confidant Lyle would pay his when it came due.[5]

The money became available to Barlow just as he began notifying those indebted to him that he required prompt payment. Turning British sterling into good bills on Paris turned out to be a lot simpler than getting good bills from his commercial ventures in the Mediterranean. He had instructed Cathalan to forward seven livre bills for payment in Paris, hoping the proceeds would relieve his immediate needs there. Only three were accepted and paid. Two came back protested, while the other two encountered difficulties, though payment was eventually "arranged." The ones that were refused had been endorsed by reputable people in Marseilles, so Barlow was reasonably sure that he would eventually be compensated, but the difficulties he encountered in transferring money within France constituted a rude reminder that many of the economic problems that the revolution had created had yet to be solved.

The Directory's "hard money" loan of December 10, 1795, had been largely subscribed in *assignats* that were overvalued at 100:1. To raise needed funds the government had no choice but continued reliance on currency finance. In March of 1796, new instruments known as "mandats territoriaux" backed by national properties first made their appearance. Barlow later complained to David Humphreys that his mission had cost him $20,000 in personal losses. The protest did not ring true because he had boasted to Ruth of the small fortune he had made in the Mediterranean trade and his inscriptions had risen to the point where, in Ruth's opinion, they constituted "a pretty fortune."[6] The losses Barlow complained about to Humphries involved the *mandats*, which—though depreciating from the moment they made their appearance—briefly acquired value for those who happened to be in the right place at the right time.

During the three months between April and July, while they were overvalued at 30:1 in relation to the depreciating *assignat*, the *mandats* were exchangeable for national properties valued in *assignats* at an artificially low rate. The arrangement set off a scramble for national properties resembling the earlier one in May 1795, while further corroding the value of the *mandats*.[7] Ruth, who showed good common sense when it came to financial matters, may have followed Daniel Parker's advice and instructed Jacques Récamier to invest any discretionary income in additional national properties.[8] Barlow's sense that he had lost heavily through his mission derived more from having missed a second chance to acquire major assets at fire-sale prices. After July 17, 1796, the depreciated *mandats* ceased to be legal tender, though they could still be exchanged for national properties at their hard money value. Even at 1 percent of face value, purchasing with them remained advantageous because of diminished demand for real estate. Parker would cap his extensive real estate acquisitions by purchasing Madame de Pompadour's former estate, the Château de Crécy, at auction in 1797.[9]

Barlow did have some reason to feel he had been left behind, though, because going on a "hard currency" standard failed to increase the money supply, despite the booty France's armies collected from their conquests. The difficulties Barlow experienced in getting his French bills paid reflected the shortage of hard money, but it did not prevent him from initiating several new commercial ventures while in the lazaretto. He ordered the captain of the *Friendship* to find a freight for America in the Mediterranean. If he succeeded in doing so, Barlow instructed him to hug the African coast after passing the Straits of Gibraltar to avoid French privateers, who were lying off the Spanish coast. If a freight could not be found for the *Friendship*, she was to come to Marseilles, where Barlow proposed to equip the vessel with a protection against French privateers. Barlow needed to document that the crew was predominantly American and the vessel American owned to insure its neutrality would be respected. The *Friendship* had already had one brush with French cruisers that had only ended happily because of papers Captain Sampson had procured in Leghorn.[10] But Barlow feared that another French cruiser might consider the *Friendship*'s American crew British subjects unless they possessed proof of their nationality. He had experienced enough anguish in wresting his fellow countrymen from the clutches of the Barbary potentates to want to avoid going through a similar process with the French.

Freights from the Mediterranean turned out to be hard to find; however, Barlow remained confident that he could sell both vessels if no freights materialized. In the meantime, he could enhance the value of the vessels by getting the Marine Ministry in Paris to issue them protections. He eventually secured a protection for the *Rachel*, but the increasing chill in Franco-American relations during the autumn of 1797 led him to hedge his bets with the *Friendship*. Her protection failed to specify that two-thirds of the crew were American, suggesting that Barlow was content to have her treated as a French vessel. Such a protection would be useful to a French purchaser, to whom Barlow eventually instructed Cathalan to sell the *Friendship*.[11]

Barlow remained in Marseilles no longer than absolutely necessary. When his quarantine ended on September 10, he and Cathalan set out immediately for nearby Aix, where they filed protests before a provincial tribunal for American vessels that had fallen prey to French privateers.[12] After disposing of this last bit of consular business, Barlow made for Paris and Ruth as fast as he could, arriving in the capital in the wake of the coup of Eighteen Fructidor.

On the night of September 4, 1797, a majority of the executive Directory, with the assistance of an army contingent, arrested and deported fifty-three allegedly royalist lawmakers who had opposed their policies. Two directors who objected to the purge were also arrested, though one of these subsequently escaped to Italy. The remaining three directors then had the legislature provide them with two more congenial colleagues. The action sent a strong message about the likely fate of anyone who opposed the reconstituted executive. Barlow failed to comment on how these developments conformed to his republican expectations, but he probably accepted the idea that the coup had been necessary to defend the Republic against a monarchical restoration. Because it had been bloodless, public order in Paris was undisturbed, and the citizenry indifferent if not apathetic. His reunion with Ruth, together with the public amusements and private amenities of the city, temporarily crowded out politics.

Ruth had recently befriended an American boarding at her pension and was eager for Barlow to meet him. Though ten or more years their junior, Robert Fulton had been in Europe longer than they had. Born near Lancaster, Pennsylvania, to a family without means, Fulton had been apprenticed to a silversmith. Having little taste either for his master or the craft, he had turned to painting portraits in his spare time and was soon able to buy back his indenture. Eventually, he assembled enough resources—with assistance from his patrons—to study painting with the American-born Benjamin West in London. Like Barlow, Fulton refused to confine himself to one occupation. Just as he was establishing his reputation as a painter, he turned to civil engineering. Rather than representing the world as it was, he—like Barlow—wanted to change it into something better. He proposed a comprehensive system of small canals for Britain, and his *A Treatise on the Improvement of Canal Navigation* (1796) argued that such a network could

Robert Fulton (1798), by John Vanderlyn. Done shortly after Barlow and Fulton had become acquainted, Vanderlyn captures an uncertainty in Fulton's personality to which both Barlows responded sympathetically. Collection of The New-York Historical Society.

connect all the major population centers of the kingdom. Fulton came to France in 1797 to patent this canal scheme before returning to America, only to become bogged down in the French bureaucracy.

Despite Barlow's assistance, Fulton would not receive a fifteen-year patent until February 1798. Well before that, Fulton, Ruth, and Barlow moved out of the pension to live together. Thus began an unconventional *ménage à trois* that was to last off and on for the next seven years. Fuller's recent biographers have noted

Joel Barlow (1798), by John Vanderlyn. Vanderlyn's charcoal and pencil portrayal of Barlow, done at roughly the same time as his sketch of Fulton, suggests why Fulton saw Barlow as an older brother or even a father figure. Courtesy National Portrait Gallery, Smithsonian Institution, gift of Mr. and Mrs. Joel Barlow.

the sexual possibilities in the living arrangement. However, the bonding that had taken place between Barlow and Ruth's older siblings in New Haven during the late 1770s and early 1780s provides a better model for understanding the relationship that initially developed between the three. The Barlows sought the reconstitution of family intimacies that had been disrupted by distance and Dudley's and Lucy's recent deaths. Fulton's youthfulness also qualified him to serve as a surrogate for the son they had never had. Fulton, for his part, appreciated the Barlows' familiarity with France and the guidance and support they offered as he strove to realize the dreams all three shared for a future based on reason and technological innovation. Fulton looked upon the Barlows as older, wiser siblings substituting for absent parents.

During the autumn of 1797, Fulton addressed a monograph to the Directory, entitled "Thoughts on Free Trade with Reasons Why Foreign Possessions And all Duties on Importation is Injurious to Nations." These were subjects very close to Barlow's heart, and he may have helped Fulton in developing them, though Fulton's economic critique of colonialism was clearly his own. Barlow probably also had a hand in a subsequent antiwar manifesto that Fulton published, entitled "To the Friends of Mankind," and in Fulton's "The Republican Creed." Finally, a recent Fulton biographer credits Barlow with lighting "the submarine spark" in his new friend.[13] Barlow quickly grasped the potential of underwater warfare for challenging Britain's naval supremacy and advised Fulton about how to interest the French government in the development of a "Nautilus."

Then, as now, submarines were expensive, and Fulton needed money up front, in addition to reasonable compensation for the time and effort he devoted to the project. Barlow helped Fulton draft a proposed agreement with the French Ministry of Marine that would secure him both. Barlow gave freely of his advice and energy because he saw Fulton as a younger version of himself and Britain's naval power as the principal barrier to the emergence of a republican world order based on the freedom of commerce.

Barlow soon realized that the Paris he had returned to was very different from the city he had left. He quickly became disillusioned with France's reconstituted Directory. Over the next fifteen months, disappointment would ripen into disgust with what he considered the corruption and incompetence of the national legislature. By January 1799, he thought that "nothing short of fructidorfying can bring them to common sense, not to say honesty."[14] But in October 1797, the French government's shortcomings were principally evident in its deteriorating relations with the United States.

During Barlow's absence in Algiers, the Washington administration had replaced Ambassador James Monroe with Charles Cotesworth Pinckney of South Carolina. The Directory interpreted the substitution of an English-educated aristocrat for a known republican enthusiast as part of the betrayal of the Franco-American alliance evidenced in the Jay Treaty. It refused to receive Pinckney and subjected him to annoying surveillance before finally ordering him out of the country on pain of being treated as a common criminal. When President John Adams learned of Pinckney's humiliation, he responded by appointing three commissioners to resolve the difficulties plaguing Franco-American relations. Each represented a different section of the country, and Adams insisted on re-appointing Pinckney for the Deep South. John Marshall, the future chief justice of the United States, represented the mid-Atlantic, and Elbridge Gerry, from Massachusetts, New England. They arrived in the French capital shortly after Barlow's return to Paris, though not before French cruisers, based in the West Indies, had begun seizing American merchant vessels.

The Directory refused to receive the commissioners, though Charles Maurice de Talleyrand-Périgord, the foreign minister, granted them an unofficial audience and issued them hospitality cards. Talleyrand advised them to be patient because the new post-Fructidor government had yet to consolidate its power. The envoys at first were hopeful because they had reason to think Talleyrand favored an accommodation with the United States. A clubfoot had forced this brilliant man, a minor noble by birth, to pursue a career in the church rather than the army. During the early days of the Revolution, Talleyrand was the only bishop in France to back the civil constitution of the clergy and had proposed the nationalization of Catholic Church properties to pay the monarchy's debts. He was on a mission to England when the monarchy fell, and he chose to seek refuge in the United States rather than join the émigrés in Europe. During his two-year sojourn in America, he had ample opportunity to take the measure of the new nation's leadership. Though Talleyrand had not much liked the New World, he possessed a better understanding of the United States than any high-ranking French official since Louis Duportail and Brissot de Warville.

Nonetheless, as time progressed, the American commissioners became suspicious that Talleyrand was stalling for a purpose. Their suspicions seemed confirmed when, after many weeks of inactivity, they were approached by several of Talleyrand's agents. The commissioners then learned that the price of accommodation would be an apology for some critical statements Adams had made to Congress about France, a large loan, and a substantial bribe. By then all Paris knew that the Directory had declined to deal directly with the commissioners. Barlow later claimed he had no knowledge of the specific demands made by Talleyrand's intermediaries, but it is clear from his correspondence that this was not the case. At the very least he had indirect access to Gerry, who let on "thorough secret whispers" to Americans like Fulwar Skipwith that the American commissioners were divided about how to deal with the Directory's demands.[15] Barlow also occasionally saw Talleyrand at social gatherings, which the commissioners

Joel Barlow (1798), attributed to John Trumbull. Trumbull's stern, romantic representation of Barlow contrasts sharply with Vanderlyn's more gentrified representation of Barlow from the same period. Photograph © 2011 Museum of Fine Arts, Boston.

made a point of shunning. While Talleyrand did not honor Barlow with an invitation to dinner, as he did John Trumbull, Trumbull painted a miniature of Barlow at this time, and the sittings would have provided an occasion for discussing the stalled negotiation.[16]

Barlow bided his time through the winter until he learned that Talleyrand had given up on Marshall and Pinckney and would only talk with Gerry. On March 4, 1798, fearing the worst, Barlow penned a long letter to his brother-in-law Abraham Baldwin about the deteriorating relations between the two republics.[17] Barlow blamed President Adams more than the Jay Treaty for the failure of the commissioners to reach an understanding with France. That was not to say that the Jay Treaty hadn't given offence, but Barlow believed that France would have been willing to forgive the injury but for the composition of the American peace commission. Americans underestimated the importance France attached to the character of the men representing a nation overseas. Jefferson had pleased them by his vigorous support of their revolution. His recall in 1789 had raised questions about the U.S. government's intentions, especially after Gouverneur Morris—described by Barlow as a "wide-mouth bawler" who fraternized with royalists and counter-revolutionaries—was named Jefferson's replacement. Pinckney had initially been dismissed because—in contrast to Monroe—he was seen as someone of Morris's ilk. The rest of the commission was not much better. Marshall had violently defended the English treaty, while Gerry was regarded as "a little make-weight man," not intended to have any influence. Gerry was known to be a republican, though, and Barlow was confident the Directory would have negotiated with him had Gerry "been sent alone, and not been shackled with the other two."

Barlow claimed that Adams's indiscreet words were resented in France almost as much as his insensitive appointments. Adams had spoken disparagingly of France as having "overturned religion" and being incapable of abiding by its treaties. Americans made a mistake in thinking that domestic utterances went unnoticed abroad. Published references made in the U.S. House of Representatives to the Directory being a "five-headed monster" did not have a soothing influence. The informed Frenchmen Barlow encountered in the cafés and salons of Paris also were aware of Adams's criticisms of the French Revolution in his *Discourses on Davilla* (1790). These writings, along with his policies, led the French to conclude that Adams was a royalist.

Barlow thought American mismanagement was responsible for bringing the two republics "to the brink of war." The remedy was to appoint ministers acceptable to the Directory. If Madison and Monroe replaced the former commissioners and Adams made a few friendly comments about France, all the difficulties between the two nations could be resolved in twenty-four hours. That assessment contrasted with Barlow's anxiety about "seeing him [Adams] give another desperate leap into the region of madness" that would lead to war between two nations that ought to be friends. Barlow feared that Pinckney and Marshall would in their dispatches seek to inflame rather than calm the tensions between the two republics.

Having no idea of the furor his March 4 letter would eventually create, Barlow expressed his anger and frustration to Baldwin without restraint. He initially decided against sending similar communications to Jefferson and Madison, though eventually he dispatched a modified version of this letter to the vice president in case Congress adjourned before Baldwin received his.[18] Barlow assumed both Baldwin and Jefferson would use his communication discretely. A Boston merchant, William Lee, carried the letters to America where, Oliver Wolcott Jr., acting for an insecure administration obsessed with the danger of foreign influence, managed to intercept and copy Barlow's letter to Jefferson but not his letter to Baldwin.[19]

Lee had purchased the *Friendship* and the *Rachel* from Barlow in order to send them to Cadiz to load with cargoes of salt for America. Barlow, along with Robert Lyle, became equal partners with Lee in the cargo. Lee was to purchase a return cargo of provisions from the salt sales in the expectation that both vessels would return to Europe before the next harvest. The venture's profitability required adherence to a tight schedule, and throughout the spring of 1798 Barlow urged Lee to speed the provisions to Europe so that they would arrive before domestic prices broke. Barlow was so optimistic about the venture's prospects that he extended a personal loan to Lyle and endorsed some bills he had authorized Cathalan to draw on Lyle.[20] Barlow assumed all three partners would be rich once the two vessels returned to Europe. Unfortunately, the first leg of the *Friendship* and the *Rachel*'s voyage failed to turn a profit. Even if it had, Barlow had not foreseen how the worsening relationship between the United States and France would affect the fortunes of Americans trying to do business on the continent.

Despite commercial and diplomatic disappointments, Barlow claimed that this period was one of the happiest in his life.[21] He and Ruth were enjoying a rare spate of good health, and the timely payment for his service in Algeria cushioned them from the hard times that affected other Americans living in France. That winter they started planning a spring visit to Switzerland. Barlow had seen enough of the Alps from a distance to be fascinated by mountains that had no parallel in New England. He was equally curious about Switzerland's republicanism. But they kept postponing their journey—allegedly in response to political disturbances that accompanied Napoleon's victorious campaigns against the Austrians—but really because no place had come to suit them both better than Paris.

The lure of Paris did not consist simply in its culture or in their newfound friend, Fulton. The Barlows had become prominent fixtures of the city's expatriate community. Their social ascent had begun prior to Barlow's departure for Algeria when Monroe brought them into his circle. Ruth subsequently reported that though she missed Barlow desperately—she complained of being unable to sleep without him—she was far from lonely. She disliked being trapped in a card-playing social round because it left no time for reading and serious conversation. However, she was dutiful in maintaining contact with their American and French friends. She reported often encountering Henri Grégoire and the translator of Thomas Paine's *The Age of Reason*, François Lanthenas, both of whom sent Barlow their regards. Helen Maria Williams, at whose table Ruth always found "good society," replaced the Monroes after their recall, and Barlow's success in Algiers further enhanced their social status after his return.[22]

Barlow was convinced that if the world's two largest republics failed to set an enlightened example, the redemptive potential of republicanism would be squandered. He supported Gerry's efforts to prevent a rupture between the two countries after Pinckney and Marshall left Paris. Because Gerry would not learn of Barlow's disparaging description of him until later, he accepted Barlow's coaching while negotiating with the Directory. Barlow then relayed optimistic reports to the United States about the progress Gerry was making. Barlow and Fulton also advised George Logan during his unauthorized peace mission to France in the summer of 1798, introducing him to the Anglophone community in Paris. Barlow complained he lacked influence in France, but he exaggerated his powerlessness. Actually, he was shy about becoming entangled in French politics after coming so near to dying "with the fathers of the Republic [the Girondins] because they were my friends," and he did not want to assume responsibility for the debacle he sensed was in the making.[23] He had fewer reservations about engaging in free-lance diplomacy back home.

Pinckney and Marshall's XYZ Dispatches describing the insults to which Talleyrand's agents had subjected the commissioners ignited fierce hostility towards France. Enraged Americans responded to what they construed as an attempt to humiliate the nation by drafting a series of belligerent addresses to President Adams. The president's formal, published answers fed the fires of public wrath. Inflamed public opinion induced the retirement of some in Congress, who had identified with the Republican opposition to Adams's policies, leaving Federalist majorities in both houses of the legislature. The Federalists used their newfound power to pass a series of measures that pointed to war with France. Congress sanctioned the arming of American merchant ships to defend themselves against French cruisers. It enlarged the navy, creating for the first time a cabinet-level post of secretary of the navy, and authorized U.S. vessels to seize or destroy France's public and private warships. Finally, Congress expanded the existing army and authorized the formation of a provisional force over which George Washington assumed titular command, though with the understanding that Alexander Hamilton would exercise actual command.

Though the Federalist leadership believed they were responding to a real threat of imminent hostilities, they also saw political advantage in their anti-French policies. They hoped tension with France would purge Americans of the anti-British prejudices they had acquired during the Revolutionary War. The Federalists assumed that in a world where one could not have good relations with one of the great powers without having bad relations with the other, alignment—if not alliance—with Britain was more in the nation's interest than alignment with France. The farce the French had repeatedly made of their constitutions showed they could not be depended upon. Because Britain looked like a stable monarchy, she could protect the United States from France's wrath in two ways. Britain's navy could serve as a barrier against French harassment and invasion while a mercantile association with the former mother country assured the young republic's prosperity and public credit. Gerry's and Barlow's efforts to mend fences in Paris ran counter to the course pursued by the Federalist-controlled Congress.

In July 1798, Barlow wrote James Watson that Gerry had gotten the Directory to agree to receive a new American minister, to drop all demands for apologies and money, and to disavow all the seizures and piracies that had taken place since the previous autumn. The French government had reacted to the hard line that the Adams administration was pursuing with little more than an embargo on American vessels in France's ports. Barlow was confident that this would soon be lifted, which made it important that the next move come from the Adams administration. Otherwise, the result would be full-scale war. Barlow warned against allying with Britain, which had barely survived the 1797 mutinies in its fleet and was nearing financial exhaustion. He predicted Britain would abandon any alliance with the United States the minute France offered peace.[24] And he discounted the significance of Britain's naval victory over the French and Spanish fleets off Portuguese Cape St. Vincent in February, 1798, perhaps already banking on the success of Fulton's submarine.

Barlow found working with Fulton more rewarding than his efforts at private diplomacy. Though the Directory had rejected Fulton's first proposal for a "Nautilus," the patent he secured for his system of small canals attracted the attention of French engineers and led to the translation of his *Treatise on the Improvement*

of Canal Navigation. When Napoleon Bonaparte heard about Fulton's ideas, he asked for more information before departing on his Egyptian campaign. Fulton also sent him a French translation of his 1797 pamphlet "On Freedom of Trade and Why Foreign Possessions and Duties on Imports, Far from Being Beneficial to Nations Are Prejudicial to Them." Predictably, it failed to appeal to someone who dreamt of conquering the Middle East.

Nonetheless, the tightening of the British blockade led the minister of marine to reconsider and appoint a commission to evaluate Fulton's "Nautilus" proposal. A presentation involving a model of the underwater craft took place on August 7, 1798, at the lodgings Fulton shared with the Barlows. The commission subsequently endorsed in principle what it called the *"bateau-poisson"* as a possible counter to Britain's naval preponderance but recommended so many modifications in design that the ministry of marine discarded it for the moment. Among other things, the morality of submarine warfare proved to be controversial.

When Barlow was not counseling Fulton about France's bureaucracy, he was dealing with the financial difficulties of his commercial partners. Prior to the salt ventures of the *Friendship* and the *Rachel*, Barlow had been concerned with Robert Lyle in the voyage of the *Nagle*. The vessel had arrived in Le Havre after Barlow departed for Algiers, and Ruth in her letters to him mentioned the possibly of the *Nagle's* cargo spoiling before it could be sold. The first sign that Lyle might be in serious trouble was his inability to pay Barlow's note for 15,000 livres when it came due in April 1798. Barlow loaned Lyle an additional 3,000 livres in June so he could stay in the salt venture. When the *Friendship* and *Rachel* failed to arrive before the new harvest, Barlow realized he might lose the 45,814 livres, or roughly $8,500, that Lyle now owed him.[25]

To recover so substantial a sum, Barlow asked Lyle to transfer some of his other assets to him. In partnership with a Virginian named John R. Dabney, Lyle had sent the Danish brigantine, *Altona*, on a slaving voyage to Africa. Her principal investors ordered her to Surinam and then Boston before returning to Europe. Barlow would not have chosen to have an interest in a slaver had Lyle possessed other assets. Even then Dabney refused to transfer Lyle's interest in the vessel until Lyle settled his accounts with Dabney. Since Lyle was in England, Barlow asked for his power of attorney and his papers. They revealed that Dabney was deeply indebted to Lyle, which eventually enabled Barlow to force Dabney's consent to the transfer. Because the vessel was at sea, the only way Barlow could be sure of securing his share was to have vessel and cargo attached when it arrived at a U.S. port. Barlow worried that other creditors would beat him to it, now that he was aware of the financial weakness of both Dabney and Lyle. He also had to fend off the claim of another American merchant in Bordeaux, who maintained Dabney had already assigned to him the interest Barlow now claimed.[26]

Dabney's problems turned out to be even greater than Lyle's. Dabney eventually had to convey all his remaining interest in the *Altona* to Hichborn and Hichborn's son-in-law. Barlow tried to keep both Lyle and Dabney afloat, though, because, apart from advertising Barlow's involvement in a trade he abhorred, the failure of the one would destroy the other. Barlow's success in doing so, while others struggled, derived from his previous investments in Parisian real estate and the compensation the U.S. government paid him in hard money for his services in Algeria. Between the two, he had the margin required both to honor his debts and to help friends like Lyle. He was even strong enough to invest in a cargo of cotton and sugar from Portugal that the firm of Strobel and Martini in Bordeaux offered him.[27]

A South Carolinian by birth, Daniel Strobel had come in the early 1790s to Bordeaux, where he entered into partnership with a Dutchman named Theodore Peters. Barlow had made their acquaintance in Paris during 1793, when they were trying to free their vessels from embargoes. After the Barlows returned to Paris in 1795, they got to know Strobel, who by then had entered a new partnership with Gotlieb Martini from Latvia. During the next decade Strobel and Martini would emerge as Bordeaux's largest commission house in the American trade. Barlow's dual citizenship proved useful to them in protecting their cargoes as Franco-American relations soured.[28]

Financial pressures in Europe did lead Barlow to try liquidating his American assets. In August he sent William Little of Boston a power of attorney to collect his debts in the United States.[29] The four shares of the Ohio Company acquired in 1787 were his most valuable possession, though he had no idea how valuable. On October 24, 1798, he gave James Watson full power to dispose of them if he thought it advantageous to do so. Barlow also tried to settle his accounts with John Fellows, the New York bookseller who had arranged for the first American publication of Barlow's *Letter to the National Convention on the defects of the Constitution of 1791; Advice to the privileged order* (Part II) and the first English translation of *Letter Addressed to the people of Piedmont*. In 1794 Barlow had consigned to Fellows a trunk containing multiple sets of the French encyclopedia, which currently ran to fifty-six volumes, hoping the sets would sell for between $250 to $300 each. Barlow wanted payment for another consignment of books he had forwarded to Fellows from Hamburg in June 1795. Finally, in 1796, Fellows had published Barlow's collected political essays. Barlow also asked Matthew Carey of Philadel-

phia to pay for the hundred unbound copies of *The Vision of Columbus* he had
sent just before he left New York in 1788. He drew on Fellows and Carey for the
full amount of what he thought was his due plus interest, which in Carey's case
consisted of almost half the total, since the debt was more than a decade old.[30]

On October 2, 1798, news from America about how the Federalists were using the
XYZ Dispatches impelled Barlow to write George Washington. Though Barlow
had known Washington in the army, he could not presume that Washington remembered him except as the author of *The Vision of Columbus* and as the American consul in Algiers who had freed 120 Americans. So Barlow got right to the
point, which was to prevent the war he thought Washington's appointment as
supreme commander of an expanded army "contemplate[d]" (395).[31] Barlow
gave his own outline of the dispute, though with considerably more tact than he
had used in writing Abraham Baldwin, attributing the current state of the Franco-
American relationship "simply and literally [to] a *misunderstanding*. . . . It is clear
that neither" of the respective governments "has an interest in going to war with
the other; and I am convinced that neither of them has the inclination" (396). But
while "the balance of inclination as well as of interest . . . is in favor of peace, . . .
each government [was] ignorant of it with respect to the other" (396–97).

Barlow sought to persuade Washington "that the French Directory is at present
sincerely desirous of restoring harmony between this country and the United
States, on terms advantageous to both parties" (397). In addition to the points he
had made in his letter to Watson, Barlow stressed two new developments. The
French had lifted their embargo on American vessels (398), and the Directory
contemplated "a just indemnity for spoliations on . . . American commerce." Barlow observed that "the Directory considers these declarations and transactions as
a sufficient overture on its part," adding "that a refusal on the part of the American
government to meet on" such an open ground would "be followed by immediate
war . . . of the most terrible and vindictive kind" (399). When Barlow saw "two great
nations rushing on each other's bayonettes [*sic*] without any cause of contention,
but a misunderstanding," he felt he had no choice but to beseech Washington to
use his influence to postpone hostilities at least "till a word of explanation can
pass" between the aggrieved parties in favor of a new attempt at negotiation (401).

Washington forwarded Barlow's letter to Adams, with a cautious endorsement.
Though he couldn't decide whether it had been written with "a very good, or a
very bad design," he was certain that "the French Directory knew about the letter"
and deferred to Adams about how to respond.[32] When Adams appointed a new
minister to France in the middle of February 1799, he went out of his way to assure

Washington that he was responding to Talleyrand's overtures rather than to Barlow. In Adams's estimate Barlow's letter to Washington betrayed "unequivocal Symptoms of blackness of heart," particularly the passages threatening war if the United States government failed to embrace an accommodation.[33] Adams had ample justification for feeling angry with Barlow's depiction of him as a mad president after Barlow's March 4 letter to Baldwin was published, but it is just as well Barlow wasn't privy to Adams's feelings. A memorandum Barlow and Fulwar Skipwith submitted to the Directory in February 1799 to promote a diplomatic resolution to the crisis depicted Adams as acting with restraint in response to France's depredations on American shipping.[34] It is unlikely that Barlow would have been able to represent Adams in so flattering a light had he known what the president thought of him.

Barlow was far more concerned with avoiding war between the French and American republics than with two Federalists measures the Fifth Congress passed towards the end of its second session. These were the Alien Friends Act, which gave the president power to deport aliens he deemed a threat to the nation's security, and the Sedition Act, which gave federal courts jurisdiction over seditious libels against the national government. Barlow had no way of knowing that both acts would seriously affect his future. The first hounded Constantine Volney out of the United States; the second led to the prosecution of Vermont congressman, Matthew Lyon, for publishing a copy of Barlow's March 4 letter to Abraham Baldwin.

Baldwin had received the letter in the midst of the Republican rout in the Fifth Congress and had sought to rally those who still opposed Federalist measures by reading passages from it aloud to them. Lyon was among the Republican stalwarts impressed by Barlow's warnings, and he asked Baldwin's permission to copy the letter. Baldwin consented after Lyon promised not to publish it, but someone subsequently persuaded Lyon's wife that Lyon's reelection depended on its publication. A version appeared on September 1, 1798, in *The Scourge of Aristocracy*, an obscure Vermont publication edited by Lyon's son James. When Lyon found out about it, he suppressed the publication as far as possible to honor his pledge to Baldwin. But that did not stop him from making all the verbal use he could of Barlow's text, nor did it stop the government from prosecuting Lyon for the seditious sentiments contained in it.[35]

In late 1798, the "angry tone" of James Watson's reply to his July letter led Barlow to suspect that his March 4 letter to Abraham Baldwin might have gotten into "the wrong hands."[36] Though Watson pretended only to report the response which "will be generally entertained by the people of this <u>Country</u>" to the Directory, it was clear that Watson now regarded Barlow as an adversary rather than a friend. Watson claimed that the American people had "never supposed that it was the object of the french government to make war upon them," while the French gained much by a "system of piracy & plunder." Neither the American government nor its people wanted anything other than peace with France, "but it must be a fair and honorable" one, "not one that invites french Anarchists to intermeddle in our elections, to debauch our citizens and to vilify our government— not one which exposes us to French insults and rapacity at home and abroad & exhibits us to the world, in the person of our envoys, as a spectacle for derision."

Watson construed the overtures in which Barlow put so much stock as "a set of new snares for our entanglement." What drew his most vehement condemnation, however, was Barlow's warning about a "terrible and vindictive" war. Watson denied the U.S. government had any intention of entering into an alliance with Britain. Instead, it hoped to preserve the nation's neutrality and independence, though it was prepared to sacrifice the former if it became inconsistent with the latter. Then it would make no difference whether Britain made peace with France. America would defend itself no matter what the cost. Far from being "moved by the terrors of a french invasion," Watson claimed Americans feared France's enmity "less than her friendship—The examples of Holland, Switzerland & the Italian States are before them & they teach them to think of france as of the beautiful female figure which crushed the bones and pierced with darts the victims it embraced."

Only toward the end of the winter of 1799 did Barlow learn for certain that his letter to Baldwin of the previous year was being used to magnify the problem he had hoped it would resolve. The letter had failed to attract much attention before November 5, 1798, when the *Connecticut Courant* published a version. Then, on November 24, "Americanus" published in Boston's *Columbian Centinel* a paraphrase of it, accompanied with a scathing denunciation. "Americanus" claimed that next to the publication of the "dispatches of our Envoys," Barlow's letter "contains the most complete discovery of the views of the five-headed monster of *France*, and of their partisans in this country." The *Centinel* also reproduced the *Courant's* introduction to the text of the letter that attributed Barlow's supposed apostasy to the "accursed demoralizing powers of that modern French philosophy which has made of *Europe* a charnel house." A month later the *Centinel* published a full copy of Barlow's letter under the heading "QUINTESSENCE OF VILLAINY." The editor attributed his delay in offering a complete text to an initial unwillingness to "promulgate the degradation of a Man, whom every American once revered for talents, patriotism, and erudition."[37]

Barlow responded to his vilification with a short essay entitled *On the system of policy hitherto pursued by our government*. In it he made no attempt to deny that he was the author of the letter the *Centinel* had republished, though he claimed "every part" of the version that had appeared there "is mutilated and distorted more or less" (366).[38] Comparison of the two texts reveals that while many words had been changed, alterations to the sense of the original were fewer than Barlow claimed. Barlow's assertions that the letter had been drafted in haste and that he had never intended it to be published were more convincing. However, he refused to retract his substantive criticism of the conduct of the U.S. executive toward France or his judgment that the United States could have settled its differences with France at much less cost "had your negotiations been properly managed" (367). All Barlow would concede was that had he realized his letter to Baldwin would be published, he would have mentioned the errors of France, among which the "villany"[sic] portrayed in the dispatches was the worst.

Barlow's American critics were not to assume he approved of France's "monstrous system of piracy and plunder" (368). He had repeatedly protested their "injustice and violence committed" (368–69) against American interests. While such actions reflected France's resentment of the Jay Treaty, Barlow had always maintained that the French response was "far greater than the occasion would justify." He also acknowledged that France had committed many "blunders, or *crimes*" in the course of its revolution (369). But when the "difficulties and incentives to ungovernable passions that have lain in the way of its leaders" were taken into account, the marvel was "why they have committed so few" rather than "why they have committed so many" (370). America had fewer excuses for squandering its opportunity for demonstrating that a "perfect liberty of commerce . . . would have a powerful tendency . . . to maintain a perpetual peace between countries separated by the ocean" (370–71).

The United States was uniquely positioned to champion this idea not just because a great ocean stood between it and most of its trading partners but also because the balance of trade was always against it. The ocean protected America against invasion, while the balance of trade placed in her hands "a most powerful weapon of defense" (372) against maritime aggression. As Barlow's 1793 memo had argued, the United States should have notified Britain that "all property taken unjustly from [our] citizens . . . [would] be compensated by so much property of the subjects [of the offending power] found within your jurisdiction." No injustice would be involved because Britain had been the aggressor (373). Nor should Americans worry about the British denying them credit or about the sequestration of debts being dishonorable. Sequestration was morally preferable to outright plunder, and the eagerness of British manufacturers to extend credit to any and all comers suggested that being denied credit was the last thing Americans need worry about.

Barlow suspected that those who stressed credit had another agenda, namely, the preservation of public credit. He repeated his assertion in Part II of *Advice to the Privileged Orders* that the capacity to borrow money was "an instrument too dangerous to be trusted in the hands" of any government (376). Now, however, he was able to point concretely to an abuse of that power. Instead of a shrinking debt and lower interest rates, the nation was accumulating debt at twice the rate of interest Hamilton had initially offered creditors in 1790. Concern for the nation's public credit had then led its Federalist leadership to align with and imitate Britain. He preferred France's condition of being "unable . . . to borrow money on any terms, even from her own citizens" (381). Despite this, France had continued to spend prodigious sums on the war.

Barlow realized that when hostilities ceased, France's "debt will be enormous, and in a very depreciated state." But he hoped she would not follow America's example of "funding it, in all its undistinguished forms and accumulated size." Instead, he preferred to see the debt "cut up into paper money, given out to the creditors, and then . . . collected and burnt, in the course of three years" through taxation. Such a policy "would be less *unjust*, and less *impolitic*, than to increase it [the debt] tenfold . . . and fix . . . it upon the nation forever at the highest rate of interest known" (381). A "middle course" might have been found in America "had there been no speculators in congress, or about the treasury" (382). Barlow evidently approved of France's funding only one-third of its consolidated debt in 1797 and forcing its creditors to accept bearer bonds for the remaining two-thirds, without much prospect that either the principal or interest on them would ever be paid.[39] The United States would be better off relying on "the debts you [are] constantly owing and renewing with all the nations that had it in their power to menace your repose" (383) for protection and should never have agreed to forego their sequestration in the Jay Treaty. Not only had that treaty produced a rupture with France, but it had ushered in an incalculable expense in the form of a navy. "It is the siphon put in suction, which can never stop, or moderate its action, till all that feeds it is exhausted" (384). America would be safer if it entirely eschewed a navy because then none of the naval powers of Europe would have an incentive to attack her.

France had "not yet reduced to practice, the liberty she has vindicated in theory," but this lapse was "owing to the prolongation of revolutionary measures, necessitated by the state of Europe, and not to a forgetfulness of principle." She had been unable to take measures to establish the freedom of the seas because "she has not yet arrived at that state of tranquility which will enable her to look beyond present exigencies, to plans of permanent improvement." In contrast, during a decade of unparalleled prosperity and peace, the U.S. government had succeeded in doing nothing besides increasing the nation's debt and imitating Europe's "follies" (392–93). Barlow had hoped that America would use its privileged position "to lay the foundation of an edifice that should . . . afford a shelter to the human race." The nation should have reformulated the law of nations, which disproportionately favored belligerent over neutral powers, upon principles of "reason, justice and . . . peace." Then, when France came to her senses, the world could have witnessed "the two greatest republics on earth, not only enjoying liberty themselves, but recommending it to others by removing the occasion of wars." If the United States was only capable of copying "precedents from old monarchies," it was time for despair because the "perfectibility of human society" would have to be abandoned in favor of men reconciling themselves "to slavery, monarchy, and perpetual war" (393).

Barlow wrote his *On the system of policy hitherto pursued by our government* to repair his injured reputation in America and sent several copies of the pamphlet —first printed in English by John Hurford Stone's Parisian press—to friends and former associates in the United States.[40] William Lee got one, which he finally acknowledged after more than a year of silence. Barlow also sent a copy to his former friend Lemuel Hopkins in Hartford with the request that he get Hudson and Goodwin of the *Connecticut Courant* to reprint it. He was aware that the *Courant* had been the vehicle for some of the abuse directed against him but assumed that it would be willing to publish the piece because "the name of an Arch Traitor like your old friend" was sure to "excite a curiosity very useful to Booksellers." Finally, he sent a copy to John Fellows in New York, urging him to arrange for its publication "without regard to copyright."[41] Despite these efforts, Barlow would have to wait until 1801 for it to be published in the United States.

CHAPTER THIRTEEN

Republican Prophet

John Fellows had withdrawn from publishing in 1798, unbeknownst to Barlow. But that did not prevent a personal letter Barlow had written Fellows from Hamburg on May 23, 1795, from appearing in the August 19, 1799, issue of the *Connecticut Courant*.[1] In responding to a proposal from Fellows to collect Barlow's political writings into a single volume, Barlow had assumed he was addressing someone sympathetic with his ideas. Barlow dismissed a report in Fellows's letter that Noah Webster was critical of his *Advice to the Privileged Orders* on the grounds that he [Webster] relied on an "English ministerial paper" for his information and therefore knew "nothing about" the French Revolution. "I have no doubt of his friendship for me. [But] His intentions are much better than his arguments." Barlow was not so indulgent about the "slavish spirit of aristocracy . . . manifest in America." He attributed it to the funding system, whose designers were described as "a phalanx of little despots" in "a retrograde march."

Barlow had then turned to the subject of religion. Because Fellows was the principal distributor of Paine's *Age of Reason* in North America, there was reason to assume he was at least sympathetic to Paine's ideas. Barlow wrote: "I rejoice in the progress of good sense over the damnable imposture of Christian mummery." He construed as a measure of that progress the publication of Thomas Paine's *Age of Reason* and a decent translation of Baron d'Holbach's *Christianisme devoilée*, which had issued from another New York press in 1795. He only wished that d'Holbach's English translator "would go on and give us the next volume, the history of that famous Montebank called St. Paul." Barlow concluded his letter to

Fellows with the injunction that he "not suffer a word of this letter to go into a newspaper."

The *Connecticut Courant* introduced Barlow's 1795 letter by accusing both Barlow and Abraham Baldwin of religious betrayal.. What manner of men could have pursued the "solemn and holy employment" of army chaplain "for the purpose of procuring its emoluments, while [they] held not only the office, but even the religion itself, which it inculcated, in the highest detestation?" In the estimation of Aaron Barlow, Barlow's letters to Fellows and Baldwin had created the impression of "your being an enemy to your native country and renouncing all religion."[2] That was a more extreme conclusion than the evidence warranted, but concerning Barlow's religion Aaron was not far off the mark. Entries Barlow made in his notebooks between 1799 and 1801 are sprinkled with references to writings that maintained there was no such thing as an intelligent God and that all religions were illusions. By 1802 these ideas had become Barlow's own. He then objected to prayers addressed to a sentient Supreme Being on the grounds that reason and intelligence were attributes of a dependent rather than an independent agent. If God were indeed sovereign, he would be the equivalent of nature and, as such, without intelligence. Barlow also rejected belief in the rewards of an afterlife, arguing that they were incompatible with notions of divine justice because they came too late to do any good. Barlow surmised many unbelievers defended religion out of expediency, but that was not a course he would pursue.

Barlow chose not to publish a confession of faith, or more accurately, his lack of it. That was less because he was ashamed of his disbelief than because of the use made of the Fellows letter in prejudicing people against his political ideas. Noah Webster's response to Barlow's letter to Baldwin left no doubt about that danger. In the *New York Spectator* of November 17, 1798, Webster accused Barlow of being "wrong in all the principles which regard the French Revolution and the connection of the United States with France." Most of Webster's letter addressed Barlow's politics, arguing that the Franco-American alliance had from the beginning cost the United States more than it was worth, but Webster concluded with a personal message "from an old friend who once loved and respected you." Webster attributed "the contemptuous manner in which you speak of the president . . . [as] striking proof of the effect of atheism and licentious examples on the civility and good manners of a well-bred man. You went from America with a good character . . . in divesting yourself of your religion, you have . . . like the French . . . commenced a rude, insulting, dogmatical egotist. . . . Do not believe, Sir, that *all* your countrymen who support their government have become ideots, that our councils are guided by 'stupidity' or 'madmen.'"[3]

It would take almost a decade before Webster and Barlow reconciled their differences to the point of again corresponding with each other. Though the political divide between them narrowed after France abandoned its republicanism, they would never recover the cordial friendship they had enjoyed as younger men. Failed relationships are painful, particularly as one grows older, and this public condemnation caused Barlow considerable unhappiness.

Coping with the intensifying economic difficulties that had been afflicting his friends since the middle of 1798 came as a merciful distraction to Barlow. In addition to the obstacles that the limited naval war with France known as the "Quasi War" imposed on trade between the two nations, adjusting to a new hard money economy propelled France into a depression. During 1797, the success of France's armies enabled her to strip her neighbors of treasure and to force Austria to come to terms. But after Britain suppressed the mutiny in her fleet during 1797, she mounted an expanded blockade of the French coast that crippled France's commerce. The Directory explored the possibility of invading Britain before deciding to strike at her South Asian possessions through Egypt and the Middle East. Nelson's victory over the French fleet in the Battle of the Nile hobbled Bonaparte's Middle Eastern operations, making conquered treasure harder to find and transport home and forcing the Directory to turn inward for financial resources.

From 1797 through 1799 taxes would account for a greater proportion of the national budget than ever before or after.[4] Heavy taxation wreaked havoc on France's economy in hitherto unprecedented ways. A sequence of good harvests produced more crops than the depleted urban areas needed, forcing down the price of food. Disorders stemming from provision shortages ceased to plague Paris and the other provincial capitals. Instead, the terms of trade shifted decisively in favor of city dwellers because increased taxation—in conjunction with the abandonment of paper money—forced what little hard money there was into the urban centers. However, the cities were far from islands of expansive prosperity. The seaports, hitherto the sites of the most dynamic economic activity, went into decline. At the same time, conscription, which did not become routine until 1798, further depleted the supply of adult males. Urban populations in general—especially the sansculottes—who had been behind most of the disorders of the earlier years— were the hardest hit. But merchants were also affected by the scarcity of hard money and resulting deflation. Their contractual obligations became harder to honor with the general diminution of all prices and the shrinking availability of capital. Everyone who participated in networks of interlocking debts and credits found themselves victimized as debts overwhelmed credits.[5]

The immunity Barlow had enjoyed from economic pressures during 1798 caught up with him early in 1799, as the normal hiatus imposed by winter on North Atlantic commerce came to an end. During the spring of 1799, several business associates whose scale of operations had dwarfed Barlow's, including Daniel Parker and James Swan, either entered into bankruptcy agreements with their creditors or were threatened with failure. Parker's creditors agreed to a settlement that compelled him to sell all his marketable assets and to mortgage the income due him from the land he had acquired in France. Since there was no guarantee that his tenants would pay their rents on time, he remained in hiding rather than risk being imprisoned for debt. The pressure of Swan's creditors led him to press Barlow to account for a small consignment of goods he had received in Hamburg during 1794 from Swan and D'allarde. The same thing occurred in Barlow's relations with C. D. Dede, though in this case the person to whom Barlow had entrusted that matter, a Mr. Whitcomb, had absconded.[6]

Barlow was determined to honor his commitments, but he found it increasingly difficult to do so because of his "losses little & great multiplying."[7] His biggest disappointment involved the voyages of the *Rachel* and the *Friendship*. When Barlow at last heard from William Lee in mid-April 1799, he learned that instead of making the three partners' fortunes as originally expected, they would be lucky to rescue $1,300 a piece from their venture.[8] That reversal forced Barlow to put off paying the debt he owed Dede, despite a previous promise, though not for long.[9] The same thing happened in connection with Barlow's wish to close his accounts with Swan and D'allarde, though here uncertainty as to whether Swan by himself could give Barlow a discharge for a debt legally due the partnership created an additional complication. Barlow acknowledged the debt and intended to pay it, but in September he requested additional time to do so.[10]

Barlow described the economy during the summer of 1799 as "much worse than the worst times [I] have ever seen here."[11] His efforts to save both Lyle and Dabney underscored the interdependence of the mercantile community during a business downturn. The strategy of diversifying one's risks by holding shares in many ventures afforded little protection. If there were any doubt as to the seriousness of the situation, Barlow had only to reflect on the number of his countrymen who were now in debtors' prison. Barlow avoided the common debacle, maintained his solvency, and was able to participate in a new venture to the West Indies sponsored by Strobel and Martini. But that enterprise went awry when a Boston consignee named Woodward ordered the vessel and its cargo from the West Indies to Boston. Woodward failed shortly afterwards, and Barlow feared Woodward's creditors would seize the cargo Strobel and Martini had entrusted to him if Woodward himself, whom Barlow suspected was a swindler, did not first make off with the partnership's property. Eventually, the venture turned out better than Barlow expected, but not before many frustrating delays in remitting its proceeds to Europe.[12]

Short of accepting a bankruptcy agreement, a creditor's most available remedy against a debtor was to have a court attach the debtor's assets. One could empower someone else to establish one's claim simply by showing plausible evidence of a valid debt. The debt did not have to be "proven" as it would in court proceedings for recovery. A debt secured in this way simply prevented the property in question from being removed or sold until the attachment was lifted, usually when the debt was paid. Courts administering this remedy honored creditors' claims in the order in which they were filed. Barlow devoted considerable time and energy during 1799 to securing attachments on the properties to which he felt he had a claim. Cumulatively, attachments adversely affected the liquidity of the larger economy by restricting sales, but Barlow knew no other way to respond to the general business downturn.

Attachment came with another disadvantage. Since it was a matter of public record, it served as a warning that someone's credit was being questioned. Thus one attachment could give rise to a flood of attachments as creditors scrambled for the limited assets of someone whose solvency was suspect. That is why Barlow was so anxious to keep the difficulties of Lyle and Dabney as quiet as possible. If their problems ever became public knowledge, the rescue Barlow was attempting would become impossible.[13] Barlow eventually succeeded in keeping Dabney afloat until 1801, when his debts to Lyle had finally been settled.

The economic difficulties that Barlow and others struggled with during 1799 contributed to the political demise of the Directory at the end of that year. The stagnating state of the French economy created few supporters prepared to defend the government in its final days. Though Barlow had construed the failure of France to establish its credit as a republican virtue in his *On the system of policy hitherto pursued by our government*, privately he denounced the Directory as unworthy of anyone's trust.[14] The predatory war the Directory waged against American vessels enhanced his dissatisfaction. Barlow maintained that France was acting against her own interests because one-eighth of her commerce continued to come from America via circuitous routes.[15] Barlow's dual citizenship allowed him to protect the ventures he and his friends sponsored, but he couldn't protect every American, nor cushion the general impact French depredations were having on the commercial environment, both American and French. Though the Directors eventually attempted to restrain France's privateers, Barlow thought the legislature contained too many members who benefited from privateering to curtail it effectively. This manner of predatory warfare made France resemble Britain more than the exemplary republic Barlow had hope she would become.

By the autumn of 1799, Barlow had come to regard the Directory as an unworthy custodian of France's republicanism and to conclude that any change would be for the better. His initial response to Napoleon Bonaparte's coup of 18 Brumaire (November 9, 1799), which replaced the Directory with a three-man consulate, was to watch and wait rather than to condemn it outright. Barlow realized that military coups were incompatible with republicanism, but he regarded all the governments that had ruled France since 1792 as revolutionary expedients thrust upon the nation by the hostility of the rest of Europe. As he wrote Baldwin shortly after Brumaire, "It has always been my opinion that they ought to have had less to do with constitutions till tranquility comes."[16]

After Napoleon's return from the Middle East, the future emperor looked less like a victorious general who would become a dictator than someone who desperately needed peace to consolidate his rule. Initially, at least, Napoleon was scrupulous about respecting the forms of republicanism. While he was careful to insure his power as first consul, he disguised his usurpation by appearing to share power with others and by invoking the nomenclature of the ancient Roman republic. He also selected a committee of fifty, drawn equally from the two branches of the previous legislature, to draft yet another constitution. The antirepublican nature of the Constitution of 1799 eventually became evident in how the franchise was to be exercised. Those qualified to vote were to choose a list of "notables" equal to one-tenth of the electors in their canton. These notables then elected a tenth of their members to an arrondissement college, which in turn chose a still smaller departmental list, from which the consuls, or their chosen agents, eventually made a final selection.[17] But these features would not become apparent until the constitution was promulgated on Christmas Day, 1799.

During the late autumn Barlow was approached for his suggestions about the shape the new constitution should take. He was flattered by the invitation because a long time had elapsed since anyone in official French or American circles had solicited his opinion about anything. The new American peace commissioners, who were momentarily expected in Paris, would shun him after they arrived at the beginning of 1800. Barlow's classmate Zephaniel Swift served as secretary to Oliver Ellsworth, a member of the commission who hailed from Connecticut. Barlow regarded Ellsworth as an enemy, and though Barlow and Swift occasionally communicated, Swift's relationship with Ellsworth forced the two former classmates to maintain more of a distance from each other than they otherwise might have.[18]

Because he had spent so much of the preceding year immersed in commercial affairs, Barlow used the constitutional commission's invitation to propose a revision of the "maritime law of nations." His short "Memoir on certain principles of Public Maritime Law," dated December 5, 1799, urged France to unilaterally foreswear commissioning privateers because they constituted a powerful "inducement for vicious individuals in all maritime countries to wish for a state of war" (460).[19] Barlow also argued that it was to France's interest to abolish privateering because "sea robbery" drew people away from more productive enterprises. As long as France remained an agricultural nation, it could not advantageously fight Britain at sea. Privateering would only serve to fill British prisons with French sailors (462).

Barlow wanted the French constitution to recognize the principle that free ships made free goods. While he acknowledged that France was not in a position to impose this principle on other nations, if she adopted it "for herself as an inviolable maxim," she would "recommend it by her great example" (467). Again, Barlow argued that this would be to France's interest because once such a measure became part of the law of nations, it would help to protect her agricultural and manufactured commodities from British seizure in neutral vessels. Barlow wanted France to abandon the concept of "*contraband of war*" (468), which Britain used to control the neutral carrying trade, and in the case of actual blockades, to have neutral vessels warned away rather than seized, unless they persisted in trying to get into port.

Barlow's December 5 memoir concluded with a draft of "a declaration of the *Rights of Nations*," (459) intended to parallel the Declaration of the Rights of Man, which he wanted appended to the new constitution. Its last five articles were designed to secure the program he had outlined in his text. But they were introduced by two of more comprehensive import. The first stated that "the French Republic will be and remain at peace with all people and at all times, so long as peace can be maintained by the strictest observance, on her part, of justice and the rights of nations" (474). The second read: "The rights of nations are, interior government and self-control; the faculty of continuing their actual forms of government, or changing them for others; the faculty of remaining neuter, and observing an impartial conduct toward neighboring nations while they may be at war" (475).

Barlow realized that his general principles would have little effect either on France or on the behavior of other nations. Nor was he surprised or disturbed that his proposed articles were ignored by those who framed the Constitution of 1799. Since he regarded a European peace as a necessary precondition for any constitutional permanency, he viewed the work of the Committee of Fifty as provisional at best. His effort was part of the larger project to revise the law of nations by articulating new principles that favored peace. At this stage, principles were far more important to him than their implementation.[20]

Drafting the "Memoir" for the French government led naturally to yet another address to his fellow Americans. Ostensibly written to counter the common reports about him lest they permanently destroy his influence in America,[21] Barlow's second letter to his fellow citizens, entitled *On certain political Measures proposed to their consideration,* outlined his vision of a republican world order. Though it was completed on the eve of the millennium, it would not be printed in the United States until the beginning of 1801. *On certain political Measures* advanced a plan for the "foundation of a pacific intercourse among all maritime nations . . . [that] may perpetuate itself and become universal." Barlow saw this international order emerging from the same substitution of "a moral [for] a physical force" that he believed lay behind the evolution of republicanism (402).[22] Experience demonstrated that "individual safety is best secured where individual [force] is least resorted to." Men had learned to "refrain from mutual injury by a habitual sense of convenience" and thus to prefer law and order. Agreement about so fundamental a matter had a power comparable in its effects to the "horror which prevents us from stepping off a precipice." By the force of public opinion, "great societies may be moved, millions of persons protected, industry and virtue universally encouraged, idleness and violence completely restrained, without lifting the hand of one man upon another" (403).

Enlightened public opinion held the key to the "progress of society, past, present, and to come. Great strides had already been taken." Anyone who compared the primitive struggle of men for survival with the current social state of human society, where industry was protected and the "comforts of life assured to himself and family," would "be convinced of a progress in human affairs, and of a tendency towards perfection." Nor was "the perfectibility of human society . . . a subject of idle speculation." In the minds of those "called to administer a representative government," it could and should act as an inspiration (404). For these men were in a unique position to "second the designs of nature by accelerating the progress of improvement" in ways that would lead to the elimination of poverty and the establishment of universal peace (405).

The same "mutual wants and aids" that had persuaded "civilized individuals

. . . of their relative dependence, and taught them the art, as well as the convenience, of living together in peace," also applied to nations (405–6). Barlow acknowledged that civility among nation states had not progressed as far as civility
among individuals. Indeed, many thought that *"the right of the strongest"* always
had and always would prevail between states, but such attitudes precluded the
continuing improvement of human society. Barlow argued that the "sense of mutual dependence" would "produce the same effects in the great sections of society
called states, as it does in the small sections called families" (406). "The mutual
dependence of man is universal, and it is perpetual." Thus a "particular *people*,
whatever extention [*sic*] we give to the meaning of the word . . . is every where a
physical and moral agent, whose interests are analogous and reciprocal with those
of another people of a like description" (407). Nor was there anything hard and
fixed about nations. They were constantly changing, as the unification of thirteen
separate states into the United States demonstrated. Barlow thought this development reflected "the tendency of civilization . . . to diminish the number of nations
and to increase their size and prosperity" (409).

The progressive dynamic Barlow saw at work among peoples had not been
operative between states until now because of the "few men, to whom the government of a state must be confided." But the United States had recently resolved
that problem by amalgamating representative democracy with federalism. Barlow
felt that France would be better off divided into twenty republics, united in a
confederacy for the pursuit of "objects of great national interest" (410). If all the
neighboring states of Europe then modeled themselves on the prototype of a fed-
eralized French Republic, Barlow believed it would provide the basis for a "*United
States of Europe*" (411) that would be neither too large in its individual compo-
nents for effective administration nor too small for effective defense.

How could Barlow assign France the task of leading the rest of Europe toward
a United States of Europe when it was conquering and looting its neighbors?
Webster's public letter of the preceding November accused the French government of subverting foreign governments in a manner "more dangerous to society
than war, famine, and pestilence." These "pretended republicans insinuate themselves among the unlettered mass of citizens, men most easily deceived and most
capable of desperate enterprizes, and among them diffuse the poison of immoral
principles and disobedience to the government of their country." Webster thought
"this dangerous and destructive practice of exciting subjects to rise against their
government . . . is more hostile to the peace and safety of society than a state of
war. . . . Against this principle, against this cowardly system of Jacobinism which
works in darkness, a *free government* is no more secure than a despotic one."[23]

Barlow dismissed Webster's concern that France might subvert America's republicanism, attributing French excesses to her circumstances. He was also sensitive to the ways America's revolutionary experience had resembled France's. Thus he claimed that in 1780, when the American Revolution had seemed on the verge of collapse, John Adams had advocated hanging all the loyalists. Maximilien Robespierre at least had wielded an axe from which he did not exempt himself.[24] Barlow thought that the United States offered the best model of what a representative democracy could become and hoped France and Europe would eventually be persuaded by that example. But he did not feel that his own country was beyond improvement. He urged Americans to explore how they could "lay the foundation of perpetual peace, at least . . . between all commercial nations" by "vindicating [their] commercial liberty, [in such a manner as] to gain the confidence of other powers" (424).

Americans' most important asset was a federal union based on interest rather than force. Barlow urged Americans to contrast their situation with that of Europe (433). The insular position of the United States made internal rather than external challenges their first priority. The greatest danger to America's liberty was an increasing public debt. Barlow felt Americans had been deceived into believing they were threatened by France; once they realized their error, they would resent the expansion of the debt to pay for unnecessary defense measures. But the assumption of the state debts in 1790 had been almost as "wanton [an] augmentation of the federal debt" as the Quasi War (433). Barlow saw two dangers in a large debt. First, he objected to the "pernicious influence" the debt was having "on the policy of our government with foreign power[s]" (434–35). Since the revenue was derived from an impost, "every stock-holder" was made "a partisan of our commercial connections with that country [Britain] whose commerce with us was supposed principally to secure this revenue; however injurious those connections might become to the general interest of the United States" (435). More fundamentally, he feared that heavy taxation would alienate the affections of the people from the national government upon which their freedom depended.

Barlow wanted everyone to be an equal stakeholder. He urged Congress to move the capital to the western reaches of the Potomac, he advocated the development of a national system of canals such as the one he had been helping Fulton promote in Europe, and he wanted universal education. All these measures would integrate the new settlements in the west into an expanding confederation, but he advanced no suggestions for how these measures might be financed except by avoiding the creation of a military establishment. Instead, Barlow banked on the future commercial development of the nation. He believed the United States

could defend its commerce—without going to the expense of maintaining a navy
—by entering maritime conventions that defined the rights of neutrals and guaranteed those rights to the signatories (445). He proposed an international judi-
ciary in the form of a "Chancery" that would rule on any violations and assess
damages against violators. These, in turn, would be enforced by commercially
boycotting the offender "until full payment shall be made," including compensation for "damages done [the] commerce" of the enforcing nations (447, 448). Barlow was prepared to admit appeals from the Chancery's decision, but he expected
his plan to work more by way of deterrence than enforcement.

Barlow even dreamed of extending this system of international governance to
"all other breaches of the rights of nations." Eventually, he hoped it would lead
to the drafting of a new law of nations and the establishment of the means to
enforce it (451). He rejected vesting the Chancery with the power to impose military sanctions as "incompatible with the object we have in view" (451–52). He also
rejected any suggestion that his vision for a new world order would not work. Instead, he repeated his claim that the United States was in a position to put his
scheme immediately into practice "because we are sufficiently indebted to those"
powers "who would be most likely to violate our rights" (455). The United States
should sequester the private or public debts due the offending power and suspend
all commercial intercourse with her.

Barlow dismissed the objection that the United States would suffer by imposing such penalties. First, he denied it would ever come to this. But if it did, the
nation could seek compensation for the trade it had lost by expanding its commerce with nations that did not injure her. Barlow reminded his readers that some
inconveniences were preferable to the "much greater one . . . of being humbled
under every species of maritime insult, and of becoming the football of rival powers
who strive which shall kick us the hardest," or, finally, of a war "in which there is
no calculating the calamities to a young republic, in fiscal derangements, commercial distresses, or loss of domestic liberty" (457). Barlow thought the "new republics of Europe [would have to] resort to this principle" at the end of the current European war "if they mean to hold the ground they have gained, in changing
their feudal for their representative constitutions" (411).

⚜

Barlow's second letter to his countrymen was completed five days before the
new French Constitution of 1799 was promulgated. Despite this constitution's
antirepublican features, Barlow remained hopeful about the future of Franco-
American relations. At the beginning of the new century, he published an article
in the Parisian press challenging the notion that Britain derived greater benefit

from the American trade than France. Barlow argued that France received more U.S. imports than Britain, despite most of that trade being forced through the circuitous channel of the Baltic ports.[25] He also believed Napoleon was seeking peace and reported optimistically to Baldwin: "we shall have peace with Austria & the Turk without another campaign." Finally, he acknowledged that the French "administration now is better than it has ever been," by which he meant more able to get things done. Though Talleyrand remained the foreign minister, Barlow predicted, "he will be so much the more pacific, as he will wish to throw the blame of the former failure on the ancient directory."[26]

Barlow clung to the idea that Napoleon was the agent of peace despite the continuing European war. When Britain remained obdurate and Austria launched a campaign in April 1800 to recover the ground that it had lost in Italy, Napoleon crossed the Alps with an army of reserves in early June and, though outnumbered by the Austrians, decisively defeated them at Marengo. This defeat forced the Austrians to accept a truce, which was only fragile, according to Barlow, because of English intrigue at the Austrian court. He was not worried about the continuation of the European war because Napoleon persisted in offering peace to both major powers. If these offers were rejected, France could make quick work of Austria, which would then isolate Britain. Barlow was also confident that a treaty would soon be forthcoming between the United States and France to bring an end to the Quasi War.[27]

Though it took considerably longer than Barlow predicted before the Treaty of Amiens—signed in March 1802—briefly pacified Europe, he had no difficulty persuading himself that Napoleon's objective remained peace.[28] It helped that Napoleon also followed republican procedure in submitting the Constitution of 1799 to the French people for their approval, despite the farcical result. The 3 million who supposedly endorsed the new constitution was twice the number that actually voted, while the 1,500 who voted "no" reflected France's political exhaustion more than the legitimacy of the new regime.[29] But any qualms Barlow entertained about the regime's legitimacy would have been assuaged by an elaborate funereal ceremony honoring Washington's memory, which took place two days after the official results of the plebiscite were announced. Part of a ten-day period of official mourning, it signaled the advent of a more conciliatory approach to the United States.

Napoleon's quest for political order in France contributed to the economic revival that secured Barlow the gentry status to which he had long aspired. As First Consul, Napoleon strove to establish an efficient financial system. He welcomed the merger of *la caisse des comptes courants*—formed in 1796—and *la caisse des d'escomptes du commerce*, established a year later, into the Banque de France in February 1800. Though to some extent modeled on the Bank of England, the Banque de France never became a truly national institution. Napoleon tried to give its notes "national" currency after 1803 by vesting it with sole power to issue bills of large denomination, but their circulation remained concentrated in Paris. Nonetheless, the consulate helped revive the economy because political stability and a loosening of credit created the conditions in which moneyed men were able to work free of their indebtedness to each other.

One can see the transformation in Barlow's commercial correspondence. During the winter of 1800, his letters to Strobel and Martini continued to deal with securing debts through attachments and blocking similar attempts by competitors.[30] But with the approach of spring, Barlow found that funds were becoming more plentiful. That, ironically, transformed him from someone who had bent over backwards to accommodate his debtor friends into a more demanding creditor.[31] Now that opportunity permitted, he was determined to achieve full liquidity. In this vein, he sent the American vice-consul at Nantes, Pierre-Frédéric Dobrée, a bond Barlow had acquired from a "desperate bankrupt," representing two shares in the French privateer *Uni*. The *Uni* had been unusually successful, and Barlow wanted to know what the bond would fetch in the Nantes market. Since Barlow had condemned privateering "as a detestable system of robbery" and realized that some American vessels had probably fallen prey to the *Uni*, he asked Dobrée to conceal his identity.[32] The answer must have been encouraging, though, because eighteen days later Barlow authorized the sale of the bond and felt rich enough from the transaction to order some good prize wine be remitted to him in addition to money.

After the first spring of the new century, Barlow was able to devote more time to his studies, even as he contended with a major change in Ruth's circumstances. Since his return from Algiers, she had been happier and healthier than at any time since the first years of their marriage. But as his financial fortunes began to improve, her health again declined. In early August 1800, Barlow and Ruth traveled to Le Havre, where they met Fulton. The summer heat did not suit Ruth, and Barlow hoped that a routine of sea bathing would restore her. She was fortunate to make the trip when she did because it enabled her to escape a terrible heat wave that gripped Paris throughout the remainder of the summer.

Fulton was in Le Havre to perfect and test a submarine he had constructed with Barlow's assistance. The project had lain dormant after 1798 while he busied himself with a rope-making project and the construction of a panorama in Paris.

Modeled on a similar attraction that had been built in London before he had left England, Fulton's circular display first projected a view of the French capital as it would have looked from above and then a representation of the British evacuation of Toulon at the end of 1793. Both proved wildly profitable. Fulton's economic windfall emboldened him to revive his submarine project during the last half of 1799.

Napoleon's appointment of a minister of marine who was friendly to the scheme led to the building of a prototype.[33] By June 1800, Fulton was ready to give a public demonstration of the *Nautilus*'s capabilities. On the appointed day, crowds lined the Seine between the Hôtel des Invalides and the Champs-de-Mars, while specially invited officials and savants viewed the spectacle from the Cours de la Reine. Fulton and a fellow American, Nathaniel Sargent, submerged the *Nautilus* for twenty minutes before resurfacing. They also maneuvered the vessel underwater. The demonstration was sufficiently successful to win an enthusiastic endorsement from the minister of marine. Though Napoleon rejected the terms Fulton demanded for loaning the *Nautilus* to the government on trial, the First Consul did consent to having the government move the vessel to Rouen. After more modifications in July, the *Nautilus* moved to Le Havre in early August, where Fulton hoped to demonstrate its potential for breaking the British blockade by sinking a British man-of-war.

By the time the Barlows joined Fulton in early August, their ménage à trois appears to have acquired a sexual dimension. Most of the evidence remains elliptical, deriving as it does from oblique allusions contained in letters Barlow wrote Ruth and Fulton after he returned to Paris. To confuse matters even more, the passages most relevant to understanding their relationship were written in a coded baby talk. They referred to Ruth and Fulton in ways that suggest Barlow wanted them to behave as husband and wife. Though this could simply have referred to their sharing a room, Barlow may also have hoped Fulton's physical attentions would be part of Ruth's cure. Significantly, Barlow did not abdicate his own identity as "Hubey," but he also used the baby talk to suggest that the triangle had a homosexual side. A decade earlier Fulton had spent a year in the establishment of the notoriously gay Duke of Devonshire. Paris during the 1790s resembled America in the late 1960s in its determination to break with previous conventions. Bourgeois women now joined aristocratic married women in taking lovers. While homosexuality remained less visible and pervasive, it was tolerated. Aside from the jocular allusions to flirtations that had peppered their previous correspondence, there is no evidence that either of the Barlows had engaged in extramarital sexual behavior before 1800.

Still they could not but have been impressed by how different the standards of sexual behavior in Paris were from those of rural Connecticut. If the ménage à trois took on a sexual cast, it likely did so more in response to the needs of Ruth and Barlow than Fulton. Both Barlows would have been experiencing the first signs of a change of life as the new century approached. Fulton was more sexually knowledgeable than either of them and may have introduced them to a new range of experiences. Barlow's gushing comments about their mutual love during that summer can be construed as reflecting the discovery of new-found pleasures. Before that, there is no hint of homosexual behavior in either Barlow's correspondence or behavior, despite his proximity for more than a year to the dey of Algiers. What is of particular note here—assuming a sexual dimension to the relationship did develop—is that neither Barlow ever sought to initiate a similar relationship with anyone else. Instead, the three remained committed to each other for the rest of their lives.

Fulton was incurring considerable risk in demonstrating his *Nautilus*, and Barlow's return to Paris in August 1800 seems like a cowardly distancing of himself from that danger. Although Barlow wrote to Ruth, denying that much risk was involved, he pestered the marine ministry in Paris for the commissions, which Fulton regarded as necessary to protect him against the possibility of being treated as a spy should he be captured while testing his submarine in combat. Barlow may have been persuaded by Fulton's confidence about the vessel's safety—nothing in fact happened to him in over a month of trials because of difficulties in approaching his targets—but Barlow dramatically underestimated the danger Fulton was running.

Perhaps Barlow decided the best chance of restraining Fulton from taking excessive risks was to offer Ruth to him. She had restrained Barlow from impulsive behavior in the past; perhaps he thought that she would have the same effect on Fulton. We shall never know whether that was part of Barlow's thinking, but we do know that Barlow assiduously ran Fulton's errands in Paris, forwarding to him the profits from his panorama and eventually the commissions that he managed to wring from reluctant bureaucrats. Barlow rejoined Ruth and Fulton in Le Havre at the beginning of October, after seeing to another matter in which they all had an interest.

🏵

Barlow had been seeking more appropriate accommodation for the three of them.[34] Finding such a place posed more of a problem for the Barlows than for Fulton because they had their American families to consider. Fulton's mother died in the summer of 1800, releasing him from any familial pull to return home. Aaron

Barlow had recently reestablished contact with Barlow; Ruth's brother, Abraham, as the only survivor among the older Baldwin siblings, maintained regular communication with them. If the Barlows meant to go home, they would have to do so reasonably soon or risk not having any family to return to. Aaron's fortunes dramatized the pressures they experienced in thinking about the future. None of his sons was interested in carrying on with his blacksmith's business. Aaron also complained that "their enemies," by which he meant Connecticut's Federalists, were exerting pressure on him to pay his debts. Aaron asked Barlow for a loan and—by Barlow's later account—was forced out of Connecticut after losing most of his property to his creditors. For his part, Abraham signaled his intention to retire from Congress, where he had served for the past twelve years, at the end of his current term.[35]

The Barlows also realized they would have to deal with hostility when they returned home. Since they would not be welcome in Connecticut, they would have to settle in another section of the country, just as Aaron shortly would. By this time Barlow had seen enough of Napoleon to realize he was as much a threat to liberty as a harbinger of it.[36] Ruth's longing to settle quietly in America had rekindled until she read some "American newspapers" that "vilify & abuse my husband . . . for supposed crimes in politicks." Ruth's despair over American politics led her to conclude that their only hope was to "look out some humble spot on this side of the water & form a little world of our own where we may be happy."[37]

Ruth's comments were made in the wake of the Barlows' purchase of a Parisian mansion that was large enough to accommodate the colony of expatriates she dreamt of harboring. In early September 1800, after searching in vain for the ideal combination of space, furniture, and board, Barlow had stumbled onto an elegant "national property." Instead of renting it, he decided to buy it as a speculation. That was compatible with postponing the decision about committing themselves either to an American or French future because real estate was cheaper than it would be when peace returned and the population of Paris recovered to its prewar level. Daniel Parker—who had been among the most active Americans in purchasing grand estates—thought the property would be worth twice as much after a year of peace.[38] Since Barlow remained reasonably confident that peace would soon be established, purchasing such a large property did not necessarily commit them to one future or the other.

We know about the house because when Barlow later tried to sell it, he supplied several prospective buyers with lengthy descriptions. A booklet written about the famous Hôtel de la Trémoille asserts, I think mistakenly, that this was the house Barlow purchased. Yet what is known about this mansion deviates significantly from what Barlow wrote about his house. Though he gave the address as 50 rue de Vaugirard—the address of the Hôtel de la Trémoille before and after the Revolution—street numbering became confused when the sections started renumbering them in 1792. They were renumbered again in 1805. In 1811–1812, Barlow gave the address of the property they had bought in 1800 as 100 rue de Vaugirard. Prerevolutionary street numbers did not reemerge until considerably later. Barlow also failed to mention that his property had a distinguished history when offering it to prospective buyers, who surely would have been interested in such information. All this suggests that Barlow's mansion probably was not the Hôtel de la Trémoille, though conclusive proof eludes us because of the destruction of the relevant section records in 1871.[39]

Nonetheless, the two mansions were not far apart from each other in the Faubourg St. Germain, which was then, as now, one of the more upscale areas of Paris. Barlow claimed his property had been constructed in 1789 or 1790 by Clermont Tonnère, who had lavished 430,000 livres (about $80,000 in 1800 or $1.375 million today) on the project. His building was shaped as a rectangle with a courtyard in the center. The portion of Barlow's building that fronted along 140 feet of the rue de Vaugirard contained a kitchen, stables for a dozen horses, and room for five carriages on the ground floor. The upper story of the front building had twenty-nine lodging rooms, serviced by sixteen chimneys. Two wings connected it with the far more elegant rear structure, leaving a courtyard in the middle roughly an acre in size "planted in the English stile" with ornamental trees and about three hundred fruit bearers. It was divided into two terraces, the rear elevated above the front one, from which three sets of stairs ascended to the ground floor of the main structure eight feet above the back terrace.

Barlow described the facing of the main structure as "perhaps the handsomest front in Paris." Its ground floor was divided into seven rooms. The central room, a "grand salon," was flanked by slightly smaller rooms on each side. These in turn formed part of "two complete apartments, each of six rooms." At the back of one of the apartments was "a genteel boudoir, bathing room & maid's chamber;" at the back of the other a library. Behind the grand saloon was a grand dining room serviced by several antechambers and side rooms. Under the mansion were "20 vaulted cellars" capable of holding at least five hundred casks of wine. Barlow claimed that the elaborate structure was so well built that neither joiner, nor mason, nor smith would have to be brought in for fifty years.[40]

Acquiring a property of this size required that Barlow have access to some hard money. It also involved a sobering change for one who hitherto had only used urban real property to generate income while living in rented premises. Barlow haggled over the purchase for the better part of a week and at one point thought he had lost it through driving too hard a bargain. After he found himself wanting to be the owner more than he feared the consequences, he closed the deal on September 8.

The property was much too big for them. They would live in one corner of the premises, "being too poor to furnish the principal apartments." Nor were they in a position to employ a large staff of servants or to entertain on the lavish scale that had been envisioned by the person who had built the mansion. Barlow undoubtedly saw the library as a place where he could pursue the studies he had never entirely abandoned during the recession of 1798–1800. But it is unlikely that his collection of books ever occupied more than a fraction of the available shelf space, even though he was a compulsive book buyer. In the event of a restoration of the monarchy, a purchaser's right to a national property would be vulnerable to challenge, but Barlow knew the hotel's former owner and found he was willing to waive all future claims to the estate for a modest fee. Sometime during the last quarter of 1801 Barlow converted his title from "national" to "patrimonial" to enhance the value of the speculation.[41] The Revolution had unexpectedly presented the Barlows with an opportunity to live, at least partially, on a scale to which neither they nor Fulton were accustomed.

CHAPTER FOURTEEN

Responding to France's Apostasy

The purchase of a Parisian mansion did not prevent Barlow's thoughts from turning homeward, but it complicated the task of returning to America. By the time he had moved their modest possessions to the new address, the progress of the American commissioners negotiating with Talleyrand, together with accounts from overseas, had convinced Barlow that American politics was moving in a new direction. The restoration of amity between the United States and France favored Thomas Jefferson's bid for the presidency, but that was not enough by itself to lure Barlow back to his native land. He also sought a mission that was more attractive than the comfortable exile his Parisian mansion now made possible. On September 15, 1800, he wrote to Jefferson suggesting an idea that had been germinating since Barlow's return to Paris from Algeria. He had come to view education as the most eligible way to protect America from the corruption and cynicism he saw subverting the Revolution in France.[1]

Washington's will—mentioning the establishment of a national university—had recently been published in France. Barlow urged that a national institute similar to the one France had created with the Constitution of 1795 be established. "The present state of knowledge presents us with little more than a confused idea of the immense . . . unknown that lies before us; and we lose the principle advantages of the little that is known for want of proper methods of teaching it to our children." Barlow's proposed "Polysophic Society" would serve four functions: expanding scientific knowledge, exploring the resources of the United States, teaching people how to communicate this knowledge to others, and furnishing schools with trained teachers by paying part of their salaries. He saw his proposal as encouraging "uniformity . . . in manners, language & sentiments of the people" and cultivating "a strict adherence to republican principles." Considering "how much their happiness depends on their political Union," both were necessary given the extent of the United States and "the variety of their pursuits."[2]

Barlow obviously was eager to head such a society, but he was equally receptive to a major diplomatic appointment in Europe. The new secretary of state, James Madison, learned from John Dawson that Barlow and Fulwar Skipwith were both prepared to serve if asked. Dawson recommended that Barlow replace William Vans Murray as ambassador to the Dutch Republic.[3] Instead, Jefferson recalled Murray, who was a Federalist, without replacing him and declined to comment on Barlow's proposal about a national learned society.

The visible tightening of Napoleon's rule after the December 24, 1800, attempt on the First Consul's life enhanced Barlow's growing disillusionment with the regime. In August 1801, he wrote Abraham Baldwin that he and Ruth were now "seriously at work" about returning to America, though he acknowledged that "after all that has been said on this subject in former years," Baldwin might not be prepared to believe him.[4] By this time several long-standing obstacles to going home had been removed. With Duer's death in 1799, Barlow no longer had to fear a suit to recover damages from the bills he had protested and refused to pay in 1790. Then Jefferson's presidency made Washington an attractive alternative to Connecticut. Barlow felt drawn to the nation's capital for the same reasons he had been drawn to Paris in the 1790s — he was becoming convinced that the future of republicanism lay there. Writing to Jefferson in August 1801, Barlow observed that if the American people ever degenerated the way the French people had, "mankind will perhaps never be compensated for your unpardonable neglect."[5]

The Barlows grew increasingly disillusioned with France's politics just as personal ties with their French friends deepened. Among the more captivating of these was Madame de Villette, a distinguished neighbor on the rue de Vaugirard. Born Philiberte de Varicourt, the daughter of an impoverished noble family near Voltaire's country estate, she had grown up to be beautiful and intelligent enough to attract that great man's attention. He supervised her education, bestowed upon her the title of "Belle et Bonne," and then enticed the wealthy second Marquis de Villette to marry her. De Villette had homosexual leanings, and the marriage was an unhappy one, but it did result in the birth of several children. The oldest to survive into adulthood, Charlotte, came to resemble her mother as she matured; a younger child named Charles eventually became the third Marquis de Villette. His father had died in 1793 of natural causes before the Terror could claim him. Because the second marquis had been part of the Girondin circle and Madame de Villette's brother had died in the queen's service, Madame was imprisoned until Thermidor.

Half of the second marquis's income terminated with his death, and his remaining properties were despoiled during Madame's incarceration. Upon being freed sometime after August 1794, she tried recovering as much of his estate as possible. As an economy measure, she moved into a building near the one the Barlows would acquire on the rue de Vaugirard, where she took in visiting Americans. Several of the peace commissioners appointed by President Adams in 1797 stayed with her. Talleyrand later identified Madame de Villette as the unnamed woman referred to in the XYZ Dispatches whom Marshall claimed had urged the American commissioners to bow to France's demands. But Marshall himself was charmed by her, and she, for her part, was genuinely drawn to Americans, preferring their forthrightness to the affectations of Parisian society.[6]

When Charlotte died from scarlet fever in 1801, Madame de Villette had difficulty accepting her daughter's death. Barlow joined several French poets in penning verses of condolence to assuage her grief, and Fulton did a portrait of Charlotte from memory that Madame considered very lifelike. Sharing her sorrow and grief made them all fast friends, and in subsequent years de Villette repeatedly overwhelmed the Barlows with her hospitality.

Some of Napoleon's domestic initiatives met with Barlow's approval. The uniform civil code that the First Consul spent a great deal of time and effort developing during 1801 was the most important of these, though its completion and full implementation had to wait until 1804. The economic benefits of Napoleonic rule, which included giving the franc a precise metallic value, were also welcome. Fiscal reforms enhanced the state's revenues, enabling the government to meet some of its obligations with hard money. That initiated an appreciation of public funds that Barlow had long expected.[7] A preliminary truce in October 1801, which eventuated in the Peace of Amiens with Britain in March 1802, pointed towards continued prosperity. Such positive developments deterred Barlow from concluding that Napoleon's rule was incompatible with Europe's liberty, despite the gradual reintroduction of facets of the ancien régime and the increasing concentration of power in one person. Nor could Barlow ever be sure the First Consul would not prove as transitory as the Directory and soon be replaced by something better.

Napoleonic prosperity allowed Barlow to trumpet his new gentility. The congratulatory letter he wrote to President Jefferson in August 1801 described his private affairs as now "on such a footing" as to allow him "to devote the remainder of my life . . . to the promotion of the solid improvements" in the "moral, political, & economical" nature of the United States.[8] But his brother Aaron's death in 1800 failed immediately to expand Barlow's sense of familial obligation, though he was willing to use his brother's male offspring to establish his Ohio claims. After one of Aaron's surviving sons visited France in 1802, Barlow gave all of them a power of attorney to settle his western lands. They would only receive the value of the improvements they made rather than full ownership. Barlow's caution reflected a number of unknowns. Apart from uncertainty about the status of his Ohio Company shares, he had little knowledge of Aaron's family. Some sons could be more worthy than others, and together they might exhaust his resources. Prudence dictated waiting until he could learn more about the family, especially as he was unfamiliar with American land values. He had yet to feel secure enough as a gentleman to rely fully on relatives he didn't know.

Barlow's sense of financial wellbeing received a boost from the rise in Parisian real estate values. Toward the end of 1801 the annual draft was suspended, and an eighth of the men who had served longest in the ranks received furloughs, signaling to an exhausted nation that it could look forward to a period of external quiet and internal reconstruction. As cities that had previously been drained of men began to recover their populations, the demand for real estate increased, making the mansion on the rue de Vaugirard appear to be a sound investment. But owning an appreciating asset in a rising market and actually selling it were two different things, as Barlow would learn when he tried to dispose of his Parisian properties. Lady Emma Hamilton, Admiral Horatio Nelson's mistress, showed no interest in Barlow's mansion when he offered it to her in 1801. In 1802 disillusionment with Napoleon led Barlow to turn to Benjamin Jarvis, an American residing in Hamburg.[9]

By then Barlow had grown anxious to free himself from all that bound him to France, and he sweetened the offer by including his other properties in the city. He also proposed that Jarvis pay for them with an annuity rather than in cash. The arrangement would give Jarvis and his heirs full title upon the death of both Barlows. There is no record of Jarvis's response to this proposal, and the Barlows remained at 50 rue de Vaugirard until the autumn of 1804. Well before they moved out, Barlow signified to Fulton that he was willing to sell for much less than his original asking price, though one that would still leave him with a profit.[10]

Barlow's improved economic circumstances never completely freed him from commerce. His involvement with ventures sponsored by Strobel and Martini continued into the new century. He also started purchasing on speculation the rights to disputed prizes and their cargoes in Britain and France. But increased economic security enabled Barlow to proclaim his gentility by undertaking several literary tasks from which he could expect little return. One was translating portions of Constantin Volney's *Les Ruines, ou méditations sur les révolutions des empires* (1791).

The work addressed the question of why the great empires of the past had all disappeared. Volney argued that the illusion of future compensation for present disappointments had permitted rulers to oppress their subjects to the point where they rebelled. The empires would have been better served by a morality rooted in experience and nature. As a Girondin sympathizer, Volney had been imprisoned at the beginning of the Terror. After his release, he emigrated to America, where he sought to remedy the deficiencies in a 1792 English translation of the *Ruines* that had appeared in London. During 1795 a second English version was published in Philadelphia that claimed to be corrected by the author. Volney was still not satisfied, however, especially after this version drew the fire of Joseph Priestley, who had recently settled in Pennsylvania.

Priestley objected to Volney's total rejection of revelation and in 1797 challenged him to debate the subject. Volney declined, though he did admit his comparative treatment of the world's religions was intended to generate a spirit of religious doubt.[11] Priestley's attack on Volney's "infidelity" brought the immigrant French philosophe into the sights of American Federalists. They made him the embodiment of the religious and political threat France posed to the United States during the Franco-American crisis of 1798. The Alien Friends Law of 1798 was directed principally at Volney. It induced him to return to France and saved John Adams the trouble of deporting him. But before Volney departed, he provided Jefferson with a French version of the *Ruines*. Jefferson translated its first twenty chapters dealing with political rather than religious matters.

The remaining four chapters comprised half of the total text, and chapter 22, entitled "The Origin and Filiation of Religious Ideas," was by far the longest. In it, Volney argued that similarities in different religious systems reflected primitive efforts to comprehend astronomical events controlling the seasons. Since the fabricators of these systems lacked concepts for extraterrestrial phenomena, they had resorted to figurative language, which accounted for the variations in their fables. The premise behind Volney's argument, that man created God rather than vice versa, was antithetical to the beliefs of American Christians, and after the Federalists started using Jefferson's religious skepticism against him, he abandoned his translation.

Barlow and Volney had known each other since the early 1790s, and Volney wasted no time upon his return to France in asking Barlow to complete the task.[12] Barlow needed little persuading because he had grown interested in finding a common source to the different religions. His exposure to a wide array of religious practices besides American and British Protestantism—including Catholicism, Islam, and Judaism—made him skeptical about the claims of each to an exclusive truth. Barlow took his translation seriously, cutting short a pleasure trip he and Ruth made during the spring of 1801 to Moulins, nestled in the foothills of the Massif central, to work on it. Barlow's translation of the last part of the *Ruines* was completed sometime later in 1801 under Volney's supervision.

The English language edition of 1802 printed in Paris remained the standard one until it was supplanted by another American version in 1822. The title page of the 1802 edition failed to identify any translator because both of the responsible parties now preferred avoiding public identification with Volney's ideas. As returning to America became more compelling, Barlow grew increasingly mindful of his reputation among his countrymen. The *Ruins* would prove to be a tough sell in an America beset by the religious fervor accompanying the Second Great Awakening.

Barlow's other literary project, a major revision of *The Vision of Columbus*, would occupy him off and on for the next five years. It is not clear when he began it since Barlow's epic was always a work in progress, but now his revisions reflected his conclusion that France's abandonment of its republicanism was irreversible. That made the 1793 Parisian edition of *The Vision of Columbus*, which still accorded France a vanguard role in disseminating revolutionary republicanism, seem inappropriate. Barlow's 1802 notebook contains many poetic ideas, as well as some lines of poetry, that eventually found their way into what became a new poem.

The plebiscite held on May 8–14, 1802, which made Napoleon First Consul for life with the power to nominate his successor, constituted a major turning point for Barlow. Charles Pinckney reported to Madison that the prospect of the plebiscite had thrown Barlow into despair, since it restored the monarchy—though not the Bourbon monarchy—in all but name.[13] Barlow's disenchantment with Napoleon was made more intense by his realization that the peace the First Consul had bestowed upon Europe did not extend to America. Well before the Treaty of Amiens went into effect, Napoleon's brother-in-law, Charles-Victor-Emmanuel Leclerc, had been dispatched with a sizeable army to reconquer Sainte Domingue. Jefferson watched this development with suspicion and seriously contemplated aligning the American republic with Britain to check Napoleon's military ambitions in the New World. Leclerc's expedition purged Barlow of any remaining inclination to view the interests of France and the United States as identical. Barlow attributed his change of heart to the growing "depravity of the men in power and the rapid degradation of those principles of liberty and morality among the leaders" of France.[14]

During the summer of 1802, Barlow received a letter from Jefferson inviting him to settle in Washington and undertake another literary project. "Mr. Madison and myself have cut out a piece of work for you, which is to write the history of the United States, from the close of the war downwards." They would provide Barlow with access to all the archives as well as personal information that had never been committed to "paper."[15] Jefferson even suggested a house the Barlows might acquire near the capitol. The letter, which ought to have seemed a heaven-sent opportunity to escape from Napoleon's tyranny, instead ignited Barlow's anxieties and conflicted feelings about leaving France. Most of them focused on the issue of real estate, suggesting he regarded ownership as a burden as much as a pleasure. Barlow worried about the cost of the Washington house, about whether the garden was a new one or one that had been fully planted, and about the property's location. One of the many tourists visiting the French capital that summer was familiar with the house. Barlow wrote Jefferson that it sounded ideal in all respects but its size and cost, which were prohibitive.[16]

There was another problem: The president and Madison were in a rush. The history they wanted Barlow to write was supposed to counteract the influence they feared John Marshall's projected biography of Washington might have on the election of 1804. Barlow was not prepared to drop everything and hazard an autumn Atlantic crossing to meet such a deadline. Furthermore, he was reluctant to abandon his involvement with some of Fulton's projects.

Fulton's attempts to perfect the *Nautilus* had stalled over the problem of delivering an explosive charge to a target. Repeated failures, together with the preliminaries of the Peace of Amiens, led Fulton to abandon the project and dismantle the *Nautilus*. Developing a steam-powered surface vessel quickly replaced work on the submarine after Fulton met Robert R. Livingston, Jefferson's newly appointed ambassador to France, at the beginning of 1802. Livingston, the patriarch of a powerful Republican family from upstate New York, had experimented with developing steam-powered vessels before coming to Europe. Though none of Livingston's designs were successful, he had secured a twenty-year monopoly of steam navigation on the Hudson from the New York legislature, conditional on successfully demonstrating that the vessel could make headway against the river's current. That gave Livingston a compelling interest in partnering with someone who could solve the technical problems, while Livingston provided much needed capital. Though Fulton was receptive to working with Livingston, neither he nor Barlow were sure that the project would not meet with the same fate as the submarine.

Barlow facilitated the collaboration as best he could because he regarded Fulton as a surrogate son and realized that Livingston had assets Fulton was unlikely to find elsewhere. But helping them was not without personal cost. Despite Livingston's Republican credentials, the new ambassador resembled Gouverneur Morris more than James Monroe. By this time Barlow was the most distinguished of the expatriate Americans living in Paris, and it would have been logical for Livingston to have sought him out. At first the two men kept their distance. That they eventually came to see each other often was largely due to Fulton making Barlow his agent in negotiating an arrangement with Livingston. The negotiation proved difficult because Livingston was reluctant to give Fulton more weight in their association than absolutely necessary. For Barlow, working out an accommodation between two headstrong egotists required time and patience. Rather than struggle with frustration in Paris, Fulton preferred to accompany Ruth to a spa at Plombières, where she could take the water cure her Parisian physicians had recommended.

Ruth's health continued to be the most imposing obstacle to the Barlows' return to America. Though she had benefited from her summer visit to Le Havre in 1800, for the remainder of their stay in Europe her health would increasingly preoccupy them both. By the summer of 1802, her complaint was described as tumors on the buttocks and genital area. If these tumors were genital warts, they would have been sexually transmitted, with Fulton the more likely agent than Barlow, assuming the triangle had acquired a sexual dimension. But it is also possible that the "tumors" were cysts that had other sources.

Barlow wrote letters to Ruth and Fulton at Plombières that referred to them as lovers. However, the relationship between Fulton and Ruth resembled more that between a mother and her favorite son, even if it had once been otherwise. If Barlow derived pleasure from thinking they were together, as some have claimed, it derived less from imagining they were lovers than from being reassured Ruth was receiving the care and attention she needed. Barlow's letters to them during that summer reveal a man obsessed with his wife's health, which initially worsened under the regime of the water cure. The evidence supporting the idea that Barlow "enjoyed" Ruth's ill health requires one to discount repeated indications to the contrary. We only have his letters, not hers to him, but to judge from his responses, she gave him a good deal to worry about. When she finally reported progress, he was genuinely relieved.[17]

Fulton's willingness to prolong his stay in Plombières with Ruth may have stemmed from a reluctance to bring her back to Paris in a worse state than when they had departed. Plombières was a considerable distance from Paris, so it was not as though they could travel back and forth with ease. Returning Ruth in an improved state of health seemed to be the least Fulton could do, given Barlow's assiduous attention to his business affairs during the summer of 1802.

Before departing for Plombières, Fulton had convinced Livingston that the crucial problem that needed to be solved was harnessing an engine's power to a device that could drive a vessel through the water. Fulton was reasonably confident that side-wheels hitched to an endless tread were the solution, provided he could reduce the hull's water resistance. Using Livingston's funds, Fulton commissioned an expert model builder in Paris to construct a miniature prototype of such a vessel. After his departure, Fulton relied upon Barlow to expedite its fabrication. The model was finally completed at the end of May, and when it arrived at Plombières, Fulton turned from the routines of spa life to experimenting with it. Before long, his experiments had become part of the spa's attractions and were witnessed by many fashionable personages, including the future empress and Napoleon's sister. The results—though not as spectacular as his initial demonstration of the *Nautilus* in Paris—were sufficiently promising that Fulton wrote Livingston an upbeat letter claiming speeds up to sixteen miles per hour were feasible.[18] Barlow thought the claim exaggerated, but since Fulton had assigned him the task of getting Livingston's consent to an arrangement in which Fulton's ideas would count as the equivalent of Livingston's capital, it at least strengthened Barlow's bargaining position.

Before undertaking these negotiations, Barlow made a brief trip to Britain. He had last been there in the autumn of 1792, when he and his radical friends were suspected of plotting treason against the crown. A decade's interval capped by the Peace of Amiens made it possible for him to pursue a claim he had acquired as a speculation to a prize cargo of 219.75 tons of wine in a captured American vessel. On October 22, 1794, James Thayer had shipped the wine from Bordeaux in the *Neptune* on his and his brother's joint account. The official clearance showed Hamburg as its destination, though the master acknowledged he was making for Charleston, South Carolina, when his vessel had been seized by HMS *Woolich* and carried into Tortola. There a local vice-admiralty court freed the vessel, which was indisputably American. But the cargo remained in dispute because of questions about Thayer's nationality, which were referred to the High Court of Admiralty.[19]

During 1802, the status of American property in the British courts had begun brightening thanks to the work of the Anglo-American commission established under article VII of the Jay Treaty. Initially, the commission's activities had been stymied because it had to pass on British counterclaims involving the unpaid debts of Americans, as well as American claims about unlawful British seizures. The commissioners spent most of their time arguing about minor details until the crown suspended their operations on July 20, 1799, because the few awards made to British creditors were not being paid. Only when the United States guaranteed the sum of six hundred thousand pounds to extinguish unpaid American debts did the commission resume its activities in February 1802.[20] Then, a controversy over whether George W. Erving, the U.S. consul-general in London, should serve simultaneously as agent for the U.S. claimants and assessor of the value of their claims threatened further to delay its operations.[21]

When the American commissioners—John Trumbull, Thomas Pinkney, and Christopher Gore—agreed with their British colleagues, Erving resigned his appointment as assessor with its salary of $1,500. The gesture cleared the way for the favorable processing of American claims arising from British seizures in the West Indies during the autumn and winter of 1793–94. Barlow got wind of the change and decided that a visit to London could not hurt. Though no one stopped him entering the kingdom at Dover, he had violated British restrictions on the movement of aliens. However, Ambassador Rufus King managed to smooth matters over by assuring the government that Barlow's business was private and that he would remain "perfectly quiet" politically.[22]

Despite his best efforts to remain incognito, Barlow was recognized soon after his arrival at a London hotel. Erving then secreted Barlow in lodgings near where he and his father lived. Erving also organized several quiet reunions with friends like Horne Tooke and Joseph Johnson. Johnson had been imprisoned in part for publishing Part I of Barlow's *Advice to the Privileged Orders* and greeted Barlow good-naturedly with the declaration, "You could not get me hanged, [though] you tried all you could."[23] Since Johnson had managed to live better in prison than he did at home, there were no hard feelings.

Erving's success in managing Barlow's contacts with his old friends led to an enduring friendship between the two men. A native of Massachusetts and the son of a loyalist, Erving had attended Oxford after the Revolutionary War. While James Monroe had been ambassador to France, Erving had shown up in Paris seeking validation of his American citizenship. Not knowing what to make of someone who sounded more British than American, Monroe refused, but that didn't stop Erving from arranging for the British publication in 1797 of the defense Monroe wrote of his diplomatic mission. On returning to the United States at the turn of the century, Erving played a role in the New York election of 1800, which proved critical to Jefferson's winning the presidency. Jefferson was grateful enough to honor Erving's request for an overseas position by appointing him consul general in London.

Erving feared the High Admiralty Court would be governed by the value of the invoice in determining damages if it ruled favorably on Thayer's nationality. That presented a problem because foreign merchants doing business in the command economy run by the Commission des subsistances customarily had used invoice figures that were 50 percent below "their real specie value in the market at that time." The permission to export the wine "was considered to be as valuable as the goods themselves."[24] Erving's advice impelled Barlow to seek an affidavit to that effect from Theodore Peters, who at the time had served as U.S. consul in Bordeaux. But since Peters also had a claim against Thayer, he refused to give Barlow the desired affidavit unless Barlow first guaranteed Peters's claim in the event Thayer recovered his property.

During his brief visit to England, Barlow also became interested in the American vessel, the *Hannah*, which had been seized by the British in the West Indies at roughly the same time as the *Neptune*. This vessel had been sold to French merchants in Bordeaux, who retained an American factor named Church as the ostensible owner to cover it with the American flag. Though Church's legal ownership of the *Hannah* was in doubt, Barlow paid £ 9,500 for Church's and the *Hannah* captain's interest in the vessel after the Jay Treaty commissioners began passing favorably on American claims.[25]

Though the rationale for his eight-day visit to London was business, Barlow found being in Britain surprisingly pleasant. He continued to view the nation as the principal threat to the freedom of the seas and indirectly to the liberty of mankind, but the very fact that Thayer's claims were being considered in an English court was refreshing. Barlow was also struck by the amenities of London life, which came close to matching those of Paris. Thanks to early industrialization, London's shops excelled those of Paris. If one wanted to buy ordinary staples of everyday life like stockings, London had the best prices. Paris remained unequaled, though, when it came to the quality and variety of custom-made, luxury goods.

Differences in lady's fashions also caught Barlow's attention. Women in London wore dresses that covered their breasts and throats "clear up to the chin," distinguishing them from the current French fashion, which exposed as much of both as possible. At times this had been carried to the extreme of baring the breast or, as was more customary for Parisian women with the appropriate figures, covering their breasts diaphanously. Some even dampened their bodices to enhance the effect. Barlow entertained Ruth and Fulton with an account of the London visit of Madame Récamier—the famous French beauty immortalized by the painter Jacques-Louis David—who had recently been exiled from Paris for spurning Napoleon's advances. When, attired in the French fashion, she alighted from her carriage for a walk in a London park, she attracted an unruly crowd. "So fierce was John to look at the little globes, that every tinker would sooner get his eyes knocked out than not have a glance," Barlow reported.[26]

The capital of the Anglophone world stirred in Barlow an unexpected sense of excitement. In London, he could never challenge Benjamin West's claim to preeminence as America's leading cultural figure. As an English author in Paris, Barlow had enjoyed a certain freedom from the standards of the metropole, but his Parisian prominence came at the cost of the stimulation he would have derived from contact with men like William Wordsworth and Samuel Coleridge, who at the time were emerging as major poets. They would leave a far more enduring legacy than William Hayley, the only English literary figure who took much interest in Barlow's work.

Barlow's wrote poignantly about viewing their old lodging at 18 Great Titchfield Street. "I felt such a glow of affection that my limbs fell a trembling & I could hardly walk away."[27] That was a strange response to seeing the residence he and Ruth had occupied after his misadventure with the Scioto Company. Had he forgotten their desperate financial circumstances and the intense effort that was required to establish his literary reputation as a republican ideologue, or had the burden of owning a Parisian mansion made his past struggles seem trivial by comparison? Despite his hostility to monarchies, Barlow could not help feeling affection for Britain because it reminded him of home. Shortly afterward, Henry Redhead Yorke recorded a conversation during which Barlow compared Britain's prospects favorably to those of France.[28]

Livingston accepted Fulton's proposals for the steamboat's design after a long conversation Barlow had with him on July 17, 1802, objecting only to the scale on which Fulton wanted to build the prototype. Livingston's desire to keep the vessel as small as possible made it less likely that the costs of construction could be met by selling fares. The realization that Livingston could always team up with another inventor weakened Barlow and Fulton's bargaining position. At the time, there was no shortage of mechanical ingenuity, both American and European, focused on constructing commercially feasible, steam-powered vessels. Barlow's attempts to reassure Fulton should Livingston abandon him were never entirely convincing. He argued that Fulton only had to demonstrate the feasibility of his model to a select group of British investors and the funds would become available for building and patenting the vessel in America. Fulton knew Barlow well enough to discount his glib optimism and realize he had best stick with Livingston.

Fulton was in no rush to return to Paris now that his experiments were giving him the upper hand. Since Ruth's health at last was showing signs of improvement, he felt she would benefit from more time at Plombières. Barlow, for his part, had embarked on another literary project premised on Fulton's collaboration. This was an epic poem about comprehensive canal systems like the one Fulton had described in his *Treatise*. Barlow thought the project would provide Fulton's genius with a new focus after the collapse of the submarine project and before either of them could be sure the partnership with Livingston was leading anywhere. The poem was entitled, "The Canal: a Poem on the application of Physical Science to Political Economy, in four Books."[29]

Attempting to render physical science and political economy into poetry did not come naturally. Barlow completed a draft of only half of one book in his customary rhymed couplets. The aborted epic drew what little life it had from two sources that continued to inspire Barlow's literary efforts. The first was the conviction that one should not be bound by past precedents in a revolutionary age. Though Richard Holmes has argued that the English poets and scientists of this age collaborated in producing what he terms "Romantic science," the results of the marriage between serious science and poetry were not yet evident. That failed to deter Barlow, who felt the attempt to join the two should be made if positive good might result. The positive good he had in mind was uniting thought to feeling, a legacy of Joseph Buckminster's insistence that religion devoid of feeling was not true religion. Barlow was not suggesting that science devoid of feeling was not true science, but he did hope that a marriage between them might capture the public's imagination and by doing so create political conditions that fostered technological innovation.[30]

When it became clear that Fulton's heart was not in the project, Barlow suggested he illustrate the reworked *Vision of Columbus*. Barlow's exposure to French standards led him to seek an elegant format for the revised version of his epic poem that made the original look primitive. He planned one illustration for each book, plus a frontispiece. He also wanted the artwork executed by an American resident in Europe because the European technique for making plates was more advanced than anything in America. Fulton eventually did a portrait of Barlow in 1805 that depicted him very much as John Vanderlyn had in 1798. (See chapter 12.)

Instead of the intense, anxiety-ridden stare shown in the 1793 likeness by Louis-Charles Ruotte and J. J. F. Le Barbier, both Vanderlyn and Fulton represent him as a relaxed, confident gentleman. Fulton's portrait conveyed the impression of an older, even more serene and gentrified Barlow than Vanderlyn's sketch, and in doing so mirrored Barlow's ambitions for his revised epic, whose task had become less to transform the world than to consolidate a world that, like the poem's author, had already been transformed.

After his return from Britain, much of Barlow's energy went into revising *The Vision of Columbus*. A notation dated December 13, 1802, indicates that he had gone through 3,474 lines of the Paris edition of 1793, striking out 526 old lines and writing 1,822 new ones, together with fourteen new notes.[31] Though it is impossible to tell exactly what part of this revision was executed when, Barlow had reworked more than half the original poem. He did this despite a busy social life that involved dining out most nights. He liked being on his own in the metropolis because it left him free to pursue his literary activities. But not all his time was entirely his own, as he was besieged by invitations from Helen Maria Williams and Margaret King, Lady Mount Cashell—Mary Wollstonecraft's most distinguished female pupil—to attend their soirées. These social distractions complemented as much as they competed with his work. Though he needed periods of solitude for his revision of *The Vision of Columbus*, similar to the isolation his brother's Redding house had afforded when he originally composed it, he also welcomed periodic release from them.

Ruth and Fulton returned to Paris in late September 1802. The English landscape artist Joseph Farington recorded the Barlows' presence at an elegant party Benjamin West hosted on September 27 for more than thirty guests. While Ruth struck Farington as being a "quiet, unassuming woman," he described Barlow as "tall & bony. His countenance is ill-favored but his look thoughtful & shrewd. To reflect & to observe seem to be his habit, and it is expressed in his appearance. His head is shrunk between his Shoulders, and constantly leans to one side; and one of his hands is invariably placed upon his breast, as it were to support his chin." Farington's dislike of Barlow's politics influenced this description. "As a *Reformer* of political constitutions," Farington held him responsible, "with others," for proving "to the world the danger of endeavouring to carry visionary Theories into practice, at the risk of all the horrors of bloodshed and confusion."[32]

A month later the Barlows attended a celebratory dinner to honor the Polish patriot and veteran of the continental army, Thaddeus Kosciuszko. The affair included more than one hundred persons and attracted the attention of the Parisian press. The Barlows, along with Livingston and Lafayette, were mentioned in published descriptions of the occasion. The story then traveled across the Atlantic, first appearing in the *Columbian Courier* of New Bedford on Christmas Eve. It was widely copied in the Republican press and eventually made its way to Washington. Abraham Baldwin read the account in the *National Intelligencer* and congratulated Ruth on the fine company she was keeping.[33] The Barlows had become celebrities.

Work on Barlow's new epic slowed after Ruth and Fulton returned to Paris, but he was glad to be relieved of the burden of negotiating with Livingston. Fulton and Livingston finally agreed to build a model steamboat that was to be powered by two side-wheels capable of towing several barges in its wake. But between Livingston's instincts for economy and the sabotage of the Seine bargemen—who feared competition and sank the first prototype before it could be tested—the demonstration of its capabilities did not take place until the summer of 1803. Ruth would be present with many of her friends at what by all accounts was a success "complet et brilliant," but both Livingston and Barlow were out of town.[34]

Livingston was on his way to Switzerland to escape the summer heat. He undoubtedly heard glowing accounts of the event, which was witnessed by many fashionable Parisians. The next step was to buy a British engine, export it to America, and install it on a vessel of American construction. Almost four years would elapse before that step was taken, however, because the resumption of the European war in 1803 led the British government to entice Fulton into resuming work on his submarine in preference to returning to America or remaining in France.

Barlow missed the demonstration of Fulton's steamboat because he was in London trying to complete the business that had taken him there the preceding spring. This second sojourn in the British capital lasted from the middle of March until the beginning of August 1803 and was inspired by the collapse of the Peace of Amiens. Barlow's claims depended on the British courts honoring the rights of neutrals, which he had reason to fear they might restrict once war resumed. Hence his frequent laments about not having pressed the matter earlier. In addition to his interest in the *Neptune*'s cargo and the *Hannah*, there was another claim identified only as "V—'s" in his correspondence, possibly Volney's royalties from his English publisher. Finally, Barlow attempted to mediate the rupture that had taken place between Benjamin West and Fulton, who had been omitted from West's elegant dinner the preceding September.[35]

Barlow would have been present on May 2 when the High Court of Admiralty finally heard Thayer's appeal. On May 27, the court awarded half the cargo to Thayer and ordered the British captors to make out a true account of the sales so that restitution could be made within a month. The court reserved the other half of the cargo to the captors.[36] The court's "prize appeals assignations" book suggests the compromise was designed to head off further legal action. On June 30, the court received the required account of the cargo's value and subsequently ordered payment on July 27.[37] What Barlow lost in the judicial compromise he made up by having the captor's proceeds in selling the wine— rather than the values listed in the invoice—taken as the measure of his restitution. Since most of the critical decisions of the High Court of Admiralty took place after the resumption of war between France and Britain in the middle of May, Barlow was relieved to have the case settled when it was.

Still, the renewal of hostilities adversely affected Barlow in several respects. "The Devil has laid his paw upon the exchanges just as I was ready to remit," he lamented in connection with two sterling bills he had sent from London to cover a debt due William Lee in France. These bills protected him from the declining value of the franc in London, but because they were due in two and three months, respectively, from the date they were drawn, long after Lee's debt was due, they had to be discounted in Paris. Barlow expected to pay a big premium as a consequence.[38]

More significantly, the resumption of the war interfered with Barlow's attempts to sell his Parisian real estate. At the end of April as the Peace of Amiens was collapsing, Barlow authorized Fulton to accept 160,000 francs for the residence on 50 rue de Vaugirard. When the former émigré owner offered Barlow 25,000 francs for a smaller property he had priced at 50,000, Barlow came down to between 40,000 and 36,000 francs because he expected the renewed war would adversely affect property values as it had the previous decade.[39]

⚜

While Barlow was in London, Livingston and James Monroe, who had arrived in France in early April, managed to acquire Louisiana from France for $11,250,000 in 6 percent stock of the United States. As part of the deal, the United States assumed the claims of U.S. citizens against French spoliations totaling $3,750,000. This sum covered cargoes not paid for, unreasonable detentions by embargoes, and prize cases in which the council of prizes had ordered restitution that had not been made. Any claims arising from captures and confiscations that were still in the process of adjudication, as well as all claims arising after the Franco-American Convention of 1800 had been signed (September 30), were excluded.

After sealing the Louisiana Purchase agreement in Paris, Monroe had crossed the channel to replace Rufus King as U.S. ambassador to Britain. There he encountered Barlow. Though they had not seen each other for eight years, the two men experienced no difficulty renewing their former friendship. From Monroe, Barlow learned of the details of the treaty, which raised the value of the "liquidations" a French Commission had issued certifying the validity of the American claims acknowledged under the Convention of 1800 but not yet provided for. Barlow was speculating in these claims much as he speculated in disputed prizes in Britain. But he was more interested in the long-term strategic implications of the Louisiana Purchase than speculative gain, as can be seen from the long letter he wrote his Yale classmate and fellow Connecticut republican, Alexander Wolcott, expressing his enthusiasm for what Monroe and Livingston had accomplished.[40]

Barlow saw the Louisiana Purchase "not merely as an acquisition of territory, but as removing, perhaps forever, the causes of war and every temptation to deviate from economy & justice and the steady pursuits of sober & well respected industry." The development was especially welcome now that the task of assuring the survival of revolutionary republicanism had fallen exclusively upon the United States. However, Barlow also realized that the acquisition of Louisiana could perpetuate racial slavery. France's recent reintroduction of slavery in its colonies heightened his sensitivity to an institution he considered "in every point of view, moral, political & economical" as "the greatest blemish of the American Republic."

Barlow still had faith in the "gradual advancement and certain triumph" of republicanism and welcomed the emancipation statutes passed by the northern states. "Slavery seems now to be nearly abolished as far south as Maryland. In that state & Virginia it is losing ground daily." He was confident that "it must certainly languish & expire by degrees" in the Deep South unless "kept in vigour by taking root in the immense regions of the west." Barlow saw the centrality of expansion in slavery's future well before many of his fellow countrymen did. He argued vigorously against it less out of consideration for "that race of men who are commonly designated for slaves" than because he thought it was "completely subversive . . . of the very ground on which [the American republic] stand[s]." It would be "impossible . . . to preserve [our] institutions, much less to improve them, under those preposterous habits of feeling, thinking & acting, that slavery in its mildest operation must inspire in the rising generations!" Barlow knew both from the experience of his own family and from his encounter with Algerian slavery what the institution did to the enslavers. "A race of hereditary masters cannot be a race of republicans, of just men."

Why did Barlow lecture Alexander Wolcott, who could not even deliver a Republican majority in Middletown, Connecticut, on the evils of slavery? Barlow may also have written to other, more influential Americans about excluding slavery from the new territory. Entries in his 1802 notebook record the ratio of slave to free states and a brief discussion of why maple sugar was more conducive to freedom than cane sugar, reflecting his growing preoccupation with the problem. Perhaps Barlow hoped that by stressing the institution's evils to Wolcott, he could give him an additional weapon with which to challenge the Federalists in Connecticut as well as the expansion of slavery into the West. The Federalists saw the Louisiana Purchase as ensuring their political death because the new territories would remain loyal to their Republican sponsors. But the Federalists also objected to acquiring Louisiana because it would expand slavery. Excluding slavery from Louisiana would deprive them of grounds for opposing the Republic's expansion.

⚜

Toward the end of his stay in London, Barlow received an alarming letter from Fulton about Ruth's health. Though she had escaped an epidemic that had killed more than ten thousand Parisians the previous winter, Barlow now judged Ruth's health too precarious to leave Europe. Since he could "not think of leaving her behind," their departure for America was again delayed.[41] Barlow talked to some of the leading physicians of London about Ruth's problems and concluded that they might understand their trade better than French physicians did. Napoleon's announcement that he planned to crown himself emperor removed Barlow's remaining reservations about leaving France.

During the ensuing year Barlow wound up most of his business affairs in France. He put his rue de Vaugirard mansion under Daniel Parker's management in the expectation of getting a better price for it when the next peace was concluded. He had no way of knowing that eventuality lay more than a decade in the future. In 1809 Fulton advised Barlow to raise an annuity "for your joint lives . . . upon the Paris property," suggesting Barlow accept $2,000 a year "if Mr. Parker will secure you." In the same letter, Fulton referred to a remittance of $35,000 (somewhat more than 600,000 current dollars) that Barlow had received from abroad, presumably from the sale of his other assets in Paris.[42] None of these strategies came to fruition, though, and the best disposition Parker could make of the rue de Vaugirard property was to have Livingston's successor, John Armstrong, move there with his legation staff at the end of 1806.[43] When the Barlows returned to Paris in 1811, they would reoccupy the mansion.

The Barlows moved to London in November 1804 and spent the winter in Bedford Square. Their departure from France led some to question Barlow's republican loyalties because he seemed to be following Fulton, who made no attempt to conceal his recent acceptance of a retainer from the British government to develop a submarine after the collapse of the Peace of Amiens. Until then

Barlow had assumed that France was the best place for bringing the submarine to fruition because her rivalry with Britain made her Fulton's logical patron. Barlow had previously collaborated with Fulton in drafting a six-thousand-word memo that survives under the title of "Fulton's Projected Letter to Pitt." The memo proposed that Britain peacefully transform herself into a republic to avoid the revolutionary consequences that were bound to attend the destruction of her navy by submarines. It echoed Barlow's *Advice to the Privileged Orders* by arguing that the nation as a whole would be vastly enriched by a free commerce unburdened by armaments, while the privileged few would be spared the horrors France had inflicted upon its ruling class.[44]

It is not clear if this memo was ever sent or whether, if sent, it had any effect beyond reinforcing the British ministry's conviction that Fulton was a mad—and therefore potentially—dangerous genius. Barlow regretted Fulton's choice of patrons but felt that the French government had mishandled his friend. He also agreed with Fulton's argument that it wouldn't make much difference who financed the submarine's development. Once the technology was perfected, it could be used by weaker naval powers against stronger ones to establish the freedom of the seas. Though Barlow refrained from attacking Napoleon's regime directly, his defense of Fulton's continuing loyalty to republicanism was in itself an implicit condemnation. As for his own loyalty to France, Barlow had no trouble sidestepping that question by saying his sole concern was Ruth's health.

The Barlows had plenty of friends in London, but they stayed out of public sight during the winter of 1805, largely because of Ruth's health. There were some pleasant evenings at Joseph Johnson's, and Fulton's association with the liberal Lord Stanhope—with whom he shared many technical interests—frequently exposed them to his lordship's company.[45] Barlow continued to cultivate his friendship with George Erving, and Ruth became acquainted with the celebrated needlework artist and schoolmistress, Mary Linwood, whom the Barlows met through Benjamin West.[46] None of these friendships were strong enough to keep the Barlows in Europe, however. They had come to the conclusion if they did not return home soon, they never would. Fulton tarried in Britain through 1806 until he came to the conclusion that the British government's support for his submarine project was no better than Frances's, but even his staying failed to detain them. In the middle of March 1805, Ruth wrote her Quaker friend Mrs. Rotch—a native of Nantucket, who with her husband had settled in France—that after a month's sojourn in the West Country near Bath and Bristol they intended to embark for America, her health permitting.[47]

Many considerations reinforced their resolve. In addition to Barlow's sense that the future of republicanism now lay in America, Jefferson continued to beckon Barlow to make the rout of Federalism permanent by writing the history of its demise.[48] Abraham Baldwin's health was declining, and if they waited much longer, none of Ruth's full siblings would be alive to welcome them. Finally, there were Barlow's lands, which were unlikely to improve with neglect. He suspected he had already lost to back taxes the Vermont lands he had purchased in 1781, and he didn't know whether his nephews had accepted his invitation to settle on his Ohio lands. That they might do so inspired Barlow to write Gen. Return Jonathan Meigs, who was agent for the Ohio Company and whose son Return Jonathan Meigs Jr. would soon be elected Ohio's governor.[49]

The senior Meigs was the older brother of Barlow's classmate, Josiah Meigs, but Barlow only mentioned that connection as an afterthought. He began his letter by referring to fellow veteran Meigs as "an old revolutionary acquaintance," asking him to assist his nephews in establishing themselves on his land. One favor, of course, deserved another, so Barlow mentioned that he was collecting "a cabinet of mineralogy" for Josiah and his university. Cashing in on revolutionary loyalties, which could not by this time have been very strongly felt, to secure his claim on a portion of the American West, meant that Barlow had resolved upon a future in America.

CHAPTER FIFTEEN

Mixed Reception

Though the Barlows had intended to sail for America in early May, they did not leave British waters until mid-June 1805. Fifty-two days later, they arrived in New York, much the worse for the wear. As Barlow commented to Abraham Baldwin, this was "as much as we expected." The voyage had been hardest on Ruth: "The dear Girl has suffered during [the] passage . . . a degree of torment equal to a half a dozen deaths." Barlow had had his share of discomfort as well, and both were relieved to have the ordeal behind them. As luck would have it, however, their arrival in New York coincided with a summer heat wave, and going to New England for relief did not seem like an option. New Haven was experiencing an outbreak of yellow fever, and Barlow wanted to learn from his friends in Connecticut, "if any such there be, that the people will not throw stones at me."[1] No one he had known was in New York City in early August. Robert R. Livingston invited them to visit him at his Clermont estate,[2] but Barlow's thoughts turned instead to scouting out Washington, D.C. While they didn't know the immediate whereabouts of Abraham Baldwin, it was possible he was still there or that President Jefferson was in town.

A chance encounter in New York with Secretary of the Treasury Albert Gallatin informed Barlow that no senior official was expected in the capital for another month. The August heat wave and Ruth's infirmities led the Barlows to plan a roundabout tour of New England by way of Albany, Ballstown, and Boston, before looping back through Providence to Connecticut. Barlow hoped the journey would rejuvenate Ruth. "It kills her to remain shut up in one place during the heats. Gentle journeying amuses & helps her very much."[3] They had also heard a rumor that Abraham was in Connecticut, and a leisurely tour would give them a chance to find him through the mails. Both Barlows longed to meet with Abraham because they looked to him more than anyone else for help in reorienting themselves to the country they called home but where they felt like strangers. Barlow worried about how the animosity directed against him in public prints would affect his reception in his native state. Circling Connecticut first might allow him to avoid bruising confrontations.[4]

Barlow was startled by the changes he saw in the country. New York now struck him as "a corner of Europe." The port's development—which included the repair of most of its war damage—caught his attention. "The country appears to be generally in a very prosperous condition." That did not mean there was no room for improvement in the realms of "Philosophy and patriotism," but Barlow was confident their seeds would flower, "as they have a good soil to trust in." America was lucky in having only "ignorance" for its enemy, while Europe had to contend with "all sorts of abuses, reasons of State, religions of State, [and] privileged orders."[5]

The Barlows were cheered by a warm note from Jefferson congratulating them on their safe arrival and inviting them to join him at Monticello for the month of September. "The mountains among which I live will offer you as cool a retreat as can any where be found and one enjoying as much health as any place in the union." Jefferson anticipated Barlow's response to his homecoming. "You will be sensible of a great change of manners generally and of principles in some. The most important change," Jefferson wrote, was "the influence gained by the Commercial towns on public opinion, & their exclusive possession of the press."[6] But by the time the Barlows received Jefferson's invitation, they had relinquished all thought of going south, though that did not stop Barlow from suggesting to the president ways to counteract the danger of Americans abandoning their revolutionary values.

Barlow's observations about the importance of education concealed an ulterior motive. He had not abandoned the project of establishing an institution that would set cultural standards for the entire nation.[7] But his anxiety about the direction the republic was moving owed more to the transformation he had witnessed in France than to self-promotion. Barlow's first public statement, replying in part to a congratulatory notice that appeared in the columns of the *American Mercury*, stressed the "great importance" of proving "to the world, and even to ourselves, that the fabric of this [the American] empire is the best organization of liberty hitherto experienced." Barlow worried about "erroneous habits of thinking . . . which seek the happiness of the few, in the depression of the many" and saw the survival of such notions as "proof that neither their own system, nor that of monarchy is well understood or appreciated."[8]

The Barlows' tour of New York and New England did not proceed as planned. Instead, they came to New Haven in early October, probably after receiving word that Abraham was there. Noah Webster saw them and afterward described Barlow as "a little convalescent, chiefly by means of Bonaparte's harsh remedies for new philosophy; but I think his [Barlow's] constitution is [so] much impaired, that a radical cure is impossible."[9] If Barlow struck Webster as chastened, it was less because of events in Europe than because of the snubs he received from former friends. Ten days later in Boston, he met with a public reception that paralleled the private ones. The Federalist *Repertory* described Barlow as "A BLOOD THIRSTY JACOBIN" whose "passion for murder" had led him to exalt at "the sacrifice of Louis and his Queen, on the scaffold" in "bacchanalian orgies." The jibe affected Barlow enough to ask Babcock to reply in kind to these "elegant samples of Boston hospitality."[10]

Federalist attacks in Massachusetts diverted Barlow's attention from the plight of Republicans in his home state. Five months later he found himself writing apologetically to Babcock to deny that he had forgotten the circumstances of "our suffering bretheren [*sic*] of Connecticut," who had been the targets of Federalist repression since Jefferson's victory in 1800.[11] In addition to a "Stand-up" Law designed to limit Republican effectiveness in elections, the Federalists had purged their opponents from state offices and ramped up libel prosecutions against those who dared to say or print anything critical of their political dominance.[12] The hardening of the Federalist stance in Connecticut pushed the state's Republicans to seek redress from Washington. Barlow's friendship with Jefferson and his intention of moving to the nation's capital led them to court him. At the beginning of November, the Republican members of the state legislature assembled at New Haven joined with "other republican citizens" in a formal address lauding his many accomplishments in America and Europe.[13] Barlow's Connecticut allies also arranged for the republication of his *Two Letters to the Citizens of the United States . . . written from Paris in the year 1799 on Political and Commercial Relations*, together with his October 2, 1798, letter to Washington.

Barlow had no desire to join Connecticut's Republicans in their struggle against the Federalists. His reply to the New Haven address showed that the hostility he had encountered was taking its toll. Why else would he have felt compelled to allege that Federalist accusations "have been hunted up and propagated with no other view than to destroy my usefulness in the cause of liberty"? He was certain they did not proceed from personal dislike, as he denied having any personal enemies. But now that the United States had become the sole "depository and the guardian of the best interests of mankind," he hoped his auditors would remain "sensible . . . of this sacred deposit, and that our patriotism, without diminishing its energy, may at all times partake of the broad and peaceful character of general philanthropy."[14] Barlow would at least be more charitable than his adversaries.

In addition to formally addressing Barlow, 150 of his Republican well-wishers treated him to a private reception at classmate Abraham Bishop's home. The reception solved a problem the Republicans would have encountered had they attempted to stage a public event. Prominent Federalists attending the legislative session would have boycotted it and, by doing so, diminished the occasion. Yale, now under the presidency of Timothy Dwight, took no notice of him. Dwight was deeply involved in promoting the Second Great Awakening and looked upon Barlow as a religious apostate. There is no record of the two men trying to revive their former friendship, and Barlow subsequently described Dwight as "a bigot and tory" with whom he wanted nothing more to do, strong language from someone who claimed he had no personal enemies.[15]

There was another former ideological ally Barlow eschewed despite their long-standing collaboration. During the Terror, Thomas Paine had entrusted Barlow with his manuscript of *The Age of Reason*, and Barlow had initially done more than any other American to get Paine released from the Luxembourg prison. When the Barlows returned to Paris in 1795, they frequently saw Paine while he recuperated at the American legation, and Barlow even considered writing an account of Paine's life.[16] After Paine departed for the United States in 1802, however, the only glimpse that we have of their subsequent relationship (aside from a letter Paine addressed to Barlow in May 1807 about a minor personal matter)[17] comes from Barlow's 1809 response to a query from James Cheetham, who was collecting materials for Paine's biography. Barlow acknowledged Paine to be "among the brightest and most undeviating luminaries of the age"; at the same time he emphasized Paine's many failings. These included a mind susceptible to flattery, a "vanity which he was too proud to conceal," and an inability to "endure the contempt [criticism] of his former friends and fellow-laborers" or "the rude scoffs of their imitators, [and] a new generation that knows him not." Barlow knew what this felt like, but he had not sought, as had Paine, "refuge in low company" or "consolation in the sordid, solitary bottle."

The catalogue of failings, possibly drawn from Barlow's observations as far back as 1795, reflected a growing distance between the two men. In America, Paine responded to the abuse he received by becoming an eccentric recluse who neglected taking proper care of himself. During the first summer and autumn the Barlows were back in America, the two men may have met either in New York or in New Rochelle. If they did, the meeting failed to revive their former friendship. Barlow concluded his Cheetham letter by observing that some of Paine's "best friends" were almost disposed to "join with his enemies, and wish, though from different motives, that he would hasten to hide himself in the grave—"[18]

The Barlows' cool reception in New England made it easier for them to turn their thoughts southward. They began their slow journey toward Washington in the middle of November, hoping to arrive in the nation's capital before Congress assembled on December 2. If Abraham was with them when they set out, he soon went ahead to attend to business preparatory to Congress's meeting. The Barlows followed at a more leisurely pace, slowed by consultations with booksellers in Philadelphia, the bad condition of the roads south of Philadelphia, and Ruth's health.[19] Webster, who still had a crush on Ruth, described her in early October as "far more precise & formal in her speech than before" and "very agreeable," though she looked sufficiently "dropsical" for him to conclude "her life & health precarious."[20]

The Barlows arrived in Washington on November 29 and took rooms at Mrs. Doyle's boarding house. Forty dollars a week bought them their meals, a bedroom, a parlor, accommodation for two servants, and a horse. Life in Paris and London had accustomed Ruth to relying on meals provided by others. Though Washington was little more than a provincial village, room and board for visiting legislators—who usually attended Congress without their wives—was the one amenity widely available. Then, as now, the town revolved around the comings and goings of influential officeholders, which in turn were determined by the seasonal activities of the government.

Barlow immediately began work on a memorial promoting a national education system. By the middle of January 1806, he was circulating a version of his proposal among members of Congress. A letter to Jefferson described it as having "excited a disposition to do something, perhaps to grant a charter" to either a university or society. Barlow asked Jefferson to comment on it before it was published under the title *Prospectus of a National Institution, to be established in the United States* on January 24.[21] The *Prospectus* argued that a national university could serve two functions—the advancement of knowledge and its dissemination —that in Europe were provided by separate institutions. Barlow felt the size of the American republic made it advisable that these functions be joined. The recent acquisition of the Louisiana territory pointed to a continental republic of such diverse interests as "will create a strong tendency to diverge and separate the views of those who shall inhabit the different regions within our limits" (482). During his tour of New England, Barlow had probably heard rumors of the secessionist plot that had been hatched during 1804 by embittered Federalists like Timothy Pickering. In Washington he would have learned that northern Federalists had been circulating such threats in Congress since the 1790s. Barlow wanted to create "a harmony of sentiment" to counteract the "tendency to a separation." He thought the citizenry should be taught to "habitually feel that community of interest on which their federal system is founded . . . by the operations of government . . . [and by] literature, sciences and arts" (483).

The vanguard role Barlow saw the United States assuming served an end that transcended the boundaries of the nation. With assistance from the physical and moral sciences, he expected political economy "to place human society on such a footing in this . . . section of the habitable world, as to secure it from farther convulsions from violence and war" (486). Though neither the first nor the last to cast the United States as secular redeemer, his invocation of the judgment of posterity touched a deep chord in revolutionary culture. History had granted the American Republic a unique opportunity, which successor generations would never forgive it for squandering.

In Barlow's thinking the national mission expanded to include the unlimited improvement of humanity. "Mankind had a right to expect this example from us. . . . Should we, by a narrowness of views, neglect the opportunity of realizing so many benefits, we ought to reflect that it can never occur to us again; nor can we foresee that it will return to any age or nation" (486). In this respect his vision resembled that being fashioned by the proponents of the Second Great Awakening. The two diverged only in Barlow's conviction that perfectibility would proceed from the development and application of scientific knowledge rather than the fulfillment of Revelation.

Barlow argued that the nation's republican government uniquely qualified it to marry scientific to moral improvement in a manner that would yield major advances in knowledge. "Our *representative* system" and "our *federal* system," by constructing a responsible government on an unprecedented scale, had created "a new world of experiment" with immense possibilities (491). The United States had fashioned a government where the power of the people, though "conveniently exercised by a few delegates," was "constantly kept within the reach of the people at large, so as to be controlled by them without a convulsion." This assured "good laws faithfully executed" (493) that would give the lie to tyrants like Napoleon, who perpetrated the falsehood that "no new principle of government has been discovered" over the past two millennia (492).

The United States had also uncovered the "mode of preserving peace among states" he had pointed to in *On certain political Measures* (1799). It involved identifying the common interests that existed between contiguous countries and then binding them "together by a federal government, composed of their . . . delegates, frequently and freely elected, to whom they can confide their common interests" (494). Seventeen years residence in Europe made Barlow support the idea that foreign experience could still contribute to improving the American system. They "will . . . give us credit for what we have done" but at the same time "point out . . . what we have omitted to do, and perhaps aid us with their lights, in bringing towards perfection a system, which may be destined to ameliorate the condition of the human race" (495).

Barlow turned to France for institutional prototypes in meeting the cultural and educational needs of the young nation. His ideas of how a national institute might be governed bore little relation to America's cultural landscape. He wanted its governing fellows selected from the top down rather than the bottom up, a method congruent with his assumption that in the arts excellence was a virtue that had to be defended against the solvent of equality. He assumed that "the legislature, as well as our opulent citizens," would be willing to assist in "making a liberal endowment for so great an object" (515). In addition to creating "a kindred mould" strengthening "the political union of the states" (521–22), it would protect Americans from "the numerous disadvantages that our young men now experience, in being obliged to obtain a European education" (521). Barlow was confident that students would benefit from the "constant examples of enlarged ideas, and paternal solicitation for the national welfare" that he expected them to be exposed to as they watched Congress and the federal courts at work (522).

Barlow's principal concern, however, remained insuring the proper transmission of revolutionary culture to the next generation. Now that the "patriarchs who framed our political systems" were "passing off the stage of public life," it had become clear that "the task of preserving liberty . . . is . . . as difficult, as that of acquiring it. To acquire liberty . . . is the work of few; to preserve it is the sober and watchful business of all" (518–19). Though France had shown that a small group of dedicated leaders could organize a revolution by tapping the momentary enthusiasm of the many, when it came to preserving liberty, "impetuosity . . . is no longer the weapon to be used." Barlow feared that once the people became master they would misuse their power if "not properly instructed." Failure to

create a national institution risked reversing the Revolution: "Children are growing up, to take the legacy we are bequeathing them, insensible of its value, and
ignorant of the means by which it can be preserved. It will seem as if we ha[ve]
labored in vain, if we leave our work but half accomplished" (518–19).

Senator George Logan of Pennsylvania agreed to sponsor legislation embodying Barlow's ideas and on February 28, 1806, asked the Senate's leave to bring in
a bill to establish a "national academy." Achieving a consensus within Congress
proved more difficult. Baldwin had failed to warn Barlow that centralization was
as antithetical to republicanism in the United States as aristocracy. Two sections
of the draft bill were deleted to preserve consensus, and Logan had reservations
about an additional section. Barlow feared these changes would make it impossible to set in motion even the modest dimensions of the surviving plan. To avoid
having his brainchild become the victim of congressional bickering, Barlow relied on Jefferson to resolve disagreements among the Republicans.[22] But Jefferson was preoccupied with other matters, in addition to being lukewarm about
centralization.

The *Essex* decision by Britain's High Court of Admiralty in July 1805 replaced the
doctrine of broken voyages—which allowed American vessels to carry French
colonial produce to France, provided they first entered an American port on their
way to Europe—with the Rule of 1756. Developed at the beginning of the Seven
Years War, this rule restricted the rights of neutrals in wartime to what they had
enjoyed in peacetime. Britain's decisive naval victory over France and Spain at
Trafalgar added to the alarm created by the *Essex* decision, inducing the merchants in the nation's principal ports to petition the federal government for redress. Jefferson responded as best he could to what he saw as a new British threat
to the freedom of the seas, but in dealing with a nation whose navy dwarfed the
U.S. Navy, his only option was to fashion a diplomatic response. Barlow remained
insensitive to the president's signals that this was not the time for his proposal,
insisting that "delays are dangerous" because the new generation was about to
succeed the men who had established republicanism in America.[23]

Jefferson's sense of the political landscape proved more realistic than Barlow's.
Logan was unable to introduce his bill until March 4, 1806, near the end of the
session. The bill proceeded to a second reading the following day but was then
referred to a committee consisting of Logan, Samuel L. Mitchell of New York,
and John Quincy Adams of Massachusetts. They reported it out without change
the following day, but it did not receive a third reading until March 14. Then, an
amendment from the floor of the Senate deleted the words "a national" preceding

the word "academy," effectively trashing the project. The Senate could agree on little more than establishing a school in the District of Columbia. On March 24, the bill was referred to another committee consisting of Logan, Abraham Baldwin, Stephen R. Bradley of Vermont, and James Hillhouse of Connecticut, where it died when Congress adjourned.[24] The House of Representatives took no notice of Barlow's plan, which hardly surprised him. If the Senate was unable to think on a grand scale, the House was even less likely to do so. Still, Barlow had trouble grasping the political moral implicit in Congress's treatment of his proposal: national institutions faced an uphill battle against local loyalties in the legislature of the federal government.

In the midst of watching Congress dispose of his proposal for a national learned society, the Barlows received a letter Robert Fulton had written in London on January 12, 1806. After Trafalgar, the British government had cooled to the development of underwater warfare devices like mines, torpedoes, and submarines. Still, it took that government the better part of a year to unburden itself of Fulton. While Fulton tried to bully the British into meeting his terms by threatening to give his secrets to the French, he contemplated marrying a wealthy widow with several children. The Barlows were horrified. Barlow reported that Fulton's announcement had "cut deep into [Ruth's] soul, constitution, [and] health." It had placed her in a situation where "she would rather die than see [the marriage] take place," at the same time that "she would rather die than it should not take place, if your happiness in the least degree is to depend upon it."

Having played on Fulton's fondness for Ruth, Barlow now turned what he claimed was the cold gaze of reason upon the proposed match. The "education, habits, feelings, character & cast of mind" of his fiancée, assuming matters had ripened to that point, "are English & London. And, what is perhaps more unfortunate for you, she has a fortune. These things render it extremely improbable that she can be happy in this country. I should think it equally improbable that you can be very happy in that country." Here Barlow played on his knowledge of Fulton's commitments. "Your patriotism, your philanthropy, your ideas of public improvement, your wishes to be a comfort to me & my wife in our declining years (if we should unluckily have many of them) would tend to make you uneasy at such a distance from the theater of so much good." In other words, by marrying this English woman, Fulton would throw away all that he and the Barlows had and still could accomplish together.

Barlow told Fulton that he and Ruth had chosen Philadelphia rather than Washington as more suitable "for our whole establishment according to the old firm" before they had received his letter. "This beau rêve we consider now at an end. . . . Young & old, Rich & Poor, Gay & Sober, Urban & Sylvan, Thames & Schuylkill, cannot harmonize so as that one soul shall animate the whole." Barlow, who described Fulton as "my inestimable friend, my younger self, my expansion & and prolongation of existence," even invoked the "scientific Poem of the Canal," which he pretended was still in the works: "Is the mighty fabric vanished? It seems forever gone." Barlow concluded what he called "these hints," offered "in perfect friendship . . . with as little regard to self as possible," by warning Fulton about the dangers of wealth and the corrupting influence it was bound to have on children.[25]

Though it is impossible to tell what tipped the scale in this affair—we do not even know the woman's name—Fulton soon broke off with her. His decision not to marry her may have been linked to the failure of his negotiations with the British government. Had Fulton stayed in Britain and any of his inventions succeeded, he might well have become a wealthy Englishman and thereby have surmounted at least some of the objections Barlow had raised against the match. Once Fulton decided to come home, however, he had no trouble giving the Barlows emotional precedence, since at this point he could not imagine living in the United States without them. Fulton's identity was too deeply involved in their shared vision of the redemptive power of republicanism for him to repudiate it and undertake constructing a new one.

In April 1806 the Barlows moved to Philadelphia. Their winter sojourn in a Washington boarding house had exposed them to the cultural limitations of the nation's capital, which offered few diversions beyond politics. Eighteen years residence in three major European cities had accustomed them to the stimulation of sophisticated urban centers. Despite New York's rapid growth, Philadelphia was still the largest city in the country. It also was the site of the nation's first learned society, the American Philosophical Society, whose *Transactions* at the time constituted the nation's sole scholarly journal. Philadelphia was also the American city most likely to have the skilled printers Barlow needed to produce a deluxe version of his epic. And the Barlows could enjoy the kind of public amusements they had grown used to in Europe; there were theaters and Charles Willson Peale's museum. While Philadelphia's climate, particularly in the summer, was little better than Washington's, relief from the heat and humidity was within easier reach.

Philadelphia also was a better location, if Fulton relented and joined them, for experimenting with a steam-powered vessel. Though neither the Delaware nor the Schulkyll had the navigational potential of the Hudson, Philadelphia's artisans included machinists who had worked with local pioneers in steam navigation like John Fitch. Fifteen years earlier, Fitch had put a steam-powered vessel into service between Philadelphia and Trenton. It had not been a commercial success; nevertheless, Philadelphia would be able to support Fulton's work more effectively than Washington.

Surprisingly little information survives about the Barlow's yearlong residence in Philadelphia. Presumably Ruth escaped the summer heat in 1806 by visiting relatives in New England, accompanied by Abraham. If Barlow remained true to his habits, he would have stayed in the city to finish revising *The Columbiad*, but it could not be published while the engravings Barlow needed remained in Europe. He had instructed Fulton to send the plates to America if he remained fixed in his determination to marry in England. Barlow waited in vain for them and did not receive Fulton's letter of September 12, from London, announcing his intention to return to the United States until well into the autumn. From the wide range of subjects the letter covers, it appears that they had not been in touch for some time.[26]

Fulton's most important news was he had broken with the British government. His bravado about his situation—"My hands are [now] free to burn, sink and destroy whom I please"—masked a chronic insecurity that led him to reaffirm an ideological objective Barlow shared. Fulton proposed "seriously set[ting] about giving liberty to the seas by publishing my system of attack." With more credibility he announced he was embarking on an autumn packet and that the Barlows should expect him sometime in the middle of November. He was aware of the risk associated with an autumn voyage because he instructed Barlow to have his drawings for a submarine attack and his plans for the construction of a steamboat published if he did not survive. Barlow could add his own ideas about how underwater warfare could contribute to establishing the freedom of the seas with "immense advantages to America and Civilization." Finally, Fulton expressed his intention of resuming their collaboration on the canal poem.

Almost as an afterthought, Fulton described the progress he had made with the engravings for *The Columbiad*. Earlier, Barlow had accepted Fulton's decision to give priority to his scientific activities after Fulton completed the portrait of Barlow that would appear as the poem's frontispiece. Fulton had recommended that John Vanderlyn be commissioned to do the remaining artwork. After doing the 1798 portraits of Barlow and Fulton in 1798, Vanderlyn returned to his native New York at the turn of the century to try his hand at American portraiture. When that effort failed, he had come back to France in 1802 to study history and landscape paintings. Aware of the difficulties Vanderlyn was having in finding a comfortable niche, Barlow had approached him about illustrating *The Columbiad* just before he and Ruth left Paris in the autumn of 1804.

Vanderlyn executed one painting depicting the Indians murdering a white woman, which later won renown as the *Death of Jane McCrea*, that was to be used as the basis for an engraving. But the price he asked for doing the remaining illustrations was far more than Barlow could afford to pay. By the time Barlow realized he had a problem, he and Fulton were in London and Vanderlyn was about to leave Paris for Italy. Barlow offered to pay Vanderlyn for the picture he had completed with the frame, though at well below Vanderlyn's asking price. He even sent Vanderlyn a draft for the amount, leaving it up to him whether to accept the money or sell to another buyer.[27] Barlow then hired an English painter named Robert Smirke to replace Vanderlyn. However, the engravings made from Smirke's work were not completed before the Barlows sailed for America in June 1805.

Just as Barlow had managed Fulton's affairs during his prolonged absences from Paris in 1800 and 1802, now Fulton assumed responsibility for having Smirke's illustrations engraved. To expedite the process, Fulton commissioned eight different engravers to execute the plates, paying for them with his own money to complete the project. He considered making the prints in Britain and leaving the plates with Benjamin West, but since Fulton had no idea of how large a printing Barlow intended, he soon abandoned that course in favor of taking the plates with him to America.

Fulton arrived in New York in December 1806 and hastened south with the plates to Philadelphia for a reunion with the Barlows. The time the three shared together was brief because on December 23 Fulton and Barlow set off for Washington.[28] Barlow hoped to procure a government commission for Fulton to survey the Mississippi, or short of that, to make contact with someone who had reliable information about the river. Fulton was interested in the Mississippi because he realized the enormous impact steam navigation could have on its future development. A canal that would connect the Hudson with the Great Lakes was also being talked about, but Fulton realized that a 363-mile water route, even with obliging assistance from the Mohawk River, might take longer to construct than he was likely to live. If he was to enjoy the celebrity he longed for, steam navigation of the Mississippi would do more for his reputation than the Hudson project. The Mississippi also provided insurance in case of any future disagreements with Livingston.

Barlow and Fulton used the occasion to cultivate another important Washingtonian, William Thornton. In addition to having an English university degree in medicine, Thornton had submitted a design for the nation's capitol that won the architectural competition. He was also an amateur inventor who fifteen years before had invested in John Fitch's efforts to introduce commercial steam navigation on the Delaware. Most important, Thornton had been placed in charge of the recently established federal patent office. Thornton allowed Fulton access to the early patents that Fitch and his rival David Rumsey had filed for different steamboat designs. Fitch had sought to transfer power from the engine to the water through oars, while Rumsey had experimented with a primitive jet. Inspection of their patents reassured Fulton that he was on the right track in seeking to transfer the engine's power to a rotating set of blades resembling a mill wheel.

Barlow and Fulton attended a banquet in Washington honoring Meriwether Lewis and William Clark, who had just returned from their overland transit of the continent. Barlow was asked to compose a short poem for the occasion and produced nine of the worst stanzas he ever wrote. In a more complex meter than he customarily used, the verses tried unsuccessfully to relate Lewis and Clark's achievement to the impact a nationwide network of waterways might have on a dispersed nation. The poem was to be read to a well-fed and liquored audience, so at least it was brief. Though widely republished in Republican newspapers, the poem made Barlow the object of mockery in a parody composed by John Quincy Adams.[29]

Barlow returned to Philadelphia and was working on the last revisions of *The Columbiad* when news arrived that his brother-in-law Abraham was dangerously ill. Barlow rushed to Washington without Ruth, arriving twenty hours after Abraham died at a lodging house on March 4, 1807. The only solace Barlow could offer Ruth was that her brother made a "placid & pleasant . . . corpse." He reported sitting by Abraham's side for two hours before the body was removed. Abraham Baldwin's funeral was attended by a great number of people who escorted the body to Rock Creek outside the District of Columbia. Barlow confided to Ruth that "it was the first time in my life that a grave appeared to me not horrible." Instead, he wished they were both there with him.[30]

Barlow's letter came as a terrible blow to Ruth. She summoned Fulton, who was conferring with Livingston in New York, back to Philadelphia. Fulton immediately obliged and remained with her for three full weeks until Barlow returned. Barlow was delayed in part by bad weather, but he was also looking for another place for them to live. Two and a half years later Barlow complained to Tench Coxe that "during all my residence in Philadelphia I knew I was regarded

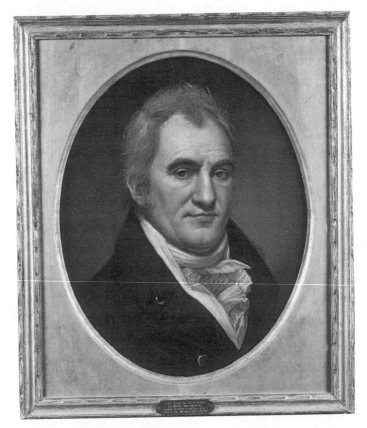

Joel Barlow (1807), by Charles Willson Peale. Though Peale's portrait of Barlow exudes confidence and self-satisfaction, it also registers Barlow's aging, making it the most realistic portrait to survive. Courtesy Diplomatic Reception Rooms, U.S. Department of State.

by the great body of the noblesse of that city as a sort of monster, against whom they must shut their doors. I did not choose to commit a burglary, & therefore I did not get into many of their houses." Barlow had hoped as "the only man in America who devotes his life entirely to literature" to be welcome in America's most liberal city.[31] Once the Barlows realized they could never make a place for themselves there, they looked to Washington as an alternative.

They had not been completely ostracized from Philadelphia society. The Coxes had been welcoming, and Charles Willson Peale had painted Barlow's portrait in the winter of 1807. This likeness comes closer to Farington's description of Barlow than the idealized portraits Vanderlyn and Fulton had done in Europe. It displays a sharp, fleshy-faced man with a quizzical, though not dissatisfied, expression. Barlow also had access to George Logan's hospitality, and a letter Barlow subsequently wrote Benjamin Rush introducing William Clark to him in 1810 suggests that Barlow knew Rush socially. But the genteel circle of Federalists surrounding Joseph Dennie and his literary magazine, *Port Folio*, snubbed the Barlows.

Despite numerous interruptions, Barlow had completed most of the revisions to his epic by May 1, 1807. In addition to serving as a testimonial to the advances Americans had made in printing and illustrating, he wanted his poem to find as wide an audience as possible. Broad appeal, however, was incompatible with the deluxe product he had in mind. Reaching different audiences required committing himself to two printing jobs, one on fine, watermarked paper, the other on common paper. The former would be bound in leather with gold trim; the latter would be sold as loose sheets. Barlow's ambition to produce over eight hundred of the deluxe volumes outstripped the resources of his Philadelphia printer. He then made arrangements with a Baltimore printer who turned out 384 imprints on a slightly inferior grade of paper. Traveling between Philadelphia and Baltimore to keep the number of errors to a minimum consumed time, energy, and money.

Barlow invested $10,000 of his own in the enterprise with little prospect of recapturing his investment unless most of the deluxe version, priced at $20 a copy—the equivalent of about $375 today—sold out. He was embarrassed by his own extravagance and pretended, in dedicating the work to Fulton, that *The Columbiad* was a gift to the American people and that Fulton had paid most of the cost of producing it. All Barlow would admit to was the "leisurely and exhilarating labor in which I always delight" of writing it. Barlow likened his poem to a child he was committing to Fulton's care and instructed Fulton to act as an adoptive rather than a "foster" parent in nurturing the work. However, Barlow had no intention of letting anyone else take charge of *The Columbiad*, which finally appeared on December 24, 1807.[32]

Though the dramatic structure of the new poem resembled that of *The Vision of Columbus*, its didactic content deviated from both the original and the 1793 Paris edition of the poem. The clearest evidence of these differences lay in *The Columbiad*'s length. It grew 41 percent from 5,182 to 7,310 lines, and it included fifty explanatory footnotes, only one of which had been in the original version of the poem. Barlow completely abandoned the effort at compression evident in the

Parisian edition of *The Vision of Columbus*. While length does not provide the only measure of change, after Books I–III, all the books of *The Columbiad* increased in size and an entirely new Book X was added at the end.

Major changes began in Book IV, when the angel Hesper escorts Columbus through European developments that have occurred since the navigator's death. Barlow had Hesper expand on the theme that North America provided a setting for humanity's gradual perfection.

> Here social man a second birth shall find,
> And a new range of reason lift his mind,
> Feed his strong intellect with purer light,
> A nobler sense of duty and of right,
> The sense of liberty; whose holy fire
> His life shall temper and his laws inspire,
> Purge from all shades the world-embracing scope
> That prompts his genius and expands his hope.   (435–42)

That passage introduces a seventy-nine-line hymn to the role of freedom in redeeming the human race (433–512). But freedom did not spring immediately, full-grown from the soil of North America. Barlow describes how the growth of freedom in colonial America brought the colonists into conflict with their mother country.

Everyone from Thomas Jefferson to Barlow's more recent biographers have lamented that Barlow preferred redoing his epic to writing a prose history of the American Revolution. But with Louis XVI's patronage no longer a concern, Barlow was able to offer a more comprehensive account of the war. Operations in which the French played no part, like the storming of Stony Point and the battle of Eutaw Springs, are developed in considerable detail, though the French role in securing the victory at Yorktown is not neglected. Book VII of *The Columbiad* also describes the naval engagement off the Capes of the Chesapeake between the French fleet, under the Comte de Grasse, and the British fleet, under Samuel Graves. Barlow claimed this was the first rendering of a major naval battle in verse. In it, he has one ship of the line from both fleets grapple and eventually blow each other up, though he acknowledges in his introduction that he has taken liberties with the record in order to convey the intensity of naval combat. His other deviation from the record, having Cornwallis personally surrender his sword to Washington, drew critical comment from the *Star* out of Raleigh, North Carolina.[33] He was not writing factually accurate history as we know it, but he did give a far more complete account of the war than he had given before.

The Columbiad diverges even more dramatically from *The Vision of Columbus* after Barlow finishes with the war. Though both poems contained the same celebration of peace, Book VIII of *The Columbiad* introduces a new theme absent from the earlier epic:

> Think not, my friends, the patriot's task is done,
> Or Freedom safe, because the battle's won.
> Unnumber'd foes, far different arms that wield,
> Wait the weak moment when she quits her shield,
> To plunge in her bold breast the insidious dart
> Or pour keen poison round her thoughtless heart.   (79–84)

Next to the improper education of the next generation, slavery posed the greatest threat to the future of the republic. A 350-line passage on slavery in Book VIII is the most elaborate statement Barlow made about the subject. His time on the Barbary Coast had taken his understanding of what it meant to be a slave far beyond what he had gleaned from his family's purchase of an African female servant before the Revolution, though neither experience stopped him from acquiring a slave in Philadelphia during 1807.[34]

Barlow acknowledged that the European enslavement of the African was a worse crime than the North African enslavement of the European.

> Far heavier vengeance, in the march of time,
> Attends them still; if still they dare debase
> And hold enthrall'd the millions of my race;
> A vengeance that shall shake the world's deep frame,
> That heaven abhors, and hell might shrink to name.   (262–66)

So extreme was the guilt of white Americans that they deserved annihilation, but Barlow also stressed appeals to self interest. Beyond assuring his readers that masters need not fear retribution from the slaves for their sufferings, it was to America's interest to do away with slavery because "Tyrants are never free; and small and great, / All masters must be tyrants soon or late" (345–46). If the nation disregarded this truth, Barlow believed it could expect its republican experiment to be wrecked. On the other hand, abolition would establish a solid foundation for the emerging empire of American liberty.

> Complete their triumph, fix their firm abode,
> Purge all privations from your liberal code,
> Restore their souls to men, give earth repose

And save your sons from slavery, wars and woes.
　　Based on its rock of Right your empire lies,
On walls of wisdom let the fabric rise;
Preserve your principles, their force unfold,
Let nations prove them and let kings behold.　　　　　　　　(391–98)

Only then did Barlow return to the rewards of victory that had been so prominent a theme in *The Vision of Columbus*. The earlier epic had pointed to geographic expansion, economic development, and the flowering of a distinctively
American culture as the principal benefits Americans would reap from independence. By the first decade of the nineteenth century, there was more evidence of
progress on all three fronts than immediately after the war, but Barlow focused
exclusively on the cultural progress the republic had made. The theme of progress
served as pretext for raising the same philosophical question in *The Columbiad*
that he had broached in *The Vision of Columbus*: "Why this progressive laboring
search of man?" (IX, 22).

Columbus's guardian angel had given an opaque answer in the earlier epic
that at least was consistent with Protestant Christianity. In 1807 Barlow had the
angel Hesper repudiate the biblical creation story.

Millions of generations toil'd and died
To crust with coral and to salt her tide,
And millions more, ere yet her soil began,
Ere yet she form'd or could have nursed her man.　　　　　　(IX, 97–100)

Barlow knew that some European thinkers felt that man's presence on earth extended further back in time than the five to six thousand years suggested in the
book of Genesis. He was also aware that different human cultures had developed
in Africa and the Middle East in prehistoric times and that "no man can trace / The
gleams of thought that first illumed his race" (IX, 137–38). He now embraced a
model for the historical development of human societies—if not the biological
evolution of the human species—that extended further back than anyone could
precisely discern. That realization changed the question he had asked in *The Vision of Columbus* from why hadn't man been created perfect to why it had taken
so long to achieve mankind's present state of development?

Human progress toward freedom had been delayed by "two settled slaveries"
that "engross their labors and debase their soul"(IX, 185–86). Two hundred lines
of Book IX are devoted to showing how a variety of cultures, including those of

ancient Greece, India, Islam, and the Norsemen, reflected that struggle. The universality of the insight leads to a second question that Barlow's Columbus asks.

> Say, friend of man, in this unbounded range,
> Where error vagrates and illusions change,
> What hopes to see his baleful blunders cease,
> And earth commence that promised age of peace? (IX, 313–16)

Barlow offers an optimistic response. Though men have made advances against oppression in the past, the real problem is how to render their intermittent gains continuous. Hesper points to the progress of European science as a central element in transforming the structure of history. By "science," Barlow means not just experimental science but culture and learning in general. After elaborating on the many technical achievements of Europe, Barlow has Hesper declare that had the ancient world known of the printing press, the Dark Ages that followed the fall of Rome would never have occurred. By making irreversible the advancement of knowledge, science also guarantees moral improvement.

Nowhere was the future of science more secure than in the United States. That prospect gets Columbus so excited that he begs for another glimpse of the rhapsodic future, which Hesper grants. The last book of *The Vision of Columbus* had pursued a similar course but with an important difference. In 1807, Barlow's version of a secular millennium involves the peaceful integration of the human family into federated republics embracing every region of the globe, with commerce, rather than being assisted by grace, the sole engine behind their unification.

> That all thy race the common wealth might share,
> Exchange their fruits and fill their treasures there,
> Their speech assimilate, their counsels blend,
> Till mutual interest fix the mutual friend. (X, 147–50)

The centrality of commerce in turn made the abolition of naval warfare central to Barlow's progressive vision of the future. The concluding, entirely new, book of *The Columbiad* underscores the utopian implications of Barlow's relationship with Robert Fulton. Barlow envisioned a radically new future once "the aspiring genius of the age / Soar[s] in the Bard and strengthen[s] in the Sage" (X, 249–50). An association between the poet and inventor had limitless possibilities. Together they could devise a way to fly as well as to tame the weather and volcanoes. Progressive improvement would continue "Till mutual love commands all strife to cease, / And earth join joyous in the songs of peace" (X, 493–94). Then "all the joys [of] descending ages" would repay the labors and pains of those who had preceded them (X, 641–42).

The Columbiad got its first major notice from an English reviewer, probably Barlow's friend Richard Phillips, writing for London's Monthly Magazine and British Register.[35] He described it as "magnificent . . . beyond any thing which modern literature has to boast, except . . . [the work of] Milton." He congratulated Barlow on having selected an event in "the discovery of America," whose "consequences comprise by far the most interesting portion of modern history," not the least of which was "giving birth to a great and civilized nation." The writer in the Monthly Magazine also congratulated Barlow on his geographic descriptions, claiming "that the mountains and rivers of the new world have [now] been better sung than those of the old." The National Intelligencer republished this review, and the Boston Patriot copied it from the Intelligencer later in the summer.[36]

Francis Jeffrey's response to The Columbiad in the Edinburgh Review was more critical. Jeffrey began by declaring that Barlow "will not be the Homer of his country; and will never take his place among the enduring poets either of the old or of the new world." He complained that Barlow's poem was constructed upon a plan where there could be "no development of character, — no unity or even connexion of action, — and consequently no interest, and scarcely any coherence . . . in the story." While Jeffrey did not doubt that Barlow was a "very good republican," his verses lacked any "play or vivacity of fancy, — any gift of simplicity or pathos, — any loftiness of genius, or delicacy of taste. . . . In his cumbrous and inflated style, he is constantly mistaking hyperbole for grandeur, and supplying the place of simplicity with huge patches of mere tameness and vulgarity." The overall effect was an "unhappy imitation of that picturesque" style "which alternatively charms and disgusts us."[37] Jeffrey was "quite certain, that his present work will have no success in" Britain, though he did concede that "the extraordinary beauty of the paper, printing, and embellishments" of the book might procure some sales.[38] The Federalist Boston Gazette republished Jeffrey's review on March 12, 1810.

Though James Dennie's Port Folio professed to support national literature, it published an equally critical assessment of The Columbiad. Dennie's reviewer summarily dismissed the work "as a whole . . . devoid of interest," despite brilliant parts. He sounded like the Edinburgh Review when he complained that Barlow had "heaped together such an immense, discordant mass of characters, facts, and descriptions" as to preclude the development of character and action. Barlow's sages were "presented to [one's] view (as you see portraits in the window of a print-shop) surrounded by air-pumps and telescopes, piles of books and heaps of chymical apparatus." The *Port Folio*'s reviewer also complained of "a certain wearisome sameness and dull repetition of favourite phrases and perpetual recurring rhymes." Finally, he took Barlow "to task for petty offences against the purity of the English language," ranking him very much as the Edinburgh reviewer had: "We place his work 'behind the foremost, and before the last,' on the same shelf with" a series of minor British authors, "but a bit below . . . the Conquest of Canaan of Dwight."[39]

Dennie subsequently acknowledged the *Port Folio*'s "caustic criticism" had "excited not a little clamour against" him "for his fancied prejudice against the Literature of his country." Dennie admitted he had published an "obnoxious criticism" in the "sterner style of the Edinburgh Review." But he protested that the "idea of deliberate hostility to this work, as an *American* production" was absurd. Dennie also denied that the reviewer's hostile view of *The Columbiad* reflected the editor's Federalist politics, asserting that the *Port Folio* was not "a *party paper.*" Instead, Dennie insisted it was "a Literary Journal, expressly intended to aggrandize the national character." Dennie added that he had personally "on many occasions . . . at the table of several literary friends, . . . frankly spoken in commendation of many passages in the Columbiad." But this was damning with faint praise, and to prove his impartiality Dennie eventually republished the review that had appeared in the *Monthly Magazine and British Register.*[40]

Magazines in the early republic had a more precarious existence than newspapers because they carried no advertising and therefore depended entirely on subscriptions. Dennie had to worry about taking a stand that might alienate potential supporters, which is why he yielded to pressure. Federalist newspapers did not have to make such concessions since they were financed by advertisements as well as subscriptions. While some accepted advertisements for the poem, those with a predominantly political orientation, like William Coleman's *New York Evening Advertiser*, the *New England Palladium*, and John Park's Boston *Repertory*, refused to take any notice of it. The intensification of the partisan conflict over the embargo of 1807–9 made them unwilling to give encouragement to a republican as notorious as Barlow.

Partisan politics, however, played only a minor role in shaping the response of the American public to *The Columbiad*. The poem touched more directly on another fissure that had developed in American society—the religious division between those who endorsed the revivalism of the Second Great Awakening and those who viewed it with indifference, if not outright hostility. Those who responded positively to the revivalists were initially far more activist in their orientation than those who did not. The Second Great Awakening led to the formation of a wide variety of religious institutions that had no precedent, including religious periodicals and societies that mobilized a predominantly female constituency. The most notable among them were the missionary societies that sought to convert the heathen. Behind the proliferation of these religious institutions lay the belief that the next great advance of Christianity would be the second coming of Christ, who would reign on earth for a thousand years. Such religious attitudes turned the growing awareness of radical change to traditional ends. These beliefs were particularly strong in New England and in the regions of the West to which migrants from the Northeast were moving, such as western New York and Ohio, but they suffused the entire nation.

Such a religiously charged culture was bound to find features of Barlow's *Columbiad*—like his abandonment of the Judeo-Christian creation myth—objectionable. Of course, most people who were likely to react that way were unlikely to read Barlow's poem. Nonetheless, their attention could be drawn to any hint of religious heterodoxy by newspaper commentators who regularly kept readers informed about such matters. In their efforts to resist the Republican triumph of Jefferson in 1800, the Federalists of New England did all they could to harness the more established Protestant sects in opposing Republican political and religious innovation. That is why Federalist editors chose to reprint so widely the letter Henri Grégoire addressed to Barlow, entitled *Critical Observations on the Poem of Joel Barlow*, outlining Grégoire's religious objections to *The Columbiad*.

Grégoire's letter began appearing in American newspapers in late August 1809 and was printed in the September edition of a Boston magazine, the *Monthly Anthology*, and eventually as a pamphlet. Instead of attacking the poem's substantive content, Grégoire restricted his criticism to Smirke's illustration titled *The Final Resignation of Prejudices*. The engraving, which appeared at the end of the poem, depicted a cross lying on the ground with other discarded symbols of authority, including a crown. Grégoire found this depiction of "the cross of Jesus Christ" deeply offensive because "the attributes of pure christianity are classed among the emblems of prejudices." Grégoire saw in such a representation "an attack against all christian societies," as well as "an act of intolerance, of persecution, which offends God and man." He acknowledged that his "infidel" countrymen had reproached Christianity "with the abuses it has experienced, as if . . . [its] abuses were the thing in itself." But this did not justify Barlow in doing so. Grégoire noted that the infidel leaders of the French Revolution had persecuted the churchmen they accused of fanaticism far more fanatically than their victims had advanced their beliefs. But the revolutionaries had done so on the assumption that "no one could be at once a christian and a republican, at once a republican and a *moderate.*" This in turn had justified an attempt to destroy Christianity. Grégoire asked, "Does not your engraving appear to retrace . . . the results, [t]hat our persecutors have executed?" The illustration offended "propriety, because, in holding out as *prejudices* the emblems of the christian religion, it is saying to all who profess it, that they are fools."[41]

Grégoire's letter also argued the utility of religion: "The cross and the gospel, in preparing us for the happiness of eternity, have civilized the world. . . . When public shame is extinct, do not expect to preserve the private virtues; and when religion is publicly insulted, it is a wound to morality, a national calamity." He continued: "The christian religion . . . well understood and rightly practiced . . . is the most certain guarantee of the purity of public and private manners." Addressing Barlow personally, he added—"Under its wings, my friend, your state of society was raised, and consolidated, and the domestic virtues hereditarily transmitted; it is to that, without doubt, that you owe, among other advantages, that of having a wife gifted with so many rare qualities and inestimable virtues. Ingratitude alone could mistake the benefits of this august and divine religion; it would be like despising the bosom of our mother."[42]

The editor of Boston's *Monthly Anthology* attempted to magnify Grégoire's authority while dismissing the favorable review that had appeared in the *Monthly Magazine* as reflecting the "unworthy tricks" of "writing articles in this country on American works, sending them to be published there, and then quoting them here as the opinions of Englishmen."[43] The *Anthology's* readers had the satisfaction of knowing that the words they were reading were those of an eminent French divine who had been a member of the National Convention and was currently a senator.

Grégoire's letter compelled Barlow "to put myself right as to the good opinion of my fellow citizens" if he were to preserve his power to do them good.[44] Fortunately, Grégoire's criticism proved easier to rebut than it would have been had Grégoire attacked some of the philosophical positions Barlow had developed in *The Columbiad.* For instance, Grégoire had discretely passed over the extensive passages in Book IX that replicated Volney's ideas about the origins and development of religions. Grégoire also confined himself to Barlow's sins of commission rather than his sins of omission. Nowhere in *The Columbiad* is there a reference to Christ or to humanity's salvation though his crucifixion. All Barlow had to do to defend himself against Grégoire's complaint was to focus on the iconography of the cross. The illustration had been done in England while Barlow was in America. That enabled him to claim he had had nothing to do with its specific design. Of course, Barlow could have elected not to use the illustration, but having done so only made him "an accomplice after the fact."[45]

Since such a defense could still be construed as a confession of guilt, Barlow took another tack that had more complex implications. He argued that New England Puritans subscribed to a version of Christianity that, in keeping with Moses' injunctions in the Ten Commandments, devalued man-made emblems of the divine and held the cross in no special reverence. Though they might regard trampling on a cross—which Dutch traders were reputed to have done when trying to convince the Japanese that they were completely different from the Portuguese—as "reprehensible" because dishonest, the action carried no other significance for the Puritans. Barlow acknowledged that "to a catholic, who identifies the cross with the gospel . . . it must appear a horrid crime; but to a protestant we may easily conceive it might appear of little moment, and by no means as a renunciation of the gospel." To underline his point Barlow asserted that he would not think twice about seeing "'the symbols of liberty, so dear to me, trampled under foot before my eyes. . . . Leave to me and my country the great realities of liberty, and I freely give you up its emblems."[46]

Barlow asked Grégoire to judge his poem "as a moral work" whose aims were drawn "from the gospel, from history, from the unlettered volume of moral nature, [and] from the experience and the inexperience of unhappy man." Barlow claimed that "the Columbiad . . . in all its parts . . . is more favorable to sound and rigid morals, more friendly to virtue, more clear and unequivocal in pointing out the road to national dignity and individual happiness, more energetic in its denunciations of tyranny and oppression in every shape, injustice and wickedness in all their forms, and consequently more consonant to what you acknowledge to be the spirit of the gospel, than all the writings of all the . . . christian authors" Grégoire had taxed Barlow with disregarding.[47] Pursuing such a defense risked making himself appear a braggart, so Barlow disclaimed any special merit. "My work is only a transcript of the tablet of my mind imprest with these images as they pass before it." As for France's abandonment of religion, Barlow suggested that "the complicated ceremonials of their worship, and what you yourself would term the non essentials of their religion" had been more important than republicanism's secular bent. "The scaffolding of your church . . . had so enclosed, perforated, overlooked and underpropt the building" that it was no wonder when "the reformer [laid] his hand, like a blind Samson, to the great substantial pillars," he overturned "the whole encumbered edifice together" and buried "himself in the ruins."[48]

Since Barlow could not count on his reply appearing in the newspapers that had published Grégoire's critique of *The Columbiad*, he had it published in pamphlet form. That allowed him to send copies to influential friends, who wrote back reassuringly. The private assurances of prominent men, however, only reflected Barlow's success in aligning himself with their evaluation of the French Revolution.[49] Their approbation conveniently ignored how vague his current religious beliefs remained. Barlow pointedly evaded Grégoire's comment that "your presbyterian countrymen will perhaps ask, if you have abjured the principles, that you professed when you were the chaplain of a regiment in the war of independence."[50] Barlow's reliance on Volney's speculations about the world's religions raised this issue, and Grégoire could have insisted on having a response. But he didn't.[51]

Instead, in his reply, dated January 28, 1810, to Barlow's letter, Grégoire accepted Barlow's apology for offending his religious sensibilities and was content to repeat his principal point that the abuse of something should not be confused with the thing itself. At the same time, Grégoire defended the use of religious emblems. His biggest gift to Barlow, however, was to declare that "you likewise recognize the immense benefits of the gospel; this naturally leads one to say, that in the order of things whatever is essentially *good* at all times and in all places, is essentially *true*; for in the last analysis these two epithets must both apply to the same object." While Grégoire was not yielding anything of what was contained in his former letter "on the principles of religion," he affirmed that they were in agreement "as to the obligation of loving our fellow creatures and laboring for their happiness."[52]

Barlow's Federalist enemies were not so kind. Once the controversy turned to his beliefs, the Federalists sensed they had the upper hand. The Federalist editor of the recently established *Connecticut Mirror*, Theodore Dwight, seized on the religious issue in a long piece that appeared on October 16, 1809, undoubtedly with the approval, if not assistance, of his brother, Timothy Dwight. The article summarized the published exchanges between Grégoire and Barlow before identifying the devious strategies Barlow had deployed in replying to Grégoire. These included flattery and attempting to throw the blame for the offending picture on someone else. However, Dwight objected principally to Barlow's notion that religious identities were a product of the society one happened to find oneself in. "If Mr. Barlow has nothing more of the Christian to boast of, than that he was *born among the puritans*, and still *adheres* to them, his title [to being a Christian] is hardly worth the trouble of renunciation." Dwight thought Barlow's claim that "the gospel had done *some good* in the world" a very tepid affirmation of faith. It would have been far more convincing to have said "'I am a Christian, and abhor Infidelity as the bane of human happiness.'"

Though Grégoire was unaware of Dwight's attack when he responded to Barlow's reply, Grégoire had noted Barlow's warning that many were republishing his letter because they think it will "destroy the effect of my republican writings."[53] Grégoire had experienced far more persecution than Barlow had from "infidels and fanatics" in France but attributed his experience to the rarity "of a man professing the same principles in 1810, which he professed in 1789." It had "roused against me the Proteus gang, who have worn every livery and followed every banner." Nonetheless, Grégoire recognized Barlow to be a fellow warrior in a righteous cause and advocated two remedies against their opponents: "one is not to resemble them, the other is to do them good" as the gospel prescribed. This was the same gospel which Barlow had lamely admitted had "done great good in the world," and that was enough for Grégoire.[54]

Barlow was sufficiently heartened after receiving Grégoire's second letter to rush it into print, probably translating it himself for the press. It did not, however, satisfy those who remained suspicious about Barlow's religious opinions, including his long-estranged Yale classmate Noah Webster. While *The Columbiad* was being printed, Barlow had tried to revive their friendship, sending Webster a copy of the postscript to the poem's notes, which explained some of the English usage the reader would encounter. It also praised Webster's "philological labors" for contributing to the "purity and regularity" of the language. Webster responded vaguely but warmly "on the score of former friendship" and because Barlow's letter informed "me of your favorable opinion of my dictionary."[55] While Webster seemed interested in Barlow's reaction to his work, self-absorbed descriptions of the numerous obstacles the lexicographer was encountering dominated his letters.[56]

Only in April 1808 did Webster mention *The Columbiad* in passing, complementing Barlow on the elegance of its printing and engravings. Even then, Webster's praise came with a hook. He grumbled that the price of the volume would make "it impossible for many of your friends & the friends of literature to purchase the Book."[57] Webster's complaints about the obstacles he faced in liberating American English from the cultural standards of the former mother country drew Barlow's attention to what separated Webster from many fellow Federalists. They continued to look upon Britain as a cultural as well as strategic barrier against French barbarism. In the summer of 1808 Barlow attempted to take advantage of this fissure by presenting himself as Webster's cultural ally, hoping thereby to gain an endorsement for the political and moral tendency of his poem. But when Barlow supplied Webster with a copy of *The Columbiad*, Webster replied only after being repeatedly pressed for a review.[58]

On October 13, 1808, Webster finally acknowledged that he "had intended to give the public a short review of your Columbiad, before this time. But two causes have prevented me." One was Webster's preoccupation with other matters, like his health. The other was "a doubt whether I can execute this purpose, in a manner to satisfy you & my own conscience at the same time." Webster was prepared to "say all . . . which you can expect or desire" about the poem, but he could not "in a review omit to pass a severe censure on the atheistical principles it contains." He bluntly informed Barlow that "the principles of irreligion which you avow . . . form the partition-wall which has separated you from many of your friends." He added, "No man on earth, not allied to me by nature or marriage, had so large a share in my affections, as Joel Barlow, until you renounced the religion, which you once preached, & which I believe." Webster concluded, "I apprehend my silence will be most agreeable to you, & most expedient for your old friend." Though Webster was prepared to forgive Barlow his politics, for religious reasons he would deny Barlow what he most wanted, despite a shared cultural agenda.[59]

The publication of *The Columbiad* nonetheless helped consolidate Barlow's reputation as a leading literary figure in the new republic. This recognition could be seen in the flow of unsolicited honors that started coming his way. In 1809 Barlow was elected to membership in the American Philosophical Society. Though international in scope, it was still very much a Philadelphia-centered institution under the influence of the people Barlow complained had treated him like a social pariah in 1807. And Josiah Meigs arranged for the University of Georgia to award Barlow an honorary doctor of laws degree. However, rebuffs from institutions he might have expected would accord him recognition accompanied these honors. He was never made a member of the Connecticut Academy of Arts and Sciences, which Timothy Dwight had established in 1801, though few of its members were as distinguished as Barlow. And when Barlow wrote to the National Institute of France that he was sending them a copy of *The Columbiad*, they congratulated him but declined to include him in their ranks. The National Institute was Napoleon's creature and was not about to waste patronage on a republican like Barlow.[60]

The Columbiad also failed to make its way into the canon of American literature because it was too rooted in problems of the moment. Though it went through seven different printings between 1807 and 1825, two of which were produced abroad, after that demand for it ceased. By contrast, his mock epic *The*

Hasty Pudding became part of the canon because its satirical "motive" enabled it to transcend the moment. It also benefited from its brevity. The avalanche of prose issuing from American presses during the nineteenth century forced poetry aside. Poetic epics continued to be written, but the heroic narrative, which John P. McWilliams Jr. has identified as "the essence of *epos*," migrated into the romantic prose of histories and the novel.[61]

The *Columbiad*'s most serious problem remained its religious implications. It is significant that *The Vision of Columbus*, which benefited from Barlow's initial desire to make Christianity and republicanism complementary systems of thought, went through more editions than the *The Columbiad* and that four of its reprintings took place after *The Columbiad* appeared. A nation in the midst of the Second Great Awakening was no more willing to forgive than Webster had been when it felt its religious convictions were being challenged.[62]

CHAPTER SIXTEEN

Washington Insider

Ruth's frailty helped draw the Barlows back to Washington during the autumn of 1807. She usually became ill with the onset of spring, and both Barlows assumed she was vulnerable to the heat, though seasonal allergies may have been the source of her problems. Despite its southerly location, Washington's small and scattered population made it more salubrious than Philadelphia. Washington summers were longer and hotter, but the chance of contracting a tropical infection like yellow fever—which had killed Joel's brother Aaron in Norfolk six years before—was less, because the capital was not a commercial center. The Barlows might visit family and friends in New England and New York during the heat, or they might retire to the mountains west of Washington. Barlow could send Ruth off ahead of him, when she was well enough to travel, because the roads were in better shape and the river crossings more manageable during the warmer months.

Now that the property Jefferson had recommended in 1802 was again available, Barlow had little difficulty deciding it was preferable to a boarding house. The house stood on twenty acres at the top of a two hundred foot hill just east of Rock Creek along the main road between Virginia and Philadelphia. From the house one had a splendid view of the White House and the Capitol four miles distant. Called "Belle Air" by previous owners, Barlow renamed it "Calorama," Greek for beautiful view. It soon came to be known as "Kalorama," a name the area still bears today.[1]

After completing *The Columbiad*, Barlow turned to writing the history of the American Revolution others had been urging him to undertake. Washington provided Barlow with convenient access to the archives of influential players like

Jefferson and Madison, but the principal attraction of the house for Barlow was its proximity to the government. After the European war entered a new phase in 1807, Barlow became even more convinced that the fate of republicanism would be decided in the American capital. During the year that Barlow completed his revisions and supervised the publication of *The Columbiad*, the nation's relations with Britain had worsened. Before Jefferson could orchestrate a diplomatic and commercial response to the replacement of the doctrine of "broken voyages" with the Rule of 1756, Britain proclaimed a blockade of France's northwestern coast and nearby dependencies. The policy taxed Britain's naval manpower to the limit, leading to an increase in her impressment of seamen from American vessels. Many British sailors were attracted to the American merchant marine by higher wages and superior conditions. Britain did not recognize the right of its subjects to renounce their allegiance. British officers—boarding American vessels to ascertain their registry and destination—often impressed as "British" seamen who were in fact Americans.

Toward the end of 1806 William Pinkney and James Monroe negotiated a treaty with the British government that granted the United States significant commercial concessions. Just as the American envoys were finalizing the agreement, however, Napoleon issued his Berlin Decree of November 21, 1806, placing the entire British Isles under blockade. The British government responded by making the Monroe-Pinkney Treaty conditional upon the United States defending its neutrality against France. Jefferson construed the condition as insulting. Since the treaty had failed to resolve the issue of impressment, he declined sending it to the Senate. The United States thus entered 1807 without an understanding with either of the great powers, though the Franco-American Convention of 1800 could be interpreted as exempting American vessels from paper blockades like the one proclaimed by the Berlin Decree.[2]

On June 22, 1807, the British frigate, HMS *Leopard*, removed any ambiguity that Britain constituted a more immediate threat than France. Because the British navy enforced her European blockades by boarding vessels as they left American waters, her men-of-war patrolling the coast found it convenient to buy provisions in American ports. Though the British seldom failed to find someone willing to sell to them, the local population retaliated by encouraging her seamen to desert. Upon learning that several deserters were on aboard the frigate USS *Chesapeake*, about to depart from Norfolk on a Mediterranean cruise, HMS *Leopard* intercepted the *Chesapeake* as she cleared the Virginia Capes. When the *Chesapeake* refused to submit to a search, the *Leopard* opened fire. Because the American frigate had failed to prepare for action, its captain surrendered his ship. The British removed four of the American frigate's crew, leaving eighteen wounded and three dead.

Such an egregious insult to the American flag ignited a war fever against Britain. Jefferson's initial anger quickly yielded to caution. Since the incident had occurred as the government dispersed for the summer, it was impossible to call Congress—which alone could declare war—back into emergency session for at least two months. Instead, Jefferson banned British warships from American waters, though the ban proved unenforceable. The British government, for her part, quickly disavowed the actions of the *Leopard*'s captain and dispatched a new minister to the United States. These developments made it pointless to call Congress back into session before it was scheduled to reassemble at the end of the year.

The Barlows moved into Kalorama just before the winter of 1807–8 began. The house was near Abraham's grave beside Rock Creek, and Ruth commented that "the idea of being once more united in death gives me a tranquil pleasure, & serves to render this spot more agreeable." Ruth's declining health inclined her to think death not far off. During their first months in Kalorama, her eyes became so inflamed that she could not spend more than ten minutes at a time with either a book or a pen. By then the publication of *The Columbiad* had progressed to a point where Barlow could take care of the remaining loose ends through a nearby printer in Baltimore.[3] Barlow was anxious to be on hand for the opening of Congress facing the choice between peace and war. While Barlow's republicanism strongly inclined him to favor peace, he was no advocate of blind submission to aggression.

Two additional developments contributed to excitement in Washington that winter: It was learned that France did not regard the Convention of 1800 as protecting American shipping from its Berlin Decree and that Britain proposed to retaliate by imposing new restrictions on neutral vessels making for Europe. These restrictions required neutral vessels to enter a British port to pay duties or else face seizure. Of the two, the British order-in-council was more threatening because Britain was better able to enforce her regulations than France. Napoleon subsequently responded with the Milan Decree, which proclaimed that any neutral vessel submitting to Britain's regulations would be a lawful prize. Suddenly, the greater part of the nation's overseas commerce had become liable to seizure and condemnation either by one great power or the other.

Jefferson realized that a declaration of war against Britain alone would dangerously divide the nation, while going to war against both great powers was beyond its capabilities. This dilemma made him receptive to Madison's preference for using commercial pressure. Jefferson concluded that a general embargo was the nation's best option, at least for the moment. As a prominent proponent of replacing warfare with commercial coercion, Barlow welcomed the president's decision. Congress quickly agreed to Jefferson's request because so much of the nation's property was vulnerable on the high seas. Sheltering it in American ports while exploring diplomatic remedies seemed the most prudent course. The imminent arrival of a new ambassador from Britain created an expectation that the embargo would only be temporary. Even if negotiations with the British ambassador collapsed, other alternatives might materialize.

Barlow was aware that some in Washington feared the British would interpret an embargo as a warlike measure, and he found it reassuring when this turned out not to be the case.[4] He and Ruth, however, remained distracted from the political drama taking place in the nearby capital during their first winter in Kalorama. An inflammation of his eyes, perhaps caught from Ruth, put him out of commission for three crucial weeks during January 1808. Then he fell, possibly because of his impaired vision, spraining his ankle badly enough to confine him to bed for a week. Their new property absorbed most of Barlow's remaining energy and time.[5] Soon after purchasing Kalorama, Barlow had added twenty more acres to his original holding.

At the end of the winter, negotiations with the British ambassador collapsed. Though Barlow had never expected much from them,[6] their termination made enforcing the embargo more difficult. Just when merchants and ship captains normally launched overseas voyages, the administration found itself having to justify the embargo more as an experiment of undefined duration than a temporary precaution. No one, including Barlow, was under the illusion that it could be maintained indefinitely. But that raised the possibility that war might become the Republicans' only option to humiliating surrender. Preparing for such a contingency was deeply distasteful, but—prodded by Albert Gallatin—they went through the motions. Congress authorized the formation of a provisional army that would be drawn from the state militias and an expansion of the gunboat force Jefferson preferred to more expensive men-of-war–like frigates.

Barlow had no scruples about channeling defense contracts in the direction of his friends. Classmate Alexander Wolcott in Middletown, Connecticut, was involved in building ten gunboats for $3,900 each, probably as a byproduct of Barlow's newly formed friendship with Secretary of War Henry Dearborn. Barlow also wrote his nephew Stephen asking whether he could have several gunboats built on the Naugatuck River for $4,000 or less. But when he learned that Jefferson intended to prune his gunboat fleet by almost half, Barlow withdrew the query. At this stage Barlow remained more witness than advisor to the government.[7]

Since their largely unfurnished house did not enable them to entertain, Barlow went back to Philadelphia in April, where he remained for most of the spring, returning only briefly to Washington during May. Northern ports were the best places to buy quality imports, and he would spend over $5,000 (around $100,000 in today's dollars) furnishing Kalorama so that Ruth could become one of Washington's first hostesses and he could indulge his passion for mixing with influential people. They also embarked on a substantial remodeling of the house, made necessary, among other things, by the imminent arrival of the Fultons.

After the success of the *Clermont* in 1807, Fulton married his partner's niece, Harriet Livingston. At the beginning of June 1808, Fulton wrote the Barlows proposing that he and Harriet, by then five months pregnant, join them at Kalorama. Fulton saw no reason why their previous arrangement could not be expanded to include his new wife and their child. He expected unprecedented opportunities to flow from uniting "our fortunes to make calorama the centre of taste beauty love and dearest friendship. . . . There Shall the Sage enjoying every blessing, prosecute with tranquil mind his literary pursuits. The artist [Fulton] his plans of Improvement Ruthlinda dear ruthlinda heart of love, and Harriet receiving Information by her example acquire all that is her most endearing."[8]

Harriet would have been a fool not to have sensed danger in this plan, but she seems to have accepted the move—which took place during the summer of 1808—as inevitable. She could have insisted on staying either with her mother or Chancellor Livingston, at least until the baby was born. Fulton had been so busy with his steamboat that Harriet had hardly ventured beyond the confines of the Livingston family since their marriage. Moving in with the Barlows would at least free her from that world and perhaps get her more attention from her husband, as well as providing a friendly place for delivering her child.

The arrival of the Fultons did not preclude the Barlows from accepting Jefferson's invitation for a prolonged visit to Monticello. No effort was made to include the Fultons because Harriet's baby was expected in October. Nor was there any need to entertain them since they were family. Instead, Barlow asked Fulton to take charge of Kalorama and to help Benjamin Latrobe—whom he had hired to design improvements for the property—with the execution of some of his plans. Over the next few years, Barlow added an orchard and two additional wings to the original house, as well as a barn, stables, and a summer cottage. He also acquired several more slaves, though not before seeking unsuccessfully to make do with free labor imported from the New England.[9] The attempt at combining the two families would prove equally unsuccessful because Ruth and Harriet competed with each other for the attention of the men. It didn't take long for all involved to realize that the ménage-à-trois of Paris would not work as a ménage-à-quatre.

Barlow expected his visit with Jefferson would yield information for his projected history of the American Revolution. On August 1, 1808, Barlow sent the president two written queries. The first related to Barlow's suspicion that the government had overreacted to the Whiskey rebels in western Pennsylvania. Barlow asked Jefferson if he knew of any evidence that Washington and Hamilton had instigated the rebellion. The other query related to a comment, attributed to Jefferson, that the Federalists had planned to replace Adams with Washington in 1800 and keep Washington in the presidency until he died. Washington's death in December 1799 had aborted the scheme, but if the allegation could be substantiated, it would show that the Federalists harbored monarchical inclinations.[10]

An August heat wave proved so severe that Barlow had to take Ruth north in search of relief before visiting Jefferson.[11] They did not return to Washington until September 7. Though Ruth's condition improved with the approach of autumn, she wanted to be on hand as Harriet's pregnancy came to term. Barlow excused his wife by telling Jefferson she was not well enough to accompany him. Without her the two men would have more time to discuss the subjects on Barlow's mind. Barlow wrote Jefferson on September 12 that he intended to set out alone the next day in a light carriage and that if the weather remained cool, "I may be with you sooner than we should otherwise contemplate."[12] He had high expectations about spending quality time with Jefferson, but they devoted as much of the visit to talking about all the other interests the two polymaths shared as they did about recent history.

Just before setting out for Monticello, Barlow forwarded to Jefferson a letter from a New England Republican about the region's rising resistance to the embargo's enforcement. The political consequences of the measure were as disturbing as the widespread evasions it inspired. The preceding March, Timothy Pickering, the junior senator from Massachusetts, had published a demagogic pamphlet accusing the administration of imposing the measure in response to Napoleon's orders. Pickering alleged that the French emperor sought to complete his continental system by excluding British goods from the United States, hoping thereby to provoke a war between the American Republic and Great Britain. Though Pickering was regarded in Washington as inconsequential, his pamphlet led to the election of a Federalist majority in the Massachusetts legislature, which then declared political war against the state's ailing Republican governor, James Sullivan.[13]

Initially, the Federalists only had their eyes on the electoral vote of Massachusetts in the upcoming presidential election, but their campaign proved so effective that they soon took aim at the embargo itself. Republicans in the northern states felt threatened and pleaded with party leaders in Washington to soften the embargo's restrictions. Barlow made light of the situation at first. In May he observed, "The embargo horse" had "all the tories in America mounted upon him & those of England are invited to get on behind." Later that month Barlow appealed to Jefferson on behalf of William Lee, his former commercial partner, for a waiver from the measure. Barlow should have approached Gallatin first but justified appealing directly to Jefferson on the grounds that the large number of seamen Lee employed would otherwise have to be supported by the public.[14]

Even after Barlow learned of the political transformation of Massachusetts, he remained unconcerned. Since the beginning of the Revolution, Massachusetts had slipped in ranking from second after Virginia to fourth largest state, yielding precedence to Pennsylvania and New York. Massachusetts remained strategically important, however, because of its shared frontier with British Canada. At that time Massachusetts included the territory that would become Maine, and its loyalty would be crucial if the United States were ever forced into a showdown with Great Britain. Nonetheless, Barlow continued to construe the Federalist agitation as a reflection of their desperation. "The embargo is the only election horse they can ride & they will wear it down to the bone." Nor was Barlow worried about a Federalist scheme to endorse Dewitt Clinton's candidacy for the presidency, thereby harnessing New York and New Jersey Republicans to split Jefferson's national coalition.[15]

Barlow's dismissive attitude toward the Federalists changed as their opposition to the administration intensified. After the Massachusetts legislature made as much political capital as it could out of the embargo, Federalists in Boston organized committees of correspondence and county conventions to encourage resistance and further violations. Barlow responded by taking a harder line on enforcement. The Federalists had only their seditious behavior to blame for the pain they were feeling. If they had obeyed the law, it would have led the belligerent powers to temper their aggressions.[16] Like Jefferson, Barlow gave no credence to the Federalist claim that a British order-in-council—issued on July 8 and opening the Iberian Peninsular to neutral vessels—represented a significant abandonment by Britain of her attempts to control American commerce. Both men viewed the British directive admitting American vessels without proper clearance papers to British ports as an attempt to bribe Americans into betraying their nation's interests.

Barlow returned to Kalorama in early October in time for the birth of the Fultons' son. The couple named their new child Robert Barlow Fulton, and Fulton insisted on calling him "Barlow." The baby's namesake spent the remainder of the autumn with Ruth readying Kalorama for the winter social season and starting his history of the American Revolution. These activities and the difficulty of incorporating Harriet and her new baby into their family occupied more of Barlow's time than did public affairs. Harriet's dissatisfaction with her living arrangement distracted Barlow from the problems Jefferson encountered that winter as he tried to keep the Republican coalition together while Congress debated whether war with Britain should replace the embargo. Finally, in February 1809, the Fultons departed for New York. To judge from the elaborate lengths to which Fulton subsequently went in reassuring Barlow that their departure had not proceeded "from any diminution of affection," their failure to integrate the two families caused them all considerable pain.[17]

Barlow remained more comfortable with his utopian dreams than the realities of international politics. He again pressed his personal agenda of a national learned society at an inopportune moment. Its only possible relevance to the concerns of his fellow Republicans was the claim that in uniting learned men across national boundaries such societies might provide the means for "confederating . . . nations by the force of one of their strongest interests."[18] But if pushing schemes of universal peace when the world seemed on the verge of universal war highlighted how disconnected Barlow had become from the current political scene, he was not alone in his confusion. Jefferson behaved more like someone who wished to be rid of his office than the leader of a national coalition. The Republican leadership in Congress focused on insuring Madison's election to the presidency that winter, rather than evaluating the consequences of modifying the embargo so that it applied only to Britain and France.

No one seemed concerned that limiting the embargo in this manner was, in effect, capitulating to Britain because Britain's naval superiority would allow her to enjoy an indirect commerce with the United States that she could deny to France. Napoleon interpreted the measure in this way and retaliated by sequestering American vessels entering French-controlled ports. David Erskine, the new British minister in Washington, construed the Nonintercourse Law—which authorized the president to direct nonintercourse exclusively against the other belligerent whenever one of them lifted its restrictions on American commerce—as an invitation to form a strategic alliance with the United States. Erskine was the son of a liberal English barrister who had defended some of Barlow's republican friends in the sedition and treason prosecutions of the 1790s. The father had recently become lord chancellor, and Barlow hoped some of his republican sympathies had rubbed off on his son.[19]

Erskine proposed that the United States and Great Britain abandon their commercial restrictions against each other, on the understanding that nonintercourse would be maintained against France. Newly elected president James Madison accepted Erskine's proposal, only to have the British government subsequently repudiate it. Madison did not wait for the British government's response before proclaiming an end of nonintercourse against Britain because he realized that with the lifting of the general embargo on March 4, American merchant vessels would inevitably serve British interests. Accepting and acting upon Erskine's proposal offered the best chance of extracting some advantage from the situation.

Barlow joined most Americans in viewing Britain's repudiation of the Erskine Agreement as treachery. They rejected the Federalist leadership's claim that Madison had known Erskine's powers were deficient and had only concluded the agreement to generate public hostility against Britain. Since the repudiation of the Erskine Agreement occurred during the summer, remedies would have to wait until the following autumn and winter when the government reassembled. Barlow did not lament the administration's slow pace in addressing its foreign problems now that he had grown accustomed to the rhythms of Washington politics. Nor was he in a rush to go anywhere that summer because of Ruth's condition. Their consolation was that Kalorama was finally furnished and they could accommodate visitors comfortably.

After Abraham's death, Ruth began cultivating relationships with her half-brother Henry, who was a rising lawyer in Pittsburgh, and Clara, a much younger half-sister. In 1803 Clara had married a South Carolinian named Joseph Kennedy and moved with him to New Orleans. There he had abandoned her. With few friends and no children to keep her in New Orleans, Clara moved back to Connecticut to look after her ailing mother, the stepmother Ruth had never been fond of, and obtained a divorce from Kennedy. Clara first visited the Barlows during the summer of 1809, when Ruth discovered they had much in common despite the quarter-century difference in their ages. Ruth found in Clara a companionable substitute for Fulton, now that he appeared to be lost to her because of Harriet.

A year later Ruth would council Clara against being over eager to remarry. "Few Men are worthy the sacrifice of liberty, & all the evils they entrain upon

Drawing of Ruth Baldwin Barlow (1798–1802), detail. It is unlikely that Ruth Barlow's bemused dignity, which endeared her to so many of her contemporaries, could have been captured by an immature artist, no matter how talented. Courtesy Connecticut Historical Society, Hartford, Connecticut.

us. . . . tho' I cannot complain for myself, having been more fortunate in my matrimony than most of my sex,—yet Love, my sister, is a soft, but delusive passion. trust it not. I have been its votary, & now know that it is not worth the pangs it costs."[20] Was Ruth really as disillusioned as this letter suggests? It is more probable that the letter was designed to guard the new relationship with the half-sister she had come to value. Ruth had perfected the art of striking poses to control those around her, and her most effective one was graceful sufferer. The only likeness we have of her is a portrait sketch in pencil, probably copied from one by

Fulton done in or around 1802, that captures what he found especially appealing about her. The sketch has been attributed to Charles de Villette, Madame de Villette's son, but who was responsible for Ruth's likeness is of less importance than the notation on it certifying that it was lifelike.[21] The sketch depicts a strong, intelligent face that expresses bemused acceptance. It offers the best insight we have into her ability to beguile those around her despite ill health. Other women at the time entertained suspicions that Ruth acted manipulatively, and Clara later acquired a similar talent, at least to judge from her ability to attract masculine attention while an invalid in Paris from 1811 through 1813.

Clara may have been present on July 4, 1809, when Barlow delivered an oration to "the Democratic Citizens" of the capital. In the early years of the Republic, celebrating the nation's birthday customarily focused on such rhetorical performances, which occasionally launched political careers. Barlow had no desire for office, but he did have a political agenda. While a hot day in the capital was not the ideal occasion on which to launch his program, it was as good a location as any for advertising it now that the furor over the nation's foreign relations had momentarily subsided. Though rumors were circulating that the British government meant to repudiate the Erskine Agreement, official confirmation would not arrive until ten days later, when the capital would be emptier than it was on the nation's official birthday.

In an effort to repair their friendship, Fulton wrote a long letter advising Barlow to eschew all references to British oppression and the triumphant outcome of the Revolutionary War and instead to concentrate on the future.[22] As a visionary obsessed with the fear that the American republic might evolve as France had, Barlow experienced no difficulty accepting Fulton's advice and stressing the importance of education. Nations resembled "individual infants" in that they "are what they are taught to be" (528). He saw *"public improvements"* as supplementing *"public instruction"* (529) in preserving the nation's political and moral unity. If it were ever forfeited, "the highest hopes of human society, the greatest promise of bettering its condition that the efforts of all generations have produced" (529–30) would be lost. Barlow ruled out force in countering tendencies to disunion. Instead, the union should "apply directly to the interest and convenience of the people" in a way that "enable[d] them to discern that interest" (530). But the scant attention the embargo had paid to public convenience left Barlow little alternative but to emphasize instruction.

The best way to insure that Americans behaved differently from the corrupt British electorate or the Parisian mob was to teach the American freeman "the

management of the power to which he is born." Because the American people—
rather than a prince or Parliament—exercised sovereignty, if they "should become
obstinate and incurable in wrong," they could "crush the state and convulse the
nation." France's example suggested this could lead to the establishment of "ferocious monarchies, prepared to act over again the same degrading scenes of
mutual encroachment and vindictive war, which disgrace modern Europe" (531).
Without public education the people might thus become "'their own worst enemies'" (533).

A tenacious practicality coexisted with Barlow's visionary disposition. His aggressive efforts to derive revenue from his publications hinted at that practicality. In
1806 he approached John Vaughan, a Wilmington printer, about issuing another version of his *Prospectus* and three years later he asked Tench Coxe to get
his July 4 oration published in Philadelphia, claiming that the Washington printer
had already sold five hundred copies. Barlow saw no more tension between his
literary ambitions and his dabbling in politics than he saw between promoting
his writings and claiming to be "the only man in America who devotes his life
entirely to literature."[23] He encouraged men like Tench Coxe to think he had
Jefferson's ear and could pass along messages to those in high office.[24] And he was
shameless about using personal connections to push for the appointment of his
friends and relations. In May 1809, he wrote Gideon Granger, Jefferson's postmaster general, soliciting a postal appointment for Ruth's half brother, Henry
Baldwin.

Barlow's letter to Granger revealed the conflicted nature of his attitudes about
entrepreneurship. While Barlow complained of the "national sin" of money making, he declared almost in the same breathe that he had no intention of personally
abstaining. If he found "that writing the Columbiad, with all the moral qualities
[of] literature & science which that work possesses" failed to place him on a par
with a Virginia planter like John Tayloe, "who is rich, why then (God damn you)
I'll be rich too."[25] The boast was not an idle one. Shortly afterward, Barlow became a director of the newly constituted Bank of Washington, despite the ideological suspicions many Republicans entertained about the potentially corrupting
power of such institutions. Though investing in a bank would contribute little
toward the visionary future Barlow imagined, it did address the financial problems
he had recently assumed. He had agreed to underwrite the education of Aaron's
youngest child, Tom, and to lend Aaron Jr. and his brother Stephen $1,000 for a
commercial venture the brothers were planning to the West Indies.

Barlow had become interested in Tom, who had taken refuge with Stephen after their father's death. Barlow shared with Tom the fate of a patrimony compromised by the death of a father. Barlow could not very well provide for Tom while ignoring Stephen, so he agreed to loan Stephen the money he needed to join Aaron Jr.'s venture in exchange for two $500 notes due in two and three years, respectively. After requesting that the brothers keep the loan secret from the rest of the family so that he would not be deluged with similar requests, Barlow sent Stephen a $1,000 check on the Bank of the United States followed by additional remittances totaling $200 between August and October to pay for Tom's preparation for college.

Barlow wanted Tom to go to Dartmouth rather than Yale because of his antipathy toward Timothy Dwight, but Tom resisted this pressure and his preference for Yale soon required the commitment of an additional $200. Barlow agreed but wanted Stephen to pay his younger brother's fees in lieu of the interest due on the notes. That seemed possible because the enterprise to the West Indies had been launched before the embargo had gone into effect. However, after Aaron's vessel was subsequently lost, Stephen had no way of retiring his debt because only the vessel had been insured. Barlow was philosophical about this misfortune, claiming, "I have lost several pretty good estates from a reluctance to go to the expence of ensurance [sic]."[26] But if he wanted to recover the loan, he would have to come up with another way for Stephen to pay him back since Stephen could barely support his family as the local postmaster of Saugatuck and proprietor of a small general store. In this context, the Bank of Washington would prove to be a godsend.

During the summer of 1809, Barlow had been approached about joining a "limited partnership" to form the bank in the District of Columbia. The partners signed an agreement capitalizing their enterprise at $1 million, long before they submitted a petition to Congress for a charter of incorporation. Theirs was not the first banking partnership to emerge in the capital area. The Bank of Potomac, capitalized at $500,000, had formed in 1804 but had avoided applying to Congress for a charter because the Bank of the United States already had a branch in the District of Columbia.[27] The Union Bank of Georgetown, also capitalized at $1 million, quickly followed the establishment of the Bank of Washington. As the expiration date of March 1, 1811, for the Bank of the United States' charter drew nearer, these banking partnerships saw an opportunity to take the national bank's place. Having several banking operations up and running in advance of Congress's decision would make rechartering the Bank of the United States seem less compelling.

Barlow was active soliciting subscriptions for the Bank of Washington before the articles of association were signed, suggesting that if he was not an originator of the enterprise, he was an early recruit.[28] He then concocted a scheme for making the bank money while restoring Stephen's fortunes. It involved circulating up to $1 million of the new bank's notes at a sufficient distance from "great cities and other banks" to make it difficult to present them for redemption in specie.[29] Bank notes in small denominations of between $1 to $10 were in high demand in the undeveloped back country, so they could be exchanged advantageously for larger notes. Barlow proposed exchanging the Bank of Washington's small notes for the larger ones of the inland banks and then presenting them for redemption. The specie procured in this fashion could then provide the basis for issuing more Bank of Washington notes. Barlow expected most of the small denomination notes to remain in circulation in the interior because their utility and the cost of redeeming them would discourage presentation at their point of issue.

As chair of the committee charged with drafting this plan, Barlow put forward Stephen as the agent to implement it. Stephen was to be compensated by a commission based on the notes he distributed that remained unredeemed at the end of each year. Barlow estimated that with proper management, 90 percent would be outstanding and that Stephen could make as much as $30,000 a year. That justified Barlow in claiming one third of Stephen's prospective earnings for signing the bond Stephen would need to post before the bank would entrust him with its notes. Barlow was willing to stand surety for Stephen after observing him closely during a visit Stephen, his wife, and Tom had paid the Barlows during the summer of 1810. Though the visitors did not fit comfortably into Kalorama's social swirl, Barlow construed his nephew's discomfort as evidence of his level-headedness.

So committed did he become to Stephen's and Tom's futures that not even a near catastrophe deterred Barlow from pursuing his plan. During the last half of that August, after Stephen and his family had left Kalorama, the Barlows visited Bedford Springs, Virginia, to escape what remained of the summer's heat. Returning home in mid-September, their carriage went off the road in the dark and "dashed down a precipice" before breaking into splinters.[30] Though no bones were fractured, Ruth was very badly bruised, and her recovery was slowed by a persistent fever. The accident had the effect of energizing Barlow's efforts to get the bank's board to authorize Stephen's agency. On October 31, Barlow wrote Stephen to come immediately to Washington to clinch the deal, and Stephen obeyed his uncle's summons.[31]

Barlow assumed that Stephen's signature was crucial to the agreement his committee had fashioned and was surprised when the directors refused to ratify it. They probably wished to secure a charter before venturing on schemes like the one Barlow was pushing, since as matters stood they would all be equally liable for any losses. Though the Bank of Washington had petitioned Congress for a charter on December 18, 1809, it would not be granted until February 1811.[32] Nonetheless, Barlow remained sufficiently enthusiastic about the project to propose that Stephen undertake a trial run without a formal agreement with the bank's board. To protect Stephen against the possibility that the contract might eventually fall through, Barlow promised that he and William Lee would find Stephen an equally lucrative position should that prove necessary. Barlow made these arrangements at a time when it seemed doubtful Ruth could "continue much longer a life of so much suffering." On December 12, 1810, William Lee confirmed Barlow's judgment, writing to his wife that "our friend Mrs. Barlow is about dying."[33]

With his uncle persisting despite his domestic circumstances, Stephen could hardly refuse to assume the risks involved in Barlow's scheme. Stephen counted on benefiting from his uncle's coaching and realized that Barlow was taking as big a leap with him as he was taking with Barlow. Unfortunately, the trial proved to be less than a complete success. At Barlow's suggestion, Stephen had contacted Ruth's brother Henry Baldwin and through him unloaded some of his first "cargo" of bills in the Pennsylvania backcountry.[34] But the Pittsburgh branch of the Bank of the United States got wind of the scheme and collected Bank of Washington notes for redemption. Of the $10,000 entrusted to Stephen, $2,500 made its way back to Washington from Pittsburgh. Barlow was alarmed lest this development discourage the bank's directors. But after the Bank of the United States' charter lapsed and its central banking ceased, he persuaded the directors to continue the experiment. A letter Barlow wrote Stephen in August 1811 declared they were in a "good humor" about the contract and advised him to keep them that way. However, Barlow's estate would eventually be charged $17,000 for what Stephen owed the bank when Barlow's accounts with it were settled in 1815.[35]

When it came to creative entrepreneurship, Barlow had few equals. His capacity to look ahead and assume risks made him a good deal of money, even though that was not his principal ambition. At the end of 1810, William Lee described him as "elegantly situated . . . [in Washington] with an ample fortune." Kalorama had a staff of four servants and three carriages. Lee's letters to his wife also alluded to Barlow's speculations in western lands. Lee himself held a quarter interest with Barlow in a land company that included Granger, Fulwar Skipwith, and Col. Seth Hunt, which Lee thought would eventually make everyone's fortune. During 1810, Barlow also invested in a Philadelphia bank and a woolen mill that Alexander Wolcott was building in Middletown, Connecticut.[36]

Once Ruth's health took a turn for the better, Barlow's involvement with politics and writing a political history of the United States revived. These passions—rather than the accumulation of wealth—remained Barlow's principal interests. Making money was something that could be done by anyone, anytime. Charting a course for the future improvement of humanity was only possible in a revolutionary age by those capable of appreciating the opportunities history offered them.

For Barlow, history and politics were inseparable. Carl von Clausewitz, the Prussian military authority, would argue in the wake of the Napoleonic conflagration that war was an extension of politics by a different means. Barlow saw history as simply another dimension of politics. While in France he had continued to toy with writing about the great events he had witnessed, until Napoleon's subversion of the republic made the effort seem futile. Jefferson's suggestion that he undertake a history of the American Revolution acquired a new urgency with the threat the revival of Federalism after 1807 posed to the Republican ascendancy. Barlow had been collecting materials about the nation's past since his return to the United States. He believed the embarrassments the Republicans encountered after 1807 made the period from 1788 to 1800 more relevant. Writing to Mercy Otis Warren at the end of 1810, Barlow referred to this postrevolutionary period as "the most important . . . in every political and moral point of view." Histories of the colonial and revolutionary periods, such as the one Warren herself had written, taught Americans how to acquire liberty. A history of the early national period would "teach them how to preserve it," since "in the present state of things . . . it is much more important to know how to preserve liberty than how to acquire it."[37]

Jefferson later complained that Barlow never wrote a word of the promised work, despite being provided with several cartons of documents at the end of Jefferson's presidency. That is not quite true. A sketch for a history of the United States survives in Barlow's papers.[38] While it is impossible to assign a firm date to the document, it was likely written during the last part of 1809 or early in 1810. The sketch moves beyond Barlow's concern about transmitting revolutionary values to focus on the specific danger he felt the Federalists posed. It turns almost immediately from the framing and adoption of the Constitution to exploring why the "federalist" party came to be synonymous in Republican thinking with a "monarchist" party. Not that Barlow believed many Federalists contemplated establishing a hereditary monarchy in America. Even those he suspected of wanting George Washington to serve as president for life realized that Washington had no children and could not have created a hereditary line of succession. Barlow was more concerned about the political tendency of Federalism to favor the few at the expense of the many and to exalt executive power.[39]

Barlow's suspicion about all Federalists prevented him from appreciating how Washington had used the renunciation of power to build political authority. If he had been pressed for an explanation of why America had taken a different course than France, Barlow would have pointed to Jefferson and Madison. Recent history led Barlow to stress the importance of leadership in the preservation of liberty. Bad leaders could corrupt the people by teaching "them to clamor at what is right & call for what is wrong in the management of public affairs." He likened the Federalist during the embargo controversy to France's extremists in the 1790s. He shuddered lest the "partial insurrections" they had sponsored would provide the pretence for "a standing military force, first to aid government & then to overturn it; perhaps to dismember the empire."[40] In this and other respects, Barlow felt the Federalists resembled the Jacobins of the French Revolution.

Barlow's inability to separate history from politics made him a poor candidate for writing an historical classic since his political commitments made it impossible for him to understand why the Federalists were behaving as they did. Not that such an understanding would have been likely to stop the Republicans and the Federalists from unproductive feuding. Each provoked the other to behave in a manner that embodied their worst nightmares. The remedy for this lay not in anything Barlow could have written but in the pacification of Europe. Napoleon's demise in 1814–15 led to a reduction in the tensions between the United States and the great powers, which permitted the emergence of new domestic politics after 1815. Barlow's death at the end of 1812 precluded his developing the perspective of a new age, but had he lived into the "Era of Good Feelings," the rapid emergence of racial slavery as a threat to the Republic's survival would probably have diverted him from his history.

Instead, Barlow's insistence that politics came first made him a player in the political crisis leading to the War of 1812. He became directly involved after Maryland senator Samuel Smith started contesting Madison's leadership of the national Republican Party. Smith thought his qualifications for the presidency superior to Madison's and was in a position to block the president's choice of Albert Gallatin as secretary of state. To head off division within the Republican coalition, Madison reluctantly offered Smith's brother, Robert, the appointment. Robert Smith was such a bad choice that Barlow feared Gallatin might resign from the treasury in protest. Given the perilous state of the Republic, Barlow felt this would be a tragedy. But Barlow was not yet close enough to Madison to approach him directly.

He turned to Jefferson, and to avoid appearing presumptuous, pretended to report "the estimation in which . . . [Smith was] held by a great majority of Congress." This was a subject about which Barlow could now speak with authority. "They have the utmost confidence in Gallatin, & they speak of [Robert] Smith with perfect contempt, both as to his morality & his talents." The Republican caucus "resent[ed] the low intrigue by which he got himself into his present place,—and . . . they . . . seem to feel it an insult to the nation that [Samuel] Smith should be suffered to carry his projects any further."[41]

Barlow did not have to tell Jefferson what those "projects" were. Samuel Smith had recently aborted an administration plan—known as Macon's Bill #1—for parrying the pressures France and Britain were exerting on the nation's commerce. The bill was designed to replace the Nonintercourse Law of 1809, which was being as widely evaded as the embargo had been. Macon's Bill #1 would have banned any public or private ship of Britain and France from entering an American port until that power's restrictions on U.S. commerce had been removed. If enacted, it would have placed the burden of enforcement on the great powers rather than on U.S. merchants and shippers. It also would have operated principally against Great Britain, the nation which, after the fiasco of the Erskine Agreement, most Americans regarded as their principal adversary. The measure had been endorsed by a large majority of the House of Representatives, but Samuel Smith managed to defeat it by claiming it was too weak a response to the provocations of the belligerents.

Smith promoted instead the idea of armed convoys with full knowledge that the Senate Federalists, on whom he had relied to defeat Macon's Bill #1, would oppose such a measure because it risked war with Britain. Because the majority of House Republicans were not ready to support armed convoys, Smith's actions stymied the Eleventh Congress in pursuing the administration's preferred response to the provocations of the belligerents. Barlow felt frustrated watching Congress thrash around during the remainder of its 1810 session, and his growing impatience revealed itself in his willingness to encourage Henry Dearborn's presidential ambitions.[42]

Dearborn, a New Hampshire native, was two years Barlow's senior. After serving with distinction during the Revolutionary War, he had settled in what is now Maine, representing his district of Massachusetts in Congress between 1793 and 1801. Jefferson chose him to be his secretary of war, and Madison might have kept him on in that capacity had not Dearborn, for financial reasons, preferred appointment as collector of the Port of Boston. Dearborn certainly looked more presidential than the scholarly and diminutive Madison, and Dearborn's military background would be an asset if war with Britain lay in the future. But Barlow wanted to avoid a war, and when the War of 1812 eventually was declared, Dearborn proved ineffectual as the senior major general of the U.S. Army.

Barlow's exaggerated estimate of Dearborn's abilities rested on a developing friendship between the Barlows and Dearborns. That intimacy suggested that were Dearborn to become president, Barlow would enjoy more of an inside track than he currently had with Madison. However, moving from collector at Boston to president of the United States was a stretch even for Dearborn, who asked Barlow whether his support was more than just flattery. Barlow protested his complete sincerity, though he could give only the lamest account of why Madison's unsurpassed familiarity with the nation's foreign relations and his enormous erudition did not make him Dearborn's superior.[43]

Barlow empathized with his Republican friends as the Smith faction and the Federalist minority prevented Congress from responding to belligerent pressures with anything short of a declaration of war. Everyone wanted to avoid war because they believed that if the nation could avoid conflicts with the great powers for a while longer, its current rate of development would soon make it invulnerable to any external power. The wisdom of pursuing a peaceful course, however, conflicted with concern over the ideological loyalties of the rising generation, which obsessed Barlow. Was there not reason to fear that humiliations like those associated with impressments, the embargo, and the Erskine Agreement might degrade republicanism in the eyes of the nation's youth, leading eventually to a reversal of the Revolution? Peace would be too costly if it jeopardized the continuation of the republican experiment in America.

The Eleventh Congress eventually agreed to replace the Nonintercourse Law with Macon's Bill #2. This measure gave the president authority to reinstitute nonintercourse against either of the great powers whenever one of them lifted its restrictions on the nation's commerce. Though ostensibly even-handed, Macon's Bill #2 was actually a one-sided invitation to France to repeal its onerous decrees. Britain would gain nothing from complying with American demands, while France could gain U.S. cooperation in exchange for revoking restrictions it could not enforce. Smith and his faction, reinforced by the Philadelphia *Aurora* and the Baltimore *Whig*, were justified in labeling it a weak response to the challenge facing the nation. But it was so only because it depended for its effectiveness on Napoleon accepting the invitation. Napoleon, however, recognized the law for what it was and tendered Madison just enough encouragement to tease the United States into a showdown with Britain.

On August 5, 1810, the Duke of Cadore, speaking for Napoleon, notified the U.S. minister in Paris, John Armstrong, that France's decrees would cease to operate against American vessels once the United States delivered on the promise contained in Macon's Law #2 to impose nonintercourse against Britain. On November 2, 1810, Madison issued Britain an ultimatum to revoke its orders-in-council by February 1, 1811, or face a termination of all commerce with the United States. Considering that it was winter and that, unbeknownst to Madison, George III was experiencing one of his periodic bouts of insanity, the ultimatum's three-month deadline guaranteed that it would not be met. But that wouldn't have troubled the president, since just before issuing it he had authorized the peaceful occupation of West Florida by American forces. Madison chose to act preemptively here because British control over West Florida would place the entire Mississippi basin at her mercy, enabling her to throttle the future development of the nation.

Madison made this strategic decision independently of Robert Smith because the president doubted the competence and loyalty of his secretary of state. The Smiths, however, posed less of a problem for Madison than France, which continued seizing American vessels and subjected those that entered continental ports to onerous restrictions and charges. France's behavior allowed the Federalists to accuse Madison of letting himself be duped by Napoleon. Of course, captures were not the same as condemnations. Even if a captured vessel was eventually condemned, the U.S. government still could press for compensation. Nor could the United States object to France imposing her own municipal regulations on the activities of foreign merchants. These were matters on which, under normal circumstances, an American minister in Paris could be expected to win concessions. From Madison's perspective, many of the difficulties in the Franco-American relationship stemmed from the absence of just such a fully accredited minister after John Armstrong had returned to the United States in 1810.

Madison delayed appointing Armstrong's replacement until a new French minister arrived in Washington in the middle of February 1811. Napoleon took his time replacing the controversial Louis-Marie Turreau with Louis-Barbé-Charles Sérurier, and the administration wanted to see what kind of minister Sérurier would be. Another Turreau—when they desperately sought clarification about the ambiguities surrounding the revocation of the French decrees—could be disastrous. Sérurier arrived in Washington just after nonintercourse against Britain went into effect. Though there was no doubt that the new French minister was an improvement over his predecessor, he brought a mixed message. Sérurier affirmed that the decrees affecting American commerce had been revoked, but he informed the administration that it could not expect restitution of American property sequestered in retaliation for the Nonintercourse Law of 1809. He also was ill informed about the new French regulations affecting American imports and exports. The explanations he offered would do little to silence Federalist protests that France was not acting in good faith.

Sérurier's arrival required the United States to appoint a minister of at least equal grade if it wanted improved relations with France. Barlow's fluent French and his friendship with many figures at the highest levels within the American government made him someone Sérurier sought out. Madison quickly realized that advantage might be gained by appointing Barlow minister to France. No one in America was better qualified than Barlow to communicate with and maneuver within the labyrinths of the French government. Madison also realized that despite Barlow's former disclaimers about being interested in an appointment, his fascination with politics would make him easy to recruit. The president had no intention of dispatching Barlow immediately to Europe. Instead, Madison wanted to use Barlow as a bargaining chip with which to win the desired clarification of French policy that seemed necessary to maintain the congressional majority needed to confront Great Britain.

Barlow was flattered by the offer and consented to his nomination, which Madison sent to the Senate on February 26, 1811. Opposition immediately surfaced from the Smith faction and the Federalists. Samuel Smith represented Barlow as "a man of small talents !! & said a commercial man was wanting in France."[44] Others alleged that Barlow's accounts from his Algerian mission remained unsettled and that he was substantially in arrears to the U.S. Treasury. In addition to being denounced as an impractical poet and visionary, he was represented as an unscrupulous entrepreneur who had mysteriously enriched himself. Finally, he was accused of being an atheist.

Nonetheless, the Senate confirmed Barlow's nomination by a margin of twenty-one to nine.[45] Questions the Treasury Department had raised about Barlow's Algerian accounts the previous December were laid to rest by a statement that they had since been settled.[46] Several Federalists supported Barlow's nomination, including senators James Lloyd and Timothy Pickering of Massachusetts. In 1797 Pickering had been sufficiently impressed by Barlow's Algerian mission to suggest he be appointed minister plenipotentiary to France,[47] and he now defended Barlow by pointing to the inconsistency in the objections raised against him. How could someone be an impractical visionary and at the same time so successful a businessman? As for Barlow's religion or lack thereof, Pickering distinguished between atheism and deism. Jefferson was a deist, and that had not deterred a majority of the nation from electing him to its highest office. Pickering's support for Barlow's nomination came with a barb, however. He referred to his prior acquaintance with Barlow in the continental army where the nominee had sustained a good character as chaplain, underscoring how far he had subsequently fallen from grace. But damning by implication was better than outright condemnation, and Pickering voted for Barlow's confirmation.[48]

Barlow's appointment as minister-designate to France took place while Madison planned Smith's removal as secretary of state. The ensuing year promised to be a critical one, and the president needed a man he could trust. Though James Monroe was the most qualified candidate, he had just become governor of Virginia, and his appointment might offend the nation's largest state. In addition, Monroe and Madison had been rivals for the presidency in 1808, and as secretary of state Madison had had a hand in Jefferson's rejection of the Monroe-Pinkney Treaty of 1807. Offering so important a position to Monroe might make amends for the congressional caucus preferring Madison. But first Madison had to sound out Monroe's Virginia supporters to make sure they wouldn't take offense and then persuade Monroe to serve. In his capacity as ambassador to both countries Monroe had developed far greater respect for Britain than he had for revolutionary France, and Madison had to reassure Monroe that he preferred a peaceful resolution to the nation's difficulties with Britain, if one were available, to win Monroe's consent.

Accomplishing the president's plan required time, though most of the pieces were in place by the middle of March 1811. The only remaining problem was removing Robert Smith without seriously damaging the Republican coalition. To preserve party harmony, Madison offered to appoint Smith minister to Russia. Smith countered by requesting London. When rebuffed on that, Smith suggested an appointment to the Supreme Court. Madison replied that Smith could not win Senate approval for the court despite his brother's influence. If Smith wanted to remain in office, the only one available was the St. Petersburg post.[49] Though not completely satisfied, Smith left the meeting apparently willing to accept Madison's offer. He published an announcement that he was being sent to Russia, then changed his mind at the behest of his brother Samuel.

At the beginning of April 1811, as Monroe assumed the duties of secretary of state, the *Aurora General Advertiser*, which had become the Smiths' mouthpiece, published an "authorized" statement listing the policy issues that had caused a rupture between the president and his former secretary of state. The statement's publication served to distract attention from the real reasons for Smith's dismissal, but it failed to assuage Smith's anger or prevent him from wanting to do the president as much harm as he felt he had received. His revenge would take the form of *An address to the people of the United States,* first serialized in the *Aurora* and the Baltimore *Whig* in June 1811. Smith blamed Madison for the inability of the Eleventh Congress to meet the challenge from abroad with anything more than Macon's Bills #1 and #2, measures Smith described as being "unwise as [well as] humiliating." Smith also announced publicly for the first time that Napoleon had refused to offer any compensation for the sequestration of American property in retaliation for the Nonintercourse Act of 1809. Finally, he questioned whether France had indeed revoked her decrees, thus reinforcing Federalist objections to Madison's policies.[50]

The Barlows realized well before the appearance of Smith's pamphlet that they were caught in a political maelstrom. Neither of them enjoyed the "torrent of abuse" that was directed at Barlow by the Federalist press.[51] William Coleman's *New York Evening Post* summarized Barlow's qualifications for ambassador by describing him as "an apostate priest and reviller of the very religion he publicly professed . . . a phrenzied and bloody-minded jacobin, a modern philosopher and a sycophant of those in power."[52] The *Boston Gazette* greeted Barlow's appointment with the statement that a "fitter man . . . could not be selected for such an office, except Genet, or Mons. Turreau. Some French citizen like [Barlow] must be selected, to carry to his Majesty, the submission of his loyal and good city of Washington." The same notice revived the rumor that Barlow had been the author of "God Save the Gullotine" — a song parodying "God Save the King."[53] The *Salem Gazette,* which was Timothy Pickering's mouthpiece in Essex County, Massachusetts, dismissed the report that Pickering had voted to confirm Barlow's nomination as a "calumny."[54] John Armstrong joined the fray by describing Barlow's speculations in disputed prizes as "prostituting" the American flag for personal gain at public expense and criticizing Fulton for continuing to work on the torpedo. What really worried Armstrong, however, was that Barlow, backed by Fulton, might improve relations between the two countries, which had soured during Armstrong's ambassadorship.[55]

A month of such abuse would lead Barlow to rethink his appointment. "The sacrifice of ease & comfort on my part is great, & the prospect of doing good to the public is little."[56] Ruth also regretted that Barlow had agreed to undertake the mission. Her only consolation was that there seemed to be an even chance that it would not actually go forward since it depended on European developments, particularly in Britain, about which the administration expected to learn with the arrival of dispatches in the USS *Essex.* Nonetheless, the Barlows had to go through the motions of preparing to depart, which neither of them enjoyed. At the end of April, Ruth reported, "my husband now regrets his acceptance almost as much as myself, yet he feels his honor concerned. he [sic] would not be thought to shrink from a difficult and arduous undertaking. his [sic] enemies would probably say he was frightened out of it." Ruth realized that Barlow had allowed Madison to trap him through his vanity and made no attempt to conceal her distaste "for this troublesome disagreeable mission."[57]

Ruth's unexpected recovery from an illness she and most of her friends assumed would prove fatal enhanced her dilemma. Her condition had led Barlow to assume he would go alone, if he went at all. Barlow did not relish a solo trip, but the notion that their separation need not be a long one could not have seemed realistic to anyone familiar with his previous sojourn in Europe. Ruth's recovery meant that, short of the mission aborting, she would have to choose between staying at home and going with her husband. Though the Barlows would linger in uncertainty for close to half a year, in early March they leased Kalorama to Sérurier for three years at $1,500 per year, subject to cancellation on three months notice if either of them was recalled. While they remained in Washington, Sérurier allowed the Barlows the use of two rooms and the library at Kalorama.[58] The arrangement permitted them to tread water while Madison used Barlow as bait to extract cooperation from France.

The much heralded appointment of a new British minister, Augustus John Foster, assisted Madison and Monroe in pursuing their strategy. Sérurier did not relish Foster's impending arrival, and getting Barlow dispatched before Foster appeared became one of the French minister's primary objectives. Were he to succeed, he could claim to have won an advantage over Britain now that it was known Ambassador William Pinkney was returning from England on the *Essex*. Madison and Monroe stalled Sérurier as best they could. A British report, reprinted the *National Intelligencer*, that Foster's appointment would lead to the resolution of the differences between the United States and Britain subsequently racheted up the pressure on Sérurier.[59] But Monroe waited until the end of June, just after Foster's arrival, and coincidentally after the appearance of Robert Smith's promised *Address to the people*, to test whether the government had gained any leverage over the French minister.

Privately, Robert Smith hoped his exposé of the inner workings of the cabinet would lead the Republicans to discard Madison in 1812. But Samuel Smith was nervous about his brother's pamphlet, as the stakes went well beyond the presidential succession. An assault from within Madison's official family compromised the president's capacity to manage the extremely delicate international situation. Barlow himself had an interest in countering Smith because his mission to France would be hampered if the administration dispatching him was perceived to be politically weak. After being the target of so much Federalist abuse, Barlow also relished the opportunity of turning his rhetorical powers on a prey like Robert Smith. William Lee boasted to his wife that he was the author of *A Review of Robert Smith's Address to the people of the United States* and that Barlow had only "corrected" Lee's draft. But Lee was in the habit of exaggerating his accomplishments, particularly to his wife, while Barlow tended to be candid about what he had and had not done.[60] The two men probably collaborated, but Barlow is properly credited as principal author of the work.

Its opening sentence showed that Barlow meant to give his adversary no quarter: "An opinion had long prevailed with many persons both in and out of Congress, that Mr. Secretary Smith, from want of capacity and want of integrity, was quite unfit for his place." After two years in office, "this conviction became so universal" that some thought it was even shared by Smith himself. Most had looked forward to the time when the government would "relieve itself from so inconvenient a burthen," and Smith would have been quickly forgotten after leaving office in March had he not first threatened and then executed an "unlucky threat. His pamphlet is before the public; and though its first characteristic is weakness, yet its wickedness is of too dangerous a tendency to be passed over without a comment" (553).[61]

Barlow accused Smith of betraying the government by "publishing the secrets of the cabinet." Smith's crime was described as being worse than perjury, so outlandish in fact that "the law ha[d] not provided for it." Still, it was unlikely that anyone would be inclined to follow Smith's example because of "the indignation of your country which must now attend you, until you will consent to be forgotten" (554). Smith had committed his act of betrayal "for the express purpose of proving to his fellow citizens that he is a man of talents worthy of his place," but he had succeeded in establishing "the reverse" (555). Exhibit one was the use Smith made of Madison's offer to appoint him ambassador to Russia. Smith had declared this to be "the most honorable appointment abroad that is in the gift of our government" and claimed that the offer demonstrated the high regard Madison had for him (556). Barlow countered that Smith vastly overrated the importance of St. Petersburg and asserted that Madison's real reason for sending Smith there was that he was the only person who could afford to live at the Russian court. To Smith's claim that he had written his pamphlet out of an obligation to the people to give an account of his resignation as secretary of state, Barlow countered that

Smith's real motive was "to resolve the President's dissatisfaction with him into other causes than his own incapacity" (558).

Barlow then addressed the policy issues over which Madison and Smith differed. He defended Macon's Bill #1 by arguing that it would have left Britain and France with the choice either of accepting a U.S. monopoly of their carrying trade or a forfeiture of American commerce until they repealed their restrictions. As for Macon's Bill #2, had it not succeeded in dividing the belligerents after becoming law? To Smith's complaint that France had not revoked her decrees in good faith, Barlow responded that while American vessels and masters "have suffered and still suffer very unjustly by French spoliation" (565), it did not follow that their misfortunes were due to the Berlin and Milan decrees. Barlow distinguished between these two decrees and the municipal regulations American property was subject to upon arrival in France. The sequestering of American property was not a violation of the nation's neutral rights, however barbarous and unfriendly it might otherwise be.

Smith's greatest crime, however, remained his treachery. He had been entrusted "by his country to manage the most delicate transaction that could be confided to a minister," touching "a point of national honor, with a rival power, jealous, haughty, lavish in her insults, and frugal in her acts of justice." To have then "betray[ed] to that rival the secret discussions of his own cabinet on that very point of honor" marked "a turpitude of heart, or a blunted, muffled, woodenheaded power of penetration and feeling too disgraceful in itself to be able to disgrace the government it betrayed." Smith could not "be trusted to carry a letter across the street" (571–72).

The misgivings Samuel Smith had entertained about his brother's challenge to the administration were borne out by the results. Once the *National Intelligencer* began serializing Barlow's *Review* on July 2, 1811, it put an end to Samuel Smith's presidential ambitions, thereby strengthening Madison's political standing among Republicans. Barlow, by contrast, was gratified by the wide circulation his *Review* was given in the Republican press.

While Barlow was demolishing the Smiths, Monroe began applying the screws to Sérurier. Monroe opened by subjecting the French minister to such a ferocious tongue-lashing that Sérurier feared an impending rupture with the United States.[62] He might not have been so concerned had he known that Foster would fare even worse at Monroe's hands. After Foster confessed on July 3 that he had nothing to offer, Monroe informed Sérurier on July 4 that Barlow would be dispatched immediately.[63] Sérurier attributed Monroe's announcement to a back channel threat he had made that the failure to dispatch Barlow would lead France to conclude that the United States was reneging on the agreement authorized by Macon's Law #2. But the French minister's claim was undercut by Monroe suspending his order until the *Essex* arrived. When the dispatches addressed to the secretary of state failed to clarify the situation for the administration, Monroe asked on July 9 whether the French minister had been more fortunate. Sérurier replied that he hadn't, occasioning another tirade from Monroe about the difficulties France was causing the administration.[64]

It is hard to believe that Barlow was not informed of the game Monroe was playing. Though there is no evidence that Monroe relied upon reports from Barlow to gauge the effect his harangues were having, sharing a common residence gave Barlow ample opportunity to observe the French minister at close quarters. Barlow was certainly among the first to learn that Monroe's July interviews with Foster had led the secretary of state to conclude that the United States should settle scores with Britain before France. What proved decisive was Foster's insistence that France's alleged failure to repeal its decrees justified Britain's intransigence. When pressed about what it would take for Britain to withdraw its orders, the British minister made the mistake of conveying the impression that France would have to lift its restrictions on British as well as American commerce. That was requiring a good deal more of the United States than any power had a right to expect.

Though such a statement from a minister was not the same thing as a government's formal declaration, Monroe could not ignore the danger posed by Foster's tactical alliance with the Federalists. Once Monroe put these pieces together, all that was needed to send Barlow on his mission was some encouraging news. An unofficial report a few days later that several previously sequestered American vessels in France had been released supplied what was needed. On July 17 Monroe again summoned Sérurier to his office, where he was asked to write a letter that interpreted this unofficial information as confirmation of the French government's intentions. The French minister complied, but in such an ambiguous way that the letter would prove useless in defending the administration against Federalist criticism. Nonetheless, Monroe announced on July 20, 1811, that Barlow would proceed to France and went immediately to work writing Barlow's instructions.[65]

⚜

Barlow realized that the game Monroe was playing with Sérurier and Foster would cease when the government broke up at the end of July to escape the summer heat. The *Constitution* had been summoned from Norfolk to Annapolis earlier in the month and the Barlows' luggage placed on board.[66] Madison left Washington for Montpelier on July 24, and Monroe completed Barlow's instructions on the twenty-sixth. Soon afterward, both Barlows departed for Annapolis, boarding the *Constitution* on August 1, 1811. Neither liked sea voyages, but the government did everything in its power to make them comfortable. Instead of a packet of three hundred tons like that in which Barlow had made his first crossing, they were aboard a giant frigate of two thousand tons and fifty-six guns. Instead of being alone, they were accompanied by two family members, Tom Barlow and Clara Baldwin. Instead of dirty little cubicles, the family would have full access to the ward room and the copious supplies of the officers' mess. William Lee, Barlow's long-time friend, who was returning as consul to Bordeaux and would serve concurrently as secretary of the American legation in Paris, and David Bailie Warden, who had been appointed consul at Paris, were also part of Barlow's official family. All were treated as honored guests by Capt. Isaac Hull.

The ship sailed immediately, and the trip down Chesapeake Bay to Norfolk, where Hull increased his complement of hands, took place in calm seas. The *Constitution* was spotlessly clean, and Barlow's party had the run of her aft of the gun deck. Barlow found his first days on the *Constitution* such a vast improvement over his previous experiences that he admitted that there "never was a fairer prospect for a good passage."[67] Still, the farewell letters he penned in American waters were suffused with melancholy. He confessed to Fulton, "my heart is heavy. I have left my country, possibly & why not probably forever." He went "with an ardent wish" for "doing good" but "without much hope," and "with the full intention, tho with feeble hope of living to return."[68]

In coming to terms with one's own mortality, one is inevitably guided by the experience of one's parents and siblings. Barlow's father had died suddenly, soon after passing 60. Nathaniel and Aaron had not fared any better, and in 1809 Barlow's sister Huldah, "the last of my mother's children that remained to me," had expired just shy of 50.[69] At 57, Barlow felt that his end could not be far off. But that concern paled before the obstacles he could expect to encounter in France.

While he still hoped war could be avoided, he was also aware of the obstacles to peace. As long as Britain was prepared to justify her commercial restrictions on grounds that the French had not really lifted hers, Napoleon could maintain tension between Britain and the United States by promising much and delivering little. That insured a better outcome for France, since complying with American expectations risked having Britain revoke her orders-in-council and an Anglo-American reconciliation. As long as the British took their signals from the Federalists, it would not require much from France to make her concessions seem superior. The only advantage Barlow could draw on for resolving this dilemma was the complementary commercial interests of the United States and France. The tactic of appealing to economic interests would have been useful had France remained a republic and her official culture more a commercial than a military one. Instead, France had become a military dictatorship, while Barlow had acquired international notoriety as a critic of France's apostasy.

CHAPTER SEVENTEEN

Europe Redux

Exactly a month later the *Constitution* hove in view of the French coast. Both Barlows fared better on this crossing than previously. Eight days out, the *Constitution* had encountered the ship *Samuel* (Captain Corran), by whom Barlow was able to send a brief note to Fulton informing him that all were well.[1] Though everyone had felt queasy at first, there had been only a few stormy intervals prior to their making landfall at the Lizard on September 2. Then they encountered headwinds that delayed their arrival at Cherbourg for another week. Nevertheless, Barlow reported to Alexander Wolcott that "my wife & self suffered less from seasickness than we ever did before."[2] For most of the passage, the biggest problem was boredom. Clara and David Warden had played backgammon while Barlow, Ruth, and William Lee spent the month talking about Barlow's mission. In the many spare moments between meals and conversations, Barlow tutored Tom in French.

Captain Hull took no chances as he approached British vessels blockading the French coast, and the *Constitution* was cleared for action when a launch from a British man-of-war pulled alongside. Neutral public ships on official business were customarily exempt from blockades, and the *Constitution* proceeded into port, where it was initially placed in quarantine. The authorities found both passengers and the ship's complement sufficiently healthy to allow Barlow and the others to disembark on September 8. They were delayed from proceeding immediately to Paris because the only transportation available, the diligence, could not accommodate their baggage. After summoning two carriages from Caen, which did not arrive until the thirteenth, they began to traverse the 120 miles between Cherbourg and the French capital. Express journeys were things of the past, and they did not arrive in the capital until six days later on the evening of the nineteenth.[3]

Jonathan Russell, the U.S. chargé d'affaires in Paris, supplied Barlow with an itinerary of where to stop along the way.[4] A graduate of Rhode Island College, now Brown University, Russell published in 1808 a political pamphlet entitled *The Whole Truth*, which rendered the conflict between Federalists and Republicans in the partisan way Jefferson desired. It traced Federalism back to American Tories who had opposed the Revolution. Somewhat less fancifully, it ably defended the Republicans against the charge of French influence and recommended that all who wished to preserve the Republic vote for Madison in the upcoming election. Russell prospered as a merchant and in 1809 embarked on a tour of Europe. When Ambassador John Armstrong came home from Paris in 1810, he placed Russell in temporary charge of the American legation in the hope that Russell would succeed him. But Madison thought Russell was too inexperienced for so important a post.[5]

Though Russell claimed he did not seek diplomatic appointment, being passed over predisposed him against Barlow. On June 27, 1811, he wrote to Armstrong, who begrudged the social standing the Barlows had enjoyed in Paris, referring to the new ambassador as a "pettifogging—canting—culture jobbing, dogerel philosopher," whose "prize speculations" and torpedo projects were "not of a character to embellish his moral beauty." Warming to what Russell knew would be an appreciative audience, he continued: "a little swindling, . . . violation of the public & private trust when set to the tune of God save the Guillotine & softened by the enlightened philanthropy, which seeks the extinction of the present generation for the benefit of opportunity" presented no obstacle to "the presumptive ambition of this adopted Frenchman." On the basis of a report that the French police had assembled a file about Barlow from former acquaintances, all of whom with the notable exceptions of Grégoire and Leavenworth were hostile, Russell predicted that Barlow would be "received but as to personal standing & personal influence he will be a non-entity."[6]

Russell changed his tune after learning from Barlow that Madison had appointed him chargé d'affaires in London.[7] The choice turned out to be one of Madison's less happy ones. Russell's failure to anticipate Britain's revocation of its orders-in-council in June 1812 helped bring on a war that need not have been fought, but his role in undermining the peace Barlow wanted desperately to preserve lay in the future. For the moment, Russell proved helpful, sharing all the information that had come his way and assisting William Lee in assuming the post of acting secretary of the legation. Barlow and Russell remained in close communication with each other until the War of 1812 began.[8]

Barlow probably sensed the contempt with which many expatriates viewed him. He may also have noticed Daniel Parker's hostility toward William Lee. Lee found it very disagreeable that Parker pointedly refused to speak to him, but since Lee was absent visiting his wife in Bordeaux from September 27 through October 23, this tension had little immediate impact on the Barlows.[9] By the time Lee returned, Barlow had decided to move the whole legation into his old residence on the rue de Vaugirard. After that, Lee had more right to be there than Parker, but Parker's behavior toward Lee mirrored the divisions that Armstrong had sown within the American community in Paris.

Nonetheless, Barlow found much to encourage him during his first weeks in Paris. He described his "reception . . . from our old friends" as "affectionate & affecting. Our ancient servants are pressing round us with tears of gratitude & attachment." So were Constantine Volney, Henri Grégoire, Lafayette, and Mme de Villette. He was also pleased to find "our old pecuniary affairs . . . in a better state than I expected." Parker had seen to the upkeep of their mansion in their absence, and the familiar surroundings contributed further to their sense of well-being. Though the garden had gone to seed, they would have little trouble restoring it. They were a bit further from St. Cloud, where the offices of the imperial government were now located, than from the center of the city. But not far enough to make a critical difference.[10]

The legation required extensive furnishings, and Ruth took charge of that task, with Lee's assistance. Their purchases drew criticism from Barlow's enemies. Leonard Jarvis complained to Russell that the Barlows were furnishing the legation to make an "Ambassadorial splash. He has got the arms of the U.S.A. on the panels of his coach & cuts a figure in cut velvet suits—Boots are under the ban—if you wish to pay your respects to the lady of the legation it must be in shoes."[11] Barlow had decided that playing the simple, virtuous republican—as Benjamin Franklin had during the American Revolution—was inappropriate in Napoleon's imperial capital.

Several personal matters required attention. A month with Tom on the *Constitution* had alerted Barlow to the deficiencies in his nephew's education. Upon their arrival in Paris, he arranged for Tom to attend several of the city's collegiate establishments. In November, Barlow reported to Stephen that Tom was taking science courses at three colleges and boarding at a fourth, where he was receiving instruction in fencing, dancing, drawing, and French, subjects that were unavailable in the curricula of American schools. The private instruction in French he had received before embarking for Europe had proved insufficient.[12]

Napoleon had "greatly embellished" Paris since Barlow was last there, making it more expensive than Barlow expected. What Congress had allocated for his "outfit"—the expenses incidental to a diplomatic mission at a European court— he complained fell woefully short. He was not the first American diplomat to be caught between congressional parsimony and the demands of European court life; he was certainly aware of the difficulties John Quincy Adams had encountered in St. Petersburg.[13] William Lee felt the same way about his consular salary and could only be persuaded to serve as secretary of the legation concurrently with being consul at Bordeaux by the prospect of two salaries.

The high cost of living confronted Barlow with an unpleasant choice. Since he did not enjoy a fortune like Robert R. Livingston, he could go into debt and trust to Congress to bail him out, or he could economize, which meant abstaining from full participation in the life of the imperial court. Since he felt Armstrong's parsimony had limited his effectiveness, Barlow asked his friends in Washington to increase his salary. He anticipated his request would be granted because "you cannot expect to find many men in our country, who are at once willing and able to" serve and "who are fit for the place."[14] Requesting more money, however, increased the pressure upon him to achieve something significant.

He knew from the correspondence of his American friends—and the public attention his mission had attracted in the European press—that expectations were high. Republicans inside and outside the administration hoped an improvement in the Franco-American relationship would strengthen Madison's hand in dealing with Britain. A letter Benjamin Latrobe wrote Barlow from Washington in mid-November 1811 illuminates the connection they saw between foreign and domestic affairs. So long as "the two great parties of our country are identified with the two belligerents of Europe, England cannot be successfully opposed on the floor of congress, unless France furnish *argument* for the public of the measures which exclude. . . . british manufactures."[15] On the same day, Dolley Madison wrote Ruth that "few have a doubt" about the success of the mission, adding "even the Enemies of *our* Minister admit his talents & Virtue, how then, can any of *them* doubt?"[16]

Barlow ignored the carping of his political enemies. Maintaining a good relationship with his sponsors and friends, however, was a different matter. Should they become disillusioned with his efforts, his situation would resemble what it had been during the Scioto fiasco. The worst thing that could happen from Barlow's perspective would be repudiation by the administration. That put pressure on Ruth to maintain the personal relationship with the Madisons that had ripened after Barlow had accepted appointment as American minister to France. In the letter conveying her high hopes for the success of Barlow's mission, Dolley Madison also requested some things for herself. "As you have every thing that is beautiful; & we nothing—I will ask the favor of you to send me by safe Vessels—large Headdresses, a few Flowers, Feathers, gloves & stockings (Black & White) or any other pritty [sic] things." Ruth was instructed to draw on the president, though Dolley added a caution to avoid extravagance.[17]

Both Barlows understood that these requests had to be honored, and William Lee dispatched a $2,000 ($72,000 in today's dollars) invoice of goods Ruth had purchased. For his part, Barlow sent Dolley a sugar beetroot weighing fourteen and a half pounds.[18] Ruth also acted as Harriet Fulton's purchasing agent in France. That was only appropriate given the exertions of Robert Fulton in straitening out Barlow's tangled accounts with his Philadelphia publisher, A. & C. Conrad. Others who thought Barlow owed them something thought nothing of imposing on him. Jefferson sent a £200 sterling draft in favor of General Thaddeus Kosciuszko. Since Barlow's salary would be paid in France and Kosciuszko's income from the funded debt of the United States was paid in America, Jefferson thought it would be advantageous in the future for Barlow to pay Kosciuszko that sum annually in Paris in exchange for a corresponding credit in Washington.[19] Joshua Gilpin, writing from London, requested that the Barlows assist two boys traveling to regain their health. Gilpin—a Philadelphia merchant, paper manufacturer, and director of the Chesapeake and Delaware Canal Company—felt authorized by his membership in the American Philosophical Society to address the American minister in a way that assumed his request would be honored. And General Presley Neville, a friend of Henry Baldwin in Pittsburgh, asked Barlow to have a bill on a Parisian merchant paid and the proceeds forwarded to Philadelphia.[20]

Far more pleasing than these chores was the long letter Barlow received from his Hamburg friend, Christoph Daniel Ebeling, who had faithfully followed Barlow's career in the American newspapers. Most of the Barlows' acquaintances during the winter of 1794–95 had died, and Ebeling himself, now completely deaf, was totally dependent on written or printed words for communication. He claimed that was a mercy because it limited his exposure to Napoleon's propaganda. However, he could not evade Napoleon's prohibition against the importation of books frowned upon in Paris. Ebeling blamed the Danes, who acted as agents of the French, for denying him access to American materials, including

The Columbiad. Ebeling had only received one letter from Barlow since July 1795, and that arrived nearly a full decade after it had been written.[21]

A steady stream of dispatches to the secretary of state on a variety of matters beyond those in his instructions occupied most of Barlow's remaining time. French privateers had robbed and burned unarmed American vessels on voyages to the Iberian Peninsula; captured American seamen—impressed on British ships—were being held in France as British prisoners of war; and U.S. policy toward the independence movements of Spain's American colonies needed clarification. Lee was kept busy drafting and copying Barlow's communications, though none of them were directly relevant to the main purpose of his mission.

Despite the warm welcome Barlow received from former friends, he remained nervous about his official reception. Though he had the advantage of fluent French, his disapproval of the emperor was no secret to those in power. Any misgivings Barlow entertained on this score, however, were initially dispelled by the cordial reception extended by the Duke of Bassano, a former acquaintance and now the French foreign minister. Though Napoleon had departed for Holland on the very day Barlow arrived in Paris, General Turreau dropped in the next morning to inform Barlow that Bassano had remained in town expressly to receive him.

Barlow made his first official call on September 21. When he expressed regret at the emperor's absence, Bassano assured Barlow that Napoleon "had foreseen the urgency of the case, and had charged him to remedy the evil . . . by dispensing with my presentation to His Majesty till his return, and that I might immediately proceed to business, as if I had been presented."[22] The next day Bassano and Barlow had a two-hour conference during which Barlow went over "the most pressing objects of my mission," throwing in "such observations as seemed to arise out of what I conceived to be the interest of France." Monroe's instructions required Barlow to secure "without delay" full compliance with "the late arrangement by which the non-importation law on the 1st May, 1811, was carried into effect against Great Britain," as well as compensation for the "injuries" to United States commerce committed "on the high seas and in French ports." America's commerce with France was still subject to "the most oppressive restraints," and the administration expected it to "be placed . . . on such a footing, as to afford it a fair market, and to the industry and enterprise of their people a reasonable encouragement." For the French to invite American trade and then rebuff it deprived the United States of any motive to continue challenging Britain over her orders-in-council.[23]

Barlow reported that Bassano "heard me with patience and apparent solicitude." He "endeavored to explain away some of the evils of which we complain" and "expressed a strong desire to remove the rest." Bassano also claimed that many of the points Barlow had raised "were new to him," and he promised to "lay them before the Emperor . . . in a manner calculated to produce the most favorable impression." To assist him in doing so, he asked Barlow to put these points in writing. Bassano left Barlow with the clear impression that between them they would be able "to remove all obstacles to a most perfect harmony between the two countries" when the emperor returned. Bassano failed to mention that Napoleon was not expected in Paris until mid-November, delaying any chance for a definitive resolution of the issues between the two countries until the beginning of 1812 at the earliest.

Barlow could have followed Bassano to Napoleon's headquarters in the Netherlands, but he decided that a better course was to start with formal notes and conduct frequent conversations with officials not distracted by other concerns.[24] Though this approach was not consistent with the speed Madison and Monroe desired, Barlow sensed that pressuring Napoleon would be counterproductive. Yet Barlow remained acutely conscious that time was running out on his hopes to avoid war with Britain. News from Washington usually arrived about one month late, so he would learn in mid-December that when the Twelfth Congress had assembled, Henry Clay, who favored a showdown with Britain, had been elected speaker of the House. He also learned that the administration had released an exchange of notes between Monroe and Foster which suggested that France would have to revoke her decrees, as they affected British as well as American commerce, before Britain would lift her orders-in-council.[25] The publication of these exchanges meant that the administration did not expect Britain to modify its position, and when Madison addressed the newly assembled Congress, he called upon them to put "the United States into an armour . . . demanded by the crisis."[26]

Though the president's quaint martial summons enhanced Barlow's standing in the French capital, he was alarmed by the tendency of events. Since the United States was heading in exactly the direction Napoleon wanted it to go, there was less need for France to yield on any of the issues in dispute between the two nations. Monroe had tried to address the problem by stressing that the "ultimate success" of the confrontational course the United States had adopted toward Britain would depend on France remaining "true to her engagement, by a faithful observance of the revocation of her decrees." It was "not sufficient" for her courts to behave as though her decrees were revoked in their admiralty judgments involving American vessels. The United States expected France to adopt "an active prohibitory policy . . . to prevent seizures" in the first place.[27]

The weakness of the American position was evident in Monroe's claim that

Britain would then have no choice but to follow France's example in removing her commercial restrictions, at least as far as the United States was concerned. Though Napoleon had repeatedly posed as the champion of commercial freedom against Britain's maritime tyranny, a war between Britain and the United States was far more to his advantage than any benefit France might derive from overseas commerce, given its ready access to Europe's continental markets. The only aspect of Monroe's communication with Barlow that might sway Napoleon was the prospect of Congress arming American merchantmen. In that eventuality, only halting the seizures would guarantee that clashes would not occur between the two nations' armed vessels. But even arming the merchantmen was unlikely to prevent Napoleon from stringing the United States along until it declared war against Britain. Barlow was left with little he could do in France beyond trying to soften the effects of French policy on American merchants.

Barlow did not accept marginalization meekly. Upon Bassano's return to Paris on November 9, Barlow proposed to him a three-point program addressing the French concern that British goods were fraudulently winning access to France's markets under the guise of being American property. Barlow's plan included the liberation of all captured and sequestered property whose ownership had been established as American, compensation for the condemnation of all property whose neutral ownership could be established after condemnation, and a new commercial treaty between the two countries that provided France with safeguards against fraudulent claims of American nationality.[28] He made this proposal before Napoleon returned from the Netherlands and a week before his official presentation to the emperor.

On November 17 Bassano greeted Barlow—dressed in his diplomatic uniform, and escorted by William Lee—at St. Cloud. The foreign minister then went through the formality of asking the emperor whether he would receive Barlow. When permission to proceed was received, protocol officers escorted Barlow into Napoleon's private quarters. Barlow confessed to Clara that despite his republican scruples, he bowed three times as he approached the emperor before delivering his commission and giving the short speech he had prepared. Napoleon stammered the customary platitudes reciprocating the American desire for improved relations before awkwardly describing himself as "great enough to be just." After this brief exchange, Barlow began withdrawing while repeatedly bowing, until, mercifully, he reached the exit.[29]

Sensing the ambiguous implications of the one unscripted statement Napoleon had made, Barlow did not attach much significance to his reception and was hardly surprised when it failed to yield immediate results. An official introduction to the society of the capital carried with it the obligation of paying a series of formal visits to everyone of political consequence in Paris. Barlow and Lee were chained to an exhausting social schedule for the next month.[30] Barlow's hopes were not raised until, at a December audience the emperor held to mark the anniversary of his coronation, Napoleon twice singled Barlow out. First the emperor congratulated him on an engagement that had taken place eight months before between an English man-of-war *Lille Belt* and the American frigate *President,* in which the British vessel had fared badly. Napoleon said, "Well, Monsieur, you know how to oppose the English." This time it was Barlow's turn to be ambiguous: "Sire, we know how to make them respect our flag." A short time later, Napoleon came back to Barlow and mentioned the note Barlow had written at Bassano's request. The emperor described it as "interesting" and promised that it would be "answered immediately and satisfactorily." Napoleon then enquired whether the *Constitution* was being held for the French reply. Barlow responded, "Sire, she waits only for that."[31]

This exchange lent authority to the back-channel assurances Barlow was receiving that Napoleon was considering fundamental changes in his commercial policy. French officials had attributed previous delays to his carefully weighing how the concessions he might grant the United States would affect his continental system. Now Napoleon himself seemed to be saying that he had figured it out and that the United States would be pleased with the results. That expectation left Barlow totally unprepared for a diplomatic feeler that came his way two weeks later, not officially from the French government but from someone representing King Joseph of Spain.

A Spanish "agent of rank who has formerly been minister at home and ambassador in France, & who now enjoys the confidence of both governments" approached Barlow with a proposal that looked as rich in possibilities as Barlow's official contacts with France had been poor in results. The agent purported to speak for the Emperor's brother, Joseph Bonaparte, whom Napoleon had recently placed on the Spanish throne. The offer was particularly intriguing because, in addition to resolving in an advantageous manner a long-standing dispute over the extent of the Louisiana Purchase, it addressed most of the more immediate problems between the United States and France.[32]

The Spanish agent proposed a treaty in which Spain confirmed the title of the United States not only to the territory purchased from France in 1803 but to all of the Floridas and much of northern Mexico. Having the government of Spain sanction the U.S. occupation of West Florida would have been incentive enough for the United States to enter such an agreement. In addition, Barlow learned, Joseph was prepared to confirm U.S. title to all lands from the river Bravo in modern Texas to the St Mary's River, which then, as now, was the recognized boundary between Florida and Georgia. Such a cession would deprive the British of any legal pretense for acquiring what remained of Spanish Florida and would secure the southern border of the United States.

More followed. Fourteen million acres of this ceded land between the Mississippi and the Bravo south of the 33rd parallel was to be set aside by King Joseph as a reserve to indemnify "American citizens for the Spoliations committed on their property contrary to the law of nations" by both France and Spain. Barlow estimated that such a reserve would cover claims amounting to 42 million francs. Awards would be made by commissioners in Paris, making it sound as though France was behind the proposal.[33] Of course, such a generous offer did not come without strings attached, but they seemed minimal. The United States was to grant Joseph private title to 6 million of the ceded acres, most of it to the west of the Mississippi. In addition, he would receive a $1 million loan in 6 percent U.S. stock redeemable in ten years. The loan was to be secured by warrants in the U.S. Treasury for Joseph's 6 million acres, on the understanding that the warrants would be released as the loan was retired at the rate of forty cents per acre. One-fifth of the loan would be retained in the U.S. Treasury to cover the cost of surveying the 14 million acres of indemnity lands. The land set aside to pay American claims would be at the disposal of the secretary of the treasury and would be sufficient to provide full indemnification for all past spoliations.

Barlow thought securing "indemnities to so many of our citizens" and "the peaceable acquisition of so great an additional territory," together with "fixing the limits of several thousand miles of our most contested frontier, and this cheaper than was ever expected and of much greater extent," would strengthen Madison domestically. He was confident the majority of Americans would approve of the addition of 200 million acres of territory and compensation for the victims of the spoliations, as the only cost was allowing the other contracting party to retain 6 million of the acres the nation was acquiring. The one-sided nature of the bargain raised the question of why the United States was being offered such advantageous terms, but his interlocutor explained that Joseph was in desperate need of cash. That explanation did not account for France's involvement in the scheme, but Barlow thought that Napoleon was persuaded of the justice of American claims and could only bring himself to pay them in this way. The American minister refused to see "in this transaction . . . [any] corruption or underhand dealing" beyond the agent making the proposal being well paid.[34]

Barlow tried to sell the scheme to Madison on the grounds that it would enable the United States "to live in peace with . . . the world, and to cultivate those natural advantages which ought to secure their greatest happiness as a nation." Barlow looked to a time when the nation would "be sufficiently populous and powerful to be able to . . . do justice, as well as command it." He assumed "habits of justice" were interdependent with "those of peace" and concluded that both would be promoted by settling "those great frontier discussions before they shall appear to be great, and while all the other parties are more willing or more complying than they ever can be hereafter." Barlow also saw the proposal exerting a decisive influence upon the outcome of "the great moral struggle between republican principles and their opposit[e]s" in America. He felt it would contribute greatly to Madison's "success; & I have accustomed myself to regard the triumph of your administration as identified in some measure with that of our constitution."[35] Left unsaid was the common perception that Madison's first term had been anything but triumphant, due to the repeated humiliations the Federalists, aided by the British, had inflicted upon the Republicans.

Madison was not as blinded as Barlow by the contrast between the generosity of this proposal and the stinginess of the French government. The president dismissed the idea that France could indemnify Americans through King Joseph. Accepting the offer would only ignite suspicions about the administration's moral probity. "Were there no other objection than the effect on the public mind here, this would be an insuperable one." But Madison saw other problems as well. "Joseph is not yet settled on the Spanish Throne," and he relied on French armies to maintain his pretensions against a widespread revolt that Britain was busy nourishing on the Iberian Peninsula. Even if France's military effort succeeded, "he will be *sovereign* neither de facto, nor de jure, of any Spanish part of this Continent." Instead, the usurpation of the Spanish crown was already providing Spain's American colonies with an opportunity to become independent from Spain. Joseph "could give us neither right, nor possession; and we should be obliged to acquire the latter by means which a grant from him would be more likely to embarrass than promote." If the French government wanted to make amends for its "flagrant wrongs," it needed to pay damages either from its treasury or in "negotiable substitutes." Without such compensation, it could expect to establish neither "cordiality nor confidence," nor "any formal Treaty on any subject."[36]

Madison suspected the French foreign ministry of planting the proposal in order to see how desperate Barlow had become. Since the president sensed that Barlow wanted to take the bait, Madison advised him to concentrate on commercial matters. The recent declaration by the French consul in Denmark that all vessels carrying colonial produce were subject to capture was an illustration of an onerous policy that needed to be changed. Madison preferred addressing specifics to negotiating a commercial treaty since he suspected that a general treaty would simply be used "to gain time."[37]

Barlow knew he needed something more tangible than the "Spanish proposal" to maintain his credibility at home. Bassano's note to him of December 27, 1811, in which the French foreign minister had blamed Britain rather than France's commercial restrictions for the anemic state of Franco-American trade, reminded Barlow of the specific matters he was expected to address. Bassano had argued that the commercial duties imposed on American produce were little more than those borne by French merchants and that they were less than Britain imposed on foreign produce. In an effort to extract something from France, Barlow presented Bassano with a memorandum proposing that French colonial goods as well as those of the United States be admitted into France in American vessels and that in the future no American ship would be detained except on the suspicion that she had forged papers. The memorandum also called for the release of all American vessels and seamen currently in detention as soon as their nationalities were established.

Barlow hoped that Bassano might sign the memo because it avoided the issue of compensation for past spoliations. But Bassano only offered verbal assurance that "every one of these principles . . . would enter into the treaty," making it pointless "to announce them in a separate declaration." He agreed to present the memorandum to Napoleon, but on December 30 Barlow learned that the emperor would not sign it. Though Napoleon was prepared to give assurances that "the principles are all adopted, and from this day forward they will be in operation,"[38] Barlow realized that this left him with very little besides Bassano's name on a joint statement they signed on December 31. Besides committing both countries to commercial negotiations, it contained a declaration that during these negotiations American vessels would be free to import U.S. produce as well as French colonial produce and that "no cause whatever shall warrant the capture or detention of an American vessel at sea, or her seizure in a French port" except "a well-grounded suspicion of forgery in her papers." The declaration still allowed every French official to be as suspicious as he wanted, leaving Franco-American commerce in the same condition as before. The free entry of American and colonial produce was further qualified by "the formalities necessary to prove the property and origin of the goods" in question.[39]

Barlow also failed to make any progress on the matter of trading licenses. Bassano's ploy here was to argue that "special licenses are a clear advantage, as far as they go, to the commerce and navigation of the United States." That might have been true had they not exposed U.S. vessels to capture and condemnation because the licenses were made out in the name of French houses so that the goods they covered appeared to be French property. Additionally, licenses confined Franco-American trade to "a few intriguing individuals" who were prepared to pay for them "to the detriment of the commercial interests generally," and thereby contributed to the radical imbalance of trade between the two countries.[40] The joint statement of Barlow and Bassano declared that "no other papers shall be required but the passport and clearance by the American authorities, and a certificate of origin by a French consul." Those certificates, though they might be preferable to licenses, would still cost those who were able to procure them a considerable sum of money. Everywhere Barlow turned, he came away empty handed.

The diplomatic impasse explains Barlow's private letter to Dolley Madison in late December expressing his mortification at having labored for three months and accomplished nothing. Barlow was afraid "the president may think I have been idle," so he begged her for reassurance: "If he should approve my conduct I wish you would let me know it." Barlow's prolonged detention of the *Constitution* until the beginning of January further embarrassed him. Though he had explained the detention to Monroe and Madison, he told Dolley that "the Emperor, who assumed such an air of goodness to me at the first audience & every time since, desired expressly that I would detain" the vessel "for the ministers answer to my . . . note." Since Barlow had been told that Napoleon was sufficiently impressed to "probably" change "his system relative to the U. States," Barlow did not think he could send the frigate off without showing disrespect for the assurances he had been given.[41]

His failure to achieve any concrete results led Barlow to fear the French government meant to string him along indefinitely until the United States declared war on Britain. War with Britain was exactly what Barlow most wanted to avoid. In addition to his ideological concerns, Barlow doubted the capacity of Madison's government to survive a war with a great power. The only option left to him was negotiating a commercial treaty between the United States and France. Barlow hoped such a treaty would reduce the pressure on the administration to vindicate its honor through a contest at arms. Assuming it contained a formal renunciation of the Berlin and Milan decrees from France, it might induce Britain to revoke her orders-in-council and lead to reconciliation between Britain and the United States. Barlow did not place much stock in the official British position that her orders were a response to Napoleon's decrees and would be removed once the emperor revoked his continental system. That was clearly something that Britain was not likely to do as long as the European war persisted. Barlow gambled instead on the United States having enough economic clout in association with France to force Britain to abandon her orders-in-council.

Barlow's proximity to Britain made him more aware of her internal condition than was the administration in Washington. He realized that her economic fortunes had changed for the worse since 1808 and that she was in the midst of a recession to which current American measures were significantly contributing. The opening of Spain's American empire to British enterprise had initially cushioned Britain against the effects of the American embargo of 1807–9. Merchandise otherwise destined for the United States had been diverted to South America, where ready buyers were quickly found. Once British merchants had satisfied the initial demand of Latin American consumers, however, a recession ensued. Debts contracted in the initial flush of the new trade had to be paid, which in turn cut down on new orders. The nonintercourse law that went into effect during the spring of 1811 hit the British economy just as its Latin American commerce was faltering, creating powerful reasons for Britain to seek an accommodation with the United States.

Barlow had access to reports about economic and political conditions in Britain through the British press, supplemented by Jonathan Russell.[42] Nor was he alone in believing that Britain's resources were strained to the limit by her blockade of the European coast. The effort involving over one thousand warships pressured Britain's financial system to the point where it seemed about to break. Surely the British would learn, as had the French, that bankruptcy was the pitfall of monarchies. However, Barlow processed this information through an ideological filter that led him to assume that a war with Britain would be a disaster for the United States because it would enlarge the public debt and lead to wholesale confiscations and conscription. The United States had survived much of the Revolutionary War without a formal federal constitution, but only barely and then only because it had possessed a powerful ally and lacked a strategic center whose seizure could bring the war to a close. Now that the United States was a full-fledged constitutional republic with a capital city, Barlow trembled over putting its institutions to the test. Either they would fail or, should they prove militarily sufficient, they would be corrupted, as the purity of republican France had been by war.[43]

This reasoning, which Barlow shared with many Republican leaders in Congress, brought them perilously close to sharing a key tenet of their Federalist enemies. The Federalists were so obsessed with the possibility that the American experiment would degrade as France's had that they interpreted everything the Republicans did as having Napoleonic implications. Their anxiety provided a moral basis for their resistance to the embargo and to war with Britain, which they would see as a war of conquest for the acquisition of Canada. Barlow certainly did not agree with the Federalists' desire to align the nation with Britain, but he did fear the length to which they were prepared to go in resisting the Republican drift toward war with her. It might tear the American republic to pieces or, short of that, compel the Republicans to become as monarchical in repressing their domestic adversaries as the Federalists had been in 1798–1800.

The frustrations of negotiating with Napoleon's court also reminded Barlow that a victorious France under the emperor would be almost as difficult to deal with as a triumphant Britain. The Federalists carried this idea to the point of being prepared to do practically anything to help Britain in her struggle against France, including tolerating the impressment of American sailors, because they saw the British navy as a barrier protecting them from Napoleon. Barlow, like most of his Republican compatriots, wished for a stable balance of power between the great powers rather than a decisive victor. Despite the economic opportunities presented by a European conflict, peace was preferable because without it there would be no chance for republicanism to expand. Peace would unfetter commerce and remind all who shared in its benefits of the interests they had in common. By contrast, wars divided nations and benefited the few at the expense of the many.

Had Barlow lived into the 1820s and 1830s, he might have been gratified by the emergence of an Atlantic world that conformed to his ideological hopes. Because he was removed from the immediate pressures of America's domestic politics, he failed to appreciate the forces pushing the Republican leadership to commit the nation's destiny to the hazards of war despite their anxieties about the consequences.[44] Just as Madison and Monroe were coming to accept war with Britain as preferable to repeated humiliations at the hands of Britain and the Federalists, Barlow grew more averse to it. When war came, Barlow would accept it because he had done his utmost to avoid it, but before war was declared Barlow continued to hope that France could be brought to cooperate in getting Britain to repeal her orders-in-council.

His efforts took two forms. One was to supply Jonathan Russell in London with information about the fate of American vessels in France. Forty American vessels had followed Barlow there since September 1811, and neither the Berlin nor Milan decrees had been invoked against any of them.[45] Unfortunately, that claim seemed contradicted by repeated reports of French seizures that even extended to vessels carrying official dispatches between Russell and Barlow. Dolley Madison complained that the administration was "annoyed" by these reports, which were not entirely without foundation.[46] Ten days after assuring Russell that American vessels were exempt from the French decrees, Barlow found himself protesting the plundering of two more American merchantmen by French ships. Piracies and mistakes could be distinguished from the official policies of a government, which disavowed the misbehavior of its agents. But official disavowals were never forthcoming, and the continued seizures certainly did not assist Barlow in his quest for peace.[47]

His other course was to pursue the commercial treaty Bassano continued to dangle before him. During the first two weeks of 1812, Barlow produced a draft treaty containing thirty articles that addressed all the difficulties plaguing Franco-American commerce, except the indemnities due the United States for French violations of her neutral rights. Barlow did this despite Madison's warning that negotiating such a treaty could be used as a pretext for postponing satisfaction on other issues. Barlow clung stubbornly to the idea "that the advantages of such a treaty as I have sketched would be very great, . . . especially if it could be concluded soon," because he still hoped to avoid war with England.[48] He also continued to report to Russell in London—as well as to friends in America—that he was making progress and that his mission was likely to succeed.[49]

At the same time, Barlow could not ignore the administration's reservations about such a treaty, a point made unmistakably clear in Monroe's April 23 commentary to the text of Barlow's draft treaty. Monroe objected to features in six of the thirty articles, adding that if the final treaty failed to "secure . . . the objects on which you were instructed, you may be assured that it will not be ratified."[50] If his own superior had so many objections, he could scarcely expect the French to have fewer.

The strain Barlow was under began to take a physical toll. Around this time he described himself to George Erving as a skeleton, which served as "tenter-frame to keep my skin stretcht upon, lest it should fall in heaps & wrinkles worse than it is now."[51] Ruth would later argue that Barlow had been fully aware of the game the French were playing and simply refused to be deterred by it. But that spring it became clear to both Barlows that the prospects of heading off a conflict with Britain were diminishing. In mid-April, Ruth wrote Dolley Madison that she expected "censure [to] fall on my husband" despite his best efforts "to promote the interest & prosperity of the country, the honor & glory of the administration." She was "sorry to see such a warlike appearance in America" and still wished, though not with much conviction, "that dreadful scourge to humanity [might]be . . . avoided." Since the government had "been so forbearing" in the past, she hoped it might consider "it right to forbear a little longer, tho' our property be taken & our flag insulted." Both seemed "a small evil in comparison to War."[52] But the plea for more time was a vain one, as they could tell from the reports they received from friends in America, the newspapers, and the communications of Monroe that informed them of each step the administration was taking in its march toward hostilities with Britain.

Though Monroe continued to hold out the possibility that the United States would draw back from conflict with France's enemy, both Barlow and the French government must have realized this was unlikely after news of the Henry affair arrived in France. The activities of the British-born, naturalized-American citizen John Henry became public in mid-March 1812. Henry had been recruited by the governor of Lower Canada, Sir James Craig, to spy on New England's opposition to the embargo of 1807–9. Henry's letters to Craig described a Federalist leadership that would have liked nothing better than to separate from the rest of the United States had circumstances permitted. But they had not. Henry's subsequent attempt to sell copies of his dispatches to the highest bidder found a willing buyer in the Madison administration. An imposter, who claimed to be a Spanish noble, Count de Crillon, and Sérurier acted as intermediaries in the sale.

Though Henry declined to disclose the precise identities of the New England Federalists he described, the administration still valued the Henry letters for what they revealed about the British government's intentions. Madison and Monroe thought they conclusively demonstrated that Britain was bent on destroying the American Republic and counted on the assistance of the Federalists to accomplish their objective. Certainly, the publication of Henry's papers hardened American public opinion against Britain. Shortly after their release, Madison had sent a message to Congress asking for an embargo—preparatory to a declaration of war—which went into effect at the beginning of April.

Barlow learned of these developments several weeks before hearing of the Prince Regent's declaration of April 21, 1812. It pledged a revocation of Britain's orders-in-council whenever "the Berlin and Milan Decrees shall, by some authentic act of the French government, publicly promulgated, be expressly and unconditionally repealed." On May 1, Barlow took to Bassano the Prince Regent's declaration, which cited American misconceptions about France's actions as the reason for persisting with their orders. Barlow demanded an explicit, official announcement that the French decrees were repealed. On this occasion, Barlow's leverage was enhanced by the recent release of a report by the French foreign minister about the commerce of neutrals. In it, Bassano failed to mention either the modification of the French decrees or their nonapplicability to the United States. Barlow now insisted that the French government "make and publish an authentic act declaring the Berlin and Milan decrees, as relative to the United States, to have ceased in November 1810," that "they have not been applied in any instance since that time, and that they shall not be applied in the future." Barlow described his position as "so just, and the necessity so urgent, that [he could not] withhold [his] confidence in the prompt and complete success of my proposition." He also tried to link the requested declaration to two other objectives he had so far sought for in vain, indemnity for "past spoliations on American property" and a commercial treaty "founded on the liberal principle of reciprocal benefit and concession."[53]

Though he would continue to be stymied on the last two matters, on May 12 Bassano handed Barlow the copy of a decree that had allegedly been issued at St. Cloud on April 28, 1811, more than a year before. It proclaimed that as a consequence of Congress's act of March 2, 1811, instituting nonintercourse against Britain, the Berlin and Milan decrees no longer applied to American shipping. The decree, which bore all the hallmarks of fraud, had to be pried out of Bassano. The French foreign minister wanted the *Moniteur*'s report to serve as the official announcement, but Barlow objected that a newspaper account in response to "an official note on so solemn a subject . . . would only serve in America to show how the French government could play with the feelings of a foreign agent." Barlow then stuck his neck out and declared that without the required declaration from the emperor and "acts conformable to it, a war against England was impracticable; but with it, it might be regarded as infallible."[54] This was exactly the card Barlow least relished playing, but by then he realized that it was probably too late to avoid war with Britain. If there were any doubts on that score, they were resolved by Dolley Madison's April 19 letter to Ruth, announcing that the embargo was considered a preliminary to hostilities.[55]

Barlow's determination to extract this declaration from the French foreign minister reflected his frustration with having so little impact on events. Bassano, for his part, probably realized that Barlow was bluffing, but since France was about to get what it wanted anyway, Bassano saw no harm in yielding this one crumb. Barlow's sense of powerlessness deepened when he learned about the uses the

Federalists were making of his private correspondence. He had continued to express optimism about his mission to his friends and even hinted that the commercial treaty he was working on might also secure the nation's title to vast new territories. Reports of a March 4 letter that Postmaster General Gideon Granger had received from Barlow drew considerable attention in the Federalist press. Since its arrival in America coincided with the release of some of the official but futile correspondence between Bassano and Barlow, Federalist newspapers dismissed as humbug the promise of a treaty, mockingly reporting that Barlow had reduced it to verse and sent it to Granger to be put to music.[56]

The first lady warned Barlow that anything he said could be used against him once it entered the public domain. Indeed, the Federalist press even used Barlow's silences against him. Some papers spread the rumor that as a citizen of France with a considerable estate there, Barlow had decided to remain in Paris permanently. Others contented themselves with describing Barlow as either the dupe of Napoleon or a fool. Without going into details, Fulton added his caution "not to say much to any of your friends until you are certain government be first informed, and not even then if very important for it may be that government will not want it made public."[57]

One of the primary agents responsible for making war with Britain more likely showed up in Paris in April 1812. Barlow would have disliked John Henry anyway for his mercenary betrayal of his former employers. Through Lafayette, Barlow learned that there was a real Comte de Crillon—Lafayette's friend—and confronted Henry with this information. Henry pretended he had been deceived and was trying to arrange for the imposter's arrest, but Barlow was not convinced. In a note to Monroe he commented, "This man [Henry] speaks of guineas as he would of . . . beans. He will probably be asking me to give him a few, as the bills received from his friend must be protested for the non-existence of the drawee." Barlow added in a postscript that the real de Crillon, who owned bank stock in Philadelphia, had instructed his banker there not to accept any drafts on his account.[58]

Barlow's contempt for Henry's behavior soon became public knowledge. In late May, Henry complained to Barlow that his reputation was being blackened by the circulation of falsehoods, which he attributed to "the resentment of individual americans now in Paris." Though he didn't accuse Barlow directly of entertaining such sentiments, Henry did say that those spreading falsehoods about him had "availed themselves of the sanction of your table to give a character of authenticity to what is . . . unfounded." Barlow replied ambiguously by promising

Henry "any protection that your character as a citizen of the U.S. & the nature of the services you have rendered to their government" might require. But while he disclaimed any responsibility for conversations overheard "at my table," he strictly enjoined Clara Baldwin from mentioning the matter to anyone in public, even as he supplied her with a copy of Henry's letters to Craig.[59]

Meanwhile, the real Comte de Crillon, Francis Denis de Cresse, traveled to the United States to protect his interests there, causing something of a sensation when he appeared in the capital. That led the secretary of state to instruct Barlow to withhold payment of any moneys that had previously been allocated for the fraudulent de Crillon. Monroe also privately instructed Barlow to try to elicit from Henry additional information that might be of use to the government. Barlow acknowledged receipt of these instructions on October 20 but didn't have time to act upon them before leaving for Vilna in response to Napoleon's summons.[60]

CHAPTER EIGHTEEN

Finale

Rumors that Congress had declared war against Britain reached Europe in early June 1812. Barlow saw the ninety-day embargo, with which Congress had responded to Madison's April 1 request for a sixty-day embargo, as postponing the dreaded event a bit longer. It preserved his slim hope that Britain's revocation of her orders-in-council—first announced on June 16 though not formally publicized until June 23—might possibly head off the conflict that James Madison proclaimed on June 19. But by late July, Barlow concluded that war had been declared or soon would be. Bitterly disappointed, he mocked his impotence, confessing to Clara Baldwin, "So . . . all my great renown built on the fact of having prevented that calamity will be let down to the ground, & it may be difficult to get it up again."[1] Official confirmation from America did not arrive until a month later and then created the impression that the conflict might be minimized and peace restored by timely negotiations, now that one of the war's principal causes had been removed.

At least war released Barlow from trying to extract concessions from Napoleon. After the French army invaded Russia in June 1812, such attempts were futile. No one familiar with the workings of the French empire expected significant diplomacy to take place before Napoleon returned to Vilna, Lithuania, where Bassano was currently holding court. Barlow continued to be summoned to St. Cloud by the Duc de Dalberg, in whose hands the commercial negotiation had been left with instructions to prolong it as long as possible. Barlow also had to protest the outrages France continued to inflict on American vessels. Addressing specific complaints was far less frustrating than trying to extract a comprehensive agreement from the emperor, and Barlow assumed his exchanges with Dalberg were unlikely to lead anywhere. The pressure on Barlow was further lightened by Madison's apparent willingness to postpone a reckoning with France until scores with Britain were settled.

Despite the absence of official notification, Barlow took all the necessary precautions. He detained public ships and supplied U.S. naval captains with funds. On July 3, when he notified the consuls in the Mediterranean and Atlantic ports of the revocation of Britain's orders-in-council, he warned them that the news might not have reached the United States in time to forestall hostilities. In early August, Barlow wrote Bassano to arrange for the accommodation of American privateers in French ports. Barlow sought exemption from all export restrictions and permission to sell prize goods in France that were not of British manufacture. He also proposed that captured British goods be deposited in warehouses for future disposal. Finally, he wanted American consuls vested with authority to render preliminary judgment in prize cases, subject to appeal in the U.S. courts. He urged these concessions on the grounds that they would hasten peace and enrich France with revenue and raw materials.[2]

When official confirmation of hostilities finally arrived, Barlow alerted the U.S. consuls in Europe to the consequences, including Algeria's declaration of war against the United States.[3] Barlow also supplied the consuls with money to aid stranded American merchant seamen. Eventually, Barlow received authorization to issue letters-of-marque to the captains of American vessels in France, which would allow them to arm and seize British shipping. Letters-of-marque required larger crews, and Britain's refusal to exchange captured seamen created a shortage of hands. The French government was willing to release the American sailors taken off British ships, provided they served on board American armed vessels. American captains, however, wanted volunteers rather than conscripts.[4] Barlow delegated the resolution of this problem to a trusted subordinate, Isaac Barnet.

During the summer of 1812, Barlow broke up the family establishment in Paris. Ruth and Clara moved in with Daniel Parker at his Draveil estate, which was close enough to the city for Barlow to move back and forth as circumstances dictated.[5] Aside from attending official functions, there was relatively little that required his attention. In place of the endless dispatches he had previously produced in multiple copies—only two survive from this period—he could at last devote more attention to his immediate family and friends.[6] Madame de Villette spent summers on her country estate, and the Barlows visited her when they were not at Parker's. Her greater distance from Paris, however, made it less convenient for Barlow to attend to what remained of his official functions in the capital when he was staying with her.

Wartime Paris had its compensations. Napoleonic rule had not completely strangled the city's cultural life as Barlow's Hamburg correspondent, Gottlieb Ebeling, complained it had Germany's. But Parisian culture had changed. Salons, like Helen Maria Williams's, which Barlow still frequented, were less politically oriented. After Napoleon crowned himself emperor, Williams courted men of science, and the German explorer and scientist Alexander von Humboldt became her hero. Barlow encountered another scientific luminary of the age, Count Rumford, at Parker's. Rumford had begun life as the Massachusetts-born loyalist Benjamin Thompson. Forced into exile by the American Revolution's outcome, he had settled in Bavaria long enough to have the title of "Count" bestowed upon him for his contributions to the field of thermodynamics. He had married the widow of the great French chemist Antoine Lavoisier more than a decade after her husband had perished on the guillotine. Now separated from her, Rumford relished the quiet of Parker's country estate. Barlow was not, as a rule, drawn to former loyalists, but he and Rumford shared much besides a friendship with Parker.[7]

If Paris, as the seat of empire, lacked the political appeal it had possessed before Napoleon had made himself first consul for life, Barlow remained at the center of a vibrant, expatriate community. In addition to his fellow countrymen, his circle included Frenchmen with American connections, a sprinkling of radical Englishmen, and exiled republicans like Thaddeus Kosciewsko. When not at Parker's or de Villette's country residences, Barlow was far from lonely. But Ruth's indisposition that summer led him to spend as much time as possible with her and Clara, who had been bedridden with a lame knee for half a year.

Clara was depressed by her prolonged immobility, and Barlow tried to cheer her, predicting that she would be married during the succeeding winter. When she misconstrued this as indicating Barlow regarded her as a burden, he responded teasingly: "You have mistaken, dear Clara, the motive I had for getting you married. It was not precisely to get you off my hands, or out of the family, though that might be a very laudable motive considering the mischief you do in exciting your sister to rebellion. —But it is rather for your own sake, to get you as soon as possible into a state of discipline, wholesome correction, regular conjugal torment for the good of your soul."[8] Barlow knew that Clara would show Ruth his letter, giving him the satisfaction of making a joke that, like the best humor, underscored a serious point. The benefits derived from committing oneself to the life and fortune of another human being required repeated sacrifices in addition to the pain of a final parting.

🔱

The long summer quietus with which the Barlows were blessed in 1812 came to an end with the receipt of a ciphered letter from Madison dated August 11. Madison had still not officially heard of the revocation of the British orders-in-council. But the president had received "an *authentic tho informal communication . . . in a dispatch ship from England. importing* that the *orders* were to be *revoked on the first of August*, subject to *renewal if . . .* the *non importation should not be forthwith re*[s]*cinded* on *the arrival of the act of revocation.*" Since "this *pledge* was given before the *declaration of war was known*," Madison could not be sure that it would be "*adher*[e]*d to.* It is not *improbable . . . that it was hurried off as a chance for* preventing an *apprehended war*; and that the same *dislike to the war* may possibly produce *advances for terminating it which if the terms be admissible will be immediately embraced.*" In that eventuality, Madison was confident that "*the full tide of indignation* with which the public *mind here is boiling will* be *directed against France* if not *obviated by a due* [reparation of] *her wrongs.*"

The wrong Madison had in mind was the St. Cloud Decree of April 28, 1811. The president claimed "*War will be* called for [against France] by the *nation almost una voce.* Even without a *peace with England* the further *refusal* and *prevarications of France* on the subject of *red*[ress] *may be* expected to *produce measures* of *hostility* at the *ensuing session of* [Congs]. This result is the more probable, as the general *exasperation will* coincide with the *calculation of not a few* that a *double war is the shortest road to peace.*" Madison authorized Barlow to turn the substance of his note "*to account . . .* in *your discussions with the French government,*" adding that Barlow should be prepared "*to retire* from *them altogether on a sudden notice so to do.*"[9]

Barlow wasted no time in communicating the substance of Madison's letter to Dalberg, who forwarded it posthaste to Bassano. But Madison's message did not reach the capital of Lithuania until almost two months after it had been written. By that time the French invasion of Russia was beginning to fall apart. Though Napoleon's Grand Army of 600,000 reached Moscow on September 14, they could not prevent the burning of the city between September 15 and 19. Deprived of a place to winter, the French had no alternative but to withdraw. Eight days before the French began their disastrous retreat, Bassano invited Barlow to come to Vilna, again offering as bait the promise of a prompt conclusion to the stalled commercial negotiations.[10]

Barlow had been manipulated enough to realize the invitation might be another false opening. He also knew that Vilna was 1,400 miles away, that there were no good roads east of Berlin, and that the further he traveled the more likely he was to encounter severe winter weather. All of these circumstances, according to Ruth, made Bassano's proposal unwelcome. On the other hand the totally unexpected character of the invitation, which was accompanied by assurances that Napoleon meant to winter in Vilna, suggested that the emperor might become more cooperative now that the tide had finally turned against him.[11] Barlow also was shown a copy of a letter Bassano had sent Dalberg on September 18, authorizing the inclusion of an indemnity provision for American vessels unjustly detained or condemned by France in the commercial treaty over which they had been haggling. This seemed like a significant concession because heretofore Napoleon's military ambitions had led him to deny responsibility for the spoliations of American property, which some thought had risen to as much as $60 million.[12]

Madison's threat to sever relations with France and possibly go to war with her unnerved Barlow more than it did Dalberg and Bassano. Because Barlow continued to view Britain as the nation's principal enemy, he could not reconcile himself to war with France. A prior communication from Monroe had suggested that the only consideration that had forestalled war with France was the expectation that an indemnity was still contemplated.[13] That, along with repeated warnings from the president and secretary of state that a commercial treaty without an indemnity provision would be unacceptable, explains the bizarre solution Barlow worked out with Dalberg. Their plan called for a syndicate of investors to create an indemnity fund. In exchange, six to eight hundred commercial licenses to import colonial produce—currently excluded on the grounds that most of it was British—would be placed at Barlow's disposal to distribute to the subscribers, proportionate to the amount of their subscriptions. The licenses exempted their possessors from Napoleon's blanket prohibition against colonial produce and from all import duties, allowing the license holders to profit from the enormous pent-up demand for colonial produce reflected in the black market price it currently fetched.[14]

The scheme had the virtue of circumventing Napoleon's reluctance to admit indemnity claims while apparently satisfying Madison's precondition for a commercial treaty. But it also contained problems. The most obvious was its reliance on licenses. Madison and Monroe had repeatedly objected to them. In William Henry Crawford's subsequent estimation, the scheme would have gone into effect before Madison learned about it and the "disposition of these licenses by the American minister . . . must have given rise to conjectures highly prejudicial to his Character."[15] Barlow had designed and committed himself to a proposal that put his reputation at risk in France and virtually insured that the commercial treaty he had worked so long and hard on would be rejected by the president. What could Barlow have been thinking when he agreed to such a scheme?

A partially coded letter Barlow wrote Madison on September 26 provides the answer. He prefaced it by observing that while the prospects for a successful resolution of the indemnities issue had "never been *brilliant*," the current discussions seem "to *promise more than I ever expected.*"[16] Barlow made much of the support the proposal had won among French officials like Dalberg, Talleyrand, and Prince Jean-Jacques-Régis de Cambacérès, who felt it was only a matter of time before the emperor himself would agree. But Barlow knew that trying to sell the indemnity arrangement as the best deal available was unlikely to persuade the president. He persevered despite the odds because he was determined to do everything in his power to dissuade Madison from embarking on the "double war" threatened in his August 11 letter.

To that end, Barlow invoked the plan for partitioning the United States between Britain and France that Aaron Burr had recently tried to promote in Europe. Barlow claimed it "was not disliked by either government. . . . The plan was laid aside for *that time* because the *parties* could not then *agree on a peace between* themselves." Barlow predicted that the minute Britain and France made peace, the plan would "be *resumed* . . . with all the force of these *two nations*" for two reasons. First, "the situation of *Spanish America* . . . greatly augments the interests naturally calculated to draw their attention to that *side of the world.*" Secondly, and more importantly, the governments of both nations "*hate the principles* of our *Government* with an *equal hatred* and would *sacrifice* a great deal to *accomplish its overthrow.* Barlow warned that "a *war declared* against them [American principles] *both at once* would have a powerful tendency to *calm the violence* of their present *animosity against* each other & smooth the way to a *speedy peace between* themselves." They would then have "*armies and navies* on hand *competent* (when *acting in concert*) to the *greatest enterprizes* ever undertaken in *distant regions.*" Barlow thought that the only thing that would restrain them from landing "*two hundred thousand* of the most *effective troops* that ever went *to war*" would be "want of *motive.*" It was to the nation's interests to encourage the emperor to turn his "*unbridled passions*" eastward, especially as Barlow did not expect Napoleon to last long. Between "the *hazards of battle* and of *assassination*" there was "more than an even chance that [Napoleon] *will not live* to revisit his *own Capitol*" if he moved against Turkey.[17]

A copy of a French translation that decodes most of this letter's coded portions ended up in the archives of the French Foreign Ministry. Since the letter contained much that Barlow would not have wanted to share with his French counterparts, it is a safe bet that it got there through an intermediary in the American legation who had access to the code and sold the translation. We shall never know for sure who the mole was, but we do know that the foreign ministry was privy to some of Barlow's secret calculations as he wound up his negotiation with Dalberg. If Barlow had known this, he would have been less sanguine about the agreement the two men forwarded to Bassano on October 18. At that time Barlow still felt there was a good chance of his being able to execute his instructions and get the commercial treaty he had labored over for so long.[18]

Barlow claimed he had accepted Bassano's invitation because he could not refuse it "without giving offense, or at least risking a postponement of a negotiation which I have reason to believe is now in a fair way to a speedy and advantageous close."[19] Left unstated was Barlow's failure up until this point to have much effect on events. But he continued to hope a commercial treaty with France would make it more difficult for the United States to declare war on her. Two days before Barlow and Tom set out by carriage for Vilna on October 27, he appointed Tom to the post of secretary of the legation. William Lee could no longer fill the post because the war required him to attend to consular duties in Bordeaux.[20] He purposely did not appoint a chargé d'affaires to supervise the routine affairs of the legation because the only available candidate was Warden, currently serving simply as consul though mistakenly credited by Bassano as consul-general. Barlow hoped to return to Paris quickly. Warden's quarrel with several legation secretaries had led Barlow to conclude that Warden placed his personal interests ahead of the public concerns.[21]

The French government offered fresh horses at each post station along the way, so Barlow had some reason for hoping they might win the race against the onset of severe weather. By traveling continuously, the two Americans reached Frankfurt in eighty-three hours. Had it not rained, turning some of the German roads into mud, they might have arrived eleven hours earlier. More than three days in a cramped carriage without any break compelled them to rest for two days before resuming their journey toward Berlin by way of Weimar and Leipzig. During the interlude, they were entertained by the French ambassador, who had been instructed to treat them as VIPs. Thanks to a brief improvement in the weather, they entered Berlin on the afternoon of the ninth day of their journey. Again greeted by the French ambassador, they were shown around the city and taken to the theater. Barlow would have preferred tarrying for another day, but the approach-

ing winter compelled them to set out the next morning for the Baltic city of
Königsberg.[22]

East of Berlin they encountered increasing difficulties. One was the effect the
autumn storms had on the sandy soils of Prussia. Eight days of uninterrupted rain
turned the roads of what is now western Poland into a sea of mud. It was impossible to proceed at night or to get out of the carriage when going up or down a
steep hill without muddying the sheepskin blanket on the floor that kept them
warm. Barlow made light of their hardships to Ruth. "The mud, the true sublime,
the real majesty of mud, you know nothing about, having seen nothing of it either
in Paris or Hartford or Maryland or Holland or any other country. My ideas have
been expanding on this subject since I crossed the Rhine. It is thick or thin, black
or brown, according to circumstances through all the kingdom of Westphalia,
Saxony is a quagmire, but the Devil's own hastypudding is in this great basin of
140 miles from Thorn to Königsberg. . . . The horses['] legs are the ladles that stir
it up, the carriage wheels whirl it over your head in a black rainbow that moves as
you move."[23]

Another difficulty stemmed from their growing proximity to the war. They
found the city gates of Kistrzy, on the River Oder, locked when they arrived there
shortly after sundown because the surrounding countryside was deemed unsafe.
This forced them to spend the night in a country inn before securing fresh horses
to continue their journey. They were lucky to find a shortcut around Thorn on
the Vistula River, but that good fortune was balanced by worsening weather. The
effects of the French invasion on the local inhabitants were also becoming evident. The only people they encountered in the barren countryside were impoverished peasants huddled in miserable huts. Accommodations were hard to find
and, when found, neither entirely safe nor comfortable. If the travelers lay down
to sleep, it would be on straw rather than a bed or pallet. When they arrived at
Kovno on the river Niemen after the city gates had been locked, they spent the
night in their unheated carriage. Had they been able to enter the town, they would
have found accommodations scarce because it was filled with French soldiers,
many of whom were sick or wounded. During the remainder of their journey to
Vilna, they would share what there was of roads and accommodations with the
four horse guards a French commander provided for their safety.[24]

Barlow continued to make light of their hardships in his letters to Ruth. During the initial, non-stop portion of the trip, he had boasted that he had slept "like
a top six hours" one night. Despite the tedium, he claimed, "I can eat & sleep &
think of Darling as well in the carriage as any where." Their physical torment
eased somewhat once it was no longer practical to travel at night. Still nineteen

days spent in continuous close quarters with only one other person grew tedious. Each day Barlow gave Tom, who "suck[ed] in ideas like a calf, . . . a great many lessons on life & manners, history & politics, science & literature." Barlow also taught his nephew what he knew of the German language.[25] Tom, for his part, read Robertson's *History of Charles V* aloud to Barlow. The only other books they carried were one copy each of *The Columbiad* and the *Iliad*.

Their carriage finally pulled into Vilna on November 18, three weeks after their departure from Paris. The last seventy-five miles of their journey made such a disagreeable impression upon Barlow that he no longer attempted to hide it from Ruth. All the natives had fled because their villages had been burned and the thatch of their roofs removed. Tom and Barlow did not have the desolate landscape to themselves, however. They passed at least six hundred open wagons loaded with wounded and sick men moving westward. Some of the wagons lacked hay for their occupants to lie on because it was being fed to the horses, who died as fast as the exposed men did. "It grows worse & worse & worse & worse the nearer you approach to the theater of glory," Barlow lamented. He reported that as many as 25,000 horses had already expired in the retreat from Moscow. The men who died were still being buried, but that was not sufficient to stifle Barlow's sense of despair. "O God! O God! What did you make mankind for. I want to know.—A creature endowed with so much intellect, foresight, calculation, prudence,—& uses them so little." Barlow estimated that a million people had perished since the French invasion had begun "in this glorious Russian war."[26]

Two days after their arrival in Vilna, rumors circulated that Napoleon had lost all his cavalry, rendering his retreating army defenseless against Cossack attacks. The rumors fed on the Russians' success in cutting off the emperor's communications with Vilna. Barlow remained confident that Napoleon would extricate himself from his current difficulties and winter in Lithuania. This conclusion received support from Bassano's efforts to maintain appearances with lavish entertainments for the diplomatic corps. But that did nothing to alleviate crowding in a town whose pre-occupation population had numbered only 37,000. Barlow fared better than most because Bassano found a house into which the diplomatic missions of four countries could squeeze. The two Americans together with their French coachman, Lewis, shared one floor with the Danish ambassador and his five servants.

No northern European state was more under the thumb of France than Denmark; next to the British and French, none had done so much damage to American commerce. However, Barlow maintained a cordial relationship with his Danish counterpart and fared better than the Prussian ambassador, who had been forced to spend a night in his carriage for want of accommodations. As for ordinary amenities, there were positive advantages to being closeted with the Danes. Since there were no restaurants in Vilna, the two ministers pooled their resources and dined together with their staffs as one family. The Danish ambassador traveled in greater style than the Americans with sixteen horses, a cook, and a special wagon loaded with supplies of wine, rum, sugar, and coffee. Barlow attempted to make light of his dependence on his Danish colleague, pretending he was entitled to what he and Tom received. "Half of the said cargo is already confiscated to the profit of the United States for having been or intended to be under English convoy, and as part payment for the cargoes of our property condemned at Copenhagen, for which Mr. Erving could get no compensation."[27]

After Jean-Baptiste Petry, whom the foreign ministry assigned as liaison to the Americans, arranged a special shipment of wines and food from Königsberg, Barlow contributed more to these living arrangements. He also managed to acquire some sheets and two blankets in the local market. The blankets were particularly precious and, together with the blanket he had brought from Paris, allowed Barlow to provide for Tom and Lewis, as well as for himself. Most attributes of normal living—like laundry—were dispensed with, though that did not stop Barlow from participating in the social occasions Bassano arranged. Barlow gave Ruth an account of a dinner where he had been seated next to a Polish princess. He described the lady in question as possessing "a pair of eyes that, if they had been made before our solar system, would have induced the architect to make two suns instead of one." Her only drawback was that she was older than Barlow. He claimed to have been so struck by the bosom of another beauty that if she had offered him "sixpence a piece to find the little snappers [body lice under her skirts] I would look all night for them without a candle." This was part of Barlow's teasing routine because he immediately added that it was "flummery" and addressed Ruth as "my darling, first begotten long beloved wife better & more & harder & softer & longer & stronger than all the poles between the south pole and the north pole."[28]

Wartime conditions failed to quench Barlow's curiosity about Vilna and its surroundings. He gave Ruth a full description of the town, which he likened in size to Boston. People dwelt in structures of brick or stone that accommodated multiple families, animals mixing freely with humans. Most of the private structures had dirt floors, and none made provision for privacy. Only the churches and the local university possessed charm. He was less specific about the surrounding countryside, though its devastation and abandonment made a deep impression on him. Vilna was not only uncomfortable but boring, so boring in fact that Barlow soon exhausted his wit on the subject of its women and turned instead to Lewis's laziness, comparing him to each of their other Parisian servants, whose shortcomings Barlow celebrated as superlative virtues when compared with the coachman.[29]

On December 5, the news of Napoleon's defeat at Berezina transformed boredom into panic. Once it became clear that the emperor was fleeing before the enemy, a mass exodus ensued. Roads clogged with carts carrying sick and wounded soldiers hindered the flight of the diplomatic corps, and the area between Vilna and Kovno turned into a charnel house, with dead horses and men strewn about the countryside. Some perished from starvation and cold, others were cut down by flying columns of Cossacks. Barlow fared better than many because he had a French carriage that was lighter and better constructed than most. He also benefited from being accompanied by Petry, who had authority to requisition suitable horses, accommodations, and supplies wherever they could be found.

Barlow, Petry, and Tom made it to Warsaw after struggling for seven days against the elements and crowds of refugees. They did so despite lending the Danish minister, whose larger carriage could not get over a hill ten miles west of Vilna, three of their horses. They were further delayed at the Niemen by having to wait a day for the river to freeze sufficiently to support their carriage because the bridge was no longer passable. Barlow had traveled 1,400 miles to see Napoleon only to have the retreating emperor pass Barlow's party by on the night of December 8, while they were taking a few hours rest at a post house. Napoleon traveled disguised as Marshall Duzac, without his customary military escort, in a carriage equipped with sleigh runners. But no one was deceived by his attempts to remain incognito since the imperial authority was repeatedly invoked to requisition the best horses and supplies. Barlow wondered whether he was flying from the severity of the winter and the Cossacks or simply wanted to beat the news of the disaster to Paris. He felt Napoleon's *"flight* from his *army* is as *shameful* as his *marshalls* ['who] will not be able to bring *off* so many of *his Troops."* As the extent of the catastrophe became more apparent, Barlow began crediting the rumor that Napoleon had been forced to flee for fear of his own men.[30]

On December 5, the news of Napoleon's defeat at Berezina transformed boredom

Despite Bassano's heroic attempt to maintain appearances in Warsaw, Barlow realized that his trip had been futile. The realization underscored "the indescribable horrors of this campaign," to which Barlow claimed words could not do justice.[31] Yet that is exactly what he did in an eighty-two-line poem, "Advice to the

Raven of Russia," most likely written during his four-day sojourn in the Polish capital.[32] The poem posits a symbiotic relationship between Napoleon and ravens, referring to "human carnage" as "that delicious fare, / That lured you hither, following still your friend, / The great Napoleon to the world's bleak end" (6–8). Ravens can find food anywhere because war's destructiveness is universal and the birds serve a useful function. "While on his slaughter'd troops your tribes are fed, / You cleanse his camp and carry off his dead" (47–48).

Barlow advises the scavenging ravens that there are better pickings than frozen corpses. The birds cannot

> tear one fiber from their breast.
> No! from their visual sockets as they lie,
> With beak and claws you cannot pluck an eye.
> The frozen orb, preserving still its form,
> Defies your talons as it braves the storm,
> But stands and stares to God, as if to know,
> In what curst hands he leaves the world below.   (56–62)

The ravens best course is to follow Napoleon in his flight to fresh fields of slaughter, where they are insured a bright future.

> Till men resume their souls, and dare to shed
> Earth's total vengeance on the monster's head,
> Hurl from his blood-built throne this king of woes,
> Dash him to dust, and let the world repose.   (80–83)

Barlow may have sensed as he was completing his poem that he would soon join the carrion on which ravens fed. Though he had repeatedly assured Ruth that his "vulgar health" had remained good during the journey to Vilna, Tom later reported that Barlow had experienced a bout of "relax" (diarrhea?) at Warsaw, from which he had not fully recovered before they had been forced to depart.[33] On the evening of December 17, Barlow uncharacteristically mentioned his "anxiety" to Ruth, though he pretended it related to getting "the business of my country done."[34] On the morning of the eighteenth, two days after Napoleon arrived in Paris, Barlow's party turned to the southwest, hoping to escape both the rigors of winter and the main thrust of the Cossack advance. An inveterate sightseer to the end, Barlow looked forward to passing for the first time through Kraków, Prague, Vienna, and Munich.

On the nineteenth, he began experiencing respiratory symptoms. Since the alternative to carrying on was to risk being caught by the Cossacks, they presse forward. The next day Barlow's condition worsened as a headache and fever set in. After they reached the town of Zarnowiec—roughly one hundred miles south southwest of Warsaw—it was clear Barlow could travel no further. Petry prevailed upon the mayor of the village to take Barlow into his home, hoping that food and warmth would be enough to revive him. Instead, Barlow continued to decline, despite the attention of a physician from a neighboring town. On the twenty-fifth, a second doctor confirmed the first's diagnosis of pneumonia that had proceeded beyond the possibility of recovery. By then Barlow was in a coma. He died the next day around noon, leaving Tom without the support and protection his famous uncle had provided and the United States without a fully accredited minister to France.

Tom wanted to transport the body to Königsberg for shipment to the United States and burial at home, but Petry quickly dissuaded him. Instead, they hastily interred Barlow in the parish churchyard at Zarnowiec, where he lies to this day, despite several efforts to repatriate his remains.[35] The two men then drafted letters about Barlow's death to the foreign ministry and to Ruth and Daniel Parker before leaving on the twenty-seventh for Kraków.[36] The Cossacks, who had begun pillaging in the neighborhood, entered the village shortly after their departure.

Barlow's death would not be known in Paris for almost three weeks because of the disruption of the mails. Napoleon's muzzling of the press also contributed to the delay, as did the foreign ministry's secretiveness. Petry wrote Ruth a misleading letter from Vienna, claiming that he had left Barlow in Warsaw too "indisposed to travel."[37] Nonetheless, the long hiatus in the flow of her husband's letters, together with garbled reports of the retreat of the Grand Army that circulated despite the emperor's censors, had prepared Ruth for the worst.

Her last letter to Barlow had declared, "all my happiness depends on my heart's friend, the love of my age, Partner of my youth of my joys, & sorrows."[38] Receipt of an official notification shortly before Tom stumbled into the legation on rue de Vaugirard left her bereft. Clara and Tom quickly informed William Lee and urged him to come to Paris to assist Ruth with the legation's affairs. The Senate had not yet confirmed Tom's appointment as secretary, and, in any case, he felt lost without his uncle's guidance. Lee was unable to leave Bordeaux until January 23 and did not arrive in the capital until the end of the month. In the meantime, David Warden stepped forward to inform Bassano that he was the only legal representative of the United States in Paris. He also hectored Ruth for the legation's papers and eventually got the French foreign ministry to declare him chargé d'affaires for United States.[39]

Ruth thought Warden acted improperly because Barlow had purposely declined to appoint him chargé d'affaires before leaving Paris. Against Parker's initial advice, she withheld the legation's seal, cipher, and papers from Warden. Ruth stood her ground against Warden's bullying, supported by Tom, Clara, Lee, and eventually even by Parker. Lee was in an awkward position because he had drawn two salaries while performing the duties of secretary of the legation. The arrangement, which Barlow had sanctioned to make Lee's circumstances more comfortable, was contrary to a congressional ban against multiple office holding.[40] This circumstance, together with Tom's youth, inexperience, and diminutive stature, not to mention the continuing enmity between Parker and Lee, compromised their efforts to check Warden.

Lee instructed Tom to insist that as the secretary to the legation he enjoyed precedence over Warden, but the foreign ministry refused to agree despite the protests Lee had Tom file with Bassano.[41] Lee also wrote Dolley Madison a long letter explaining why they had resolved to keep the seal and cipher out of Warden's hands. They feared he would give it to the French, though Warden claimed he sought possession of the cipher as a precaution against Parker gaining access to it. Lee understood the importance of having a functioning legation in France during a war with Britain, and he would have welcomed appointment as chargé d'affaires. But to avoid further scrutiny he recommended George Erving, then minister to Denmark, for the position.

Lee felt less compunction about exploiting sympathy for Ruth in attacking Warden and accused him of having greatly increased her suffering.[42] Clara had already given the first lady a graphic description of Warden's behavior. She told Dolley why Barlow had never fully trusted Warden. He was a man of inferior abilities whom Barlow had tolerated but had only trusted with minor tasks like the disposition of prisoners. Clara added that as a naturalized citizen of the United States Warden lacked the American connections that family and property might have created. She particularly objected to the way Warden had behaved to Ruth, claiming he seemed determined to "kill my poor dear sister" whose "agitated mind & delicate health are not adequate to the burden fate has allotted her to bear."[43] Warden had hinted to Ruth that once Madison found out about the terms of the indemnity provision in the treaty Barlow had negotiated, her husband would be discredited.[44]

At first Ruth thought Tom should set out as soon as possible for the United States, despite having "suffered much . . . & [being] quite ill" with "a dreadful cold & pain in his breast." Ruth felt that no one else had the information Tom possessed. But Warden carried matters to such extremes that the family decided Tor had better stay "to protect the papers."[45] That left the French government watching the spectacle of a callow youth challenging the credentials of an older man, while denying Warden crucial assets that a chargé d'affaires needed. In effect, the Franco-American relationship would remain immobilized by internal squabbles until Ambassador William H. Crawford arrived the following summer. After reviewing the situation, Crawford recommended Warden's removal as consul general.

In addition to diplomatic collapse, Barlow's death left a big hole in the lives of all those associated with him. Lee spoke publicly for them in acknowledging their grievous loss. Ruth sustained hers with the dignity she had displayed during her illnesses, fortified first by shock and then by the affectionate support of many prominent French and American friends. Lafayette and Pierre Samuel Dupont offered their sympathy, and the expatriate American community went into public mourning, framing an address of condolence to Ruth, to which Warden refused to subscribe.[46] It helped Ruth to have so many personal friends share her sorrow. It must also have been reassuring that her unofficial authority over the legation was supported by Barlow's closest friends, including Parker, Madame de Villette, and Erving after he arrived in Paris.

Fulton, in New York, learned of Barlow's death at the end of February 1813, only hours after the death of his partner Robert R. Livingston. As surrogate father and faithful friend for sixteen years, Barlow, more than anyone besides Ruth, had offered the support and guidance that helped Fulton make something of his genius. His death left Fulton feeling "abandoned and exposed." "None knew him as well as I did," he lamented to Jefferson.[47] It did not help Fulton in absorbing his double loss that his circumstances were generally unhappy. Even after the recent birth of a third child, Harriet and Fulton were not content in their marriage. He also had financial difficulties, despite the success of his steamboats. If Ruth had been around to console him, it would not have helped his marriage, since his relationship with the Barlows had been a source of tension with Harriet and would remain so in the future.[48]

Nonetheless, Fulton went out of his way to stay close to "Ruthlinda." In June 1813, he asked her to approach the sculptor Houdon about doing busts of Washington, Jefferson, Franklin, Barlow, and himself, authorizing her to commission the work if the price was five thousand francs or less. He also offered to sell the $12,000 investment Barlow had in Alexander Wolcott's Middletown Manufacturing Company, which had yet to pay a dividend, and put the money into an enterprise he promised would yield $2,000 to $3,000 per annum. Wartime interest rates were high, but Fulton must have had one of his steamboats in mind. Ruth was not to worry, though, because Fulton still claimed to have a fortune of $30,000 per year. "Tooty [the Barlows' nickname for Fulton] is always the same and will ever be disinterested and kind," he assured her.[49]

In 1814, Fulton discovered that the title to some Illinois lands, which Barlow, Seth Hunt, Gideon Granger, and Joseph Nancrede had speculated in and sold, had been called into doubt by a French baron, who claimed he still owned them. Fulton was concerned for Barlow's reputation: "In as much as I sincerely loved Barlow and his fame was as dear to me as my own, and in an intimate acquaintance of 12 years I never knew a dishonest Act or Sentiment in him, this affair grieves me exceedingly."[50] Fulton blamed the misfortune on Nancrede, a controversial Frenchman who was a naturalized American citizen. But because Barlow's estate would be liable to those who had bought the land, Fulton agreed with Granger that "the honor of Barlow's fame" required his partners "to get in the title" whatever the cost.[51] Fulton was less concerned about Ruth's financial well-being, since the $20,000 she had inherited from her brother Abraham was immune to any claims brought against Barlow's estate.

Barlow had died a rich man. The inventory of his estate made before his departure for Vilna and the will Ruth made from that inventory in August 1813 before returning to America listed well over $100,000 in bank, canal, and manufacturing stock, plus title to extensive western lands. Questions about the solvency of his estate never arose because the claims against it never exceeded $35,000. After Ruth was forced to part with some bank stock to settle Barlow's debts, she worried briefly that there was not much left besides bad debts and houses she couldn't sell. That turned out to be an exaggeration, despite the government's procrastination in settling Barlow's accounts.[52] Ruth would never be in need, and she lived on till 1818, eventually dying at Kalorama. Upon her death, the house passed to Tom, who then sold it to Clara and her new husband, Col. George Bomford. They lived there until the mid-1840s. To a greater extent than Barlow realized, his dreams of achieving financial independence for himself and his family had become reality.

Barlow would remain almost as controversial in death as he had been in life. In 1834 John Armstrong was still circulating a scurrilous version of Barlow's private diplomacy during the Quasi War of 1798–1800, allegedly based on information Armstrong had obtained from Parker.[53] Armstrong claimed that Talleyrand had put Barlow up to writing his 1798 letter to Washington in exchange for receiving an exclusive privilege to import American tobacco into France. Barlow had then transferred the franchise to Lee as part of their business arrangements, but Lee had been unable to derive any benefit from it. The only way Barlow could cover the loss was to prevail on Jefferson to make Lee U.S. consul in Bordeaux, which forced Isaac Barnet's dismissal from that post. Armstrong's twisted interpretation of events did not specify what Barlow had received from Lee that required a tobacco monopoly as compensation, nor could it explain why Barnet was on such good terms with Barlow at the end of Barlow's life. It does, however, draw our attention to the conflicting passions Barlow inspired among his contemporaries, which in turn have survived in recent accounts of their lives.

The controversies Barlow inspired raise questions about the larger significance of his life. Though the many inconsistencies that characterized his career invited criticism, the intensity of the condemnations he met went beyond what the circumstances warranted. It would be a mistake to attribute these criticisms solely to the partisan divide that emerged between Federalists and Republicans during his last twenty years. Instead, they had a deeper source. In an age that historians now celebrate as giving rise to modern nationalisms, Barlow's cosmopolitanism was emblematic of a complex relationship to his times and ours. Though he ended up touting the United States as the last best hope of republicanism, he did so only because France's militarism had led her to betray her republicanism. Barlow's writings always strove to provide a global diagnosis of the human condition and to envision ecumenical solutions. That approach makes him especially relevant today when humanity faces a range of issues like global warming and the control of nuclear weapons that defy the capacity of any one nation, no matter how powerful, to resolve.

While Barlow often fell victim to his own grandiose visions, and never more so than during his last mission, he was neither as devious nor as impractical as his critics claimed. Much of what he advocated now enjoys wide currency if not universal acceptance: his republicanism, his belief in the liberating power of technology, his call for a national educational system, his vision of a peaceful world order based on commerce and presided over by the community of nations, his ecumenical view of human history, and even his secularization of the Christian millennium. Despite being born and nurtured in a premodern culture, Barlow speaks to us today in a modern idiom, underscoring the enduring nature of many of the axioms that underpin our lives. Barlow's visionary perspective antagonized some of his contemporaries. They thought that dealing with the world as it was was more urgent than dreaming about the way it should be. Barlow succeeded in living gracefully with the hostility his ideas provoked because he realized they inflamed the fears of those who distrusted a world in tumultuous transition. That world subjected everyone to conflicting pressures, involving them in contradictions that Barlow's life exemplified—more than most—because of his wide-ranging activities.

Two hundred years later, our world is undergoing a similar ferment. Visionaries like Barlow, who strive to address the big picture, invariably incur the antagonism of those who feel threatened by change and are preoccupied with the immediacy of their parochial interests. Yet in unsettled times like our own, we need visionaries even more than those who are focused on coping with the exigencies of the moment. Without a healthy tension between the grounded "realists" and those whose gaze is fixed on the larger dimensions of what might be, the best options for tomorrow will elude us. Joel Barlow's attempts to reconcile his commitment to defining the larger mission of his generation with his quest for economic security, political influence, and gentility were often not successful. But, during the Age of Revolution, he spoke as one of humanity's better angels, and any age, including our own, that ignores such figures does so at its peril.

Acknowledgments

I am indebted to the staffs of many libraries and museums—too numerous to be acknowledged—in the United States and Europe for assistance in researching this book. However, I cannot refrain from mentioning a few individuals who were especially helpful. They include Peter Drummey of the Massachusetts Historical Society, Anne B. Shepherd of the Cincinnati Historical Society Library, Roy E. Goodman of the American Philosophical Society, Thomas G. Lannon of the New York Public Library, Edward O'Reilly of the New York Historical Society, Judy Schiff of the Manuscripts and Archives division of the Yale University Library, and Lizanne Reger of the National Portrait Gallery.

Quotations referenced by the abbreviation BPL are printed courtesy of the trustees of the Boston Public Library, Rare Books; those referenced by HB (the Hay Library at Brown University), courtesy of the Brown University Library; those referenced by NYPL, courtesy of the Manuscripts and Archives Division of the New York Public Library, Astor, Lenox and Tilden Foundations. Special thanks are due to the University Press of Virginia, and particularly David Sewell, for allowing me temporary access to the *Dolley Madison Digital Edition*, edited by Holly C. Shulman, so that I might check the accuracy of Samuel Olmsted's transcriptions of documents contained therein.

I am grateful to Kate Wessling, M.D., for some of the medical information in the text; to Charles A. Couch for taking me on a tour of historic Redding, Connecticut; to Robert Mankin of the University of Paris, for helping me with local arrangements; to Philipp Ziesche, who shared the draft of two chapters from his *Cosmopolitan Patriots: Americans in Paris in the Age of the French Revolution* (2010) with me; and to Peter Onuf, Jean-François Dunyach, and Howard G. Brown for reading and commenting on all or portions of the manuscript. The book has benefited from the editorial suggestions of Robert J. Brugger and the editing of Julia Ridley Smith and Kimberly F. Johnson.

Without an emeritus fellowship from the Andrew W. Mellon Foundation during 2005–2007, I would never have undertaken this biography. Without the continuing support of the Olin Memorial Library at Wesleyan University, I could not have brought the book to completion. I am especially indebted to John Wareham, of Wesleyan's Information Technology Services, for processing the illustrations that appear in the book; and to Emilie Bremond-Poule, my research assistant in Paris, who helped me navigate the intricacies of France's historical archives. My greatest debt, though, is to my wife, Marilyn, who carefully read the manuscript at several stages in its development and who has encouraged and supported all my scholarly efforts.

Abbreviations

MANUSCRIPT ARCHIVES

The Joel Barlow Papers in the Houghton Library at Harvard University, Cambridge, MA (MS Am 1448), are designated by BPH. The collection includes letters from Barlow organized alphabetically by recipient and then chronologically (items 64–529). These precede Barlow's incoming correspondence (items 530–645), also arranged alphabetically and chronologically by sender. Last are letters to and from others pertaining to Barlow (items 646–79), together with miscellaneous materials assembled by the family after Barlow's death, including accounts and receipts from his Algerian mission and legal papers (items 680–720). In addition I have cited four Barlow letter books, designated in the notes as BPH:LB (items 1–4); a Bank of Washington Letter Book, designated as BPH:LB (item 6); two brief diaries (1788), designated as H: Diary (items 9 & 10); various manuscript writings, designated as BPH:Litmss (with item no.); and several notebooks, designated as BPH:Notebook (with item no.). Members of the Baldwin and Barlow families have been assigned the following codes for this and the other manuscript collections referenced in this work:

AaB	Aaron Barlow
AbB	Abraham Baldwin
CB	Clara Baldwin Bomford
HB	Henry Baldwin
JB	Joel Barlow
RB	Ruth Baldwin Barlow
SB	Stephen Barlow
TB	Thomas Barlow

Additional locations and major manuscript collections are abbreviated as follows:

AAS   American Antiquarian Society, Worcester, MA
      ACP   Andrew Craigie Papers
      JBP   Joel Barlow Papers
AE   Archives des Affaires étrangères, Paris
      Cd   Correspondance diplomatique: Etats-Unis, vols. 30–31
      Cp   Correspondence politique: Etats-Unis, vols. 51, 65–72
AN   Archives nationales, Centre historique, Paris
      AD   Series d'Archives (microfilm)
      MIN   Minutier central des notaries de Ville de Paris
APS   American Philosophical Society, Philadelphia, PA
      SHMOP Smith, Houston, Morris, Ogden Papers
BLC   Baker Library, Columbia University, New York
      GMP   Gouverneur Morris Papers
BPL   Boston Public Library
CHS   The Connecticut Historical Society, Hartford
      BP   Barlow Papers
      OWP   Oliver Wolcott Jr. Papers
CIN   Cincinnati Historical Society Library, Cincinnati Museum Center, Cincinnati, OH
      Gal   Gallipolis Papers, Mss fG171c RM
CSL   Connecticut State Library, Hartford
      P   Probate files
      RWR   Revolutionary War Records
HB   Hay Library, Brown University, Providence, RI
      JRP   Jonathan Russell Papers
HL   Huntington Library, San Marino, CA
      BFP   Baldwin Family Papers, BN 73
HSP   Historical Society of Pennsylvania, Philadelphia
      TCP   Tench Coxe Papers
LC   Library of Congress, Washington, DC
      DBWP David Bailie Warden Papers
      H-SP   Henley-Smith Papers
      JHP   John Henry Papers
      JMonP James Monroe Papers
      JMadP James Madison Papers
      L-PP   Lee-Palfrey Papers

TJP   Thomas Jefferson Papers, General Correspondence
WLP   William Lee Papers
WSP   William Short Papers
MaHS   Massachusetts Historical Society, Boston
BTP   Bowdoin Temple Papers in the Winthrop Family
        Papers
HDP   Henry Dearborn Papers
HKP   Henry Knox Papers
JRP   Jonathan Russell Papers
MOW   Mercy Otis Warren Papers
TFDP   T. F. Dwight Papers
WLFP   William Livingston Family Papers
WSP   Winthrop Sargent Papers
NA   National Archives, Silver Spring, MD. Record Groups as noted.
CC   Consular Correspondence
DC   Diplomatic Correspondence
PCC   Papers of the Continental Congress
NPG   National Portrait Gallery, Washington, DC
NWU   Charles Deering McCormick Library of Special Collections, North-
        western University Library, Evanston, IL
MCP   Manasseh Cutler Papers
NYHS   New York Historical Society, New York
JBP   Barlow Papers
RFP   Robert Fulton Papers
SCP   Scioto and Ohio Land Company Papers
WDP   William Duer Papers
NYPL   Manuscripts and Archives Division, New York Public Library, New York
JMonP   James Monroe Papers
PRO   Public Records Office, Kew Gardens, London
HCA   High Court of Admiralty Records
RLR   Redding, CT, Land Records
UGa   Courtesy of Hargrett Rare Book and Manuscript Library / University of
        Georgia Libraries, Athens
ABP   Abraham Baldwin Papers
YB   Yale University, Beinecke Library, New Haven, CT
BPBarlow Papers (Za Barlow)
BPq   Barlow Papers on loan from the Pequot Library,
        Southport, CT

YS   Yale University, Manuscripts and Archives, Sterling Memorial Library,
New Haven, CT
HMO   Humphreys-Marvin-Olmstead Collection MS 857
K   Knollenburg Collection MS 1017
MM   Miscellaneous Manuscripts MS 352, folders 71–71

PUBLISHED PRIMARY SOURCES

AmMercury   *American Mercury* (Hartford)
AP   *Archives Parlementaires* (Paris)
AR   *Annual Register* (London)
ARAHA   *Annual Report of the American Historical Association*, 1912
ASP   *American State Papers, Documents Legislative and Executive,
of the Congress of the United States . . . Foreign Relations.*
6 vols. Washington, DC: Gales and Seaton, 1832–59.
BW   Joel Barlow. *The Works of Joel Barlow in Two Volumes.*
Introduction by William K. Bottorff and Arthur L. Ford.
2 vols. Gainesville, FL: Scholars' Facsimiles and Reprints,
1970.
ColCentinel   *Columbian Centinel* (Boston)
CtCourant   *Connecticut Courant* (Hartford)
CtMirror   *Connecticut Mirror* (Hartford)
DMDE   *The Dolley Madison Digital Edition.* Ed. Holly C. Shulman.
Charlottesville: University of Virginia Press, Rotunda, 2004.
DPCUS   *The Debates and Proceedings of the Congress of the United
States . . .* Washington, DC: Gales and Seaton, 1834–56.
JCC   *Journals of the Continental Congress, 1774–1789.* 34 vols.
Ed. Worthington Chauncey Ford. Washington, DC: GPO,
1904–37.
MA   *Monthly Anthology* (Boston)
MHSC   *Massachusetts Historical Society, Collections.* 2nd. Ser., 8
(1826): 269–70.
Mon   *Gazette nationale, ou le Moniteur universel* (1792–1804)
Morris, *Diary*   Gouverneur Morris. *A Diary of the French Revolution . . .*
Ed. Beatrix Cary Davenport. 2 vols. Boston: Houghton
Mifflin Co., 1939.
NI   *National Intelligencer* (Washington, DC)

PAH   *The Papers of Alexander Hamilton.* Ed. Harold C. Syrett.
                   27 vols. New York: Columbia University Press, 1961–87.
PGW:P   *Papers of George Washington, Presidential Series.* Ed. Dorothy
                   Twohig, Mark A. Mastromarino, Jack D. Warren Jr., Chris-
                   tine Sternberg Patrick, and David R. Hoth. 14 vols. to date.
                   Charlottesville: University Press of Virginia, 1987–.
PGW:R   *Papers of George Washington, Retirement Series.* Ed. W. W.
                   Abbot and Edward G. Lengel. 5 vols. Charlottesville: Univer-
                   sity Press of Virginia, 1998–99.
PJMad:PS   *The Papers of James Madison. Presidential Series.* Ed. Robert
                   A. Rutland, J. C. A. Stagg, and Angela Kreider. 6 vols to date.
                   Charlottesville: University Press of Virginia, 1984–.
PJMad:SS   *The Papers of James Madison. Secretary of State Series.* Ed.
                   Robert J. Brugger, Mary A. Hackett, and Paul Mattern. 8 vols.
                   to date. Charlottesville: University Press of Virginia, 1986–.
PMarsh   *The Papers of John Marshall.* Ed. Herbert A. Johnson,
                   Charles T. Cullen, and Charles A. Hobson. 12 vols. Chapel
                   Hill: University of North Carolina Press, 1974–2006.
PTJ   *The Papers of Thomas Jefferson.* Ed. Julian P. Boyd, Charles T.
                   Cullen, John Catanzariti, and Barbara B. Oberg. 36 vols. to
                   date. Princeton: Princeton University Press, 1950–.
Stiles, *LitDiary* Ezra Stiles. *The Literary Diary of Ezra Stiles, D.D., L.L.D.*
                   Ed. Franklin B. Dexter. 3 vols. New York: Scribner's, 1901.
SUS   *The Susquehannah Company Papers.* Ed. Julian P. Boyd and
                   Robert J. Taylor. 11 vols. Ithaca, NY: Cornell University Press,
                   1968–1971.
WJMon   James Monroe. *The Writings of James Monroe . . .*
                   Ed. Stanislaus M. Hamilton. 7 vols. New York: G. P. Putnam's
                   Sons, 1898–1903.

Notes

1. JB to RB, July 8, 1796, in BPH, #271.

1. Charles B. Todd, *The History of Redding, Conn., from its first settlement to the present time* (New York: John A. Gray Press, 1880), 175; mss genealogy supplied by Clara Hill to Samuel L. Mitchell Barlow, June 30, 1935, in BPH, #680.

2. CSL:P.

3. JB to Oliver Wolcott Jr., Nov. 4, 1779, in CHS:BP.

4. Patricia Crain, *The Story of A: The Alphabetization of America from* The New England Primer *to* The Scarlet Letter (Stanford: Stanford University Press, 2000).

5. RLR: II, 64.

6. William E. Grumman, *The Revolutionary Soldiers of Redding, Connecticut* . . . (Hartford, CT: Hartford Press, 1904), 33.

7. CSL:P.

8. The letter, dated July 15, in JB's hand is in AB's commonplace book, UG:ABP, 97–92:2, folder 81.

9. This quotation and the following one come from Eleazer Wheelock to Napht-alie Daggett, Nov. 8, 1774, in Theodore A. Zunder, *The Early Days of Joel Barlow, A Connecticut Wit* . . . (New Haven: Yale University Press, 1934), 18.

10. JB to Esther Barlow, July 6, 1775, in BPH, #105.

11. JB's account book, in YB:BPq, M886.

12. See Book VII, lines 23–34.

13. Book VIII, lines 58–68.

14. CSL:P.

15. Leon Howard, *The Connecticut Wits* (Chicago: University of Chicago Press, 1943), 23.

16. *A Catalogue of the Society of Brothers in Unity, Yale College, founded in 1768* (New Haven, CT: Hitchcock and Stafford, 1841).

17. Zunder, *Early Days of Barlow*, 100.

18. Ibid., 40.

19. Brooks M. Kelley, *Yale: A History* (New Haven, CT: Yale University Press, 1974), 86.

20. CSL:RWR, 1st ser., 20: 277 and 278.

21. Pierre Samuel Dupont de Nemours, "Notice Sur La Vie De M. Barlow," in *Mercure de France*, April 10, 1813; Konrad Englebert Oelsner, *Notice sur la vie et les écrits de M. Joël Barlow, ministre plénipotentaire des États-Unis d'Amérique auprês de s. m. l'empereur des Français* (Paris, 1813), 4.

22. Damon G. Douglas, *The Bridge Not Taken: Benedict Arnold Outwitted* (Westport, CT: Westport Historical Society, 2002), 10 ff., for this and what follows.

23. James R. Case, *An Account of Tryon's raid on Danbury in April, 1777* . . . (Danbury, CT: The Danbury Publishing Co., 1927), 13–14.

24. "O'er Reading Hills / High flaming Danbury the welkin fills," Bk. V, lines 503–4.

25. Richard M. Rollins, ed., *The Autobiographies of Noah Webster: From the Letters and Essays, Memoir, and Diary* (Columbia: University of South Carolina Press, 1989), 67–68.

26. Stiles, *LitDiary*, 2:227.

27. Ibid., 288. The numbers in parentheses refer to the lines of the poem.

28. Joseph Buckminster to JB, Oct. 5, 1778, in YB:BPq, M952.

CHAPTER 2: AMBITIOUS GOALS

1. Stiles, *LitDiary*, 2:294.

2. Joseph Buckminster to JB, Oct. 5, 1778, in YB:BPq, M952.

3. Joseph Buckminster to JB, Jan. 11, 1779, in YB:BPq, M953.

4. JB to Joseph Buckminster, Mar. 19, 1779, in LC:H-SP.

5. Charles C. Baldwin, *The Baldwin Genealogy from 1500 to 1881* (Cleveland, OH: 1881), 419, 1084; RB to JB, Feb. 13, 1782, addenda dated Feb. 22, in YB:BP, #14.

6. See AbB to RB, June 9, 1794, in BPH, #649.

7. JB to Noah Webster, Jan. 30, 1779, in BPH, #518.

8. Elizabeth Whitman to JB, Feb. 19, 22, Mar. 29, 1779, in Caroline W. H. Dall, *The Romance of the Association; or, One last glimpse of Charlotte Temple and Eliza Wharton. A Curiosity of literature and life* (Cambridge, MA: J. Wilson and Son, 1875), 80, 83 (quote), 86. Most but not all of the originals reprinted in Dall are currently in HL:BFP. Despite minor deviations in Dall's transcriptions (Feb. 19 in Dall is Feb. 16 in the original), I have used Dall's texts because they are more accessible.

9. Elizabeth Whitman to JB, Mar. 17, 1779, in Dall, *Romance*, 85.

10. Elizabeth Whitman to JB, Feb. 22 and Apr. 15, 1779, in Dall, *Romance*, 84, 88.

11. Joseph Buckminster to JB, Mar. 9, 1779, in YB:BPq, M954.

12. JB to Oliver Wolcott Jr., Mar. 17, 1779, in CHS:BP.

13. See JB receipt to James Barlow for $200 continental currency, dated Oct. 15, 1779, in NYPL, Joel Barlow Papers.

14. In BPH:Litmss, #43.

15. JB to Joseph Buckminster, Mar. 19, 1779, in LC:H-SP; Joseph Buckminster to JB, Apr. 5, 1779, in YB:BPq, M955.

16. JB to Joseph Buckminster, Mar. 19, 1779, in LC:H-SP.

17. JB to Noah Webster, Jan. 30, 1779, in BPH, #518; JB to Oliver Wolcott Jr., Mar. 11, 1779, in CHS:BP.

18. Elizabeth Whitman to JB, May 10, 1779, in Dall, *Romance*, 91.

19. JB to RB, July 26, 1779, in BPH, #109.

20. JB to RB, Sept. 2, 1779, in BPH, #110; JB to Noah Webster, Aug. 17, 1779, in BPH, #519.

21. In BPH:Litmss, #51.

22. JB to RB, Sept. 26, 1779, in BPH, #111.

23. Elizabeth Whitman to JB, Oct. 17, 1779, in Dall, *Romance*, 93, 94.

24. JB to RB, n.d. (Oct. ?) and Oct. 12, 1779, in BPH, #114, #112.

25. Joseph Buckminster to JB, Oct. 26, 1779, in YB:BPq, M957.

26. JB to Noah Webster, Oct. 21, 1779, in BPH, #520.

27. JB to Oliver Wolcott Jr., Dec. 13, 1779, in CHS:BP.

28. Elizabeth Whitman to JB, Nov. ?, 1779 in Dall, *Romance*, 95.

29. Elizabeth Whitman to JB, Feb. 25, 1780, and May 12, 1781, in Dall, *Romance*, 98, 99.

30. AbB to JB, Dec. 31, 1779, in YS:MM, folder 71.

31. AbB to JB, Dec. 21 and 31, 1779, in YS:MM, folder 71; AbB to JB, Feb. 2, 1781, in BPH, #535.

32. In UGa:ABP, 97–92a:2, folder 81.

33. JB to RB, Sept. 11, 1780, in BPH, #126; Theodore A. Zunder, *The Early Days of Joel Barlow, A Connecticut Wit* (New Haven: Yale University Press, 1934), 108.

34. JB to RB, Oct. 18, 1780, in BPH, #131.

35. JB to RB, Oct. 2 and 18, 1780, in BPH, #129, #131.

36. JB to RB, Sept. 11 and 23, 1780, in BPH, #126, #128.

37. JB to RB, Oct. 29, 1780, in BPH, #132.

38. JB to RB, Oct. 18, 1780, in BPH, #131.

39. JB to RB, Oct. 29, 1780 in BPH, #132.

40. In BPH, #134.

41. From the sketch in Franklin Bowditch Dexter, *Biographical sketches of the graduates of Yale college with accounts of the college history . . .*, 6 vols. (New York: Henry Holt and Co., 1885–1913), 3:637.

42. See JB to RB, Apr. or (May?) 4, 1780, in BPH, #123.

43. JB to RB, Apr. 17, 1781, in BPH, #140; their relationship probably resembled Capac and Oella's in *The Vision of Columbus*, Book II, lines 479 ff.

CHAPTER 3: UNCHARTED WATERS

1. JB to RB, Feb. 11 and 12, 1781, in BPH, #136, #137.

2. JB to RB, Feb. 12 and 26, 1781, in BPH, #137, #138.

3. JB to RB, Feb. 12, 1781, in BPH, #137.

4. JB to RB, Mar. 12, 1781, in BPH, #139.

5. Theodore A. Zunder, *The Early Days of Joel Barlow, A Connecticut Wit* (New Haven, CT: Yale University Press, 1934), 122.

6. JB to RB, June 19, 1781, in BPH, #142.

7. JB to RB, June 10, 1781, in BPH, #141.

8. JB to RB, July 19, 1781, in BPH, #143.

9. JB to RB, July 21 and 22, 1781, addenda to JB to RB, July 19, 1781, in BPH, #143.

10. Stiles, *LitDiary*, 2:556.

11. Ibid., 2:553.

12. Ibid., 2:556–57.

13. In the *New York Packet*, Oct. 25, 1781.

14. JB to RB, Oct. 25, 1781, in BPH, #148.

15. JB to RB, Nov. 29, 1781, in BPH, #149.

16. JB to RB, Jan. 5, 1782, in BPH, #150.

17. JB to Noah Webster, Aug. 31, 1782, in BPH, #531.

18. JB to RB, Jan. 19, 1782, in BPH, #153.

19. With JB to RB, Jan. 5, 1782, in BPH, #150.

20. AbB to RB, Jan. 23, 1782 (misdated 1781), in BPH, #646.

21. JB to RB, Nov. 15, 1782, in BPH, #171.

22. JB to RB, Feb. 21, 1782, in BPH, #155.

23. AbB to RB, Jan. 23, 1782 (misdated 1781), in BPH, #646.

24. RB to JB, Feb. 13, 1782, in YB:BP, #14.

25. JB to RB, Feb. 21, 1782, in BPH, #155.

26. JB to RB, Mar. 9, 1782, in BPH, #156.

27. AbB to RB, Mar. [?], 1782, in BPH, #648.

28. JB to RB, Mar. 16, 1782, in BPH, #157.

29. JB to Michael Baldwin, Mar. 20, 1782, in BPH, #160, filed with letters to RB.

30. JB to RB June 18, 1782, in BPH, #162.

31. See *CTCourant*, Jan. 1, 1787.

32. JB to RB, Aug. 12, 1782, in BPH, #164.

33. Ibid.

34. JB to Jeremiah Wadsworth, Oct. 4, 1782, in MaHS:TFDP, II.

35. JB to RB, Oct. 24, 1782, in BPH, #168.

36. Ibid.

37. JB to RB, Nov. 2–4, 1782, in BPH, #169.

38. Ibid.

39. JB to RB, Nov. 12, 1782, in BPH, #170.

40. JB to RB, Nov. 15, 1782, in BPH, #172.

41. JB to Elias Boudinot, Jan. 10, 1783, NA:PCC, M247.

42. JB to RB, May 6 and 19, 1783, in BPH, #173, #174.

43. JB to Benjamin Lincoln, May 26, 1783, in NYPL, Thomas Addis Emmet Collection.

44. In CHS:BP.

45. Zunder, *Early Days*, 169.

46. In ibid., Oct. 14, 1783.

47. JB to Nathaniel Greene, Mar. 21, 1784, in Anson P. Stokes, *Memorials of Eminent Yale Men* (New Haven: Yale University Press, 1914), 1:134.

48. JB to RB, June 11, 1784, in BPH, #176.

49. *AmMercury*, Jan. 31, 1785.

50. JB to RB, June 11, 1784, in BPH, #176.

51. JB to RB, June 8, 1785, in BPH, #175 (misdated 1784, see Carla Mulford, "Joel Barlow's Letters, 1775–1788," Ph.D. diss., University of Delaware, 1983, 348.

CHAPTER 4: DEAD ENDS

1. *AmMercury*, Sept. 6, 1784.

2. *CtCourant*, Nov. 15, 1784.

3. Richard M. Rollins, ed., *The Autobiographies of Noah Webster: From the Letters and Essays, Memoir, and Diary* (Columbia: University of South Carolina Press, 1989), 206.

4. Ibid., 235.

5. *CtCourant*, Nov. 23, 1784.

6. Stiles, *LitDiary*, 3:156.

7. *The Political green-house, for the year 1798. Addressed to the readers of the Connecticut Courant, January 1, 1799* (Hartford, 1799), 14 fn.

8. *AmMercury*, Aug. 8, 1785.

9. Ibid., Nov. 3 and 31, 1785.

10. *CtCourant*, Mar. 20, 1786.

11. P. 13.

12. *AmMercury*, Oct. 10, 1785.

13. Rollins, *Autobiographies*, 208–9.

14. JB to Jeremiah Wadsworth, Sept. 10, 1783, in CHS:BP.

15. As reported in the *AmMercury*, Oct. 18, and *CtCourant*, Oct. 19, 1784.

16. AE:Cd, 31: 72.

17. Ibid., 30: 77; BW, 2:103–5.

18. AE:Cd, 31: 72, LC photocopy.

19. Rollins, *Autobiographies*, 207–8.

20. JB to Jeremiah Wadsworth, Sept. 10, 1783, in CHS:BP.

21. Manuscript of Barlow's legal dissertation is in BPH:Litmss, #57.

CHAPTER 5: LITERARY RECOGNITION

1. July 21, 1785, in MaHS:WLFP II.

2. June 5, 1786, in Frank L. Humphreys, *Life and Times of David Humphries, Soldier—Statesman—Poet*, 2 vols. (New York: G. P. Putnam's Sons, 1917), 1:354, 353.

3. "Lemuel Hopkins," *Monthly Magazine and American Review* (1799), 1:468–70, attributed to Elihu H. Smith.

4. *The Anarchiad: A New England Poem, (1786–1787)* . . . , ed. Luther G. Riggs (1861) (Gainsville, FL: Scholars' Facsimiles and Reprints, 1967), 56.

5. Ibid., 8, 11–12.

6. Ibid., 13.

7. Ibid., 16–17.

8. Ibid., 31.

9. Ibid., 34.

10. Ibid., 35.

11. *BW*, 2:191.

12. Ibid., 178–79.

13. Ibid., 184.

14. Ibid., 189.

15. Ibid., 187.

16. Stephen Blakemore, *Joel Barlow's Columbiad: A Bicentennial Reading* (Knoxville: University of Tennessee Press, 2007), 57–58.

17. *BW*, 2:342–43.

18. Ibid., 343–44.

19. Page 22.

20. *AmMercury*, Aug. 25, 1788.

21. Vol. 65: 34–35.

22. Page references in parentheses in the following text are to the text as reproduced in *BW*, vol. 1.

CHAPTER 6: LAND FEVER

1. Andrew R. L. Crayton, *The Frontier Republic: Ideology and Politics in the Ohio Country, 1780–1825* (Kent, OH: Kent State University Press, 1986), 22–25.

2. *AmMercury*, Jan. 3–Feb. 7, Feb. 21, 1785.

3. *AmMercury*, Feb. 21, 1785.

4. *SUS*, 9:74; subsequently cited by Pennsylvania Congressmen, in *SUS*, 10:38, 75.

5. Ibid., 9:132.

6. "Manasseh Cutler," *American National Biography*, ed. John A. Garraty and Mark C. Cones, 24 vols. (New York: Oxford University Press, 1999), 5:939.

7. Journal, Jan. 21, 1787, in NWU:MCP.

8. *JCC*, 24:366.

9. Copies are in NWU:MCP.

10. In BPH, #522.

11. Archer B. Hurlbert, ed., *The Records of the Original Proceedings of the Ohio Company*, 2 vols. (Marietta, OH: Marietta Historical Commission, 1917), 1:lxxvi.

12. Cf. YS:K.

13. Hurlbert, *Records*, 1:26.

14. Joseph Stancliffe Davis, *Essays in the Earlier History of Corporations* (Cambridge, MA: Harvard University Press, 1917), 140 ff.

15. Andrew Craigie to William Duer, Aug. ?, 1787, in NYHS:SCP; also William Duer to Winthrop Sargent, Feb. 17, 1788, in MaHS:WSP.

16. Extract from Manasseh Cutler's Journal, May 10, 1787, in CIN:Gal, IIIB. For Barlow's attitude towards Duer, see JB to Benjamin Walker, October 19, 1791, in CIN:Gal, I.

17. In CIN: Gal, I.

18. Winthrop Sargent to Royal Flint, Apr. 14, 1791, in MaHS:WSP.

19. Theodore A. Zunder, "Joel Barlow and Seasickness," Yale Journal of Biology and Medicine 1 (1929): 389.

20. Daniel Parker to Andrew Craigie, Sept. 26, 1788, in AAS:ACP.

21. JB to William Duer, June 25, 1788, in CIN:Gal, I (copy).

22. Ibid.

23. John Trumbull to William Short, July 21, 1788, in LC:WSP.

24. JB to Nathan Hazard, Aug. 27, 1788, in YB:BPq, M896.

25. BPH:Diary, # 9, Aug., 30, 1788.

26. JB to Nathan Hazard, Aug. 27, 1788, in YB:BPq, M896.

27. Daniel Parker to Andrew Craigie, Sept. 9, 1788, in AAS:ACP.

28. Davis, Essays, 153.

29. Ibid., 159–63.

30. Brissot de Warville to William Duer, Jan. 31, 1789, in NYHS:SCP.

31. James H. Billington, Fire in the Minds of Men: The Origins of Revolutionary Faith (New York: Basic Books, 1980), 25–33.

32. See William Short to Gouverneur Morris, Apr. 11 and July 27, 1789, in BLC:GMP.

33. Morris, Diary, 1:378.

34. JB to Benjamin Walker, Dec. 21, 1790, in NWU:MCP.

35. JB to Winthrop Sargent, Aug. 25, 1789, in MaHS:WSP.

36. JB to RB, Dec. 9, 1789, in YB:BPq, #898.

37. JB to RB, July 28, 1789, in YB:BPq, #897.

38. JB to Benjamin Walker, Dec. 21, 1790, in NWU:MCP.

39. Ibid.

40. Copy in CIN:Gal, IIIA, 40–52.

41. JB to Winthrop Sargent, Aug. 25, 1789, in MaHS:WSP.

42. Thomas Jefferson to John Jay, Aug. 27, 1789, in PTJ, 15:358.

43. JB to Benjamin Walker, Dec. 21, 1790, in NWU:MCP.

44. Copy in CIN:Gal, IIIA, 72–78.

45. JB to William Duer, Nov. 29, 1789, in NYHS:SCP, copy in CIN:Gal, I; JB to Winthrop Sargent, Nov. 28, 1789, in AAS:ACP.

46. In CIN:Gal, I.

47. As recorded in AN:MIN, Étude CXVI.

48. John Trumbull to Oliver Wolcott Jr., Dec. 9, 1798, in George Gibbs, Memoirs of the Administrations of Washington and John Adams, Edited from the Papers of Oliver Wolcott, Secretary of the Treasury, 2 vols. (New York: Scribner's, 1846), 1:25.

49. AbB to JB, May 1 and 8, 1790, in YS:MM, folder 72.

CHAPTER 7: DISGRACE

1. JB to RB, Jan. 1, 1790, in BPH, #178; JB to Andrew Craigie, Jan. 30, 1790, in AAS:ACP.

2. JB to Winthrop Sargent, Nov. 28, 1789, and to Benjamin Tupper, Dec. 8, 1789 (quotes), in AAS:ACP.

3. JB to [?] Boulogne or Bourogne, Jan. 1, 1790, in NYHS:WDP.

4. Henri Carré, "Les Emigrés Français en Amérique," *La Revue de Paris* 5 (May–June, 1898): 311–13, 318–19.

5. JB to William Duer, Dec. 8 and 29, 1789, in NYHS:SCP.

6. Sylvia Harris, "Search for Eden: An Eighteenth-Century Disaster. *Mémoires of Count de Lezay-Marnésia*," *Franco-American Review* 2 (1937): 51.

7. Morris, *Diary*, 1:407.

8. Dated May 19, 1790, in *PAH*, 6:421.

9. As recorded in AN:MIN, Étude CXVI.

10. AbB to JB, May 8, 1790, in YS:MM, folder 72.

11. *Journal Général de la Court et de la Ville*, May 7, 1790.

12. JB to William Duer, Dec. 25, 1790, in CIN:Gal, I, and Dec. 29, 1790, in NYHS:SCP.

13. JB to William Duer, Jan. 25, 1791, in NYHS:SCP.

14. William Playfair to William Duer, Dec. 27, 1790, in CIN:Gal, I; JB to William Duer, Mar. 3, 1790, in NYHS:SCP.

15. William Playfair to William Duer, Dec. 27, 1790, in CIN:Gal, I.

16. *Le Spectateur National*, Jan. 27 and 30, 1790; also *Observations générales et impartiales sur L'Affair du Scioto* (Paris: P. F. Didot le jeune, 1790), 12.

17. *Mon*, Mar. 6 and 16, Apr. 12, 1790; *Chronique de Paris*, Mar. 15, 1790.

18. *Le Nouveau Mississippi ou les dangers d'habiter sur les bords du Scioto, par un patriote voyageur* (Paris, 1790).

19. See William Short to Alexander Hamilton, Apr. 4, 1790, in *PAH*, 6:353; also Short to John Jay, Jan. 2 and 12, 1790, in *PAH*, 6:228 fn.

20. Morris, *Diary*, 1:407.

21. Gouverneur Morris to Thomas Jefferson, Dec. 24, 1790, in *PTJ*, 18:364.

22. Feb. 1, 1791, in AAS:ACP.

23. AbB to JB, May 1 and 8, 1790, in YS:MM, folder 72; for the invitation, see JB to RB, Dec. 8, 1789, in YB:BPq, M898.

24. JB to RB, Mar. 9, 1790, in BPH, #181.

25. William Duer to JB, Apr. 21, 1790, in CIN:Gal, I.

26. Andrew Craigie to JB, May 24, 1790, in AAS:ACP; Morris, *Diary*, 1:536.

27. June 20, 1790, in BPH, #182.

28. JB to RB, June 29 and July 9, 1790, in BPH, #184.

29. Text in *PTJ*, 15:241 n.

30. Text from *Gazette of the United States*, Nov. 27, 1790.

31. JB to RB, July 11, 1790, in BPH, #185.

32. Mona Ozouf, *Festivals and the French Revolution*, trans. Alan Sheridan (Cambridge, MA: Harvard University Press, 1988), 49.

33. JB to RB, July 15, 1790, in BPH, #186.

34. In BPH, #187.

35. In CIN:Gal, I.

36. Playfair declaration, July 30, 1790, in ibid.

37. Rufus Putnam to William Duer, Jan. 28, 1791, in CIN:Gal, I; draft in NWU: MCP.

38. Etienne Nicolas Marie de Rochefontaine to William Duer, Aug. 15, 1790, in NYHS:SCP.

39. Rufus Putnam to William Duer, Jan. 28, 1791, in CIN:Gal, I.

40. Col. David S. Franks to William Duer, Sept. 11 and Oct. 29, 1790, in CIN: Gal, I.

41. Jean Joseph de Barthe to Rufus Putnam, Nov. 8, 1790, in CIN:Gal, I.

42. Rufus Putnam to William Duer, Jan. 28, 1791, in CIN:Gal, I.

43. JB to Winthrop Sargent, Aug. 25, 1789, in MaHS:WSP; also JB to Benjamin Walker, Dec. 21, 1790, in NWU:MCP.

44. JB to RB, July 19, 1790, in BPH, #187.

45. JB to RB, July 8, 1796, in BPH, #271.

46. Andrew Craigie to JB, May 24, 1790, in AAS:ACP.

47. Contract between JB and Etienne Suplice Hallet, Aug. 14, 1790, in NYPL.

48. *Archives Parlementaires*, 17:505.

49. Morris, *Diary*, 1:584; Phyn, Ellices, and Inglis to Gouverneur Morris, Oct. 12, 1790, in APS:SHMOP.

50. Assuming two months for the east-west passage of the protest across the Atlantic, see William Duer to JB, Nov. 4, 1790, in NYHS:SCP.

51. Morris, *Diary*, 2:50, 60.

52. JB to Benjamin Walker, Dec. 21, 1790, in NWU:MCP.

53. RB to Mary Woolsey Dwight, Oct. 3 and 4, 1790, in BPH, #650.

54. Samuel Breck, *Recollections of Samuel Breck with Passages from his Note-Books (1771–1862)*, ed. H. E. Scudder (Philadelphia: Porter and Coates, 1877), 171–72.

55. Theodore T. Belote, *The Scioto Speculation and the French Settlement of Gallipolis. A Study in Ohio Valley History* (New York: Burt Franklin, 1907), 74.

56. Morris, *Diary*, 2:95, 108.

57. Phyn, Ellices, and Inglis to Gouverneur Morris, Nov. 5, 1790, in APS:SHMOP.

58. William Playfair to William Duer, Dec. 27, 1790, in CIN:Gal, I.

59. William Playfair to Alexander Hamilton, Mar. 30, 1791, in *PAH*, 8:231.

60. Benjamin Walker to Alexander Hamilton, Dec. 28, 1790, in *PAH*, 7:388–89.

61. William Playfair to Alexander Hamilton, Sept.–Dec., 1791, in *PAH*, 9:254.

62. Royal Flint[?] to Benjamin Walker, Mar. 26, 1791, in CIN:Gal, I.

63. William Playfair to Alexander Hamilton, Mar. 30, 1791, in *PAH*, 8:229, 232–33; JB to Benjamin Walker, Apr. 10, 1791, copy in BPH, #529.

64. *Mon*, Apr. 16, 1791.

65. See CIN:Gal, III, 114–37, for what the Scioto associates did for the settlers.

66. My evaluation of the settlers' treatment diverges from that of Jocelyne Moreau-Zanelli, *Gallipolis: Histoire d'un mirage américain au XVIIIe siècle* (Paris: l'Hartmattan, 2000), who stresses their victimization.

67. William Duer to Benjamin Walker, Nov. 30, 1790, in CIN:Gal, I; Bruce H. Mann, *Republic of Debtors: Bankruptcy in the Age of American Independence* (Cambridge, MA: Harvard University Press, 2002), 114.

68. JB to AbB, May 3, 1791, in BPH; #65; also JB to Benjamin Walker, Oct. 19, 1791, in CIN:Gal, I.

69. JB to Benjamin Walker, Apr. 10, 1791, copy in BPH, #529.

70. Craigie had facilitated the accommodation; see his letters to JB, June 16, 1790, and to Brissot de Warville, Aug. 31, 1790, in AAS:ACP.

71. JB to AbB, May 3, 1791, in BPH, #65.

72. JB to John Warner, July 16, 1791, in YB:BPq, M900.

73. In YB:BPq, M984.

CHAPTER 8: REVOLUTIONARY ADVENTURER

1. James H. Billington, *Fire in the Minds of Men: The Origins of Revolutionary Faith* (New York: Basic Books, 1980), 30.

2. Richard Price, *Discourse on the Love of our Country* (London: T. Cadell, 1789), 49, 50, 51.

3. JB to AbB, Oct. 17, 1791, in BPH, #66; to William Hayley, Mar. 6, 1792, in HL: BFP; and to Jeremiah Wadsworth, Feb. 2, 1792, in CHS:BP.

4. JB to AbB, Oct. 17, 1791, in BPH, #66.

5. Ford K. Brown, *The Life of William Godwin* (New York: E. P. Dutton, 1926), 39, 40; David Williams, *Incidents of My Own Life Which Have Been Thought of Some Importance* (Brighton, UK: University of Sussex, 1980), 77.

6. Moncure D. Conway, *The Life of Thomas Paine* (New York: G. P. Putnam's Sons, 1909), 1:321.

7. Page numbers in parentheses refer to the pagination of *BW*, vol. 1, rather than that of the original publication.

8. Ensuing references are to lines.

9. JB to Oliver Wolcott Jr., Mar. 18, 1792, in CHS:OWP; and to David Humphreys, Sept. 28, 1792, in YS:HMO.

10. *Morning Chronicle*, Apr. 14, 1792.

11. Lyndall Gordon, *Vindication: A Life of Mary Wollstonecraft* (New York: Harper Collins, 2005), 161, 163.

12. James Swan to Gouverneur Morris, Feb. 15, July 18, and Dec. 12, 1791, in APS: SHMOP.

13. JB to RB, Apr. 25, 1792, in BPH, #189, for this and what follows.

14. JB to RB, May 20, 1792, in BPH, #190.

15. JB to RB, May 31, 1792, in BPH, #191.

16. Morris, *Diary*, 2:444.

17. Ibid., 450.

18. JB to RB, June 10, 1792, in BPH, #193.

19. In BPH, #194.

20. JB to RB, June 25, 1792, in BPH, #195.

21. Morris, *Diary*, 2:446, allegedly using Greene's words.

22. *Annual Register* 35 (1792): 207.

23. At least according to Joseph Johnson, see Thomas Bayly Howell and Thomas Jones Howell, *Cobbett's Complete Collection of State Trials and Proceedings for High Treason . . .* , 34 vols. (London: R. Bagshaw, 1809–29), 24:518.

24. Leon Howard, *The Connecticut Wits* (Chicago: University of Chicago Press, 1943), 289–90.

25. Quotes from Mary Wollstonecraft to her sister, Everina, Feb. 23, June 20, and Sept. 14, 1792, in Ralph L. Wardle, ed., *Collected Letters of Mary Wollstonecraft* (Ithaca, NY: Cornell University Press, 1979), 209, 211, 215.

26. Page numbers in parentheses refer to the pagination of *BW*, vol. 1, rather than that of the original publication.

27. Antoine de Baecque, *Glory and Terror: Seven Deaths under the French Revolution*, trans. Charlotte Mandell (New York: Routledge, 2001), 65.

28. Address of the Society for Constitutional Information to the National Convention in France, Nov. 1792, in *Annual Register* 34 (1792): 73–74.

29. JB to RB, Nov. 26, 1792, in BPH, #221 (misfiled as 1794).

30. *Mon*, Nov. 29, 1792.

31. Jenny Graham, *The Nation, the Law and the King, Reform Politics in England, 1789–1799* (Lanham, MD: University Press of America, 2000), 401.

32. *Annual Register* 34 (1792): 92.

33. Ibid., 94, 95.

34. Graham, *Nation*, 166, 167.

35. Eugene C. Black, *The Association: British Extraparliamentary Political Organization 1769–1793* (Cambridge, MA: Harvard University Press, 1963), chap. 7.

36. RB to JB, Jan. 1 and 9, 1793, in BPH, #538, #539.

37. JB to RB, Nov. 26 (mistakenly dated 1794), Dec. 4, 1792, in BPH, #221, #196; cf. also Henri Grégoire to JB, Mar. 16, 1793, in BPH, #601.

38. In BPH, #198.

39. Page numbers in parentheses refer to the pagination of *BW*, vol. 1, rather than that of the original publication.

40. Line numbers are given in parentheses.

41. In BPH:Litmss, #20.

42. Quoted in JB to RB, Feb. 13, 1793, in BPH, #249.

43. Ezra Stiles to JB, Mar. 20, 1793, in BPH, #632.

44. See unidentified Dartmouth graduate's letter to his father, Oct. 25, 1794, courtesy of the Dartmouth College Library; Benjamin Silliman, *Journals of Travels in England, Holland, and Scotland, and of Two Passages over the Atlantic, in the Years 1805 and 1806, with Considerable Additions*, 2 vols., 3rd ed. (New Haven: S. Converse, 1820), 1:211.

CHAPTER 9: THE TERROR

1. Morris, *Diary*, 2:602.

2. RB to JB, Jan. 28, 1793, in BPH, #538.

3. JB to RB, Feb. 13, 1793, in BPH, #201.

4. The National Assembly acted on Feb. 17, but Barlow's certificate of citizenship is dated Mar. 22, 1793, in YB:BPq, M977; Michael Rapport, *Nationality and Citizenship in Revolutionary France: The Treatment of Foreigners, 1789–1799* (Oxford: Clarendon, 2000), 145.

5. Peter Sahlins, *Unnaturally French: Foreign Citizens in the Old Regime and After* (Ithaca, NY: Cornell University Press, 2004), 278.

6. JB to Thomas Jefferson, Mar. 7, 1793, in *PTJ*, 25:336; also JB to Oliver Wolcott Jr., Mar. 8, 1793, in CHS:OWP.

7. John R. Alden, *Stephen Sayre: American Revolutionary Adventurer* (Baton Rouge: Louisiana State University Press, 1983), 177; Caracciolo Parra-Pérez, *Miranda et la revolution française* (Paris: J. Dunoulin, 1925), lvi–lvii, 8, 33–36.

8. *American Historical Review* 3 (1897–98): 490–516, 650–71.

9. Mar. 5, 1793, in BPH, #202.

10. JB to RB, Mar. 6 and 21, 1793, in BPH, #203, #207.

11. David V. Erdman, *Commerce des Luminières: John Oswald and the British in Paris, 1790–1793* (Columbia: University of Missouri Press, 1986), 226; Benedetta Craveri, *The Age of Conversation*, trans. Teresa Waugh (New York: New York Review of Books, 2005), 357 ff.

12. Gita May, *Madame Roland and the Age of Revolution* (New York: Columbia University Press, 1970), 220, 230–31; M. Ray Adams, "Helen Maria Williams and the French Revolution," in *Wordsworth and Coleridge: Studies in Honor of George McLean Harper*, ed. Earl Leslie Griggs (Princeton, NJ: Princeton University Press, 1939), 88, 104–5.

13. Lionel D. Woodward, *Une Anglaise Amie de la Révolution Française: Hélène-Maria Williams et ses Amis* (Paris: Librairie Ancienne Honoré Champion, 1930), 60; Helen Maria Williams, *Memoirs of the Reign of Robespierre* (London: J. Hamilton Ltd, 1929), 15.

14. JB to RB, Apr. 5, 15, and 19, 1793, in BPH, #208, #209, #210.

15. JB to RB, Apr. 15, 1793, in BPH, #209.

16. Ibid., and JB to RB, Apr. 19, 1793, in BPH, #210.

17. Woodward, *Une Anglaise Amie*, 102 n.

18. Vincente Dávila, ed., *Archivo del General Miranda*, 24 vols. (Caracas: Parra León Hermanos, Editorial Sur-América, 1929–50), 12:158.

19. JB to RB, May 2, 1793, in BPH, #211; Gouverneur Morris to Thomas Jefferson, Apr. 19, 1793, in *PTJ*, 25:574; M. J. Sydenham, *The Girondins* (London: Athlone, 1961), 159.

20. Janet Todd, ed., *The Collected Letters of Mary Wollstonecraft* (New York: Columbia University Press, 2003), 234–35.

21. James Swan to Henry Knox, Dec. 21, 1793, in MaHS:HKP.

22. Both portraits survive as engravings. The portrait shown in this chapter is by Jean Jacques François LeBarbier, engraved by Louis C. Ruotte, see NPG. 76. 42. The other, not shown here, is by Jean-Simon Fournier, engraved by Gilles-Louis Chretian, NPG. 71. 54.

23. JB to RB, May 7, 1793, in BPH, #212.

24. Printed at the beginning of the Paris edition.

25. James Stanier Clarke to JB, Mar. 25, 1791, in YB:BPq, M986; Lewis Leary, "Joel Barlow and William Hayley: A Correspondence," *American Literature* 21 (1949): 331. See also Philipp Ziesche, *Cosmopolitan Patriots: Americans in Paris during the French Revolution* (Charlottesville: University of Virginia Press, 2010), chap. 3.

26. Page numbers in parentheses refer to the pagination of *BW*, vol. 1, rather than that of the original publication.

27. Jack Fruchtman Jr., *The Political Philosophy of Thomas Paine* (Baltimore: Johns Hopkins University Press, 2009), 123 ff.

28. John Trumbull, *M'Fingal: A Modern Epic Poem in Four Cantos* (London: J. S. Jordan, 1792), 136 fn.

29. In BPH:Litmss, #59, manuscript pages in parentheses.

30. See Frederick Nussbaum, *Commercial Policy in the French Revolution: A Study of the Career of G. J. A. Ducher* (Washington, DC: American Historical Association, 1923), and Allan Potofsky, "The Political Economy of the French-American Debt Debate: The Ideological Uses of Atlantic Commerce, 1787 to 1800," *William & Mary Quarterly*, 3rd ser., 58 (2006): 489–516.

31. Donald Greer, *The Incidence of the Terror during the French Revolution: A Statistical Interpretation* (Cambridge, MA: Harvard University Press, 1935), 113.

32. Brissot de Warville, *New Travels in the United States of America; including the Commerce of America with Europe; particularly with France and Great Britain* (London, 1794), 2:lix.

33. Deborah Kennedy, *Helen Maria Williams and the Age of Revolution* (Lewisburg, PA: Bucknell University Press, 2002), 111.

34. Elizabeth W. Latimer, *My Scrapbook of the French Revolution* (Chicago: A. C. McClurg and Co., 1898), 41, 46.

35. Dated 3 Frimaire 2 (Nov. 23, 1793), in AE:Cp: Espagne, 636, folio 391.

36. Nussbaum, *Commercial Policy*, 193.

37. AN:AD/XXc/72–73, document 126, referred to in Maurice Tourneau, *Bibliographie de l'histoire de Paris pendant la revolution française* (Paris, 1913), 2:263.

38. John G. Alger, *Paris in 1789–1794* (London: George Allen, 1902), 152.

39. *Mon*, Jan. 29, 1794. The text of the appeal to the Committee of Surety is dated 12 Ventôse 2 (Mar. 2, 1794), in AN:F7/4774/61. See also John Keane, *Tom Paine: A Political Life* (Boston: Little Brown and Co., 1995), 404–8.

40. Bronislaw Baczko, *Ending the Terror: The French Revolution after Robespierre*, trans. Michel Petheram (Cambridge: Cambridge University Press, 1994), 197–99, 202–7.

41. JB to AbB, Feb. 10, 1794, in BPH, #67.

CHAPTER 10: COMMERCIAL INTERLUDE

1. Joseph Fenwick's consular dispatches from Bordeaux, Sept. 28, 1792, and Jan. 20, Feb. 11, Apr. 4, and June 28, 1793, in NA:CC, RG 59.

2. Dated July 8, 1793, in BPH, #692, filed at the end of "Bacri accounts 1795–1796."

3. James Anderson's consular dispatches from Nantes, Sept. 19 and Oct. 5, 1793, in NA:CC, RG 59.

4. *Mon*, Aug. 4 and 8, Sept. 29, Oct. 4, 20, and 28, 1793.

5. Joseph Fenwick's consular dispatch, Dec. 12, 1793, NA:CC, RG 59.

6. James Anderson's consular dispatch, Dec. 1, 1793, NA:CC, RG 59.

7. Joseph Fenwick's consular dispatches, Jan. 4 and Apr. 23, 1794; James Anderson's consular dispatch, Feb. 7, 1794, NA:CC, RG 59.

8. John G. Alger, *Paris in 1789–1794* (London: George Allen, 1902), 82.

9. Pierre Caron, ed., *La Commission des subsistances de l'an II: procès-verbaux et acts* (Paris: E. Leroux, 1925), 2:482, 660, 662, 664, 666.

10. *Biographie universelle, ancienne et moderne: ou, Histoire, par ordre alphabétique, de la vie publique et privée de tous les hommes qui se sont fait remarquer par leurs écrits, leurs actions, leurs talents, leurs vertus ou leurs crimes*, 45 vols. (Paris: A. T. Desplaces, 1843–65), 2:493–94.

11. Caron, *Commission des subsistances*, 2:88.

12. Ibid., 2:102; Pierre Léon et al., *Histoire économique et sociale de la France*, Vol. 3: *L'avenement de l'ère industrielle (1789–années 1880)* (Paris: Presses Universitaires de France, 1976), 38.

13. William James, *The Naval History of Great Britain, from the Declaration of War by France in 1793 to the Accession of George IV*, 6 vols. (London: Richard Bentley and Son, 1886), 1:138, 140.

14. Ibid., 1:191.

15. Christina and David Bewley, *Gentleman Radical: A Life of John Horne Tooke, 1736–1812* (London: Tauris Academic Studies, 1998), 134–40; Albert Goodwin, *The Friends of Liberty: The English Democratic Movement in the Age of the French Revolution* (Cambridge, MA: Harvard University Press, 1979), 338.

16. Janet Todd, ed., *The Collected Letters of Mary Wollstonecraft* (New York: Columbia University Press, 2003), 253 and 255.

17. Wil Verhoven, *Gilbert Imlay: Citizen of the World* (London: Pickering and Chatto, 2008), 194, conditionally absolves Barlow but in a manner that leaves him Verhoven's chief suspect.

18. See JB to RB, July 8, 1796, in BPH, #271.

19. RB to Betsy Wolcott, Sept. 21, 1794, in CHS:BP.

20. In BPH, #215.

21. AbB to RB and JB, June 9, 1794, in BPH, #649. For the date of receipt, see JB to Oliver Wolcott Jr., Nov. 6, 1794, in CHS:OWP.

22. JB to AbB, Feb. 10, 1795, in BPH, #67.

23. Oliver Wolcott Jr. to JB, June 10, 1794, in BPH, #645.

24. JB to Oliver Wolcott Jr., Nov. 6, 1794, in CHS:OWP.

25. JB to RB, Jan. 16, 1796, in BPH, #236.

26. JB to Ezra Stiles, May 28, 1794, in *Massachusetts Historical Society, Collections*, 2nd ser., 8 (1826): 269–70, for this and what follows. Also see Christoph D. Ebeling to Jeremy Belknap, Sept. 20, 1794, in *Proceedings of the American Antiquarian Society*, n.s., 35 (1925): 284 n.

27. Josephine Seaton, *William Winston Seaton of the "National Intelligencer"* . . . (Boston: J. R. Osgood and Co., 1871), 66–70.

28. RB to Betsy Wolcott, Sept. 21, 1794, in CHS:BP.

29. JB to RB, Jan. 16, 1796, in BPH, #236.

30. JB to a Mr. Ashmore, May 1, 1796 in BPH:LB: #1, and JB affidavit, May 1796, in LC:DBWP, vol. 2. Nonetheless, on Feb. 24, 1797, the High Court of Admiralty condemned the *Sally* as enemy property; see HCA 22. After Barlow's death, Ashmore swore out an affidavit denying Barlow had acquired any right to either the *Sally* or the *Margaritta* and their cargoes through fictitious sales; see the affidavit dated May 31, 1813, in LC:DBWP, vol. 2.

31. JB to David Humphreys, Jan. 6, 1796, in BPH:LB, #1.

32. In BPH, #510. The vessel was probably the brig *Peggy* (Capt. Parks), reported in Hamburg in the *New York Daily Advertiser*, Sept. 1, 1794.

33. BPH:LB, #1:85.

34. *WJMon*, 2:259.

35. JB to AbB, Feb. 10, 1795, in BPH, #67.

36. JB to Oliver Wolcott Jr., Apr. 27, 1796, in BPH:LB, #1.

37. BPH:Notebook, #18 entitled "Notes for the hist. of the F.R." (pps. 17 and 18 of unnumbered pages).

38. Evgenii Tarlé, *Germinal et Prairial* (Moscow: Éditions en langues étrangères, 1959), chaps. 6–7, esp. 177 ff.

39. Monroe to Edmund Randolph, Aug. 1, 1795, in *WJMon*, 2:334.

40. AbB to JB, June 9, 1794 in YS:MM, folder 72.

CHAPTER 11: MISSION TO ALGIERS

1. See accounts between the United States and Joel Barlow, agent to Barbary, in BPH, #5.

2. François Crouzet, *La Grande inflation: la monnaie en France de Louis XVI à Napoléon* (Paris: Fayard, 1993), 400–405.

3. The development of this market can be traced in *Mon*, Jan.–May 1797.

4. JB to Jacques Récamier, Dec. 21, 1796, in BPH, #512.

5. Howard G. Brown, *Ending the French Revolution: Violence, Justice, and Repression from the Terror to Napoleon* (Charlottesville: University of Virginia Press, 2006), 140.

6. In BPH, #542.

7. Described at length in JB to Timothy Pickering, Aug. 28, 1797, in BPH:LB, #4.

8. JB to RB, Jan. 1, 1796, in BPH, #223.

9. Richard B. Parker, *Uncle Sam in Barbary: A Diplomatic History* (Gainesville: University Press of Florida, 2004), 31.

10. JB to RB, Jan. 10, 1796, in BPH, #230.

11. JB to RB, Jan. 14, 1796, in BPH, #234.

12. JB to RB, Feb. 23, 1796, in BPH, #253.

13. JB to RB, Mar. 8, 1796, in BPH, #257.

14. Parker, *Uncle Sam*, 2; see, also, JB to Timothy Pickering, Aug. 24, 1797, in BPH: LB, #4.

15. JB, "Estimate of the Advantages and expences of maintaining a peace with Barbary for the United States," n.d., but probably late Apr. 1796, "Submitted to the Secretary of State," in BPH:LB, #1.

16. JB to RB, Apr. 26, 1796, in BPH, #262; also JB to James Monroe, May 19, 1796, in BPH:LB, #1.

17. See JB to James Monroe, May 24, 1796, in BPH:LB, #1.

18. Aug. 7, 1796, in BPH:LB, #1.

19. Aug. 31, 1796, in BPH:LB, #1.

20. JB to RB, Oct. 12, 1796, in BPH, #279.

21. JB to Timothy Pickering, Oct. 19, 1796, in BPH:LB, #2.

22. JB to RB, Mar. 8 and Apr. 2, 1796, in BPH, #257, #259.

23. JB to Timothy Pickering, Oct. 18, 1796, in BPH:LB, #2.

24. JB to David Humphreys, May 23, 1797, in BPH:LB, #3.

25. JB to RB, Oct. 9, 1796, in BPH, #278.

26. At least to judge from the way Ruth rationalized his absence, see RB to JB, Apr. 12, 1796, in BPH, #555.

27. JB to RB, Dec. 30, 1796, in BPH, #288.

28. JB to William Little, Dec. 20 and 31, 1796, in BPH:LB, #2.

29. JB to Robert and John Montgomery, Feb. 3, 1797, in BPH:LB, #3.

30. JB to David Humphreys, Mar. 14, 1797 in BPH:LB, #3.

CHAPTER 12: FRANCO-AMERICAN CRISIS

1. JB to RB, July 30, and Aug. 1, 1797, in BPH, #307, #308.

2. JB to Stephen Cathalan, Aug. 1 and 4, 1797, in BPH:LB, #4.

3. JB to Timothy Pickering, Aug. 17, 1797, in BPH:LB, #4.

4. JB to David Humphreys, Aug. 10, 1797, in BPH:LB, #3.

5. JB to Samuel Williams, Dec. 19 and 27, 1797, in BPH:LB, #4.

6. JB to David Humphreys, Aug. 1, 1797, in BPH:LB, #4, and RB to JB, May 31, 1797, in BPH, #580.

7. François Crouzet, *La Grande Inflation: la monnaie en France de Louis XVI à Napoléon* (Paris: Fayard, 1993), 412–13, 419–20.

8. RB to JB, Mar. 26 and Apr. 3, 1797, in BPH, #295, #296.

9. Yvon Bizardel, "French Estates, American Landlords," *Apollo* 101 (1975): 110.

10. JB to Mr. Felicchi, Sept. 2, 1797, in BPH:LB, #4.

11. JB to Stephen Cathalan, Sept. 3, 1797, in BPH:LB, #4.

12. JB to RB, Sept. 10, 1797, in BPH, #328.

13. Kirkpatrick Sale, *The Fire of His Genius: Robert Fulton and the American Dream* (New York: Free Press, 2001), 66.

14. JB to Jesse Putnam, 30 Nivôse 7 (Jan. 19, 1799), in BPH:LB, #4.

15. Fulwar Skipwith to Thomas Jefferson, Mar. 17, 1798, in *PTJ*, 30:186; also *PMarsh*, 3:158–242; 383–88.

16. Carl L. Lokke, "The Trumbull Episode: A Prelude to the 'XYZ Affair,'" *New England Quarterly* 7 (1934): 219–29.

17. Copy in BPH:LB, #4.

18. JB to Thomas Jefferson, Mar. 12, 1798, in BPH:LB, #4.

19. William Stinchcombe, *The X Y Z Affair* (Westport, CT: Greenwood, 1980), 119.

20. JB to Stephen Cathalan, 24 Prairial 6 (June 12, 1798), in BPH:LB, #4.

21. JB to Lemuel Hopkins, Mar. 14, 1798, BPH:LB, #4.

22. RB to JB, Jan. 6, 14, 18, 20, 28, Feb. 7, Apr. 9, 1796; Jan. 28, and Mar. 26, 1797, in BPH, #542, #543, #545, #546, #550, #551, #554, #557, #571, # 575.

23. JB to Stephen Cathalan, 26 Prairial 7 (June 14, 1799), in BPH:LB, #4.

24. JB to James Watson, July 26, 1798, in BPH:LB, #4.

25. JB to Robert Lyle, July 31 and Dec. 4, 1796, in BPH:LB, #4.

26. JB to J. B. Dabney, Sept. 29, Nov. 20, 1798, and Jan. 19 and 27, 1799, in BPH:LB, #4.

27. JB to Strobel and Martini, 18 Brumaire 6 (Nov. 8, 1798), in BPH:LB, #4.

28. Silvia Martzagalli, "Establishing Transatlantic Trade Networks in Time of War: Bordeaux and the U.S., 1793–1815," *Business History Review* 79 (2005): 811–44.

29. JB to William Little, Aug. 2, 1798, in BPH:LB, #4.

30. JB to James Watson, Oct. 24, 1798; to John Fellows, Oct. 25, 1798; and to Matthew Carey, Oct. 25, 1798, in BPH:LB, #4.

31. Page numbers in parentheses refer to the pagination of *BW*, vol. 1, rather than that of the original publication.

32. George Washington to John Adams, Feb. 1, 1799, in *PGW:R*, 3:350.

33. John Adams to George Washington, Feb. 19, 1799, in ibid., 387.

34. Feb. 12, 1799, copies in English and French, in BPH:LB, #4; also AE:Cp, 51, LC photocopies.

35. Aleine Austin, *Matthew Lyon: "New Man" of the Democratic Revolution, 1749–1822* (University Park: Pennsylvania State University Press, 1981), 114.

36. James Watson to JB, Oct. 26, 1798, in CHS:BP. Also, see JB to Watson Apr. 17, 1800, in BPH:LB, #4.

37. In the Dec. 22, 1798, issue.

38. Page numbers in parentheses refer to the pagination of *BW*, vol. 1, rather than that of the original publication.

39. Léon Say, *Dictionaire des finances* (Paris: Berger-Levrault et Cie, 1889–94), 1:434.

40. James Woodress, *A Yankee's Odyssey: The Life of Joel Barlow* (Philadelphia: J. B. Lippincott, 1958), 322.

41. JB to Lemuel Hopkins, Apr. 12, 1799, and to John Fellows, Apr. 13, 1799, in BPH:LB, #4.

CHAPTER 13: REPUBLICAN PROPHET

1. For what follows, see *CtCourant*, Aug. 19, 1799.

2. AaB to JB, Sept. 24, 1799, in BPH, #536.

3. Noah Webster, *Letters of Noah Webster*, Harry R. Warfel, ed. (New York: Library Publishers, 1953), 188, 193–94.

4. Eugene N. White, "The French Revolution and the Politics of Government Finance, 1770–1815," *Journal of Economic History* 55 (1995): 230.

5. François Crouzet, *La Grande Inflation: la monnaie en France de Louis XVI à Napoléon* (Paris: Fayard, 1993), chap. 16.

6. JB to C. D. Dede, Mar. 14, 1799, in BPH:LB, #4.

7. JB to Robert Lyle, June 27, 1799, in BPH:LB, #4.

8. JB to Robert Lyle, May 1, 1799, in BPH:LB, #4.

9. JB to C. D. Dede, Mar. 14, July 30, and Sept. 22, 1799, in BPH:LB, #4.

10. JB to Swan and D'allarde, Sept. 29, 1799, in BPH:LB, #4.

11. JB to Robert Lyle, July 28, 1799, in BPH:LB, #4.

12. As documented in JB to Strobel and Martini, 23 Fructidor 7 (Sept. 9, 1799), 2 and 24 Pluviôse 8 (Jan. 22 and Feb. 13, 1800), 23 Floréal 8 (May 13, 1800), June 18, 1800, 29 Thermidor 8 (Aug. 17, 1800), and 8 Pluviôse 9 (Jan. 28, 1801), in BPH:LB, #4.

13. JB to J. B. Dabney, 29 Pluviôse 7 (Feb. 17, 1799), in BPH:LB, #4.

14. JB to Robert Lyle, Sept. 23, 1799, in BPH:LB, #4.

15. BPH:Notebook, #12 (1798–1801).

16. JB to AbB, Jan. 1, 1800, in BPH, #71; see, also, BW, 1:423.

17. Irene Collins, *Napoleon and His Parliaments, 1800–1815* (London: Edward Arnold, 1979), 47–49.

18. JB to RB, Aug. 23 and 24, 1800, in BPH, #338, #339. See also JB to Alexander Wolcott, Oct. 6, 1800, in BPH, #526.

19. References in parentheses are to the pagination in *BW*, vol. 1, rather than the original edition.

20. JB to AaB, Oct. 1, 1800, in BPH, #103.

21. Ibid. and JB to AbB, Oct. 3, 1798, in BPH, #70.

22. An English language edition in Paris (1800) preceded the three separate U.S. editions that appeared in 1801. All bore the completion date of Dec. 20, 1799. References in parentheses are to the pagination in *BW*, vol. 1, rather than the original editions.

23. Quotes from Webster, *Letters*, 192–93.

24. BPH:Notebook, #17 (1802).

25. The article appeared in the *Publiciste*, 25 Nivôse 8 (Jan. 15, 1800). A manuscript version is in YB:BPq, M931.

26. JB to AbB, Jan. 1, 1800, in BPH, #71.

27. JB to RB, Aug. 22 and 27, 1800, in BPH, #337, #341.

28. JB to AbB, Jan. 3, 1801, in BPH, #74.

29. Jean Tuland, *Napoleon: The Myth of the Saviour*, trans. Teresa Waugh (London: Weidenfeld and Nicholson, 1984), 86.

30. JB to Strobel and Martini, Jan. 22 and 30, 1800, in BPH:LB, #4.

31. JB to Strobel and Martini, Feb. 28 and Mar. 19, 1800, and to James Watson, Apr. 17, 1800, in BPH:LB, #4.

32. JB to Pierre-Frédéric Dobrée, Mar. 1, 1800, in BPH:LB, #4.

33. Cynthia O. Philip, *Robert Fulton: A Biography* (New York: Franklin Watts, 1985), 96–7.

34. JB to Josiah Meigs, Oct. 6, 1800, in BPH, #506.

35. AbB to JB, Mar. 30 and Apr. 24, 1799, in YS:MM, folder 72; AaB to JB, Sept. 24, 1799, in BPH, #536.

36. JB to AaB, Oct. 1, 1800, in BPH, #103.

37. RB to Jesse Putnam, Mar. 10 and June 14, 1801, in BPH, #657, #658.

38. JB to RB, Aug. 28 and 29, 1800, in BPH, #342, #343; Yvon Bizardel, "French Estates, American Landlords," *Apollo* 101 (1975): 110.

39. Jeanne Pronteau, *Les numérotages des maisons de Paris, du quinzième siècle à nos jours* (Paris: Préfecture de la Seine, Service des travaux historiques, 1966), chaps. 4 and 5. The booklet in question is Yvon Bizardel, *Hôtel de La Trémoïlle, rue de Vaugirard* (n.p., France: Alençonnaise, 1979).

40. JB to Lady Emma Hamilton, Sept. 21, 1801, and to Benjamin Jarvis, Jan. 5, 1802, in BPH:LB, #4; also Henry R. Yorke, *Letters from France in 1802*, 2 vols. (London: for H. D. Symonds, 1804), 2:371.

41. JB to Benjamin Jarvis, Jan. 5, 1802, in BPH:LB, #4.

CHAPTER 14: RESPONDING TO FRANCE'S APOSTASY

1. In *PTJ*, 32:141–43.

2. Ibid., 142.

3. *PJMad:SS*, 1:191.

4. JB to AbB, Jan. 3 and Aug. 21, 1801, in BPH, #74. The latter letter is transcribed and misidentified as addressed to Josiah Meigs, in BPH, #509.

5. JB to Thomas Jefferson, Aug. 25, 1801, in LC:TJP.

6. Jean Stern, *Belle et Bonne* (Paris: Hachette, 1938), 173; see, also, AN, F7 6152 [d.918].

7. Michael D. Bordo and Eugene N. White, "A Tale of Two Currencies: British and French Finance During the Napoleonic Wars," *Journal of Economic History* 51 (1991): 314.

8. JB to Thomas Jefferson, Aug. 25, 1801, in LC:TJP.

9. JB to Benjamin Jarvis, Jan. 5, 1802, in BPH:LB, #4.

10. JB to RB and Robert Fulton, Apr. 22, 1803, in BPH, #428.

11. Constantin-François Volney, *Volney's answer to Doctor Priestley, on his pamphlet entitled, "Observations on the increase of infidelity . . ."* (Philadelphia, 1797), 13.

12. William Vans Murray to Timothy Pickering, Jan. 31, 1799, in *Annual Report of the American Historical Association* (1912), 514.

13. *PJMad:SS*, 3:248.

14. JB to James Monroe, Mar. 17, 1802, in BPH:LB, #4.

15. Thomas Jefferson to JB, May 3, 1802, in LC:TJP.

16. JB to RB, July 30 and Aug. 1, 1802, in BPH, #403, #404.

17. I take exception to Cynthia Owen Philip's interpretation of the relationship in *Robert Fulton: A Biography* (New York: Franklin Watts, 1985), chaps. 7 and 8.

18. Ibid., 131.

19. HCA 45/40, in PRO.

20. Hunter Miller, ed., *Treaties and Other International Acts of the United States of America* (Washington, DC: GPO, 1931–48), 1:488–90.

21. "Minutes of the Proceedings of the Commissioners appointed in pursuance of the VII Article of the Treaty of Amity Commerce and Navigation between His British Majesty and the United States of America 10 October 1798–13 Apr. 1803," in HCA 30/885, PRO.

22. See George W. Erving to James Madison, June 10, 1802, in *PJMad:SS*, 3:299; JB to RB and Robert Fulton, July 1 and 6 (quote), 1802, in BPH, #389, #391; and JB to Rufus King, June 29, 1802, in Rufus King Papers, NYHS.

23. JB to RB and Robert Fulton, July 12, 1802, in BPH, #394.

24. JB to James Thayer, Aug. 24, 1802, in BPH:LB, #4.

25. Barlow's involvement with the *Hannah* is discussed in the *New York Evening Post*, Mar. 18, 1811, and in JB to Robert Fulton, Apr. 8, 1811, in YB:BP, #21. See also JB affidavit, Jan. 13, 1806, in YB:BPq, M908–910 and M912.

26. JB to RB and Robert Fulton, July 16, 1802, in BPH, #396.

27. JB to RB and Robert Fulton, July 6, 1802, in BPH, #391.

28. Henry R. Yorke, *Letters from France in 1802*, 2 vols. (London: for H. D. Symonds, 1804), 2:372–75.

29. Texts in YB:BPq, M932, M933.

30. Richard Holmes, *Age of Wonder: How the Romantic Generation Discovered the Beauty and Terror of Science* (London: Harper, 2008), xv–xix.

31. BPH:Notebook 1802, #17.

32. Joseph Farington, *The Farington Diary*, 2nd. ed., ed. James Greig, 8 vols. (London: Hutchinson and Co., 1923–28), 2:36.

33. AbB to RB, Feb. 7, 1803, in HL:BFP.

34. From *Journal des Debates*, Aug. 11, 1803, and used by Philip, *Fulton*, as the title of chap. 9.

35. Kirkpatrick Sale, *The Fire of His Genius: Robert Fulton and the American Dream* (New York: Free Press, 2001), 108–9.

36. HCA 44/44, in PRO.

37. HCA 44/45, in PRO.

38. JB to Robert Fulton, Aug. 10, 1803, in BPH, #433.

39. JB to RB and Robert Fulton, Apr. 22, 1803, in BPH, #428.

40. JB to Alexander Wolcott, July 28, 1803, in BPH, #527.

41. Ibid.

42. Robert Fulton to JB, Mar. 1, 1809, in HL:BFP.

43. See JB to David Bailie Warden, Apr. 28, 1808, in LC:DBWP; C. Edward Skeen, *John Armstrong, Jr., 1758–1843: A Biography* (Syracuse, NY: Syracuse University Press, 1983), 59.

44. In YB:BPq, M 915.

45. Benjamin Silliman recorded meeting Barlow at the end of May 1805 and being introduced through him and Fulton to Stanhope, Chandos M. Brown, *Benjamin Silliman: A Life in the Young Republic* (Princeton, NJ: Princeton University Press, 1989), 172–73.

46. Mary Linwood to RB, Mar. 4, 1805, and Nov. 1810, in HL:BFP.

47. RB to Mrs. Rotch, Mar. 16, 1805, in MaHS.

48. Thomas Jefferson to JB, Jan. 19, 1804, in LC:TJP.

49. JB to Return J. Meigs, Sept. 6, 1804, in BPH:LB #4.

CHAPTER 15: MIXED RECEPTION

1. JB to AbB, Aug. 4, 1805, in BPH, #77.

2. See JB to Robert R. Livingston, Sept. 18, 1807, in Haverford College Archives.

3. JB to AbB, Aug. 20, 1805, in BPH, #78.

4. Such as those appearing in the *CtCourant*, Nov. 12, 1798, May 20 and June 8, 1799, Sept. 15 and Dec. 24, 1800.

5. JB to Josiah Meigs, Aug. 26, 1805, transcript in BPH, #506.

6. Thomas Jefferson to JB, Aug. 14, 1805, in LC:TJP.

7. JB to Thomas Jefferson, Sept. 2, 1805, in LC:TJP.

8. *AmMercury*, Aug. 15 and Nov. 7, 1805.

9. Noah Webster to Stephen Jacob, Oct. 3, 1805, in BPL.

10. *Repertory*, Oct. 15, 1805; JB to Elisha Babcock, Oct. 30, 1805, in NYPL, Joel Barlow papers.

11. JB to Elisha Babcock, Dec. 11, 1805, in YB:BP, #12.

12. See *NI*, Apr. 1, 1806.

13. Address to Barlow, in *AmMercury*, Nov. 7, 1805.

14. *AmMercury*, Nov. 7, 1805.

15. JB to SB, Oct. 12, 1808, in BPH, #461.

16. See JB to James Monroe, Feb. 26, 1796, in BPH:LB, #1.

17. John Keane, *Tom Paine: A Political Life* (Boston: Little, Brown, 1995), 404, 425, 449, and 524–25.

18. JB to James Cheetham, Aug. 11, 1809, is reprinted in Charles L. Todd, *Life and Letters of Joel Barlow, LL.D. Poet, Statesman, Philosopher . . .* (New York: G. P. Putnam's Sons, 1886), 237–39, quotes from 237.

19. See JB to AbB, Nov. 28, 1805, in BPH, #79.

20. Noah Webster to Stephen Jacob, Oct. 3, 1805, in BPL.

21. JB to Thomas Jefferson, Jan. 17, 1806, in LC:TJP; references in parentheses are to the pagination of *BW*, vol. 1.

22. In LC:TJP.

23. JB to Thomas Jefferson, Jan. 17, 1806, LC:TJP.

24. *DPCUS*, 9th Cong., 1st sess., 144, 161, 163, 183.

25. JB to Robert Fulton, Mar. 30, 1806, in BPH, #494.

26. In YB:BPq, M979.

27. JB to John Vanderlyn, Dec. 20, 1804, in BPH, #514.

28. JB to AbB, Dec. 22, 1806, in BPH, #80.

29. Original in *NI*, Jan. 16, 1807; for the parody attributed to John Quincy Adams, *Monthly Anthology* 7 (1807): 143–44; *Hampshire Federalist*, Apr. 27, 1807.

30. JB to RB, Mar. 6, 1807, in YB:BPq, M918.

31. JB to Tench Coxe, Sept. 29, 1809, in HSP:TCP.

32. *The Columbiad* (Philadelphia: C. and A. Conrad and Co., 1807), iv, not republished in *BW*, vol. 2.

33. In the issue of Feb. 2, 1809.

34. See certificate made out in JB's name dated Apr. 28, 1807, in BPH, #715.

35. For the attribution, see JB to Richard Philips, July 21, 1809, in YB:BP, #27.

36. Text taken from *NI*, June 2 and 9, 1809. See also *Boston Patriot*, July 1 and 8, Aug. 2, 1809.

37. Quotes from *Edinburgh Review* 15, no. 29 (Oct. 1809): 24, 25, 26; Leon Howard, *The Connecticut Wits* (Chicago: University of Chicago Press, 1943), 323.

38. Quotes from ibid., 39 and 40.

39. *Port Folio*, n.s. (3rd), 1 (Jan. 1809): 64, 65, 67, 68, 69, 70.

40. *Port Folio*, n.s. (3rd), 5 (May 1809): 432–33; cf., also, *Republican Watch Tower*, Apr. 28, 1809.

41. Henri Grégoire, *Critical Observations on the Poem of Joel Barlow*, The Columbiad (Washington, DC: Roger C. Weightman, 1809), 4, 5, 6, 7, 9, 10.

42. Ibid., 9, 13, and 14.

43. *Monthly Anthology* 7 (1809): 3.

44. JB to Tench Coxe, Sept. 29, 1809, in HSP:TCP.

45. Joel Barlow, *Letter to Henri Gregoire, bishop, senator, compte of the empire and member of the institute of France, in Reply to his Letter on the Columbiad* (Washington, DC: Roger. C. Weightman, 1809), 3.

46. Ibid., 6 and 7.

47. Ibid., 8–9.

48. Ibid., 9 and 10.

49. Cf. Benjamin Smith Barton to JB, Apr. 22, 1808, and Sept. 27, 1809, in YB:BPq, M946 and M947.

50. Grégoire, *Critical Observations*, 10.

51. Stephen Blakemore, *Joel Barlow's Columbiad: A Bicentennial Reading* (Knoxville: University of Tennessee Press, 2007), 315.

52. *Richmond Enquirer*, June 29, 1810.

53. Barlow, *Letter to Henri Gregoire*, 13.

54. My interpretation of Barlow's relationship with Grégoire differs from that advanced by Alyssa G. Sepinwall, "The Abbé Gregoire and the Atlantic Republic of Letters," *Proceedings of the American Antiquarian Society* 116 (2006): 317–35.

55. *BW*, 2:856: Noah Webster to JB, Oct. 19, 1807, in BPH, #636.

56. Noah Webster to JB, Oct. 19 and Nov. 12, 1807, in BPH, #636, #637.

57. Noah Webster to JB, Apr. 5, 1808, in BPH, #638.

58. JB to Noah Webster, June 17 and Aug. 1, 1807, in BPH, #523, #524. Barlow made a similar appeal to Josiah Meigs, see JB to Meigs, June 10, 1809, in YB:BP, #25.

59. Noah Webster to JB, Oct. 13, 1808, in BPH, #641.

60. *Monthly Anthology and Boston Review* 7 (1809): 284.

61. See *The American Epic: Transforming a Genre, 1770–1860* (Cambridge: Cambridge University Press, 1989), 6.

62. See the religious critique of *The Columbiad* published by the *Panoplist, and Missionary Magazine* 9 (1813): 499, and 10 (1814): 30–32.

CHAPTER 16: WASHINGTON INSIDER

1. Martha Mitchell, "Kalorama: Country Estate to Washington's Mayfair," *Records of the Columbia Historical Society* 48 (1971–72): 164, 166.

2. Hunter Miller, ed., *Treaties and Other International Acts of the United States of America*, 8 vols. (Washington, DC: GPO, 1931–48), 2:46–47, 470–72.

3. RB to Pamela Jacob, Nov. 10, 1807, in BPL; also JB to John Wheelock, Feb. 11, 1808, in BPL.

4. JB to Tench Coxe, Dec. 16, 1807, and Feb. 13, 1808, in HSP:TCP.

5. RB to Dorcas Dearborn, n.d., in BPL; JB to Tench Coxe, Feb. 13 and 20, 1808, in HSP:TCP; JB to SB, Feb. 20, 1808, in BPH, #458.

6. Cf. JB to Tench Coxe, Dec. 16, 1807, in HSP:TCP.

7. JB to SB, Jan. 24, 1808, in BPH, #457.

8. Robert Fulton to JB and RB, June 8, 1808, in YB:BPq, M980.

9. See BPH, #707; JB to SB, Dec. 15, 1807, Jan. 8, 1808, Dec. 11, 1808, in BPH, #455, #456, #462.

10. JB to Thomas Jefferson, Aug. 1, 1808, in LC:TJP.

11. JB to Tench Coxe, Aug. 2, 1808, in HSP:TCP.

12. In LC:TJP.

13. See Richard Buel Jr., *America on the Brink* . . . (New York: Palgrave Macmillan, 2005), chap. 2.

14. JB to Tench Coxe, May 15, 1808, in HSP:TCP; JB to Thomas Jefferson, May 26, 1808, in LC:TJP.

15. JB to Thomas Jefferson, Sept. 12, 1808, in LC:TJP; also JB to Tench Coxe, July 3, 1808, in HSP:TCP.

16. See JB to SB, Oct. 12, 1808, in BPH, #461.

17. Robert Fulton to JB, Mar. 1, 1809, fragment, in HL:BFP.

18. JB to Thomas Jefferson, Dec. 4, 1808, in LC:TJP.

19. JB to SB, Apr. 18, 1807, in BPH, #447.

20. RB to CB, June 10, 1810, in HL:BFP.

21. De Villette may have copied a portrait by Fulton, but he could have been no older than twelve when the original likeness was most likely made; see Jean Stern, *Belle et Bonne, une fervente amie de Voltaire (1757–1822)* (Paris: Librairie Hachette, 1938), and Gilbert Stenger, *La Société française pendant le Consulat* (Paris: Perrin et cie, 1905), 3e sér., 513–16.

22. Robert Fulton to JB, June 23, 1809, in NYHS:RFP.

23. JB to John Vaughan, July 21, 1806, in HSP:Gratz Collection; JB to Tench Coxe, July 19 and Sept. 29, 1809, in HSP:TCP.

24. JB to Tench Coxe, Mar. 20, 1808; also Dec. 16, 1807, and Apr. 28, 1810; all in HSP:TCP.

25. JB to Gideon Granger, May 3, 1809, in YB:BPq, M923.

26. JB to SB, May 28, 1810, in BPH, #466.

27. DPCUS, 11th Cong., 1st and 2nd sess., 1368–73.

28. Cf. Francis Corbin to JB, Aug. 6 and 27, 1809, in YB:BPq, M962–3.

29. JB to SB, Sept. 23, 1810, in BPH, #468, for this and what follows.

30. Ibid.

31. In BPH, #472.

32. DPCUS, 11th Cong., 1st sess., 747; 3rd sess., 1305–11.

33. JB to SB, Oct. 31, 1810, in BPH, #472; William Lee to Susannah Lee, Dec. 12, 1810, in LC:L-PP.

34. JB to SB, Dec. 27, 1810, in BPH, #474.

35. JB to SB, Aug. 5, 1811, in BPH, #477; RB to CB, Jan. 26, 1815, in HL:BFP.

36. William Lee to Susannah Lee, Jan. 9 and Oct. 20 (quote), 1810, in LC:L-PP; also JB to William Whann, Jan. 10, 1810, in HSP; and JB to Alexander Wolcott, Sept. 26, 1811, in BPH, #528.

37. JB to Mercy Warren, Dec. 29, 1810, in MaHS:MOW.

38. "Sketch of History of the U.S.," in YB:BPq, M934 for what follows.

39. Addenda to above, in YB:BPq, M935.

40. YB:BPq, M934.

41. JB to Thomas Jefferson, Jan. 15, 1810, in LC:TJP.

42. JB to SB, Apr. 8, 1810, in BPH, #465.

43. JB to Henry Dearborn, Feb. 5, 1810, in MaHS:HDP.

44. As reported by George W. Erving to James Bowdoin, Mar. 11, 1811, in MaHS: BTP.

45. William Lee to Susannah Lee, Mar. 6, 1811, in LC:L-PP; see also, George W. Erving to James Bowdoin, Mar. 11, 1811, in MaHS:BTP.

46. G. Duvall to JB, Dec. 4, 1810, and JB reply, Dec. 6; and G. Duvall to JB, Feb. 27, 1811, and JB to Joseph B. Varnum, Feb. 28, 1811, all in BPH, #700–#704. An announcement that Barlow's accounts were settled appeared in the NI, Mar. 2, 1811.

47. Timothy Pickering to Alexander Hamilton, Apr. 29, 1797, PAH, 27:71.

48. See Josephine Seaton, William Winston Seaton of the "National Intelligencer" . . . (Boston: J. R. Osgood and Co., 1871), 101–4.

49. Madison's notes on their discussion are in PJMad:PS, 3:255–63.

50. Quote from Robert Smith, An address to the people of the United States (Baltimore, 1811), 4.

51. RB to Pamela Jacob, Apr. 28, 1811, in CHS:BP.

52. New York Evening Post, Mar. 5, 1811.

53. Boston Gazette, Mar. 4, 1811.

54. Mar. 8, 1811.

55. See *New York Evening Post*, Mar. 18, 20, 21, 1811, and JB to Robert Fulton, Apr. 8, 1811, in YB:BP, #21.

56. JB to Henry Dearborn, Apr. 11, 1811, in MaHS:HDP.

57. RB to Pamela Jacob, Apr. 28, 1811, in CHS:BP.

58. See indenture dated Mar. 28, 1811, in YB:BP, #33; see, also, JB to Henry Dearborn, Apr. 11, 1811, in MaHS:HDP.

59. See Apr. 18, 1811.

60. Compare William Lee to Susannah Lee, Sept. 9, 1811, in LC:L-PP, with JB to Tench Coxe, Dec. 16, 1809, in HSP:TCP.

61. Pagination as it appears in *BW*, vol. 1.

62. I follow Henry Adams, *History of the United States during the Administrations of James Madison* (New York: Library of America, 1986), 330 ff., for the tug of war between Monroe and Sérurier. It is based on Sérurier to Bassano, June 30, 1811, in AE: Cp, 65, LC photocopy.

63. Peter P. Hill, *Napoleon's Troublesome Americans: Franco-American Relations, 1804–1815* (Washington, DC: Potomac Books, 2005), 126.

64. Sérurier to Bassano, July 5 and 10, 1811, in AE:Cp, 65, LC photocopy.

65. Adams, *History*, 337.

66. William Lee to Susannah Lee, July 1, 1811, in LC:L-PP.

67. JB to Robert Fulton, Aug. 2 and 5, 1811, in BPH, #500, #501.

68. JB to Robert Fulton, Aug. 2, 1811, in BPH, #500.

69. See JB to Tench Coxe, July 19, 1808, in HSP:TCP.

CHAPTER 17: EUROPE REDUX

1. JB to Robert Fulton, Aug. 14, 1811, in BPH, #501.

2. JB to Alexander Wolcott, Sept. 26, 1811, in BPH, #528; see also, William Lee to Susannah Lee, Sept. 9, 1811, in LC:L-PP; and David Warden's journal of the voyage in *Maryland Historical Magazine* 11 (1917): 124–44, 204–17.

3. William Lee to Susannah Lee, Sept. 17, 1811, in LC:L-PP.

4. Jonathan Russell to JB, Sept. 19, 1811, in MaHS:JRP.

5. See *PJMad:PS*, 3:68 n., 184.

6. In HB:JRP.

7. JB to Jonathan Russell, Sept. 9, 1811, in ibid.

8. JB to Jonathan Russell, Sept. 28 and Oct. 5, 1811, in MaHS:JRP; also JB to Jonathan Russell, Oct. 21, 1811; Mar. 12 and 31, and May 12, 20, and 22, 1812, in MaHS:JRP; Jonathan Russell to JB, Nov. 11, 1812, in BPL.

9. William Lee to Susannah Lee, Oct. 31, 1811, in LC:L-PP.

10. JB to Alexander Wolcott, Sept. 26, 1811, in BPH, #528, and JB to Wolcott, Nov. [?], 1811, in YB:BPq, M927; JB to Samuel Eliot, Mar. 6, 1812, in BPH:LB #6; also William Lee to Susannah Lee, Oct. 25, 1811, in LC:L-PP.

11. Leonard Jarvis to Jonathan Russell, Dec. 14, 1811, in HB:JRP.

12. JB to SB, Nov. 21, 1811, in BPH, #478.

13. See JB to Robert Fulton, Apr. 8, 1811, and JB to Benjamin Latrobe, Feb. 29, 1812, in YB:BP, #21 and #23.

14. JB to James Monroe, Nov. 21, 1811, in NA:DC, RG 59, NA; *DPCUS*, 14th Cong., 1st sess., 1740; JB to Stephen Bradley, Jan. 2, 1812, in YB:BP, #18.

15. Nov. 15, 1811, in BPH, #619.

16. Dolley Madison to RB, Nov. 15, 1811, in *DMDE*.

17. Ibid.

18. JB to Dolley Madison, Dec. 21, 1811, *DMDE*.

19. Thomas Jefferson to JB, May 11, 1811, in LC:TJP.

20. Presley Neville to JB, June 6, 1811, in YB:BP, #34; Joshua Gilpin to JB, July 11, 1811, in BPH, #599.

21. Christoph D. Ebeling to JB, n.d., probably early 1812, in *Proceedings of the American Antiquarian Society* 35 (1896):409–11.

22. JB to James Monroe, Sept. 29, 1811, in *ASP*, 3:512.

23. James Monroe to JB, July 26, 1811, in *ASP*, 3:509, 510. Also in NA:DC, RG 84, Correspondence, American Legation Paris, Dispatches to the Department of State, July 26, 1811–Nov. 23, 1812, 3–16.

24. JB to James Monroe, Oct. 29, 1811, in *ASP*, 3:512.

25. Benjamin Latrobe to JB, Nov. 15, 1811, in BPH, #619.

26. In *PJMad:PS*, 4:3.

27. James Monroe to JB, Nov. 21, 1811, in *ASP*, 3:513–15.

28. Ibid., 3:513.

29. JB to James Monroe, Nov. 21, 1811, with JB's translation of his remarks to the emperor, in NA:DC, RG 59; William Lee to Susannah Lee, Nov. 17, 1811, in LC:L-PP; and CB to Anna Thornton, Nov. 19, 1811, in HL:BFP.

30. William Lee to Susannah Lee, Nov. 17, 22, 26, 29, and Dec. 3, 1811, in LC: L-PP.

31. JB to James Madison, Dec. 19, 1811, in *PJMad:PS*, 4:77.

32. The substance of what follows is in JB to James Madison, Dec. 30, 1811, *PJMad: PS*, 4:97–103.

33. Ibid., enclosure, 4:102.

34. Ibid., 4:100, 101.

35. Ibid., 4:100.

36. James Madison to JB, Feb. 24, 1812, ibid., 4:201.

37. Ibid., 4:200.

38. JB to James Monroe, Dec. 31, 1811, in *ASP*, 3:515–16.

39. The declaration is in ibid., 3:517.

40. The abuses associated with licensing are discussed in William Lee to James Madison, Jan. 1, 1812, LC:L-PP. For Barlow's account of Bassano's retort, see JB to James Monroe, Dec. 31, 1811, in *ASP*, 3:516.; also *PJMad:PS*, 4:201.

41. JB to Dolley Madison, Dec. 21, 1811, in *DMDE*. See also TB to Daniel Barlow, Jan. 20, 1812, in BPH, #660.

42. Jonathan Russell to JB, Nov. 23 and Dec. 12, 1811, in HB:JRP.

43. See JB to James Madison, Apr. 22, 1812, in *PJMad:PS*, 4:338.

44. These are explored in Richard Buel Jr., *America on the Brink* . . . (New York: Palgrave Macmillan, 2005), chaps. 3–5.

45. JB to Jonathan Russell, Mar. 2, 1812, in *ASP*, 3:518–19.

46. Dolley Madison to RB, Apr. 19, 1812, *DMDE*.

47. JB to Bassano, Feb. 6, 1812, in *ASP*, 3:520.

48. JB to James Madison, Jan. 28, Mar. 11, and Apr. 22, 1812, in *ASP*, 3:518–20; a draft of Barlow's treaty can be found in NA:DC, RG 59, M34, r 16.

49. JB to Jonathan Russell, Jan. 14 and Mar. 25, 1812, in HB:JRP.

50. James Monroe to JB, Apr. 23, 1812, in NA:DC, RG 59.

51. JB to George W. Erving, Mar. 22, 1812, in BPH, #492.

52. RB to Dolley Madison, Apr. 15, 1812, in *DMDE*.

53. JB to James Monroe, May 12, 1812, in *ASP*, 3:603.

54. JB to James Madison, May 12, 1812, in *PJMad:PS*, 4:379.

55. Dolley Madison to RB, Apr. 19, 1812, in *DMDE*.

56. See Boston *Repertory*, Apr. 21, 1812.

57. See Dolley Madison to RB, Apr. 19, 1812, in *DMDE*, and Robert Fulton to JB, Apr. 19, 1812, in BPH, #597. For the Federalist press, see *Poulson's American Daily Advertiser*, May 31, 1812, and *Newburyport Herald*, June 12, 1812.

58. JB to James Monroe, Apr. 17, 1812, in LC:JHP in code; also decoded in BPH, #608.

59. John Henry to JB, May 29, 1812, and JB to Henry, June 1, 1812, in BPH, #609 and #502. Also JB to CB, Aug. 10, 1812, in HL:BFP.

60. This story can be traced in Eliza Clarke Custis to CB, Aug. 14, 1812, in HL:BFP; James Monroe to Barlow, n.d. (next to Sept. 11, 1812), in LC: JMonP, and James Monroe to JB, Sept. 15, 1812, in NYPL: JMonP; see also JB to James Monroe, Oct. 20, 1812, in NA:DC, RG 59.

CHAPTER 18: FINALE

1. JB to CB, July 25, 1812, in BPH, #86.

2. JB to Edward Caffarena, July 3, 1812, transcript in BPH, #484; JB [circular to consuls] July 17, 1812, in NA:DC, RG 59; and JB to Bassano, Aug. 8, 1812, in ibid.

3. JB to Edward Caffarena, Sept. 10, 1812, transcript in BPH, #485.

4. Isaac Cox Barnet to JB, Dec. 2, 1812, and R. Beasley to JB, Dec. 3, 1812, in LC: JMonP.

5. CB to Anna Thornton, Aug. 10, 1812, in HL:BFP.

6. They are dated July 13 and Sept. 25, 1812, in NA:DC, RG 59.

7. Evidence of their acquaintance is in CB to Anna Thornton, Aug. 10, in HL:BFP; JB to CB, July 27, 1812, in BPH, #87; and George W. Erving to RB, Dec. 21, 1813, in HL:BFP.

8. JB to CB, June 13, 1812, in BPH, #85.

9. In *PJMad:PS*, 5:144–45, coded portions in italics.

10. Bassano to JB, Oct. 11, 1812, in AE:Cp, 69, LC photocopy.

11. RB to Dolley Madison, Nov. 10 and 25, 1812, *DMDE*.

12. JB to James Monroe, Oct. 20, and JB to Bassano, Oct. 25, 1812, in NA:DC, RG 59.

13. James Monroe to JB, June 16, 1812, in LC:JMonP.

14. Outlined in AE:Cp, 69, 273, LC photocopy.

15. See Crawford's Aug. 15, 1813 evaluation of the plan in "Communications June 15, 1813–Apr. 26, 1815," 12, in NA:DC, RG 84.

16. Printed in *PJMad:PS*, 5:354–55, coded portions in italics.

17. Ibid., 5:536, coded portions in italics.

18. In AE:Cp 68, 203, LC photocopy.

19. JB to James Monroe, Oct. 25, 1812, in NA:DC, RG 59.

20. According to TB to Bassano, Feb. 2, 1813, in AE:Cp 67, LC photocopy; also JB to James Monroe, Nov. 23, 1812, in BPH, #507.

21. For the Warden affair, see David B. Warden to JB, June 16, and JB to Warden, June 29, 1812, in NA:DC, RG 59.

22. The trip is documented in JB's letters to RB, beginning on Oct. 28, 1812, in LC:H-SP.

23. JB to RB, Nov. 11, 1812, in ibid.

24. JB to RB, Nov. 17, 1812, in ibid.

25. JB to RB, Oct. 28 and 29, 1812, in ibid.; JB to CB, Nov. 12, 1812, in BPH, #93.

26. JB to RB, Nov. 18, 1812, in LC: H-SP.

27. JB to RB, Nov. 22, 1812, in ibid.

28. Idem and JB to RB, Nov. 30, 1812, in ibid.

29. JB to RB, Nov. 25, 1812, in ibid.

30. JB to RB, Dec. 13, 1812, in ibid., coded portions in italics.

31. Ibid. for quote and JB to RB, Dec. 17, 1812, in ibid.

32. Manuscript copies can be found in LC:H-SP and HL:BFP. The poem is reprinted in James Woodress, *A Yankee's Odyssey: The Life of Joel Barlow* (Philadelphia: J. B. Lippincott, 1958), 338–39, and Arthur L. Ford, *Joel Barlow* (New York: Twayne, 1971), 103–5. References in parentheses are to lines.

33. JB to RB, Nov. 7, 1812 in LC:H-SP; TB to James Monroe, Jan. 25, 1813, in NA: DC, RG59.

34. JB to RB, Dec. 17, 1812, in LC:H-SP

35. See U.S. House, 54th Cong., 1st sess., *Report on the Bill (H.R. 6889) for the Removal of the Remains of Joel Barlow* (Washington: GPO, 1896); U.S. Senate, 71st Cong., 2nd sess., *A Bill (S. 2503) Authorizing the Erection of a Memorial to Joel Barlow* (Washington: GPO, 1930).

36. TB to RB, Dec. 27, 1812, in BPH, #667.

37. RB to David B. Warden, Jan. 12, 1813 in LC:DBWP.

38. RB to JB, Nov. 12, 1812, in HL:BFP.

39. David Warden to Bassano, Jan. 15, 1813, in LC:DBWP.

40. Cf. William Lee to Susannah Lee, Mar. 6, 1811, in LC:L-PP.

41. TB to Bassano, Feb. 2, 9, and Mar. 4, 1813, in AE:Cp 67, LC photocopy.

42. William Lee to Dolley Madison, Mar. 20, 1813, in *DMDE*.

43. CB to Dolley Madison, Feb. 16, 1813, in *DMDE*.

44. William H. Crawford to James Monroe, Sept. 3, 1813, in NA:DC, RG 84.

45. CB to Dolley Madison, Feb. 16, in *DMDE*; also CB to Anna Thornton, Feb. 2, 1813, in HL:BFP.

46. Dated Jan. 26, 1813, and reprinted in *NI*, Apr. 15, 1813.

47. Cynthia O. Philip, *Robert Fulton: A Biography* (New York: Franklin Watts, 1985), 290; Robert Fulton to Thomas Jefferson, Apr. 7, 1813, in LC:TJP.

48. Robert Fulton to CB, Mar. 13, 1814, and Mar. 7, 1815, in HL:BFP.

49. Robert Fulton to RB, June 12, 1813, in BPH, #676.

50. Robert Fulton to HB, Dec. 8, 1814, in NYHS:RFP.

51. See Gideon Granger to Robert Fulton, Jan. 10, 1815, in NYHS:RFP. Buying up the title to protect Barlow's reputation proved difficult; see Madeleine B. Sterns Papers relating to Joseph de Nancrede (Papineau Papers), docs. #640, #641, #642, #644, and #648, in Special Collections, University of Delaware Library.

52. Barlow's inventory, dated Oct. 26, 1812, is in BPH, #710; Ruth's will is dated Aug. 24, 1813, in HL:BFP; see, also, RB to CB, Mar. 25, 1814, in HL:BFP.

53. John Armstrong to Henry Lee, Nov. 17, 1834, in NYHS.

Essay on Sources

Seven book-length studies of Joel Barlow have appeared since the late nineteenth century, though none have given a comprehensive account of his multifaceted career. The first, Charles L. Todd, *Life and Letters of Joel Barlow, LL.D. Poet, Statesman, Philosopher* (New York: G. P. Putnam, 1886), published some of Barlow's personal correspondence, including an important letter about Thomas Paine that, so far as I know, is currently unavailable elsewhere. A half-century later, Victor L. Miller's narrowly focused *Joel Barlow: Revolutionist, London, 1791–1792* (Hamburg: Friedrichsen, de Gruyter, and Co., 1932) preceded by two years Theodore A. Zunder's *The Early Days of Joel Barlow, A Connecticut Wit* (New Haven: Yale University Press, 1934). Zunder's work is still authoritative for Barlow's early career but ignores completely the last twenty-five eventful years of Barlow's life. In 1954, Milton Cantor's Columbia Ph.D. dissertation, "The Life of Joel Barlow," attempted to remedy that defect. But it was never published, perhaps because James Woodress's *A Yankee's Odyssey: The Life of Joel Barlow* (Philadelphia: J. B. Lippincott) appeared in 1958. Woodress came closest to writing a comprehensive biography, but he ignored most of Barlow's entrepreneurial activities and slighted his importance as a republican ideologue. In 1971 Arthur L. Ford published a short literary biography, *Joel Barlow* (New York: Twayne). That was followed in 1985 by Samuel Bernstein's *Joel Barlow: A Connecticut Yankee in the Age of Revolution* (New York: Routledge), who tried to remedy one of the limitations of the Woodress volume by placing Barlow's thought in a European context. However, that effort ignored the fact that—with the exception of four pamphlets in the mid-1790s—the bulk of Barlow's oeuvre was addressed to American audiences. Finally, in 2007 Steven Blakemore published *Joel Barlow's Columbiad: A Bicentennial Reading* (Knoxville: University of Tennessee Press), which, as the title suggests, is a literary study of one work.

My attempt at a comprehensive biography is based on Barlow's published works, most of which are available in *The Works of Joel Barlow in Two Volumes* (Gainesville, FL: Scholars Facsimiles and Reprints, 1970), and his voluminous unpublished correspondence. Many libraries in diverse locations hold letters to and from Barlow, but the largest collection by far is in the possession of the Houghton Library of Harvard University. (For the organization of this collection, see the abbreviations preceding the notes.) Users need to watch for misattributions and chronological confusions within this collection, as occasionally noted in my references.

The second most important group of Barlow manuscripts is held by Yale University. The Beinecke Library has a small Barlow Collection of its own (Za Barlow) as well as a larger one consisting of two and a half boxes of loose manuscripts on loan from the Pequot Library in Southport, Connecticut. Za Barlow includes two revisions of the 1793 edition of *The Vision of Columbus* that became *The Columbiad* and copies of Barlow's diplomatic correspondence with the French foreign minister (1811–12) in bound volumes, together with manuscript drafts of *The Columbiad* and a box of loose correspondence (35 items). In addition, the Manuscripts and Archives division of the Sterling Memorial Library has some Barlow materials in three separate collections: two Abraham Baldwin folders in the Miscellaneous manuscript collection (MS 352), the Humphreys-Mason-Olmstead Papers (MS 857), and the Knollenberg Collection (MS 1017), as well as a few fugitive items in other collections.

The Library of Congress owns a wide scattering of Barlow related materials. In addition to a very small collection of Barlow Papers, relevant manuscripts can be found in the John Henry Papers, the Thomas Jefferson Papers (now digitally available and searchable), the James Madison Papers, the James Monroe Papers, the William Lee Papers, the Henley-Smith Family Papers, the Lee-Palfrey Papers (most of which can be found in Mary Ellen Mann, ed., *A Yankee Jeffersonian: Selections from the Diary and Letters of William Lee of Massachusetts, Written from 1796 to 1840* [Cambridge, MA: The Belknap Press of Harvard University Press, 1958]), the William Short Papers, and the David B. Warden Papers, which includes copies of the Warden Papers in the possession of the Maryland Historical Society. The manuscript division also holds photocopies of the diplomatic correspondence currently in the Archives des Affaires étrangères in Paris relating to Barlow's mission to France in 1811–12.

The American counterpart to the French Foreign Ministry's archives dealing with Barlow's mission to Algiers, as well as to France, can be found in Record Group 59 of the National Archives and Records Administration's facility in College Park, Maryland. Consular reports in the same record group, particularly from Nantes, Bordeaux, and Hamburg during 1793–95, provide insight into the commercial landscape of Western Europe during the 1790s. I searched Record Group 84 in vain for the records of the U.S. consular courts in France, which do not seem to have survived. However, an interesting copy of William H. Crawford's report about Barlow's mission can be found there in addition to some of Robert Fulton's correspondence with the British government about the development of the torpedo.

The Baldwin Family Papers in the Huntington Library at San Marino, California, is the last major manuscript collection bearing on Barlow's life. Though the bulk of it consists of letters to and from members of Ruth Barlow's family, it also contains copies of Barlow's early correspondence with Elizabeth Whitman, most of which is reproduced in Caroline W. H. Dall, *The Romance of the Association; or, One last glimpse of Charlotte Temple and Eliza Wharton. A Curiosity of literature and life* (Cambridge, MA: J. Wilson and Son, 1875). Smaller collections of Barlow correspondence or materials relevant to him can be found in the Joel Barlow and the Andrew Craigie Papers of the American Antiquarian Society; the Charles Willson Peale Papers in the American Philosophical Society; the Joel Barlow and Oliver Wolcott Jr. Papers at the Connecticut Historical Society; the David B. Warden Papers in the Maryland Historical Society; the Scioto Company Papers, William Duer Papers, and Robert Fulton Papers in the New York Historical Society; the Tench Coxe Papers at the Historical Society of Pennsylvania; the Jonathan Russell Papers at the Hay Library of Brown University; the Manasseh Cutler Papers at Northwestern University, and the Dolley Madison Papers (now in a searchable digital edition) at the University of Virginia. Additionally, various collections of the Massachusetts Historical Society, the New York Public Library, and the Dartmouth and Haverford College rare books and manuscripts divisions contain individual documents of considerable importance. Finally, the University of Georgia holds the manuscript of a commonplace book dating from the 1770s that Abraham Baldwin and Barlow seem to have shared.

The Cincinnati Historical Society's three bound volumes of manuscripts, mostly copies of originals, are helpful in deciphering the complex operations of the Scioto Company with which Barlow was associated. In addition, the Smith, Houston, Morris, and Ogden Papers in the American Philosophical Society shed critical light on Gouverneur Morris's relationship with Barlow. Finally, the Connecticut State Library contains the probate materials associated with settling Samuel Barlow's estate, while the Redding Land Records are useful in understanding the world into which Joel Barlow was born.

Though Barlow spent more than half his adult life in Europe, evidence of his extended presence there is largely confined to two archival collections. The first is the Minutier central des notaries de Ville de Paris in the Archives nationales, where I attempted to trace the land sales of the Scioto Company during 1789–91. The second is the High Court of Admiralty Records in the Public Records Office in London, which yielded insight into Barlow's speculations in prizes under litigation. However, extracting useful information from these archives can be very unrewarding unless one knows exactly what to look for.

Students of the American and French Revolutions benefit from the extensive publication of each country's public archives. The first such publications for the United States began appearing in the mid-nineteenth century with the *American State Papers, Documents Legislative and Executive, of the Congress of the United States* (Washington, DC: Gales and Seaton, 1832–59). It was quickly followed by *The Debates and Proceedings of the Congress of the United States* (Washington, DC: Gales and Seaton, 1834–56). Both are now available in electronic format to subscribers. The recent digitization of the *Early American Newspapers, Series 1–7 (1690–1922)* is a godsend to anyone investigating the early republican period because it allows one to search multiple newspaper files for references to particular subjects. The availability of *Early American Imprints, Series I (1639–1800) & Series II (1801–1819)* online allows similar searches in the books, pamphlets, and broadsides of the period, as does the *American Periodicals, 1740–1900,* for the magazine literature, though it is less comprehensive than either the newspaper or imprints series.

The digitization of European documents has not been pursued on the same scale as in the United States. But students can search *Eighteenth Century Collections On Line* for the digital texts of works published in Britain. However, this archive is not complete and attributes to Barlow several items that he did not write. Students may profit more from exploring the *Annual Register* for each year of the period spanned by Barlow's European career, as well as the relevant files in *Early English Newspapers* on microfilm. In France, only the *Archives Parlementaires* are now digitized, though many more such projects are in contemplation. The publication I relied on most is the *Gazette nationale, ou le Moniteur universel,* which first appeared on November 24, 1789. It became the official paper of the French Revolution even before Napoleon declared it to be such in December 1799. Finally, some of the scholarly work done on the French Revolution at the end of the nineteenth century is still useful, especially Maurice Tourneau, *Bibliographie de l'histoire de Paris pendant la révolution française,* 5 vols. (Paris: Imprimerie nouvelle, 1890). The Bibliothèque nationale de France has the best collection of pamphlets generated by the controversy over the Scioto Company, while the British Library has the most complete collection of texts Barlow published in Britain in their various editions.

The published correspondence of prominent members of America's founding generation contains a treasure trove of information in an easily readable format. These include *Papers of George Washington, Presidential Series,* ed. Dorothy Twohig, Mark A. Mastromarino, Jack D. Warren Jr., Christine Sternberg Patrick, and David R. Hoth, 14 vols. to date (Charlottesville: University Press of Virginia, 1987–); *Papers of George Washington, Retirement Series,* ed. W. W. Abbot and Edward G. Lengel, 5 vols. (Charlottesville: University Press of Virginia, 1998–99); *The Papers of Alexander Hamilton,* ed. Harold C. Syrett et al., 27 vols. (New York: Columbia University Press, 1961–87); *The Papers of Thomas Jefferson,* ed. Julian P. Boyd, Charles T. Cullen, John Catanzariti, and Barbara B. Oberg, 36 vols. to date (Princeton: Princeton University Press, 1950–); *The Papers of James Madison: Secretary of State Series,* ed. Robert J. Brugger, Mary A. Hackett, and David B. Mattern, 8 vols. to date (Charlottesville: University Press of Virginia, 1986–), and *The Papers of James Madison: Presidential Series,* ed. Robert A. Rutland, J. C. A. Stagg, and Angela Kreider, 6 vols. to date (Charlottesville: University Press of Virginia, 1984–); *The Papers of John Marshall,* ed. Herbert A. Johnson, Charles T. Cullen, and Charles A. Hobson, 12 vols. (Chapel Hill: University of North Carolina Press, 1974–2006). All these series with the exception of the Hamilton Papers, the Marshall Papers, and the Washington Papers Retirement Series are incomplete, but some of the holes can be filled by reference to older though less comprehensive collections of writings by these men. For James Monroe, there is little alternative to *The Writings of James Monroe* . . . , ed. Stanislaus Murray Hamilton, 7 vols. (New York: G. P. Putnam Sons, 1898–1903).

In addition, various editions of the published records relating to lesser figures, such as Gouverneur Morris, *A Diary of the French Revolution* . . . , ed. Beatrix Cary Davenport, 2 vols. (Cambridge, MA: Riverside, 1939); Richard M. Rollins, ed., *The Autobiographies of Noah Webster: From the Letters and Essays, Memoir, and Diary* (Columbia: University of South Carolina Press, 1989); Ezra Stiles, *The Literary Diary of Ezra Stiles, D.D., L.L.D.,* ed. Franklin B. Dexter, 3 vols. (New York: Charles Scribner's Sons, 1901); Noah Webster, *Letters,* ed. Harry R. Warfel (New York: Library

Publishers, 1953); and Archer B. Hurlbert, ed., *The Records of the Original Proceedings of the Ohio Company*, 2 vols. (Marietta, OH: Marietta Historical Commission, 1917), are helpful for anyone investigating Barlow's life.

Counterparts to such multivolume North American publication projects are less prevalent elsewhere, but I found volume 12 of the *Archivo del General Miranda*, ed. Vincente Dávila, 24 vols. (1929–1950), entitled *Revolucion Francesa: Causas Judiciales Proceso Militar y Prison Politica de Miranda 1793 a 1795*, ed. Léon Hermanos (Caracas, Venezuela: Editorial sur-América, 1931), essential in understanding Barlow's role in Miranda's defense, and Pierre Caron, ed., *La Commission des subsistances de l'an II: procès-verbaux et acts*, 2 vols. (Paris: E. Leroux, 1925), useful in tracking Barlow's commercial activities at the end of 1793. Ralph L. Wardle, ed., *Collected Letters of Mary Wollstonecraft* (Ithaca, NY: Cornell University Press, 1979), and Janet Todd, ed., *The Collected Letters of Mary Wollstonecraft* (New York: Columbia University Press, 2003), covered everything relevant to her relationship with the Barlows that can be found in Lord Abington's Shelly-Godwin Collection at the Bodleian Library at Oxford. Volume 24 of Thomas Bayly Howell and Thomas Jones Howell, *Cobbett's Complete Collection of State Trials and Proceedings for High Treason . . .* (London: Longman, 1816) contains testimony bearing on Barlow's activities in Britain between 1791 and 1792.

The published observations of Barlow's contemporaries about him and the places he lived, especially Paris, are sometimes useful. I found unique information in Henry R. Yorke, *Letters from France in 1802*, 2 vols. (London: H. D. Symonds, 1804), and *The Farington Diary, by Joseph Farrington*, 2nd ed., ed. James Greig, 8 vols. (London: Hutchinson and Co., 1923–28). *Paris as it was and as it is; or A Sketch of the French Capital, illustrative of the effects of the Revolution* (London: C. and R. Baldwin, 1803), written by a visiting Englishman, also contains information that Parisians would have failed to note because it was part of their everyday life but which struck the eye of a foreigner. Much of that information later found its way into John G. Alger, *Paris in 1789–1794* (London: George Allen, 1902).

In keeping track of Barlow's many associates in the United States, Britain, and France, I have made ample use of the standard biographical reference works: the *American National Biography*, ed. John A. Garraty and Mark C. Carnes, 24 vols. (New York: Oxford University Press, 1999), for the United States and the *Dictionary of National Biography*, ed. H. C. G. Matthew and Brian Harrison, 60 vols. (New York: Oxford University Press, 2004), for Britain, supplemented by Franklin Bowditch Dexter, *Biographical Sketches of the Graduates of Yale College with Accounts of the College History . . .*, 7 vols. (New York: H. Holt and Co., 1885–1913). For Barlow's French associates, I used *Biographie universelle, ancienne et moderne: ou, Histoire, par ordre alphabétique, de la vie publique et privée de tous les hommes qui se sont fait remarquer par leurs écrits, leurs actions, leurs talents, leurs vertus or leurs crimes*, comp. J. F. and L. G. Michuad, 45 vols. (Paris: A. T. Desplaces, 1843–1865).

Many secondary works provided a context for understanding Barlow's life and writings. Among the most useful for his early years were Brooks M. Kelley, *Yale: A History*

(New Haven, CT: Yale University Press, 1974); William Edgar Grumman, *The Revolutionary Soldiers of Redding, Connecticut . . .* (Hartford: Hartford Press, 1904); and Leon Howard, *The Connecticut Wits* (Chicago: University of Chicago Press, 1943).

For Barlow's involvement in the Scioto Land Company, see Andrew R. L. Cayton, *The Frontier Republic: Ideology and Politics in the Ohio Country, 1780–1825* (Kent, Ohio: Kent State University Press, 1986); Theodore T. Belote, *The Scioto Speculation and the French Settlement of Gallipolis: A Study in Ohio Valley History* (Cincinnati, OH: University of Cincinnati Press, 1907); Joseph Stancliffe Davis, *Essays in the Earlier History of Corporations: Essay II William Duer, Entrepreneur, 1744–1799* (Cambridge, MA: Harvard University Press, 1917). Anyone dealing with the French migration to Ohio needs to look at Joscelyne Moreau-Zanelli, *Gallipolis: Histoire d'un mirage américain au XVIIIe siècle* (Paris: L'Harmattan, 2000). I think Moreau-Zanelli overdoes the victimization of the French emigrants, despite the support that Sylvia Harris, "Search for Eden: An Eighteenth-Century Disaster. *Mémoires of Count de Lezay-Marnésia*," *Franco-American Review* 2 (1937): 50–60, lends to such an approach.

For Barlow's relationship to British radicals, I have relied on Albert Goodwin, *The Friends of Liberty: The English Democratic Movement in the Age of the French Revolution* (Cambridge, MA: Harvard University Press, 1979); Eugene Charlton Black, *The Association: British Extraparliamentary Political Organization 1769–1793* (Cambridge, MA: Harvard University Press, 1963); Lyndall Gordon, *Vindication: A Life of Mary Wollstonecraft* (New York: Harper Collins Publishers, 2005); and Jenny Graham, *The Nation, the Law and the King, Reform Politics in England, 1789–1799*, 2 vols. (Lanham, MD: University Press of America, 2000).

For understanding the radical phase of the French Revolution and the relationship of resident Americans to it, I turned to François Furet, *French Revolution, 1770–1814*, trans. Antonia Nevill (Cambridge, MA: Blackwell, 1996); Donald Greer, *The Incidence of the Terror during the French Revolution: A Statistical Interpretation* (Cambridge, MA: Harvard University Press, 1935); Mona Ozouf, *Festivals and the French Revolution*, trans. Alan Sheridan (Cambridge, MA: Harvard University Press, 1988); Melanie R. Miller, *Envoy to the Terror: Gouverneur Morris and the French Revolution* (Dulles, VA: Potomac Books, 2005); and Phillip Ziesche, *Cosmopolitan Patriots: Americans in Paris during the French Revolution* (Charlottesville: University of Virginia Press, 2010).

For the revolutionary economy of France, I am beholden to François Crouzet, *La Grande Inflation: La monnaie en France de Louis XVI à Napoléon* (Paris: Fayard, 1993); Frederick Nussbaum, *Commercial Policy in the French Revolution: A Study of the Career of G. J. A. Ducher* (Washington, DC: American Historical Association, 1923); Léon Say, *Dictionaire des Finances*, 2 vols. (Paris: Berger-Levrault et Cie, 1889–94); J. F. Bosher, *French Finances, 1770–1795: From Business to Bureaucracy* (Cambridge: Cambridge University Press, 1970); Pierre Léon et al., *Histoire économique et sociale de la France*, Vol. 3: *L'avenement de l'ère industrielle (1789–années 1880)* (Paris: Presses Universitaires de France, 1976); and Michael D. Bordo and Eugene N. White, "A Tale of Two Currencies: British and French Finance during the Napoleonic Wars," *Journal of Economic History* 51 (1991): 303–16.

For the end of the Terror and Barlow's diplomatic mission to Algiers, Howard G. Brown, *Ending the French Revolution: Violence, Justice, and Repression from the Terror to Napoleon* (Charlottesville: University of Virginia Press, 2006); Bronislaw Baczko, *Ending the Terror: The French Revolution after Robespierre*, trans. Michel Petheram (New York: Cambridge University Press, 1994); and Richard B. Parker, *Uncle Sam in Barbary: A Diplomatic History* (Gainesville: University of Florida, 2004).

For the Franco-American crisis of 1798–1800 and Barlow's growing disenchantment with France, William Stinchcombe, *The X Y Z Affair* (Westport, CT: Greenwood, 1980); Jean Stern, *Belle et bonne, une fervente amie de Voltaire (1757–1822)* (Paris: Librairie Hachette, 1938); and Lionel D. Woodward, *Une Anglaise Amie de la Révolution Française: Hélène-Maria Williams et ses Amis* (Paris: H. Champion, 1930).

For the political background to Barlow's last mission, Henry Adams, *History of the United States during the Administrations of James Madison* (New York: Literary Classics of the United States, 1986), which first appeared at the end of the nineteenth century, still is worth reading. I also found useful Bradford Perkins, *Prologue to War: England and the United States 1805–1812* (Berkeley and Los Angeles: University of California Press, 1961), and Peter P. Hill, *Napoleon's Troublesome Americans: Franco-American Relations, 1804–1815* (Dulles, VA: Potomac Books, 2005).

For Barlow's association with prominent figures like Thomas Paine, Robert Fulton, and others, see Craig Nelson, *Thomas Paine: Enlightenment, Revolution, and the Birth of Modern Nations* (New York: Viking Penguin, 2006); John Keane, *Tom Paine: A Political Life* (Boston: Little Brown, 1995); Cynthia Owen Philip, *Robert Fulton: A Biography* (New York: Franklin Watts, 1985); Kirkpatrick Sale, *The Fire of His Genius: Robert Fulton and the American Dream* (New York: Free Press, 2001); Eloise Ellery, *Brissot de Warville: A Study in the History of the French Revolution* (New York: AMS, 1970); Wil Verhoeven, *Gilbert Imlay: Citizen of the World* (London: Pickering and Chatto, 2008); Howard C. Rice, "James Swan: Agent of the French Republic, 1794–1796," *New England Quarterly* 10 (1937): 464–86; and Alyssa G. Sepinwall, "The Abbé Gregoire and the Atlantic Republic of Letters," *Proceedings of the American Antiquarian Society* 116 (2006): 317–35.

For the religious environment of the United States during the early Republican period, there is no better summary than Gordon S. Wood's chapter on "Republican Religion" in *Empire of Liberty* (New York: Oxford University Press, 2009). For an interesting discussion of the relationship between history and biography, the reader can consult a recent round table entitled "Historians and Biography" in the *American Historical Review* 114 (2009): 573–661.

Index